THE SONGS THE BEATLES PLAYED

AN EXPANDED COMPENDIUM

The Songs the Beatles Played

An Expanded Compendium

Steve Lambley

SLIDE Books

By the same author

And the Band Begins to Play:
The Definitive Guide to the Songs of the Beatles

The Beatles' Recordings:
A Compendium

ISBN: 978-94-91868-03-0
©2017, 2019 Steve Lambley

Front cover image: from photograph of Neumann U47 microphone, taken by the author at Abbey Road Studio Two

SLIDE Books, London / The Hague
Typeset by Steve Lambley Information Design

10 9 8 7 6 5 4 3 2

Contents

Introduction 1

A–Z of Songs 7

Calendar of Recording Sessions 1963–1969 313

The Recording Sessions 319

Catalogue of Releases 333

Introduction

This book contains information about every song recorded and released by the Beatles between 1958 and 2018. In addition to the official canon of the group's recordings made in the Abbey Road studios, the book incorporates home recordings, sessions for BBC radio, concert recordings, film versions, TV appearances, plus over eighty key songs that the group played live but did not record.

For every recorded track, details are given of the takes and overdubs recorded at each session, and where that session took place. The relevant mono/stereo editing and mixing information is given, again with dates and locations.

The section "BBC and other performances" includes recordings made for the BBC, and specifically for BBC radio, unless otherwise noted. Between March 1962 and June 1965, the Beatles made 53 shows for the BBC Light Programme, playing a total of 275 songs. The recording and broadcast date of each song are given. All (worldwide) non-mimed TV appearances are also listed, but in terms of radio only the BBC performances are given.

It is impossible to list all the songs that the band played live. As Mark Lewisohn points out in *Tune In*, in Hamburg they would by necessity play entire LPs of material – including every track on the debut LPs of Carl Perkins, Buddy Holly, Johnny Burnett, Gene Vincent and Elvis Presley, as well as all of *Elvis' Golden Records*, for example. For this reason, the listing of the songs that the group played live is limited to the most important songs and those that were played most often.

A list of the releases featuring the various versions of the song is given, showing which mix was used for each release, and the peak position reached in the UK or US (or both) as appropriate. The list includes the principal compilation albums issued by Parlophone/Apple and Capitol. In addition, where a particular mix appears exclusively on another album, such as the first stereo mix of 'I Want To Hold Your Hand' on the German *The Beatles' Greatest*, that album is listed for that particular track only.

Each listing concludes with some points of interest on each song, sometimes trivial, sometimes not.

The studio sessions are broadly divided into recordings for each of the thirteen "official" LPs, as listed in the "The Recording Sessions" section at the back of the book. From 1963 onwards, the focus of any series of recording sessions was an LP. Singles and EP tracks would usually fall out of these sessions, with a song either having been recorded specifically as a single, or later having been decided that it would be better as a single than an LP track. In later years, there was a degree of overlap between LP recordings, but the main track that was recorded on a particular day is used to determine which LP that day's session falls under. Exceptionally, the *Let It Be* track 'Across The Universe' was recorded along with 'Lady Madonna' at the start of the White Album sessions on 3 February 1968, and so that session is filed under both the White Album and *Let It Be*. More typically, the 8 February 1968 session involved a brief recording of backing vocals for 'The Inner Light', but substantial work on 'Across The Universe', and so that session falls under *Let It Be*.

If sessions ran, or even started, after midnight, the date given is that of the start of the booked session. So, for instance, the vocal overdub for 'Eleanor Rigby' took place in the early hours of 7 June 1966, but as the session was booked for 6 June, that date given.

In general, the mix numbers that are given are only for recordings that were released. These are usually in the form RM5 (remix mono number 5), or RS3 (remix stereo number 3).

The exact dates for mixes that were carried out by Capitol are not known – the dates given are those on which the relevant US LP was mastered. The mono *Meet The Beatles!* and *Help!* tracks are simply the stereo versions with left and right channels combined.

A guide to the information given in the body of this book can be found on page 5. The session numbers used are detailed in "The Recording Sessions", and a list of every release listed in the book is given in "Catalogue of Releases" – both of these sections are at the back of the book.

The precise nature of the overdubs, particularly for the earlier recordings, does involve a fair degree of educated guesswork. Although EMI studio documentation is second to none as regards dates, times and personnel, and take and mix numbers – and naturally Mark Lewisohn's excellent *The Complete Beatles Recording Sessions* and *The Complete Beatles Chronicle*, together with the three-volume *The Beatles' Recorded Legacy* by John C. Winn are bedrocks for all research in this area – few of the sessions have bequeathed us detailed notes of who played what on which particular take. There are exceptions – such as those published by George Martin in his fascinating 2003 memoir *Playback*. However, with some detective work it is possible to make a fair estimate of the sequence of events. Photographs taken during the sessions help, as does the fact that, for the most part, four tracks of tape were used for the recordings. Thanks to the efficient working methods of those involved, we can often determine how the sound was built.

Experts in the field are Kevin Ryan and Brian Kehew, who published their findings in 2006 as part of the magnificent *Recording The Beatles* publication.

Some later LP compilations, such as the 1977 *Love Songs*, are largely collections of the standard releases. In such cases, details are given only for tracks where a non-standard version was used (in this case, for example, George Martin's new mixes of 'Girl' and 'Nowhere Man'). This is also the case for certain LPs released outside the UK and US that use a special mix, such as for a number of tracks on the Canadian *Long Tall Sally* LP, or the German version of *With The Beatles*.

The CD versions of the "Red" and "Blue" albums, *The Beatles 1962–1966* and *The Beatles 1967–1970*, are only included if the track differs from that which appeared on both the UK and US LPs.

The 2009 CD remasters and the 2012 and 2014 vinyl reissues are so meticulously based on the original masters that separate mixing dates are not listed.

Details of variations for these releases are given in "Catalogue of Recordings" at the back of the book.

The *1* release from 2000 is not included as a it is more of a remaster than a remix. The revamped *1+* is included, but of course the mix dates are given only for new mixes.

The chart positions are as in the "official" UK *Record Retailer* listings, and the US *Billboard* charts. Prior to the *Record Retailer* chart appearing in March 1960, the *NME* chart has been used as the standard listing.

In 1967, what was the *Billboard* top 150 LP listing became a chart of the top 200 LPs. The *Billboard 200* does not list CD reissues of LPs, and so these are not included here.

Throughout the 1950s and 1960s, *Billboard* would give separate listings for either side of a single, depending upon the title requested at the point of sale. It was not uncommon for both sides to enter the charts – between 1956 and 1961, Elvis made the *Billboard* top 40 with both sides of 21 out of his first 26 hits. The practice naturally had the effect of compromising chart positions, as can be seen from looking at his peak positions over these five years. For most of these double chart entries, one side vastly outsold the other – his first hit 'Heartbreak Hotel' got to number one, while the flipside 'I Was The One' peaked at number 19. However, where both sides sold well, neither achieved the position that the combined sales would have managed – within a string of number one hits, 'One Night' peaked at number 4, because the flipside 'I Got Stung' itself proved popular and reached number 8; 'His Latest Flame' also only made it to number 4, because the flip, 'Little Sister' peaked at 5.

The Beatles achieved top ten positions with both sides of a release on four separate occasions, although amazingly on each occasion, one side did get to number one. On 29 November 1969, while both sides of a Beatles single were in the top ten for a fifth time, *Billboard* changed the rules and began to combine sales for titles on the same disc that would previously have had separate runs. This made its mark on the Beatles' last single of the 1960s. Two weeks before the change to the rules, 'Come Together' was at number 2 and 'Something' at number 3. The following week, 'Come Together' had dropped to number 7, while 'Something' hadn't moved. Then, on 29 November, under the new rules, 'Come Together'/'Something' came together, combined their sales, and topped the *Billboard* chart.

	15 November 1969		22 November 1969		29 November 1969	
1	5th Dimension	Wedding Bell Blues	5th Dimension	Wedding Bell Blues	The Beatles	Come Together/ Something
2	The Beatles	Come Together	R.B. Greaves	Take A Letter Maria	Blood, Sweat & Tears	And When I Die
3	The Beatles	Something	The Beatles	Something	5th Dimension	Wedding Bell Blues
4	Blood, Sweat & Tears	And When I Die	Blood, Sweat & Tears	And When I Die	R.B. Greaves	Take A Letter Maria
5	Smith	Baby It's You	Flying Machine	Smile A Little Smile For Me	Steam	Na Na Hey Hey Kiss Him Goodbye
6	The Temptations	I Can't Get Next To You	Steam	Na Na Hey Hey Kiss Him Goodbye	Flying Machine	Smile A Little Smile For Me
7	Elvis Presley	Suspicious Minds	The Beatles	Come Together	Peter, Paul & Mary	Leaving On A Jet Plane

Not all songs from all the group's films are listed – notably the wide range of songs used for *Yellow Submarine* – as specific mix dates for the movie versions are generally not known. However, the *Let It Be* recordings are well documented, particularly thanks to exhaustive research by Doug Sulpy and Ray Schweighardt. Their 1997 book *Get Back*, first published in the US in *910* magazine as *Drugs, Divorce and a Slipping Image*, allocated take numbers for every song and improvisation recorded by the group between Thursday 2 January and Friday 31 January 1969 – a staggering 1,045 of them. Subsequent research uncovered even more recordings, but the original take numbers are used here. These number are of the form "24.73", which signifies the 73rd take recorded on 24 January.

For much more information on the songs of the Beatles, check out And The Band Begins To Play *by the same author, also available from SLIDE Books.*

A guide to the page layout

Title and composer

Who played what

Please Mister Postman
[Dobbins-Garrett-Holland-Bateman-Gorman]

John – lead vocals, rhythm guitar
Paul – backing vocals, bass
George – backing vocals, lead guitar
Ringo – drums

Date and location of session

Studio recording and mixing
30 July 1963 – Studio Two – With The Beatles session 3 out of 9
Takes 1–2

LP session number

Overdubs onto take 2 – vocals > take 3
Takes 4–7
Overdubs onto take 7 – vocals, handclaps > take 9

Mix number

21 August 1963 – Studio Two control room
RM9 [1] – mono mix from take 9

Date of broadcast

29 October 1963 – Studio Two control room
RS9 [2] – stereo mix from take 9

17 March 1964 – Capitol

Date of recording

[3] – mastering of stereo mix from [2]
[4] – mastering of mono mix from [2]

BBC and other performances
7 March 1962 – 8 March 1962 edition of *Here We Go*
10 July 1963 [5] – 30 July 1963 edition of *Pop Go The Beatles*
28 February 1964 – 30 March 1964 edition of *From Us To You*

Mix cross-reference –
the mix labelled [5] was
used for *Live At The BBC*

Releases   UK/US peak
With The Beatles LP (1963) – Parlophone PMC 1206 [1], PCS 3045 [2]   1
With The Beatles LP (Germany, 1963) – Odeon O 83 991 [1], Odeon STO 83 568 [2]   –
'Roll Over Beethoven' / 'Please Mister Postman' single (Canada, 1963) Capitol 72133 [1] –
The Beatles' Second Album LP (US, 1964) – Capitol T 2080 [4], ST 2080 [3]   1
The Beatles' Second Album EP (US, 1964) – Capitol SXA 2080 [3]   –
Four By The Beatles EP (US, 1964) – Capitol EAP 1-2121 [3]   92
Live At The BBC CD (1994) – Apple 8 31796 2 [5]   1/3

Year of release in UK
unless otherwise stated

═══════════════ **NOTES** ═══════════════

♪ The first of three Tamla tracks on *With The Beatles*.
♪ Performed by the Beatles on their first radio broadcast in March 1962.

Song-related trivia

Performance on UK or US chart, as appropriate

Where two entries are given, the same release appeared
in the UK and US – so, for example, *Live At The BBC*
peaked at #1 in the UK and at #3 in the US

A – Z of Songs

Across The Universe

[Lennon-McCartney]

John – lead vocals, acoustic guitar, lead guitar; backing vocals (WWF version)
Paul – piano; backing vocals (WWF version)
George – sitar, tamboura, guitar, maracas; backing vocals (WWF version)
Ringo – percussion, drums (*Let It Be* version)
George Martin – possible organ (WWF version)
Lizzie Bravo, Gayleen Pease – backing vocals (WWF version)
Session musicians – eighteen violins, four violas, four cellos, three trumpets, three trombones, two guitars, harp, fourteen-voice female choir (*Let It Be* version)

Studio recording and mixing

3 February 1968 – Studio Three – Let It Be session 1 out of 17
Takes 1–2
Overdubs onto take 2 – tamboura (possibly on 4 February)

4 February 1968 – Studio Three – Let It Be session 2 out of 17
Takes 4–7
Overdubs onto take 7 – vocals
Tape reduction of take 7 > take 8
Overdubs onto take 8 – backwards bass, drums (unused)
Sound effects takes 1–3

8 February 1968 – Studio Two – Let It Be session 3 out of 17
Overdubs onto take 8 – guitar, maracas, piano, vocals

8 February 1968 – Studio Two control room
RM2 [1] – mono mix from take 8

7 January 1969 – Twickenham Film Studios – Let It Be rehearsal session
Takes 7.78, 7.83 [2, edited]

2 October 1969 – Room 4
RS2 [3] – stereo mix from take 8

1 April 1970 – Studio Three control room
Tape reduction take 8 > take 9

1 April 1970 – Studio One
Overdubs onto take 9 – orchestra and choir

2 April 1970 – Room 4
RS13 [4] – stereo mix from take 9

1995 – *EMI*
[5] – stereo mix from take 2

2003 – *EMI*
[6] – stereo mix from take 7

2018 – *EMI*
[7] – stereo mix from take 6

Releases

	UK/US peak
No One's Gonna Change Our World LP (1969) – Regal Starline SRS 5013 [3]	–
Let It Be LP (1970) – Apple PXS1, PCS 7096 [4]	1
Let It Be LP (US, 1970) – Apple AR 34001 [4]	1
Let It Be movie (1970) [2]	
The Beatles 1967–1970 LP (1973) – Apple PCSP 718 [4]	2
The Beatles 1967–1970 LP (US, 1973) – Apple SKBO 3404 [4]	1
Rarities LP (1978) – Parlophone PCM 1001, PSLP 261 [3]	71
Rarities LP (US, 1980) – Capitol SHAL 12060 [3]	21
The Beatles Ballads LP (1980) – Parlophone PCS 7214 [3]	17
Past Masters 2 CD (1988) – EMI CDP 7 90044 2 [3]	46/–
Anthology 2 CD (1996) – Apple 8 34448 2 [5]	1/1
Let It Be… Naked CD (2003) – Apple 24359 57142 [6]	7/5
Mono Masters CD (2009) – Apple 6 849582 4 [1]	–
The Beatles Deluxe CD (2018) – Apple 0602567571957 [7]	4/6

NOTES

♪ Proceeds from the *No One's Gonna Change Our World* LP went to the World Wildlife Fund.
♪ WWF version is preceded by the sound of birds flocking.
♪ The mono version is only available on the *Mono Masters* collection.

Act Naturally

[Russell-Morrison]

Ringo – lead vocals, drums, percussion
Paul – harmony vocals, bass
John – acoustic guitar
George – lead guitar

Studio recording and mixing

17 June 1965 – *Studio Two – Help! session 13 out of 13*
Takes 1–13
Overdubs onto take 13 – vocal, percussion

18 June 1965 – *Studio Two control room*
RM1 [1] – mono mix from take 13
RS2 [2] – stereo mix from take 13

1987 – *EMI*
[3] – stereo mix from take 13

BBC and other performances

1 August 1965 – *Blackpool Night Out* (Associated British Corp. TV, live)
14 August 1965 [4] – *The Ed Sullivan Show* broadcast on 12 September 1965 (CBS TV)
15 August 1965 – *The Beatles At Shea Stadium* (live), broadcast by BBC TV on 1 March 1966

Releases   *UK/US peak*

Help! LP (1965) – Parlophone PMC 1255 [1], PCS 3071 [2]	1
'Yesterday' / 'Act Naturally' single (US, 1965) – Capitol 5498 [1]	47
"Yesterday"... And Today LP (US, 1966) – Capitol T 2553 [1], ST 2553 [2]	1
Yesterday EP (1966) – Parlophone GEP 8948 [1]	1
Help! CD (1987) – EMI CDP 7 46439 2 [3]	61
The Four Historic Ed Sullivan Shows DVD (2003) – EREDV 372 [4]	

═══ NOTES ═══

♪ Performed by the Beatles in concert in 1965.
♪ The last full cover version to be released by the Beatles.
♪ The original by Buck Owens reached #1 on the *Billboard* country singles chart in 1963.
♪ The Shea Stadium recording was poor and so the audio track was replaced by an edited copy of the studio version for transmission.

Ain't She Sweet

[Ager-Yellen]

John – lead vocals, rhythm guitar
Paul – bass
George – lead guitar
Pete Best– drums (1961)
Ringo – drums (1969)

Studio recording and mixing

22 June 1961 – *Friedrich-Eberts-Halle, Hamburg*
Unknown take numbers

24 June 1961 – *Polydor, Hamburg*
[1] – stereo mix from unknown take number

1964 – *Polydor, Hamburg*
[2] – mono mix from [1]

1964 – *Atlantic Studios, USA*
Overdubs onto [2]
[3] – mono mix from overdubbed track

24 July 1969 – *Studio Two* – *Abbey Road session 27 out of 42*
Unnumbered take

1995 – *EMI*
[4] – stereo mix from unnumbered take

Releases   UK/US peak

	UK/US peak
'Ain't She Sweet' / 'If You Love Me Baby' single (1964) – Polydor NH 52317 [2]	29
'Ain't She Sweet' / 'Nobody's Child' single (US, 1964) – Atco 45-6308 [3]	19
Beatles First LP (1967) – Polydor 236 201 [1]	–
The Early Tapes Of The Beatles CD (1985) – Polydor 823701-2 [1]	–
Anthology 1 CD (1995) – Apple 8 34445 2 [3]	2/1
Anthology 3 CD (1996) – Apple 8 34451 2 [4]	4/1

=== NOTES ===

♪ The song was originally published in 1927, though John knew it from Gene Vincent's 1956 version.
♪ Performed by the Quarry Men/Beatles between 1957 and 1962.

Ain't That A Shame

[Domino-Bartholomew]

Lead vocals, **John** or **Paul**. The song was played by the Quarry Men/Beatles until 1961. A US #1 for Pat Boone in 1955, while making #10 on the *Billboard* Juke Box charts for Fats Domino. In the UK, Boone reached #7 in 1955, and Domino #23 in 1957. George Martin produced a version by the Southlanders in 1955, but this failed to chart. John recorded a version for his 1975 *Rock 'n' Roll* LP.

All I've Got To Do

[Lennon-McCartney]

John – lead vocals, rhythm guitar
Paul – harmony and backing vocals, bass
George – backing vocals, lead guitar
Ringo – drums

Studio recording and mixing

11 September 1963 – Studio Two – With The Beatles session 4 out of 9
Takes 1–14
Overdubs onto take 14 – possibly guitar or vocals > take 15

30 September 1963 – Studio Two control room
RM15 [1] – mono mix from take 15

29 October 1963 – Studio Three control room
RS15 [2] – stereo mix from take 15

19 December 1963 – Capitol
[3] – mastering of stereo mix from [2]
[4] – mastering of mono mix from [3]

Releases	UK/US peak
With The Beatles LP (1963) – Parlophone PMC 1206 [1], PCS 3045 [2]	1
Meet The Beatles! LP (US, 1964) – Capitol T 2047 [4], ST 2047 [3]	1
Meet The Beatles! EP (US, 1964)– Capitol SXA 2047 [3]	–

=== NOTES ===
♪ Paul plays chords on the bass.

All My Loving

[Lennon-McCartney]

Paul – lead vocals, bass
John – harmony and backing vocals, rhythm guitar
George – harmony and backing vocals, lead guitar
Ringo – drums

Studio recording and mixing

30 July 1963 – Studio Two – With The Beatles session 3 out of 9
Takes 1–4, 6–11
Overdubs onto take 11 – vocals > takes 12–14

21 August 1963 – Studio Two control room
RM14 [1] – mono mix from take 14

29 October 1963 – Studio Three control room
RS14 [2] – stereo mix from take 14

19 December 1963 – Capitol
[3] – mastering of stereo mix from [2]
[4] – mastering of mono mix from [3]

1993 – EMI
[5] – stereo mix from take 14

BBC and other performances

2 December 1963 – *The Morecambe And Wise Show* broadcast on 18 April 1964 (ATV)
7 December 1963 – *It's The Beatles* broadcast the same day (BBC TV)
17 December 1963 – 21 December 1963 edition of *Saturday Club*
18 December 1963 [6] – 26 December 1963 edition of *From Us To You*
7 January 1964 – 15 February 1964 edition of *Saturday Club*
12 January 1964 – *Sunday Night At The London Palladium* (ATV, live)
9 February 1964 [7] – *The Ed Sullivan Show* (CBS TV, live)
16 February 1964 [8] – *The Ed Sullivan Show* (CBS TV, live)
28 February 1964 [9] – 30 March 1964 edition of *From Us To You*
17 June 1964 – *The Beatles Sing For Shell* broadcast on 1 July 1964 (Channel 9 TV, Australia)
23 August 1964 [10] – Hollywood Bowl (live)

Releases   *UK/US peak*

Release	UK/US peak
With The Beatles LP (1963) – Parlophone PMC 1206 [1], PCS 3045 [2]	1
With The Beatles LP (Germany, 1963) – Odeon O 83 991 [1], Odeon STO 83 568 [2, untrimmed]	–
Meet The Beatles! LP (US, 1964) – Capitol T 2047 [4], ST 2047 [3]	1
All My Loving EP (1964) – Parlophone GEP 8891 [1]	1
'All My Loving' / 'This Boy' single (Canada, 1964) – Capitol 72144 [1]	45
Meet The Beatles! EP (US, 1964) – Capitol SXA 2047 [3]	–
Four By The Beatles EP (US, 1964) – Capitol EAP 1-2121 [4]	92
The Beatles 1962–1966 LP (1973) – Apple PCSP 717 [2]	3
The Beatles 1962–1966 LP (US, 1973) – Apple SKBO 3403 [3]	3
The Beatles At The Hollywood Bowl LP (1977) – Parlophone EMTV 4 / Capitol SMAS 11638 [10]	1/2
The Beatles Ballads LP (1980) – Parlophone PCS 7214 [2]	17
The Beatles 1962–1966 CD (1993) – EMI CDP 7 97036 2 [5]	3
Live At The BBC CD (1994) – Apple 8 31796 2 [9]	1/3
Anthology 1 CD (1995) – Apple 8 34445 2 [7]	2/1
The Four Historic Ed Sullivan Shows DVD (2003) – EREDV 372 [7] [8]	
The Beatles Bootleg Recordings 1963 (2013) – iTunes [6]	–
Live At The Hollywood Bowl CD (2016) – Apple 6025 57054972 [10]	3/7

┌─────── **NOTES** ───────┐

  ♪ The first song played on the first Ed Sullivan Show.
  ♪ Won the Ivor Novello Award for best British song in 1963.
  ♪ Performed in concert in 1963–64.

└─────────────────────┘

All Shook Up

[Blackwell-Presley]

Lead vocals, **Paul**. Played by the Quarry Men until at least 1960, and may have been performed on 6 July 1957, when John met Paul for the first time. A US and UK #1 for Elvis Presley in 1957.

All Things Must Pass

[Harrison]

George – vocals, guitars

Studio recording and mixing

25 February 1969 – unknown studio – Abbey Road rehearsal session
Demo takes 1–2
Overdubs onto take 2 – guitar

1996 – EMI
[1] – stereo mix from demo take 2

Releases   *UK/US peak*

Anthology 3 CD (1996) – Apple 8 34451 2 **[1]**   4/1

═══════ **NOTES** ═══════

♪ The demo version was engineered by
  Ken Scott.
♪ The title track of George's 1970 triple-LP set.
♪ Covered by Billy Preston as 'All Things (Must)
  Pass' on his 1970 LP *Encouraging Words*, his
  second and final LP on the Apple label.

All Together Now

[Lennon-McCartney]

Paul – lead vocals, acoustic guitar, bass
John – lead and harmony vocals, acoustic guitar, banjo, harmonica
George – harmony vocals
Ringo – harmony vocals, drums, finger cymbals

Studio recording and mixing

12 May 1967 – Studio Two – Yellow Submarine session 5 out of 15
Takes 1–9
Overdubs onto take 9 – vocals, bass, percussion
RM6 **[1]** – mono mix from take 9

29 October 1968 – *Studio Three control room*
RS1 [2] – stereo mix from take 9

25 November 1968 – *EMI*
[3] – mono mix from [2]

1999 – *EMI*
[4] – stereo mix from take 9

Releases
UK/US peak

Yellow Submarine movie (1968) [1]	
Yellow Submarine LP (1969) – Apple PMC 7070 [3], PCS 7070 [2]	3
Yellow Submarine LP (US, 1969) – Apple SW 153 [2]	2
Yellow Submarine Songtrack CD (1999) – Apple 5 21481 2 [4]	8/15
Mono Masters CD (2009) – Apple 6 849582 4 [1]	–

> ════════════ **NOTES** ════════════
>
> ♪ Recorded and mixed in less than six hours, in George Martin's absence.
> ♪ The song appears twice in the film, re-appearing in an abridged version during the live action sequence at the end of the film.

All You Need Is Love

[Lennon-McCartney]

John – lead vocals, harpsichord, banjo
Paul – backing and harmony vocals, bass, double bass
George – backing and harmony vocals, violin, guitar
Ringo – drums
George Martin – piano
Session musicians – four violins, two cellos, two trumpets (one piccolo trumpet and one doubling on flügelhorn), two trombones, two tenor saxophones, accordion
Chorus

Studio recording and mixing

14 June 1967 – *Olympic Sound – Yellow Submarine session 9 out of 15*
Takes 1–33
Tape reduction of take 10 > take 10

19 June 1967 – *Studio Three – Yellow Submarine session 10 out of 15*
Overdubs onto take 10 – vocals, drums, piano, banjo

23 June 1967 – *Studio One – Yellow Submarine session 11 out of 15*
Tape reduction of take 10
Overdubs onto take 10 – orchestra > takes 34–43

24 June 1967 – *Studio One* – *Yellow Submarine session 12 out of 15*
Overdubs onto take 10 – orchestra > takes 44–47

25 June 1967 – *Studio One* – *Yellow Submarine session 13 out of 15*
Overdubs onto take 10 – orchestra, vocals > takes 48–57
Overdubs onto take 10 – orchestra, bass, drums, guitar, vocals > take 59 (telecast)
Overdubs onto take 59 – vocals

26 June 1967 – *Studio Two* – *Yellow Submarine session 14 out of 15*
Overdubs onto take 59 – drums

26 June 1967 – *Studio Two control room*
RM4 [1] – mono mix from take 59

1967 – *Capitol*
[2] – mock stereo mix from [1]

1 November 1967 – *Room 53*
RM11 [3] – mono mix from take 59

29 October 1968 – *Studio Two control room*
RS6 [4] – stereo mix from take 59

25 November 1968 – *EMI*
[5] – mono mix from [4]

1999 – *EMI*
[6] – stereo mix from take 59

2004–06 – *EMI*
[7] – stereo mix from take 59: includes samples from 'Ticket To Ride' (guitar); 'Sgt Pepper's Lonely Hearts Club Band', 'Baby You're A Rich Man', 'Rain', 'The Beatles' Third Christmas Record' (vocals); 'Good Night' (orchestra)

2015 – *EMI*
[8] – stereo mix from take 59

Releases   UK/US peak

'All You Need Is Love' / 'Baby You're A Rich Man' single (1967) – Parlophone R 5620 [1]	1
'All You Need Is Love' / 'Baby You're A Rich Man' single (US, 1967) – Capitol 5964 [1]	1
Magical Mystery Tour LP (US, 1967) – Capitol MAL 2835 [1], SMAL 2835 [2]	1
Yellow Submarine movie (1968) [3]	
Yellow Submarine LP (1969) – Apple PMC 7070 [5], PCS 7070 [4]	3
Yellow Submarine LP (US, 1969) – Apple SW 153 [4]	2
The Beatles 1967–1970 LP (1973) – Apple PCSP 718 [4]	2
The Beatles 1967–1970 LP (US, 1973) – Apple SKBO 3404 [4]	1
Reel Music LP (1982) – Parlophone PCS 7218 / Capitol SV-12199 [4]	–/19
20 Greatest Hits LP (1982) – Parlophone PCTC 260 / Capitol SV-12245 [4]	10/50
Yellow Submarine Songtrack CD (1999) – Apple 5 21481 2 [6]	8/15

Love CD (2006) – Apple 0946 3 80790 2 6 [7]   3/4
1+ CD/DVD (2015) – Apple 6205 47567727 [8]   5/6

=== **NOTES** ===

♪ The first single to credit George Martin.
♪ George plays violin and John plays banjo on
  the backing track.
♪ Played to an estimated TV audience of around
  400 million.

Almost Grown

[Berry]

Lead vocals, **John**. Played by the Beatles until 1962, and during the *Let It Be* sessions on 24 January 1969. It was a minor US hit for Chuck Berry in 1959.

And I Love Her

[Lennon-McCartney]

Paul – lead vocals, bass
John – acoustic guitar
George – acoustic lead guitar, possibly claves
Ringo – bongos

Studio recording and mixing

25 February 1964 – Studio Two – A Hard Day's Night session 2 out of 12
Takes 1–2

26 February 1964 – Studio Two – A Hard Day's Night session 3 out of 12
Takes 3–19

27 February 1964 – Studio Two – A Hard Day's Night session 4 out of 12
Takes 20–21
Overdubs onto take 21 – claves, vocals

3 March 1964 – Studio One control room
RM1 [1] – mono mix from take 21

22 June 1964 – Studio One control room
RM2 [2] – mono mix from take 21
RS1 [3] – stereo mix from take 21

1964 – Capitol
[4] – stereo mix from [3], edited

1964 – United Artists
[5] – panned mono mix made from [1]

1993 – EMI
RS1 [6] – stereo mix from take 21

1995 – EMI
[7] – mono mix from take 2

BBC and other performances

19 July 1964 – *Blackpool Night Out* (Associated British Corp. TV, live)
14 July 1964 – 16 July 1964 edition of *Top Gear*

Releases   UK/US peak

	UK/US peak
A Hard Day's Night LP (1964) – Parlophone PMC 1230 [2], PCS 3058 [3]	1
A Hard Day's Night LP (US, 1964) – United Artists UAL 3366 [1], UAS 6366 [5]	1
'And I Love Her' / 'If I Fell' single (US, 1964) – Capitol 5235 [1]	12
Something New LP (US, 1964) – Capitol T 2108 [1], ST 2108 [3]	2
Something New LP (Germany, 1964) – Odeon STO 83 756 [4]	–
Something New EP (US, 1964) – Capitol SXA 2108 [1]	–
The Beatles 1962–1966 LP (1973) – Apple PCSP 717 [3]	3
The Beatles 1962–1966 LP (US, 1973) – Apple SKBO 3403 [3]	3
Love Songs LP (1977) – Parlophone PCSP 721 / Capitol SKBL 11711 [3]	7/24
Rarities LP (US, 1980) – Capitol SHAL 12060 [4]	21
The Beatles Ballads LP (1980) – Parlophone PCS 7214 [3]	17
Reel Music LP (1982) – Parlophone PCS 7218 / Capitol SV-12199 [3]	–/19
The Beatles 1962–1966 CD (1993) – EMI CDP 7 97036 2 [6]	3
Anthology 1 CD (1995) – Apple 8 34445 2 [7]	2/1

═══ NOTES ═══

♪ The first all-acoustic guitar/percussion recording released by the group.
♪ The German version has an extra two guitar riffs edited in at the end, giving six instead of four.
♪ Mix [1] has single-tracked lead vocals, all others are mainly double-tracked.
♪ The version on *A Hard Day's Night* released as part of the 13-CD set *The U.S. Albums* in 2014 is mix [1], but runs a little slow.

And Your Bird Can Sing

[Lennon-McCartney]

John – lead vocals, rhythm guitar
Paul – harmony vocals, bass, lead guitar
George – harmony vocals, lead guitar
Ringo – drums, tambourine

Studio recording and mixing

***20 April 1966** – Studio Two – Revolver session 10 out of 33*
Takes 1–2
Overdubs onto take 2 – vocals

***26 April 1966** – Studio Two – Revolver session 13 out of 33*
Takes 3–13
Overdubs onto take 10 – vocals

***12 May 1966** – Studio Three control room*
RM7, RM8 – mono mix from takes 10 and 6
[1] – edit of RM7 and RM8

***13 May 1966** – Capitol*
[2] – mastering of mock stereo mix from [1]

***20 May 1966** – Studio Three control room*
RS1, RS2 – stereo mix from takes 10 and 6
[3] – edit of RS1 and RS2

***6 June 1966** – Studio Three control room*
RM9, RM10 – mono mix from takes 10 and 6

***8 June 1966** – Studio Three control room*
[4] – edit of RM9 and RM10

***1995** – EMI*
[5] – stereo mix from take 2

Releases   UK/US peak

	UK/US peak
Revolver LP (1966) – Parlophone PMC 7009 [4], PCS 7009 [3]	1
"Yesterday" … And Today LP (US, 1966) – Capitol T 2553 [1], ST 2553 [2] [3]	1
Anthology 2 CD (1996) – Apple 8 34448 2 [5]	1/1
Tomorrow Never Knows (2012) – iTunes [3]	44/24

═══════ **NOTES** ═══════

♪ John's original title was 'You Don't Get Me'.
♪ Take 2 features much giggling and tomfoolery.

Anna (Go To Him)

[Alexander]

John – lead vocals, acoustic guitar
Paul – backing vocals, bass
George – backing vocals, lead guitar
Ringo – drums

Studio recording and mixing

11 February 1963 – Studio Two – Please Please Me session 5 out of 8
Takes 1–3

25 February 1963 – Studio One control room
[1] – mono mix from take 3
[2] – stereo mix from take 3

1965 – Capitol
[3] – stereo mix from [2]
[4] –mono mix from [3]

BBC and other performances

17 June 1963 [5] – 25 June 1963 edition of *Pop Go The Beatles*
1 August 1963 [6] – 27 August 1963 edition of *Pop Go The Beatles*

Releases   *UK/US peak*

Please Please Me LP (1963) – Parlophone PMC 1202 [1], PCS 3042 [2]	1
Introducing... The Beatles LP (US, 1963) – Vee Jay VJLP 1062 [1], VJSR 1062 [2]	2
The Beatles (No. 1) EP (1963) – Parlophone GEP 8883 [1]	2
Souvenir Of Their Visit To America EP (US, 1964) – Vee Jay VJEP 1903 [1]	–
The Early Beatles LP (US, 1965) – Capitol T 2309 [4], ST 2309 [3]	43
On Air – Live At The BBC Volume 2 CD (2013) – Apple 6025 37491698 [6]	12/7
The Beatles Bootleg Recordings 1963 (2013) – iTunes [5]	–

=== **NOTES** ===

♪ Arthur Alexander's original release
   got to #68 in the US in 1962.
♪ Performed live in 1962–63.

Another Beatles Christmas Record

[Lennon-McCartney-Harrison-Starkey]

John, Paul, George, Ringo – vocals, piano, effects

Studio recording and mixing

26 October 1964 – Studio Two – Beatles For Sale session 8 out of 8
Takes 1–5 – Christmas message for fan club members

26 October 1964 – Studio Two control room
[1] – edit of takes 1–5

Releases   *UK/US peak*

From Then To You LP (1970) – Apple LYN 2153/2154 [1]	–

═══════════ **NOTES** ═══════════

♪ The second Christmas flexidisc sent out to members of the fan club.
♪ Mainly spoken messages scripted by Tony Barrow, with a little piano busking.

Another Girl

[Lennon-McCartney]

Paul – lead vocals, bass, lead guitar
John – harmony vocals, acoustic guitar
George – harmony vocals, rhythm guitar
Ringo – drums

Studio recording and mixing

15 February 1965 – Studio Two – Help! session 1 out of 13
Take 1
10 unnumbered edit pieces (unused)

16 February 1965 – Studio Two – Help! session 2 out of 13
Overdubs onto take 1 – guitar, tom tom, vocals

18 February 1965 – Studio Two control room
RM1 [1] – mono mix from take 1

23 February 1965 – Studio Two control room
RS1 [2] – stereo mix from take 1

1965 – Capitol
[3] – mono mix made from [2]

1987 – EMI
[4] – stereo mix from take 1

Releases   *UK/US peak*

Help! LP (1965) – Parlophone PMC 1255 [1], PCS 3071 [2]	1
Help! LP (US, 1965) – Capitol MAS 2386 [3], SMAS 2386 [2]	1
Help! CD (1987) – EMI CDP 7 46439 2 [4]	61

═══════════ **NOTES** ═══════════

♪ Written by Paul in Hammamet, Tunisia, in early February 1965.
♪ The unused edit pieces were guitar flourishes for the end of the song.

Any Time At All

[Lennon-McCartney]

John – lead vocals, acoustic guitar
Paul – lead vocals, bass, possibly piano
George – lead guitar
Ringo – drums

Studio recording and mixing

2 June 1964 – Studio Two – A Hard Day's Night session 10 out of 12
Takes 1–11

3 June 1964 – Studio Two – A Hard Day's Night session 11 out of 12
Overdubs onto take 11 – vocals, piano

22 June 1964 – Studio One control room
RM2 [1] – mono mix from take 11
RM3 [2] – mono mix from take 11
RS1 [3] – stereo mix from take 11

Releases   *UK/US peak*

A Hard Day's Night LP (1964) – Parlophone PMC 1230 [1], PCS 3058 [3]	1
Something New LP (US, 1964) – Capitol T 2108 [2], ST 2108 [3]	2
Extracts From The Album 'A Hard Day's Night' EP (1964) – Parlophone GEP 8924 [1]	7
Rock 'n' Roll Music LP (1976) – Parlophone PCSP 719 / Capitol SKBO 11537 [3]	11/2

═ NOTES ═

♪ The middle eight is without vocals as there was no time to complete the recording – Ringo contracted tonsillitis the day before embarking on the 1964 world tour.
♪ The overdubs may have been recorded on 2 June.
♪ The pianist may be George Martin.

Ask Me Why

[McCartney-Lennon]

John – lead vocals, rhythm guitar
Paul – harmony and backing vocals, bass
George – harmony and backing vocals, lead guitar
Pete Best – drums (6 & 11 June 1962)
Ringo – drums

Studio recording and mixing

6 June 1962 – Studio Two or Three – Please Please Me session 1 out of 8
Unknown take numbers

26 November 1962 – Studio Two – Please Please Me session 4 out of 8
Takes 1–6

30 November 1962 – Studio Two control room
[1] – mono mix from take 6

25 February 1963 – Studio One control room
[2] – mono mix from take 6
[3] – stereo mix from take 6

1965 – Capitol
[4] – stereo mix from [3]
[5] – mono mix from [4]

BBC and other performances

11 June 1962 – 15 June 1962 edition of *Here We Go*
December 1962 [6] – Star-Club, Hamburg (live)
16 January 1963 – 25 January 1963 edition of *Here We Go*
22 January 1963 – 29 January 1963 edition of *The Talent Spot*
2 July 1963 – 16 July 1963 edition of *Pop Go The Beatles* (not broadcast)
3 September 1963 [7] – 24 September 1963 edition of *Pop Go The Beatles*

Releases

	UK/US peak
'Please Please Me' / 'Ask Me Why' single (1963) – Parlophone 45-R 4983 [1]	2
'Please Please Me' / 'Ask Me Why' single (US, 1963) – Vee Jay VJ 498 [1]	–
Please Please Me LP (1963) – Parlophone PMC 1202 [2], PCS 3042 [3]	1
Introducing… The Beatles LP (US, 1963) – Vee Jay VJLP 1062 [2], VJSR 1062 [3]	2
All My Loving EP (1964) – Parlophone GEP 8891 [2]	1
Souvenir Of Their Visit To America EP (US, 1964) – Vee Jay VJEP 1903 [1]	–
The Early Beatles LP (US, 1965) – Capitol T 2309 [5], ST 2309 [4]	43
Live! At The Star-Club In Hamburg, Germany; 1962 LP (1977) – Lingasong LNL 1 [6]	–
On Air – Live At The BBC Volume 2 CD (2013) – Apple 6025 37491698 [7]	12/7

=== NOTES ===

♪ The first Lennon-McCartney track to be played for the BBC.
♪ Only Capitol release is on *The Early Beatles*.
♪ Performed live from 1962–63.

Baby It's You

[David-Bacharach-Williams]

John – lead vocals, rhythm guitar
Paul – backing vocals, bass
George – backing vocals, lead guitar
Ringo – drums
George Martin – celeste

Studio recording and mixing

11 February 1963 – Studio Two – Please Please Me session 5 out of 8
Takes 1–3

20 February 1963 – Studio One – Please Please Me session 6 out of 8
Overdubs – piano (unused), celeste > takes 4–6

25 February 1963 – Studio One control room
[1] – mono mix from take 5
[2] – stereo mix from take 5

1965 – Capitol
[3] – stereo mix from [2]
[4] –mono mix from [3]

BBC and other performances

1 April 1963 – 22 April 1963 edition of *Side By Side*
1 June 1963 [5] – 11 June 1963 edition of *Pop Go The Beatles*

Releases

	UK/US peak
Please Please Me LP (1963) – Parlophone PMC 1202 [1], PCS 3042 [2]	1
Introducing… The Beatles LP (US, 1963) – Vee Jay VJLP 1062 [1], VJSR 1062 [2]	2
The Early Beatles LP (US, 1965) – Capitol T 2309 [4], ST 2309 [3]	43
Live At The BBC CD (1994) – Apple 8 31796 2 [5]	1/3
'Baby It's You' single (1995) – Apple 8 82073 2 [5]	7/67
1+ CD/DVD (2015) – Apple 6205 47567727 [5]	5/6

========= **NOTES** =========

♪ Performed in concert from 1962–63.
♪ The Shirelles' original got to #8 in the US in February 1962.
♪ George Martin plays the celeste overdub – although the
   Beatles happened to be in London at the time, appearing live
   on the BBC's *Parade Of The Pops*.

Baby Let's Play House

[Gunter]

Lead vocals, **John**. Performed on 6 July 1957, when John met Paul for the first time, being one of two songs captured on tape on that day. It was played by the Beatles until 1962. It was the first Elvis Presley song to chart nationally, making #5 on the *Billboard* country singles chart in 1955. John used the opening lines in his song 'Run For Your Life'.

Baby You're A Rich Man

[Lennon-McCartney]

John – lead vocals, piano, clavioline
Paul – backing vocals, bass, piano
George – backing vocals, guitar
Ringo – drums, tambourine, maracas
Session musician – vibraphone

Studio recording and mixing

11 May 1966 – Olympic Sound – Yellow Submarine session 4 out of 15
Takes 1–12
Tape reduction of take 12 > takes 1, 2
Overdubs onto take 2 – guitar, clavioline, vocals, backwards piano, vibraphone
[1] – mono mix from take 2

1967 – Capitol
[2] – mock stereo mix from [1]

1970 – Capitol
[3] – mock stereo mix from [1]

22 October 1971 – AIR Studios
[4] – stereo mix from take 2

1999 – EMI
[5] – stereo mix from take 2

Releases

	UK/US peak
'All You Need Is Love' / 'Baby You're A Rich Man' single (1967) – Parlophone R 5620 [1]	1
'All You Need Is Love' / 'Baby You're A Rich Man' single (US, 1967) – Capitol 5964 [1]	34
Magical Mystery Tour LP (US, 1967) – Capitol MAL 2835 [1], SMAL 2835 [2] [3]	1
Magical Mystery Tour LP (Germany, 1971) – Hör Zu SHZE 327 / Apple 1C 072-04449 [4]	–
Magical Mystery Tour cassette (1976) – Parlophone TC-PCS 3077 [4]	–
The Beatles EP (1981) – Parlophone SGE 1 [4]	
Magical Mystery Tour CD (1987) – EMI CDP 7 48062 2 [4]	52
Yellow Submarine Songtrack CD (1999) – Apple 5 21481 2 [5]	8/15

╔══════════════ **NOTES** ══════════════╗

♪ John's song 'One Of The Beautiful People'
   combined with Paul's chorus.
♪ The first session to be held at Olympic –
   the first track recorded and mixed outside
   Abbey Road.
♪ Not mixed for stereo until 1971.

╚══════════════════════════════════════╝

Baby's In Black

[Lennon-McCartney]

John – lead vocals, acoustic guitar
Paul – harmony vocals, bass, tambourine
George – lead guitar
Ringo – drums

Studio recording and mixing

11 August 1964 – Studio Two – Beatles For Sale session 1 out of 8
Takes 1–14
13 unnumbered edit pieces (unused)

26 October 1964 – Studio Two control room
RM2 [1] – mono mix from take 14

4 November 1964 – Studio Two control room
RS1 [2] – stereo mix from take 14

BBC and other performances

11 April 1965 – *NME 1964–65 Annual Poll-Winners' Concert*
20 June 1965 – *Les Beatles* (Europe 1 TV, France, live)
15 August 1965 – *The Beatles At Shea Stadium* (live), broadcast by BBC TV on
   1 March 1966
29 August 1965 [3 intro] – Hollywood Bowl (live)
30 August 1965 [4] – Hollywood Bowl (live)
24 June 1966 – *Die Beatles* broadcast on 5 July 1966 (ZDF TV, Germany)

Releases   *UK/US peak*

Beatles For Sale LP (1964) – Parlophone PMC 1240 [1], PCS 3062 [2]	1
Beatles '65 LP (US, 1964) – Capitol T 2228 [1], ST 2228 [2]	1
Beatles For Sale (No. 2) EP (1965) – Parlophone GEP 8938 [1]	5
'Real Love' single (1996) – Apple 8 82646 2 [edit of 3, 4]	4/11
Live At The Hollywood Bowl CD (2016) – Apple 6025 57054972 [4]	3/7

```
═══════ NOTES ═══════
```

♪ In triple time (6/8).
♪ George's guitar swell achieved by manual adjustment of the volume control rather than by foot pedal.
♪ Performed live until 1966.

Back In The U.S.S.R.

[Lennon-McCartney]

Paul – lead vocals, piano, lead guitar, bass, drums, percussion
John – backing vocals, lead guitar, six-string bass, drums, percussion
George – backing vocals, lead guitar, six-string bass, percussion, possibly drums

Studio recording and mixing

May 1968 – Kinfauns, Esher
Demo recording

22 August 1968 – Studio Two – White Album session 48 out of 81
Takes 1–5

23 August 1968 – Studio Two – White Album session 49 out of 81
Overdubs onto take 5 – drums, bass, piano, guitar
Tape reduction of take 5 > take 6
Overdubs onto take 6 – vocals, handclaps

23 August 1968 – Studio Two control room
RM1 [1] – mono mix from take 6

13 October 1968 – Studio Two control room
RS1 [2] – stereo mix from take 6

2004–06 – EMI
[3] – stereo mix from take 6: includes alternative vocals

2018 – EMI
[4] – stereo mix from take 6
[5] – stereo mix from demo
[6] – stereo mix from take 5

Releases   *UK/US peak*

The Beatles LP (1968) – Apple PMC 7067–7068 [1], PCS 7067–7068 [2]	1
The Beatles LP (US, 1968) – Apple SWBO-101 [2]	1
The Beatles 1967–1970 LP (1973) – Apple PCSP 718 [2]	2
The Beatles 1967–1970 LP (US, 1973) – Apple SKBO 3404 [2]	1
Rock 'n' Roll Music LP (1976) – Parlophone PCSP 719 / Capitol SKBO 11537 [2]	11/2
'Back In The U.S.S.R.' / 'Twist And Shout' single (1976) – Parlophone R 6016 [2]	19

Love CD (2006) – Apple 0946 3 80790 2 6 [3]	3/4
Tomorrow Never Knows (2012) – iTunes [2]	44/24
The Beatles Deluxe CD (2018) – Apple 0602567571957 [4] [5] [6]	4/6

NOTES

♪ Ringo quit during the recording.
♪ The 1976 single was to promote the *Rock 'n' Roll Music* LP.

Bad Boy

[Williams]

John – lead vocals, rhythm guitar, possibly organ
Paul – bass, electric piano
George – lead guitar
Ringo – drums, tambourine

Studio recording and mixing

10 May 1965 – Studio Two – Help! session 9 out of 13
Takes 1–4
Overdubs onto take 4 – guitar, piano, tambourine, vocals

10 May 1965 – Studio Two control room
RM1 [1] – mono mix from take 4
RS1 [2] – stereo mix from take 4

1976 – Capitol
[3] – stereo mix from take 4

Releases   *UK/US peak*

Beatles VI LP (US, 1965) – Capitol T 2358 [1], ST 2358 [2]	1
A Collection Of Beatles Oldies LP (1966) – Parlophone PMC 7016 [1], PCS 7016 [2]	7
Rock 'n' Roll Music LP (1976) – Parlophone PCSP 719 [2]	11
Rock 'n' Roll Music LP (US, 1976) – Capitol SKBO 11537 [3]	2
Rarities LP (1978) – Parlophone PCM 1001, PSLP 261 [2]	71
Past Masters 1 CD (1988) – EMI CDP 7 90043 2 [2]	49/–

NOTES

♪ A Larry Williams single from 1959, performed live from 1960 to 1962.
♪ Recorded for the US market – the UK release was over 18 months
after its recording.
♪ The lead track on a Japanese EP from May 1967 – ahead of
'Strawberry Fields Forever', 'Penny Lane' and 'Good Day Sunshine'.

Bad To Me

[Lennon-McCartney]

John – lead vocals, acoustic guitar
Paul – lead vocals, acoustic guitar

Studio recording and mixing

May 1963 – unknown location
[1] – demo version

Releases
UK/US peak

The Beatles Bootleg Recordings 1963 (2013) – iTunes [1]
—

NOTES

♪ Written by John for Billy J Kramer and the
  Dakotas, who took it to #1 in August 1963 and
  to #9 in the US in 1964.
♪ Paul was present for Kramer's recording at
  Abbey Road on 27 June 1963.

The Ballad Of John And Yoko

[Lennon-McCartney]

John – lead vocals, acoustic and electric guitars, percussion
Paul – harmony vocals, bass, drums, piano, maracas

Studio recording and mixing

14 April 1969 – Studio Three – Abbey Road session 2 out of 42
Takes 1–11
Overdubs onto take 10 – bass, piano, guitar, maracas, percussion

14 April 1969 – Studio Three control room
RS5 [1] – stereo mix from take 10

Releases
UK/US peak

'The Ballad Of John And Yoko' / 'Old Brown Shoe' single (1969) – Apple R 5786 [1]	1
'The Ballad Of John And Yoko' / 'Old Brown Shoe' single (US, 1969) – Apple 2531 [1]	8
Hey Jude LP (US, 1970) – Apple SW 385 [1]	2
The Beatles 1967–1970 LP (1973) – Apple PCSP 718 [1]	2
The Beatles 1967–1970 LP (US, 1973) – Apple SKBO 3404 [1]	1
20 Greatest Hits LP (1982) – Parlophone PCTC 260 [1]	10
Past Masters 2 CD (1988) – EMI CDP 7 90044 2 [1]	46/–
1+ CD/DVD (2015) – Apple 6205 47567727 [1]	5/6

The Beatles' 1968 Christmas Record

[Lennon-McCartney-Harrison-Starkey]

John, Paul, George, Ringo, Mal Evans, Tiny Tim – vocals, piano, guitars, effects

Studio recording and mixing

1968 – various locations
Unnumbered takes – Christmas message for fan club members

1968 – Kenny Everett studio
[1] – edit of unnumbered takes

Releases   *UK/US peak*

From Then To You LP (1970) – Apple LYN 2153/2154 [1]   –

The Beatles' Christmas Record

[Lennon-McCartney-Harrison-Starkey]

John, Paul, George, Ringo – vocals, percussion, effects

Studio recording and mixing

17 October 1963 – Studio Two – With The Beatles session 8 out of 9
Unnumbered takes – Christmas message for fan club members

October 1963 – Studio Two control room

[1] – edit of unnumbered takes

Releases _____ *UK/US peak*

From Then To You LP (1970) – Apple LYN 2153/2154 **[1]**   –

═══════════════ **NOTES** ═══════════════

♪ The first Christmas flexidisc sent out to members of the fan club.
♪ Messages from the four, scripted by Tony Barrow.

The Beatles' Seventh Christmas Record
[Lennon-McCartney-Harrison-Starkey]

John, Paul, George, Ringo, Yoko Ono – vocals, guitars, effects

Studio recording and mixing

1969 – various locations

Unnumbered takes – Christmas message for fan club members

1969 – Kenny Everett studio

[1] – edit of unnumbered takes

Releases _____ *UK/US peak*

From Then To You LP (1970) – Apple LYN 2153/2154 **[1]**   –

═══════════════ **NOTES** ═══════════════

♪ The final Christmas flexidisc, mainly featuring John and
Yoko interviewing each other, and a song by Paul.
♪ Again, the various contributions were recorded separately,
and then edited and mixed by Kenny Everett.

The Beatles' Third Christmas Record
[Lennon-McCartney-Harrison-Starkey]

John, Paul, George, Ringo – vocals, guitars, percussion, effects

Studio recording and mixing

8 November 1965 – Studio Two – Rubber Soul session 13 out of 15

Takes 1–3 – Christmas message for fan club members

9 November 1965 – Room 65

[1] – edit of takes 1–3

Releases *UK/US peak*

From Then To You LP (1970) – Apple LYN 2153/2154 **[1]** –

═══ NOTES ═══

♪ Includes badly busked versions of 'Yesterday', and a mention by John of "we'll gather lilacs in an old brown shoe".

♪ The last Christmas disc to be co-written and produced by Tony Barrow.

Beautiful Dreamer

[Foster-Keller-Goffin]

Paul – lead vocals, bass
John – backing vocals, rhythm guitar
George – backing vocals, lead guitar
Ringo – drums

BBC and other performances

22 January 1963 **[1]** – 26 January 1963 edition of *Saturday Club*

Releases *UK/US peak*

On Air – Live At The BBC Volume 2 CD (2013) – Apple 6025 37491698 **[1]** 12/7

═══ NOTES ═══

♪ Written by Stephen Foster in 1864, a hit for Al Jolson in 1951.

♪ Jack Keller and Gerry Goffin wrote new lyrics for a version by Tony Orlando in 1962.

Be-Bop-A-Lula

[Vincent-Davis]

John – rhythm guitar
Paul – bass
George – lead guitar
Ringo – drums
Fredi Fascher – vocals

BBC and other performances

December 1962 **[1]** – Star-Club, Hamburg (live)

Releases *UK/US peak*

Live! At The Star-Club In Hamburg, Germany; 1962 LP (1977) – Lingasong LNL 1 /
   Lingasong LS 2 7001 **[1]**   –

```
═══════ NOTES ═══════
```
♪ A *Billboard* #7 and UK #16 single by Gene
   Vincent from 1956.
♪ Vocals by Fredi Fascher, one of the
   brothers who kept things in line at the
   Star-Club – normally vocals would be by
   John.
♪ Appears on John's *Rock 'n' Roll* LP.

Because

[Lennon-McCartney]

John – harmony vocals, guitar
Paul – harmony vocals, bass
George – harmony vocals, Moog synthesiser
George Martin – electric harpsichord

Studio recording and mixing

1 August 1969 – Studio Two – Abbey Road session 33 out of 42
Takes 1–23
Overdubs onto take 16 – vocals

4 August 1969 – Studio Two – Abbey Road session 34 out of 42
Overdubs onto take 16 – vocals

5 August 1969 – Room 43 – Abbey Road session 35 out of 42
Overdubs onto take 16 – Moog

12 August 1969 – Studio Two control room
RS2 **[1]** – stereo mix from take 16

1996 – EMI
[2] – stereo mix from take 16 (vocals only)

2004–06 – EMI
[3] – stereo mix from take 16: includes sample from 'Across The Universe' (bird sound
effects); wood pigeon and other sound effects

Releases *UK/US peak*

Abbey Road LP (1969) – Apple PCS 7088 **[1]**	1
Abbey Road LP (US, 1969) – Apple SO 383 **[1]**	1
Anthology 3 CD (1996) – Apple 8 34451 2 **[2]**	4/1

> ### ═══════ NOTES ═══════
>
> ♪ The vocals consist of three sets of three-part harmonies, nine voices in all.
> ♪ The Moog synthesiser was first used on a Beatles track on 5 August.
> ♪ The recording involved all four Beatles, although Ringo does not appear on the finished track.

A Beginning
see 'Don't Pass Me By'

Being For The Benefit Of Mr Kite!

[Lennon-McCartney]

John – lead vocals, organ
Paul – harmony vocals, bass, guitar
George – harmonica, tambourine
Ringo – drums, harmonica
George Martin – harmonium, Hammond organ
Mal Evans, Neil Aspinall – harmonicas

Studio recording and mixing

17 February 1967 – Studio Two – Sgt Pepper session 29 out of 56
Takes 1–7
Tape reduction of take 7 > takes 8, 9
Overdubs onto take 9 – vocals

20 February 1967 – Studio Three – Sgt Pepper session 30 out of 56
Unnumbered takes – editing of calliope tapes

28 March 1967 – Studio Two – Sgt Pepper session 50 out of 56
Overdubs onto take 9 – harmonica, organ, guitar, tambourine

29 March 1967 – Studio Two – Sgt Pepper session 51 out of 56
Overdubs onto take 9 – calliope effects

31 March 1967 – Studio Two – Sgt Pepper session 53 out of 56
Overdubs onto take 9 – glockenspiel, organ

31 March 1967 – Studio Two control room
RM4 [1] – mono mix from take 9

7 April 1967 – Studio Two control room
RS8 [2] – stereo mix from take 9

1995 – EMI

[3] – stereo mix from takes 1, 2
[4] – stereo mix from take 7

2004–06 – EMI

[5] – stereo mix from take 9, in medley with 'I Want You (She's So Heavy)' take 1 and 'Helter Skelter' take 21: includes samples from 'Cry Baby Cry' (accordion); 'Good Morning Good Morning' (sound effects); 'Helter Skelter' (vocals); laughter possibly from 'Piggies' session

2016/17 – EMI

[6] – stereo mix from takes 1, 4
[7] – stereo mix from take 9

Releases

	UK/US peak
Sgt Pepper's Lonely Hearts Club Band LP (1967) – Parlophone PMC 7027 [1], PCS 7027 [2]	1
Sgt Pepper's Lonely Hearts Club Band LP (US, 1967) – Capitol MAS 2653 [1], SMAS 2653 [2]	1
Anthology 2 CD (1996) – Apple 8 34448 2 [3] [4]	1/1
Love CD (2006) – Apple 0946 3 80790 2 6 [5]	3/4
Sgt Pepper's Lonely Hearts Club Band Deluxe CD (2017) – Apple 0602557455328 [1] [6] [7]	1/3

NOTES

♪ Calliope tapes were cut up and randomly reconstructed to create organ effect.
♪ Automatic double-tracking was added to the vocals during the mixing.

Besame Mucho

[Velazquez-Skylar]

Paul – lead vocals, bass
John – harmony vocals, rhythm guitar
George – harmony vocals, lead guitar
Pete Best – drums (January & June 1962)
Ringo – drums

Studio recording and mixing

1 January 1962 – Decca Studios
Studio test recorded in mono

6 June 1962 – Studio Two or Three – Please Please Me session 1 out of 8
Unknown take numbers

29 January 1969 – Apple Studio – Let It Be rehearsal session
Takes 29.12–29.15 [1, edited]

1984 – AIR Studios
[2] – editing unknown take number

BBC and other performances

11 June 1962 – 15 June 1962 edition of *Here We Go*
December 1962 [3] – Star-Club, Hamburg (live)

Releases   *UK/US peak*

Let It Be movie (1970) [1]
Live! At The Star-Club In Hamburg, Germany; 1962 LP (1977) – Lingasong LNL 1 /
    Lingasong LS 2 7001 [3]   –
Anthology 1 CD (1995) – Apple 8 34445 2 [2]   2/1

```
┌──────────────────── NOTES ────────────────────┐
│                                                │
│   ♪ Written in 1940 by Consuelo Velázquez,    │
│     with English lyrics added in 1944 by       │
│     Sunny Skylar.                              │
│   ♪ A single by the Coasters from 1960 with    │
│     King Curtis on sax.                        │
│                                                │
└────────────────────────────────────────────────┘
```

Birthday

[Lennon-McCartney]

Paul – lead and harmony vocals, bass, piano
John – lead and harmony vocals, lead guitar
George – harmony vocals, lead guitar, tambourine
Ringo – drums
Pattie Harrison, Yoko Ono – backing vocals

Studio recording and mixing

18 September 1968 – Studio Two – White Album session 63 out of 81
Takes 1–21
Four- to eight-track tape copying of take 19 or 20 > take 22
Overdubs onto take 22 – vocals, piano, tambourine, handclaps

18 September 1968 – Studio Two control room
RM1 [1] – mono mix from take 22

14 October 1968 – Studio Two control room
RS1 [2] – stereo mix from take 22

2018 – EMI
[3] – stereo mix from take 2
[4] – stereo mix from take 22

Releases
UK/US peak

The Beatles LP (1968) – Apple PMC 7067–7068 [1], PCS 7067–7068 [2]	1
The Beatles LP (US, 1968) – Apple SWBO-101 [2]	1
Rock 'n' Roll Music LP (1976) – Parlophone PCSP 719 / Capitol SKBO 11537 [2]	11/2
The Beatles Deluxe CD (2018) – Apple 0602567571957 [3] [4]	4/6

NOTES

♪ Yoko and Pattie Harrison on backing vocals.
♪ Midway through recording, the group nipped round to Paul's house to watch *The Girl Can't Help It* on TV.
♪ The LP's only true Lennon-McCartney collaboration (also with contributions from the others).

Blackbird

[Lennon-McCartney]

Paul – lead vocals, acoustic guitar

Studio recording and mixing

May 1968 – Kinfauns, Esher
Demo recording

11 June 1968 – Studio Two – White Album session 10 out of 81
Takes 1–32 (unannounced)
Overdubs onto take 32 – vocals

11 June 1968 – Studio Two control room
RM1–RM6 – mono mixes from take 32

13 October 1968 – Studio Two control room
RS1 [1] – stereo mix from take 32 with sound effects overdub
RM10 [2] – mono mix from take 32 with sound effects overdub

1996 – EMI
[3] – stereo mix from take 4

2004–06 – EMI
[4] – stereo mix from take 32, in medley with 'Yesterday' take 2: possibly includes sample from 'Girl' (guitar)

2018 – EMI
[5] – stereo mix from demo
[6] – stereo mix from take 28
[7] – stereo mix from take 32 with sound effects overdub

Releases

	UK/US peak
The Beatles LP (1968) – Apple PMC 7067–7068 [2], PCS 7067–7068 [1]	1
The Beatles LP (US, 1968) – Apple SWBO-101 [1]	1
The Beatles Ballads LP (1980) – Parlophone PCS 7214 [1]	17
Anthology 3 CD (1996) – Apple 8 34451 2 [3]	4/1
Love CD (2006) – Apple 0946 3 80790 2 6 [4]	3/4
The Beatles Deluxe CD (2018) – Apple 0602567571957 [5] [6] [7]	4/6

═══ **NOTES** ═══

♪ Just Paul – the recording was made while John was recording sound effects for 'Revolution 9' in Studio Three.
♪ The tapping sound is not a metronome, but Paul's feet, specially miked.

Blue Jay Way

[Harrison]

George – lead vocals, Hammond organ
Paul – backing vocals, bass
John – backing vocals, possibly organ
Ringo – drums, tambourine
Session musician – cello

Studio recording and mixing

6 September 1967 – Studio Two – Magical Mystery Tour session 13 out of 30
Take 1

7 September 1967 – Studio Two – Magical Mystery Tour session 14 out of 30
Tape reduction of take 1 > take 2
Overdubs onto take 2 – vocals
Tape reduction of take 2 > take 3
Overdubs onto take 3 – vocals

6 October 1967 – Studio Two – Magical Mystery Tour session 23 out of 30
Overdubs onto take 3 – cello, tambourine

7 November 1967 – Studio Two control room
RM27 [1] – mono mix from take 3, edited
RS12 [2] – stereo mix from take 3, edited

See 'Something' [3] for *Love* CD info.

Releases

	UK/US peak
Magical Mystery Tour EP (1967) – Parlophone MMT-1 [1], SMMT-1 [2]	2
Magical Mystery Tour LP (US, 1967) – Capitol MAL 2835 [1], SMAL 2835 [2]	1

```
======= NOTES =======
```
♪ Composed by George on a keyboard rather than a guitar.
♪ The backward vocal effects appear on the stereo version only.

Blue Moon

[Rodgers-Hart]

Paul – lead vocals, acoustic guitar
John – skulls
Ringo – percussion

Studio recording and mixing

16 September 1968 – Studio Two – White Album session 61 out of 81
Studio jam

2018 – EMI
[1] – stereo mix from studio jam

Releases   *UK/US peak*

The Beatles Deluxe CD (2018) – Apple 0602567571957 [1]   4/6

```
======= NOTES =======
```
♪ An international #1 for the Marcels in 1961.
♪ Recorded by Elvis Presley for his debut LP.

Blue Moon Of Kentucky

[Monroe]

Lead vocals, **Paul**. Played by the Quarry Men/Beatles between 1957 and 1961. Written by bluegrass singer Bill Monroe and recorded by Elvis Presley in 1954. It was released with 'That's All Right', but failed to chart nationally.

Blue Suede Shoes

see 'Rip It Up/Shake, Rattle And Roll/Blue Suede Shoes'

Bony Maronie

[Williams]

Lead vocals, **John**. Part of the Quarry Men/Beatles' set between 1957 and 1961. The second of Larry Williams' two hits, #14 in the US, #11 in the UK. It appears on John's 1975 *Rock 'n' Roll* LP.

Boppin' The Blues

[Perkins-Griffin]

Played by the Quarry Men/Beatles until around 1961 with **John** singing lead. Carl Perkins took it to #9 on the *Billboard* country & western chart in 1956.

Boys

[Dixon-Farrell]

Ringo – lead vocals, drums
John – backing vocals, rhythm guitar
Paul – backing vocals, bass
George – backing vocals, lead guitar

Studio recording and mixing

11 February 1963 – Studio Two – Please Please Me session 5 out of 8
Take 1

25 February 1963 – Studio One control room
[1] – mono mix from take 1
[2] – stereo mix from take 1

1965 – Capitol
[3] – stereo mix from [2]
[4] –mono mix from [3]

1976 – Capitol
[5] – stereo mix from take 1

BBC and other performances

1 April 1963 [6] – 13 May 1963 edition of *Side By Side*
21 May 1963 – 25 May 1963 edition of *Saturday Club*
4 April 1963 – 24 June 1963 edition of *Side By Side*
17 June 1963 [7] – 25 June 1963 edition of *Pop Go The Beatles*
3 September 1963 [8] – 17 September 1963 edition of *Pop Go The Beatles*
7 December 1963 – *It's The Beatles* broadcast the same day (BBC TV)
18 December 1963 – 26 December 1963 edition of *From Us To You*
19 April 1964 [9] – *Around The Beatles* (Rediffusion TV, not broadcast)
17 July 1964 – 3 August 1964 edition of *From Us To You*
23 August 1964 [10] – Hollywood Bowl (live)
3 October 1964 – *Shindig* broadcast on 7 October 1964 (American
 Broadcasting Co. TV)

Releases   *UK/US peak*

Please Please Me LP (1963) – Parlophone PMC 1202 [1], PCS 3042 [2]   1

Introducing… The Beatles LP (US, 1963) – Vee Jay VJLP 1062 [1], VJSR 1062 [2]	2
The Early Beatles LP (US, 1965) – Capitol T 2309 [4], ST 2309 [3]	43
'Kansas City/Hey, Hey, Hey, Hey' / 'Boys' single (1965) – Capitol Starline 6066 [4]	102
Rock 'n' Roll Music LP (1976) – Parlophone PCSP 719 [2]	11
Rock 'n' Roll Music LP (US, 1976) – Capitol SKBO 11537 [5]	2
The Beatles At The Hollywood Bowl LP (1977) – Parlophone EMTV 4 / Capitol SMAS 11638 [10]	1/2
'Baby It's You' single (1995) – Apple 8 82073 2 [6]	7/67
Anthology 1 CD (1995) – Apple 8 34445 2 [9]	2/1
On Air – Live At The BBC Volume 2 CD (2013) – Apple 6025 37491698 [7]	12/7
The Beatles Bootleg Recordings 1963 (2013) – iTunes [6] [8]	–
Live At The Hollywood Bowl CD (2016) – Apple 6025 57054972 [10]	3/7

═ NOTES ═

♪ The B-side of the Shirelles' US #1 'Will You Love Me Tomorrow'.

♪ Previously sung by John with the Beatles, and by Ringo with Rory Storm & Hurricanes.

♪ Performed by the Beatles live until 1964.

Can You Take Me Back

[Lennon-McCartney]

Paul – lead vocals, acoustic guitar
John – skulls
Ringo – percussion

Studio recording and mixing

16 September 1968 – Studio Two – White Album session 61 out of 81
Take 1 (from take 19 of 'I Will')

16 October 1968 – unspecified control room
RM [1] – mono mix from take 1
RS [2] – stereo mix from take 1

2018 – EMI
[3] – stereo mix from take 1

Releases   *UK/US peak*

The Beatles LP (1968) – Apple PMC 7067–7068 [1], PCS 7067–7068 [2]	1
The Beatles LP (US, 1968) – Apple SWBO-101 [2]	1
The Beatles Deluxe CD (2018) – Apple 0602567571957 [2] [3]	4/6

```
┌══════════════ NOTES ══════════════┐
│                                                │
│ ♪ Officially untitled and uncopyrighted snippet, │
│   ad-libbed by Paul during takes for 'I Will'. │
│ ♪ Uncredited insert between 'Cry Baby Cry' and │
│   'Revolution 9'.                              │
│ ♪ [3] is the full version, and an extended version │
│   appears on the Love CD – see 'Come Together'. │
│                                                │
└════════════════════════════════════┘
```

Can't Buy Me Love

[Lennon-McCartney]

Paul – lead vocals, bass
John – acoustic guitar
George – lead guitar
Ringo – drums

Studio recording and mixing

29 January 1964 – EMI Pathé Marconi, Paris – A Hard Day's Night session 1 out of 12
Takes 1–4

25 February 1964 – Studio Two – A Hard Day's Night session 2 out of 12
Overdubs onto take 4 – guitar, vocals

26 February 1964 – Studio Two control room
RM1 [1] – mono mix from take 4

10 March 1964 – Studio Two – A Hard Day's Night session 6 out of 12
Possible overdubs onto take 4 – hi-hat

10 March 1964 – Studio Two control room
RS1 [2] – stereo mix from take 4

1964 – United Artists
[3] – panned mono mix made from [1]

1993 – EMI
[4] – stereo mix from take 4

1995 – EMI
[5] – mono mix from edit of takes 2, 1

BBC and other performances

28 February 1964 [6] – 30 March 1964 edition of *From Us To You*
31 March 1964 – 4 April 1964 edition of *Saturday Club*
19 April 1964 [7] – *Around The Beatles*, mimed performance recorded on 28
    April and broadcast on 6 May 1964 (Rediffusion TV)
26 April 1964 – *NME 1963–64 Annual Poll-Winners' Concert*

1 May 1964 – 18 May 1964 edition of *From Us To You*
17 June 1964 – *The Beatles Sing For Shell* broadcast on 1 July 1964 (Channel 9 TV, Australia)
20 June 1965 – *Les Beatles* (Europe 1 TV, France, live)
15 August 1965 – *The Beatles At Shea Stadium* (live), broadcast by BBC TV on 1 March 1966
30 August 1965 **[8]** – Hollywood Bowl (live)

Releases

	UK/US peak
'Can't Buy Me Love' / 'You Can't Do That' single (1964) – Parlophone R 5114 **[1]**	1
'Can't Buy Me Love' / 'You Can't Do That' single (US, 1964) – Capitol 5150 **[1]**	1
The Beatles' Million Sellers EP (1965) – Parlophone GEP 8946 **[1]**	1
A Hard Day's Night LP (1964) – Parlophone PMC 1230 **[1]**, PCS 3058 **[2]**	1
A Hard Day's Night LP (US, 1964) – United Artists UAL 3366 **[1]**, UAS 6366 **[3]**	1
A Collection Of Beatles Oldies LP (1966) – Parlophone PMC 7016 **[1]**, PCS 7016 **[2]**	7
Hey Jude LP (US, 1970) – Apple SW 385 **[2]**	2
The Beatles 1962–1966 LP (1973) – Apple PCSP 717 **[2]**	3
The Beatles 1962–1966 LP (US, 1973)– Apple SKBO 3403 **[2]**	3
The Beatles At The Hollywood Bowl LP (1977) – Parlophone EMTV 4 / Capitol SMAS 11638 **[8]**	1/2
Reel Music LP (1982) – Parlophone PCS 7218 / Capitol SV-12199 **[2]**	–/19
20 Greatest Hits LP (1982) – Parlophone PCTC 260 / Capitol SV-12245 **[2]**	10/50
The Beatles 1962–1966 CD (1993) – EMI CDP 7 97036 2 **[4]**	3
Anthology 1 CD (1995) – Apple 8 34445 2 **[5]**	2/1
Live At The BBC CD (1994) – Apple 8 31796 2 **[6]**	1/3
1+ CD/DVD (2015) – Apple 6205 47567727 **[7]**	5/6
Live At The Hollywood Bowl CD (2016) – Apple 6025 57054972 **[8]**	3/7

=== NOTES ===

♪ The first recording not held at Abbey Road studios at the only session held outside London.
♪ Performed in concert until 1965.
♪ *Around The Beatles* performance has both Paul and John miming vocals.
♪ Sold 940,225 copies in the US on the first day of release.

Carol

[Berry]

John – lead vocals, rhythm guitar
Paul – bass
George – lead guitar
Ringo – drums

BBC and other performances

2 July 1963 [1] – 16 July 1963 edition of *Pop Go The Beatles*

Releases   *UK/US peak*

Live At The BBC CD (1994) – Apple 8 31796 2 [1]   1/3

┌─────────────── NOTES ───────────────┐
│ ♪ A Chuck Berry single from 1958, also covered │
│   by the Rolling Stones on their debut LP.   │
└──────────────────────────────────────┘

Cathy's Clown

[Everly-Everly]

Lead vocals, **John** and **Paul**. Part of the Beatles' set until 1962. On the earliest surviving (partial) Beatles set list written by Paul in mid-1960. A US and UK #1 in 1960 for the Everly Brothers.

Catswalk

[McCartney]

An instrumental, written by Paul in 1958/59. It appears on a rehearsal tape recorded in the Cavern club in late 1962. It was recorded under the title 'Cat Call' by trad jazz trombonist Chris Barber in 1967, with Paul on keyboards, but failed to chart.

Cayenne

[McCartney]

Paul – acoustic guitar
John – acoustic guitar
Stuart Sutcliffe – bass

BBC and other performances

early 1960 – amateur recording made in Liverpool

1995 – EMI
[1] – edited from source tape

Releases   *UK/US peak*

Anthology 1 CD (1995) – Apple 8 34445 2 [1]   2/1

┌─────────────── NOTES ───────────────┐
│ ♪ One of a number of Paul's guitar-based instrumentals from 1959. │
└──────────────────────────────────────┘

Chains

[Goffin-King]

George – lead vocals, guitar
John – harmony vocals, rhythm guitar, harmonica
Paul – harmony vocals, bass
Ringo – drums

Studio recording and mixing

11 February 1963 – Studio Two – Please Please Me session 5 out of 8
Takes 1–4

25 February 1963 – Studio One control room
[1] – mono mix from take 1
[2] – stereo mix from take 1

1965 – Capitol
[3] – stereo mix from [2]
[4] –mono mix from [3]

BBC and other performances

16 January 1963 – 25 January 1963 edition of *Here We Go*
1 April 1963 [5] – 13 May 1963 edition of *Side By Side*
17 June 1963 [6] – 25 June 1963 edition of *Pop Go The Beatles*
3 September 1963 [7] – 17 September 1963 edition of *Pop Go The Beatles*

Releases

	UK/US peak
Please Please Me LP (1963) – Parlophone PMC 1202 [1], PCS 3042 [2]	1
The Beatles (No. 1) EP (1963) – Parlophone GEP 8883 [1]	2
Introducing… The Beatles LP (US, 1963) – Vee Jay VJLP 1062 [1], VJSR 1062 [2]	2
The Early Beatles LP (US, 1965) – Capitol T 2309 [4], ST 2309 [3]	43
On Air – Live At The BBC Volume 2 CD (2013) – Apple 6025 37491698 [6]	12/7
The Beatles Bootleg Recordings 1963 (2013) – iTunes [5] [7]	–

=**NOTES**=

♪ A #17 hit in the US for the Cookies, backing group for Neil Sedaka.
♪ Released in November 1962, it was the most recent of the *Please Please Me* covers to be a hit.
♪ Performed live until 1963.

Child Of Nature

[Lennon]

John – lead vocals, acoustic guitar

Studio recording and mixing

May 1968 – Kinfauns, Esher
Demo recording

2018 – EMI
[1] – stereo mix from demo

Releases

The Beatles Deluxe CD (2018) – Apple 0602567571957 [1]   4/6

> ## ═NOTES═
>
> ♪ Like Paul's 'Mother Nature's Son', it was inspired by a lecture given by Maharishi in Rishikesh.
> ♪ The song was given a new set of lyrics and became 'Jealous Guy', recorded by John for his LP *Imagine*.

Christmas Time (Is Here Again)

[Lennon-McCartney-Harrison-Starkey]

John – vocals, timpani
Paul – vocals, piano
George – vocals, acoustic guitar
Ringo – vocals, drums

Studio recording and mixing

6 December 1966 – Studio Two – Sgt Pepper session 5 out of 56
[1] – Christmas messages for Radio London and Radio Caroline

28 November 1967 – Studio Three – Magical Mystery Tour session 30 out of 30
Take 1 (music)
Takes 1–10 (speech)
Overdubs onto edit of take 1 (music), 2, 6, 10 (speech) [2] – sound effects

29 November 1967 – Studio One control room
[3] – mono mix from edit of take 1 (music), 2, 6, 10 (speech)

1995 – EMI
[4] – stereo mix from edit of [1] and [2]

Releases

From Then To You LP (1970) – Apple LYN 2153/2154 [3]   –
'Free As A Bird' single (1995) – Apple 8 82587 2 [4]   2/6

====== **NOTES** ======

♪ [3] is the fifth Christmas flexidisc for fan club members.
♪ The first and last parts of [4] are in stereo, run longer and include parts not used on the Christmas record.

Circles

[Harrison]

George – lead vocals, organ

Studio recording and mixing

May 1968 – Kinfauns, Esher
Demo recording

2018 – EMI
[1] – stereo mix from demo

Releases   *UK/US peak*

The Beatles Deluxe CD (2018) – Apple 0602567571957 [1]   4/6

====== **NOTES** ======

♪ Finally released on George's 1982 *Gone Troppo*.

Clarabella

[Pingatore]

Paul – lead vocals, bass
John – rhythm guitar
George – lead guitar
Ringo – drums

BBC and other performances

2 July 1963 [1] – 16 July 1963 edition of *Pop Go The Beatles*

Releases   *UK/US peak*

Live At The BBC CD (1994) – Apple 8 31796 2 [1]   1/3

====== **NOTES** ======

♪ A 1956 B-side by the Jordimars, former members of Bill Haley's Comets.
♪ Performed by Billy Preston on the US show *Shindig!* in August 1965.

C'mon Everbody

[Cochran-Capehart]

Lead vocals, **John** or **Stuart Sutcliffe**. Played by the Quarry Men/Beatles until around 1962. A UK #6 in 1959 for Eddie Cochran.

Come And Get It

[McCartney]

Paul – lead vocals, piano, bass, maracas, drums

Studio recording and mixing

24 July 1969 – Studio Two – Abbey Road session 27 out of 42
Take 1
Overdubs onto take 1 – vocals, maracas, bass, drums

24 July 1969 – Studio Two control room
[1] – stereo mix from take 1

Releases
UK/US peak

Anthology 3 CD (1996) – Apple 8 34451 2 [1]   4/1

=== NOTES ===

♪ A one-man recording by Paul for Badfinger who were about change their name from the Iveys.
♪ Paul produced the Badfinger session, telling them "it's got to be exactly like this demo".
♪ The single reached #4 in the UK and #7 in the US in early 1970.

Come Go With Me

[Quick]

Lead vocals, **John**. Played by the Quarry Men at St Peter's Church fete on 6 July 1957, the day Paul met John. The group would play it until the Quarry Men name was dropped. A 1956 single by the doo-wop group the Del-Vikings, it was written by their bass vocalist Clarence Quick and reached #4 on *Billboard*.

Come Together

[Lennon-McCartney]

John – lead and harmony vocals, guitars
Paul – harmony vocals, bass, electric piano
George – guitar
Ringo – drums, maracas

Studio recording and mixing

21 July 1969 – Studio Three – Abbey Road session 24 out of 42
Takes 1–8
Four- to eight-track tape copying of take 6[8?] > take 9

22 July 1969 – Studio Three – Abbey Road session 25 out of 42
Overdubs onto take 9 – vocals, piano, guitar, maracas

23 July 1969 – Studio Three – Abbey Road session 26 out of 42
Overdubs onto take 9 – guitar

25 July 1969 – Studio Two – Abbey Road session 28 out of 42
Overdubs onto take 9 – vocals

29 July 1969 – Studio Three – Abbey Road session 30 out of 42
Overdubs onto take 9 – guitar

30 July 1969 – Studio Three – Abbey Road session 31 out of 42
Overdubs onto take 9 – guitar

7 August 1969 – Studio Two control room
RS1 [1] – stereo mix from take 9

1996 – EMI
[2] – stereo mix from take 1

2004–06 – EMI
[3] – stereo mix from take 9, in medley with 'Dear Prudence' take 1 and 'Cry Baby Cry' take 12 (including 'Can You Take Me Back'): includes samples from 'Eleanor Rigby' (strings); 'A Day In The Life' (orchestra); 'Let It Be' (drums)

Releases

	UK/US peak
'Something' / 'Come Together' single (1969) – Apple R 5814 [1]	4
'Something' / 'Come Together' single (US, 1969) – Apple 2654 [1]	2 (1)
Abbey Road LP (1969) – Apple PCS 7088 [1]	1
Abbey Road LP (US, 1969) – Apple SO 383 [1]	1
The Beatles 1967–1970 LP (1973) – Apple PCSP 718 [1]	2
The Beatles 1967–1970 LP (US, 1973) – Apple SKBO 3404 [1]	1
Anthology 3 CD (1996) – Apple 8 34451 2 [2]	4/1
Love CD (2006) – Apple 0946 3 80790 2 6 [3]	3/4
1+ CD/DVD (2015) – Apple 6205 47567727 [1]	5/6

═ NOTES ═

♪ Inspired by Timothy Leary's request to John for a campaign song.
♪ See 'Something' for details of the *Billboard* chart position.

The Continuing Story Of Bungalow Bill

[Lennon-McCartney]

John – lead vocals, acoustic guitar, organ
Paul – harmony vocals, bass
George – harmony vocals, acoustic guitar
Ringo – harmony vocals, drums, tambourine
Yoko Ono, Maureen Starkey and others – backing vocals
Chris Thomas – Mellotron

Studio recording and mixing

May 1968 – Kinfauns, Esher
Demo recording

8 October 1968 – Studio Two – White Album session 76 out of 81
Takes 1–3
Overdubs onto take 3 – Mellotron, vocals

9 October 1968 – Studio Two control room
RS2 **[1]** – stereo mix from take 3
RM1 **[2]** – mono mix from take 3

2018 – EMI
[3] – stereo mix from demo
[4] – stereo mix from take 2
[5] – stereo mix from take 3

Releases   *UK/US peak*

The Beatles LP (1968) – Apple PMC 7067–7068 **[2]**, PCS 7067–7068 **[1]**	1
The Beatles LP (US, 1968) – Apple SWBO-101 **[1]**	1
The Beatles Deluxe CD (2018) – Apple 0602567571957 **[3] [4] [5]**	4/6

=== **NOTES** ===

♪ John's first character-based song.
♪ About an American student, Richard A Cooke III,
   who was with the Beatles in Rishikesh.
♪ The guitar flourish at the beginning is a sample
   from the Mellotron.

Corinne, Corrina

[Trad.]

Lead vocals, **John**. A traditional country blues song, played by the Beatles around 1961–62. Bill Haley & His Comets released it as a single in 1958 and a 1960 recording by Ray Peterson, produced by Phil Spector, reached #9 on *Billboard*.

Cry Baby Cry

[Lennon-McCartney]

John – lead vocals, acoustic guitar, piano, whistling
Paul – harmony vocals, bass, whistling
George – lead guitar
Ringo – drums, tambourine
George Martin – harmonium

Studio recording and mixing

May 1968 – Kinfauns, Esher
Demo recording

15 July 1968 – Studio Two – White Album session 26 out of 81
Unnumbered takes

16 July 1968 – Studio Two – White Album session 27 out of 81
Takes 1–10
Tape reduction of take 10 > takes 11, 12
Overdubs onto take 12 – harmonium, piano

18 July 1968 – Studio Two – White Album session 28 out of 81
Overdubs onto take 12 – vocals, harmonium, tambourine, sound effects

15 October 1968 – Studio Two control room
RS3 [1] – stereo mix from take 12
RM1 [2] – mono mix from take 12

1996 – EMI
[3] – stereo mix from take 1

2018 – EMI
[4] – stereo mix from demo
[5] – stereo mix from unnumbered rehearsal
[6] – stereo mix from take 12

Releases   UK/US peak

	UK/US peak
The Beatles LP (1968) – Apple PMC 7067–7068 [2], PCS 7067–7068 [1]	1
The Beatles LP (US, 1968) – Apple SWBO-101 [1]	1
Anthology 3 CD (1996) – Apple 8 34451 2 [3]	4/1
The Beatles Deluxe CD (2018) – Apple 0602567571957 [4] [5] [6]	4/6

═══ **NOTES** ═══

♪ The fraught studio atmosphere caused Geoff Emerick
to temporarily stop working for the Beatles.
♪ Leads into the unlisted 'Can You Take Me Back'.

Cry For A Shadow

[Harrison-Lennon]

John – rhythm guitar
Paul – bass
George – lead guitar
Pete Best – drums

Studio recording and mixing

22 June 1961 – Friedrich-Eberts-Halle, Hamburg
Unknown take numbers

22 June 1961 – Polydor, Hamburg
[1] – stereo mix from unknown take number

c. 1962 – Polydor, Hamburg
[2] – mono mix from [1]

Releases   *UK/US peak*

'Cry For A Shadow' / 'Why (Can't You Love Me Again)' single (1964) – Polydor NH 52275 [2]	–
'Why' / 'Cry For A Shadow' single (US, 1964) – MGM K13227 [2]	–
Beatles First LP (1967) – Polydor 236 201 [1]	–
The Early Tapes Of The Beatles CD (1985) – Polydor 823701-2 [1]	–
Anthology 1 CD (1995) – Apple 8 34445 2 [1]	2/1

=== NOTES ===

♪ The first Beatles original song (it is an instrumental) to be recorded in a studio.
♪ Probably part of the Beatles' set around 1961.

Crying, Waiting, Hoping

[Holly]

George – lead vocals, lead guitar
John – backing vocals, rhythm guitar
Paul – backing vocals, bass
Pete Best – drums (1962)
Ringo – drums

Studio recording and mixing

1 January 1962 – Decca Studios
Studio test recorded in mono

BBC and other performances

16 July 1963 [1] – 6 August 1963 edition of *Pop Go The Beatles*

Releases   *UK/US peak*

Live At The BBC CD (1994) – Apple 8 31796 2 [1]   1/3

```
┌══════════ NOTES ══════════┐
  ♪ Buddy Holly's 1959 B-side to
    'Peggy Sue Got Married', his first
    posthumous single.
  ♪ Performed live by the Beatles
    from 1960–62.
└═══════════════════════════┘
```

Cumberland Gap

[Trad.]

Lead vocals, **John**. The song was played by the Quarry Men until around 1959, and may have been another of the songs performed on 6 July 1957, when Paul and John met for the first time. It is an Appalachian folk song from about 1924. It was a UK #1 for Lonnie Donegan in 1957, at the same time as a George Martin-produced version by the Vipers Skiffle Group made it to #10.

Dance In The Street

[Davis-Welch]

Lead vocals, **Paul**. The song was played by the Beatles until 1962. The earliest movie footage of the Beatles – silent but in colour from early 1962 – shows the group performing this song. It was originally released by Gene Vincent in September 1958.

Darktown Strutters' Ball

[Brooks]

Lead vocals, **George**. Performed by the Beatles throughout the first three Hamburg seasons. Written in 1917, the Beatles heard the version by Joe Brown, which got to #34 in the UK, his first chart hit. Fats Domino also covered the song in 1958.

A Day In The Life

[Lennon-McCartney]

John – lead vocals, acoustic guitar, tambourine, piano
Paul – lead vocals, bass, piano
George – maracas
Ringo – drums, congas, piano
George Martin – harmonium
Mal Evans – piano

Session musicians – twelve violins, four violas, four cellos, two double basses, harp, two clarinets, oboe, two flutes, three trumpets, three trombones, tuba, two bassoons, two French horns, percussion

Studio recording and mixing

19 January 1967 – Studio Two – Sgt Pepper session 20 out of 56

Takes 1–4
Overdubs onto take 4 – vocals, piano

20 January 1967 – Studio Two – Sgt Pepper session 21 out of 56

Tape reduction of take 4 > takes 5–7
Overdubs onto take 6 – vocals, bass, drums, percussion

30 January 1967 – Studio Three control room

RM1 [1] – mono mix from take 6

3 February 1967 – Studio Two – Sgt Pepper session 24 out of 56

Overdubs onto take 6 – vocals, bass, drums, tom toms, maracas, tambourine

10 February 1967 – Studio One – Sgt Pepper session 27 out of 56

Tape reduction of take 6 > take 7
Overdubs onto take 7 – orchestra
Tape reduction of take 7 with overdubs onto take 6
Edit pieces takes 8–11
Edit of take 9 onto take 7

22 February 1967 – Studio Two – Sgt Pepper session 32 out of 56

Edit pieces 1–9 – piano chord

22 February 1967 – Studio Two control room

RM6–RM9 – mono mixes from takes 6, 7
[2] – edit of RM9 and edit piece 9

23 February 1967 – Studio Two control room

RS10–RS12 – stereo mixes from takes 6, 7
[3] – edit of RS12 and edit piece 9

1995 – EMI

[4] – mix from takes 1, 2, 6 and RM1

2004–06 – EMI

[5] – stereo mix from takes 1, 6, 7 and edit piece 9: includes additional sound effects

2015 – EMI

[6] – mix from takes 6, 7 and edit piece 9

2016/17 – EMI

[7] – stereo mix from take 1
[8] – stereo mix from take 2

[9] – stereo mix of overdub onto take 7
[10] – stereo mix of edit piece takes 8–11
[11] – stereo mix of edit piece 9
[12] – stereo mix from takes 6, 7 and edit piece 9

Releases   UK/US peak

Sgt Pepper's Lonely Hearts Club Band LP (1967) – Parlophone PMC 7027 [2], PCS 7027 [3]	1
Sgt Pepper's Lonely Hearts Club Band LP (US, 1967) – Capitol MAS 2653 [2], SMAS 2653 [3]	1
The Beatles 1967–1970 LP (1973) – Apple PCSP 718 [3]	2
The Beatles 1967–1970 LP (US, 1973) – Apple SKBO 3404 [3]	1
'Sgt Pepper's Lonely Hearts Club Band' / 'With A Little Help From My Friends' / 'A Day In The Life' single (1978) – Parlophone R 6022 [3]	63
'Sgt Pepper's Lonely Hearts Club Band' / 'With A Little Help From My Friends' / 'A Day In The Life' single (US, 1978) – Capitol 4612 [3]	–
The Beatles 1967–1970 CD (1993) – EMI CDP 7 97039 2 [3, without crossfade]	4
Anthology 2 CD (1996) – Apple 8 34448 2 [4]	1/1
Love CD (2006) – Apple 0946 3 80790 2 6 [5]	3/4
1+ CD/DVD (2015) – Apple 6205 47567727 [6]	5/6
Sgt Pepper's Lonely Hearts Club Band Deluxe CD (2017) – Apple 0602557455328 [1] [2] [7] [8] [9] [10] [11] [12]	1/3

===== NOTES =====

♪ A promotional film was made but not shown in its entirety until 1983, probably due to the BBC ban on the song.
♪ The orchestral interlude is a combination of five separate takes.
♪ John's hand-written lyrics sold for $1.2 million at a New York auction in 2010, having fetched £56,600 in 1992.

Day Tripper

[Lennon-McCartney]

John – lead and harmony vocals, guitars
Paul – lead and harmony vocals, bass
George – lead guitar
Ringo – drums, tambourine

Studio recording and mixing

16 October 1965 – Studio Two – Rubber Soul session 3 out of 15
Takes 1–3
Overdubs onto take 3 – vocals, guitar, tambourine

26 October 1965 – Studio Two control room
RS1 [1] – stereo mix from take 3

29 October 1965 – *Studio Two control room*
RM3 [2] – mono mix from take 3
10 November 1966 – *Studio Two control room*
RS2 [3] – stereo mix from take 3
2015 – *EMI*
[4] – stereo mix from take 3, edited

Releases   UK/US peak

'We Can Work It Out' / 'Day Tripper' single (1965) – Parlophone R 5389 [2]	1
'We Can Work It Out' / 'Day Tripper' single (US, 1965) – Capitol 5555 [2]	5
A Collection Of Beatles Oldies LP (1966) – Parlophone PMC 7016 [2], PCS 7016 [3]	7
"Yesterday" … And Today LP (US, 1966) – Capitol T 2553 [2], ST 2553 [1]	1
The Beatles 1962–1966 LP (1973) – Apple PCSP 717 [3]	3
The Beatles 1962–1966 LP (US, 1973) – Apple SKBO 3403 [1]	3
20 Greatest Hits LP (1982) – Parlophone PCTC 260 [3]	10
Past Masters 2 CD (1988) – EMI CDP 7 90044 2 [3]	46/–
The Beatles 1962–1966 CD (1993) – EMI CDP 7 97036 2 [3]	3
1+ CD/DVD (2015) – Apple 6205 47567727 [4]	5/6

═══════════════ **NOTES** ═══════════════

♪ A promotional film was made on 23 November 1965 and appears on 1+.
♪ The group's first double A-sided single.
♪ Performed live until 1966.
♪ The edit corrects a gap after the middle eight where the guitar was
briefly faded out to remove a spurious squeak – the edit was also
carried out for 1 in 2000.

Dear Prudence

[Lennon-McCartney]

John – lead vocals, guitar, tambourine
Paul – backing vocals, bass, drums, piano, flügelhorn
George – backing vocals, lead guitar
Mal Evans – backing vocals, tambourine
John McCartney, Jackie Lomax – backing vocals

Studio recording and mixing

May 1968 – *Kinfauns, Esher*
Demo recording

28 August 1968 – *Trident Studios – White Album session 50 out of 81*
Take 1
Overdubs onto take 1 – guitar

29 August 1968 – *Trident Studios – White Album session 51 out of 81*
Overdubs onto take 1 – bass, vocals, tambourine

30 August 1968 – *Trident Studios – White Album session 52 out of 81*
Overdubs onto take 1 – piano, flügelhorn

13 October 1968 – *Studio Two control room*
RS1 [1] – stereo mix from take 1
RM5 [2] – mono mix from take 1

2018 – *EMI*
[3] – stereo mix from demo
[4] – stereo mix from take 1 (guitar, drums, vocals)
[5] – stereo mix from take 1

See 'Come Together' [3] for *Love* CD info.

Releases	UK/US peak
The Beatles LP (1968) – Apple PMC 7067–7068 [1], PCS 7067–7068 [2]	1
The Beatles LP (US, 1968) – Apple SWBO-101 [2]	1
The Beatles Deluxe CD (2018) – Apple 0602567571957 [3] [4] [5]	4/6

=== **NOTES** ===

♪ Recorded at Trident, with Paul on drums.
♪ The first song title mentioning a real woman, Prudence Farrow, who was with the Beatles in Rishikesh.

Devil In Her Heart

[Drapkin]

George – lead vocals, lead guitar
John – harmony and backing vocals, rhythm guitar
Paul – harmony and backing vocals, bass
Ringo – drums, maracas

Studio recording and mixing

18 July 1963 – *Studio Two – With The Beatles session 2 out of 9*
Takes 1–3
Overdubs on take 3 – vocals, maracas > takes 4–6

21 August 1963 – *Studio Three control room*
RM6 [1] – mono mix from take 6

29 October 1963 – *Studio Three control room*
RS6 [2] – stereo mix from take 6

17 March 1964 – Capitol
[3] – mastering of stereo mix from [2]
[4] – mastering of mono mix from [2]

BBC and other performances

16 July 1963 [5] – 20 August 1963 edition of *Pop Go The Beatles*
3 September 1963 [6] – 24 September 1963 edition of *Pop Go The Beatles*

Releases   UK/US peak

With The Beatles LP (1963) – Parlophone PMC 1206 [1], PCS 3045 [2]	1
The Beatles' Second Album LP (US, 1964) – Capitol T 2080 [4], ST 2080 [3]	1
The Beatles' Second Album EP (US, 1964) – Capitol SXA 2080 [3]	–
'Baby It's You' single (1995) – Apple 8 82073 2 [5]	7/67
On Air – Live At The BBC Volume 2 CD (2013) – Apple 6025 37491698 [6]	12/7

NOTES

♪ A 1962 B-side by the Donays, the single ('Bad Boy') was their only released recording.
♪ Performed live from 1962–63.
♪ The only *With The Beatles* cover not to have charted anywhere.

Dig A Pony

[Lennon-McCartney]

John – lead vocals, lead guitar
Paul – harmony vocals, bass
George – lead guitar
Ringo – drums
Billy Preston – electric piano

Studio recording and mixing

7 January 1969 – Twickenham Film Studios – Let It Be rehearsal session
Take 7.85 [1]

22 January 1969 – Apple Studio – Let It Be rehearsal session
Rehearsal

30 January 1969 – Apple rooftop – Let It Be session 9 out of 17
Take 30.8 [2]

23 March 1970 – Room 4
RS2 [3] – stereo mix from take 30.8, edited

1996 – EMI
[4] – stereo mix from rehearsal

2003 – EMI
[5] – stereo mix from take 30.8, edited

Releases   *UK/US peak*

Let It Be LP (1970) – Apple PXS1, PCS 7096 [3]	1
Let It Be LP (US, 1970) – Apple AR 34001 [3]	1
Let It Be movie (1970) [1] [2]	
Anthology 3 CD (1996) – Apple 8 34451 2 [4]	4/1
Let It Be… Naked CD (2003) – Apple 24359 57142 [5]	7/5

=== NOTES ===

♪ The only new all-John song on the LP.
♪ Edit is removal of "All I want is you" lines at the beginning and end.

Dig It

[Lennon-McCartney-Harrison-Starkey]

John – lead vocals, acoustic guitar
Paul – piano
George – rhythm guitar
Ringo – drums
Billy Preston – organ
George Martin – shaker

Studio recording and mixing

24 January 1969 – Apple Studio – Let It Be session 4 out of 17
Take 24.73 (speech)

26 January 1969 – Apple Studio – Let It Be session 6 out of 17
Take 26.27 [1]

27 March 1970 – Room 4
RS1 [2] – stereo mix from edit of takes 26.27, 24.73

Releases   *UK/US peak*

Let It Be LP (1970) – Apple PXS1, PCS 7096 [2]	1
Let It Be LP (US, 1970) – Apple AR 34001 [2]	1
Let It Be movie (1970) [1]	

=== NOTES ===

♪ The LP features a 50-second excerpt from a 12½-minute recording.

Dizzy Miss Lizzy

[Williams]

John – lead vocals, rhythm guitar
Paul – bass, possibly electric piano
George – lead guitar
Ringo – drums, cowbell

Studio recording and mixing

10 May 1965 – Studio Two – Help! session 9 out of 13
Takes 1–2
Takes 3–7
Overdubs onto take 7 – electric piano, cowbell, guitar

10 May 1965 – Studio Two control room
RM1 [1] – mono mix from take 7
RS1 [2] – stereo mix from take 7

1987 – EMI
[3] – stereo mix from take 7, with added vocal echo

BBC and other performances

26 May 1965 [4] – 7 June 1965 edition of *The Beatles Invite You To Take A Ticket To Ride*
15 August 1965 – *The Beatles At Shea Stadium* (live), broadcast by BBC TV on 1 March 1966
29 August 1965 [5] – Hollywood Bowl (live)
30 August 1965 [6] – Hollywood Bowl (live)

Releases   *UK/US peak*

Help! LP (1965) – Parlophone PMC 1255 [1], PCS 3071 [2]	1
Beatles VI LP (US, 1965) – Capitol T 2358 [1], ST 2358 [2]	1
'Dizzy Miss Lizzy' / 'Yesterday' single (1965) – Parlophone DP 563 [1]	–
Rock 'n' Roll Music LP (1976) – Parlophone PCSP 719 / Capitol SKBO 11537 [2]	11/2
The Beatles At The Hollywood Bowl LP (1977) – Parlophone EMTV 4 / Capitol SMAS 11638 [edit of 5, 6]	1/2
Help! CD (1987) – EMI CDP 7 46439 2 [3]	61
Live At The BBC CD (1994) – Apple 8 31796 2 [4]	1/3
Live At The Hollywood Bowl CD (2016) – Apple 6025 57054972 [edit of 5, 6]	3/7

═══════ **NOTES** ═══════

♪ A Larry Williams single from 1958, backed with 'Slow Down'.
♪ Performed live 1960–62, then dropped until 1965.
♪ Significant echo was added for the CD release in 1987.

Do You Want To Dance

[Freeman]

Lead vocals, **John**. Played by the Quarry Men/Beatles until 1962. A *Billboard* #5 for Bobby Freeman in 1958. It is also on John's *Rock 'n' Roll* LP.

Do You Want To Know A Secret

[McCartney-Lennon]

George – lead vocals, lead guitar
John – backing vocals, rhythm guitar
Paul – backing vocals, bass
Ringo – drums

Studio recording and mixing

11 February 1963 – Studio Two – Please Please Me session 5 out of 8
Takes 1–6
Overdubs onto take 6 – drumsticks > takes 7, 8

25 February 1963 – Studio One control room
[1] – mono mix from take 8
[2] – stereo mix from take 8

1965 – Capitol
[3] – stereo mix from [2]
[4] –mono mix from [3]

2013 – EMI
[5] – stereo mix from take 7

BBC and other performances

6 March 1963 [6] – 12 March 1963 edition of *Here We Go*
21 March 1963 – 28 March 1963 edition of *On The Scene*
1 April 1963 – 22 April 1963 edition of *Side By Side*
21 May 1963 [7] – 25 May 1963 edition of *Saturday Club*
24 May 1963 – 4 June 1963 edition of *Pop Go The Beatles*
10 July 1963 [8] – 30 July 1963 edition of *Pop Go The Beatles*

Releases*UK/US peak*

Please Please Me LP (1963) – Parlophone PMC 1202 [1], PCS 3042 [2]	1
Twist And Shout EP (1963) – Parlophone GEP 8882 [1]	1
Introducing… The Beatles LP (US, 1963) – Vee Jay VJLP 1062 [1], VJSR 1062 [2]	2
'Do You Want To Know A Secret' / 'Thank You Girl' single (US, 1964) – Vee Jay VJ 587 [1]	2
The Early Beatles LP (US, 1965) – Capitol T 2309 [4], ST 2309 [3]	43
'Do You Want To Know A Secret' / 'Thank You Girl' single (US, 1965) – Capitol Starline 6064 [4]	–
The Beatles Ballads LP (1980) – Parlophone PCS 7214 [2]	17

On Air – Live At The BBC Volume 2 CD (2013) – Apple 6025 37491698 **[8]**   12/7
The Beatles Bootleg Recordings 1963 (2013) – iTunes **[6] [7]**   –

================================ **NOTES** ================================

> ♪ Performed in concert in 1963.
> ♪ Billy J Kramer's version was held off #1 by 'From Me To You'.

Doctor Robert

[Lennon-McCartney]

John – lead vocals, rhythm guitar, harmonium
Paul – harmony vocals, bass, possibly piano
George – lead guitar, maracas
Ringo – drums

Studio recording and mixing

17 April 1966 – Studio Two – Revolver session 8 out of 33
Takes 1–7

19 April 1966 – Studio Two – Revolver session 9 out of 33
Overdubs onto take 7 – vocals

12 May 1966 – Studio Three control room
RM4 **[1]** – mono mix from take 7, edited

13 May 1966 – Capitol
[2] – mastering of mock stereo mix from **[1]**

20 May 1966 – Studio One control room
RS1 **[3]** – stereo mix from take 7, edited
RS2 **[4]** – stereo mix from take 7, edited

21 June 1966 – Studio Three control room
RM6 **[5]** – mono mix from take 7, edited

Releases   *UK/US peak*

Revolver LP (1966) – Parlophone PMC 7009 **[5]**, PCS 7009 **[4]**   1
"Yesterday" … And Today LP (US, 1966) – Capitol T 2553 **[1]**, ST 2553 **[2] [3]**   1

================================ **NOTES** ================================

> ♪ Fades to a final chord.
> ♪ Post-1973 *"Yesterday" … And Today* releases have true stereo version.
> ♪ The first Lennon-McCartney song about a real person.

Don't Bother Me

[Harrison]

George – lead vocals, lead guitar
John – rhythm guitar, tambourine
Paul – bass, claves
Ringo – drums, bongo

Studio recording and mixing

11 September 1963 – Studio Two – With The Beatles session 4 out of 9
Takes 1–4
Overdubs onto take 4 > takes 5–7

12 September 1963 – Studio Two – With The Beatles session 5 out of 9
Remake, takes 10–13
Overdubs onto take 13 – vocals, claves, tambourine, bongo > takes 15–19

30 September 1963 – Studio Two control room
RM15 [1] – mono mix from take 15

29 October 1963 – Studio Two control room
RS15 [2] – stereo mix from take 15

19 December 1963 – Capitol
[3] – mastering of stereo mix from [2]
[4] – mastering of mono mix from [3]

Releases

	UK/US peak
With The Beatles LP (1963) – Parlophone PMC 1206 [1], PCS 3045 [2]	1
Meet The Beatles! LP (US, 1964) – Capitol T 2047 [4], ST 2047 [3]	1
Meet The Beatles! EP (US, 1964) – Capitol SXA 2047 [3]	–

=== NOTES ===

♪ The first George composition to be recorded.
♪ The first Beatles recording featuring claves as a percussive instrument.

Don't Ever Change

[Goffin-King]

George – lead vocals, lead guitar
Paul – harmony vocals, bass
John – rhythm guitar
Ringo – drums

BBC and other performances

1 August 1963 [1] – 27 August 1963 edition of *Pop Go The Beatles*

Releases   *UK/US peak*

Live At The BBC CD (1994) – Apple 8 31796 2 [1]   1/3

> **═ NOTES ═**
>
> ♪ The single by the Crickets got to #5
> in the UK in 1962, but failed to make
> the *Billboard* charts.

Don't Forbid Me

[Singleton]

Lead vocals, **Paul**. Played by the Beatles in 1960–61. Appears on the earliest surviving complete set list from early 1961. Pat Boone reached #1 in the US and #2 in the UK in 1957.

Don't Let Me Down

[Lennon-McCartney]

John – lead vocals, rhythm guitar
Paul – harmony vocals, bass
George – lead guitar
Ringo – drums
Billy Preston – electric piano

Studio recording and mixing

6 January 1969 – Twickenham Film Studios – Let It Be rehearsal session
Take 6.36 [1]

28 January 1969 – Apple Studio – Let It Be session 8 out of 17
Take 28.4

30 January 1969 – Apple rooftop – Let It Be session 9 out of 17
Takes 30.3 [2], 30.12

7 April 1969 – Olympic Sound – Let It Be session 11 out of 17
Overdubs onto take 28.4 – vocals

7 April 1969 – Olympic Sound
RM1 [3] – mono mix from overdubbed take 28.4
RS1 [4] – stereo mix from overdubbed take 28.4

2003 – EMI
[5] – stereo mix from edited takes 30.3, 30.12

Releases   _UK/US peak_

	UK/US peak
'Get Back' / 'Don't Let Me Down' single (1969) – Apple R 5777 [3]	1
'Get Back' / 'Don't Let Me Down' single (US, 1969) – Apple 2490 [4]	35
Hey Jude LP (US, 1970) – Apple SW 385 [4]	2
Let It Be movie (1970) [1] [2]	
The Beatles 1967–1970 LP (1973) – Apple PCSP 718 [4]	2
The Beatles 1967–1970 LP (US, 1973) – Apple SKBO 3404 [4]	1
Past Masters 2 CD (1988) – EMI CDP 7 90044 2 [4]	46/–
Let It Be… Naked CD (2003) – Apple 24359 57142 [5]	7/5
1+ CD/DVD (2015) – Apple 6205 47567727 [5]	5/6

═ NOTES ═

- ♪ A promotional film was made for the US.
- ♪ One of just two new songs (with 'Dig A Pony') that John contributed to the *Get Back* sessions.
- ♪ The last Beatles B-side to make the *Billboard* charts.

Don't Let The Sun Catch You Cryin'

[Greene]

Lead vocals, **Paul**. Played by the Beatles around 1960. Recorded by Ray Charles in 1959.

Don't Pass Me By

[Starkey]

Ringo – lead vocals, piano, percussion
Paul – piano, bass, drums
Jack Fallon – violin

Studio recording and mixing

5 June 1968 – Studio Three – White Album session 7 out of 81

Takes 1–3
Tape reduction of take 3 > takes 4, 5
Overdubs onto take 5 – vocals, bass
Tape reduction of take 5 > take 6

6 June 1968 – Studio Two – White Album session 8 out of 81

Overdubs onto take 5 – vocals
Tape reduction of take 5 > take 7
Overdubs onto take 7 – bass

12 July 1968 – *Studio Two* – *White Album session 25 out of 81*
Overdubs onto take 7 – violin, bass, piano

22 July 1968 – *Studio Two* – *White Album session 30 out of 81*
Edit piece takes 1–4 – orchestral introduction (unused)

11 October 1968 – *Studio Two control room*
RM1 [1] – mono mix from take 7, edited
RS1 [2] – stereo mix from take 7, edited

1996 – *EMI*
[3] – stereo mix from takes 3, 5

2018 – *EMI*
[4] – stereo mix from take 7, edited
[5] – stereo mix from take 7, unedited, with orchestral introduction

Releases   *UK/US peak*

The Beatles LP (1968) – Apple PMC 7067–7068 [1], PCS 7067–7068 [2]   1
The Beatles LP (US, 1968) – Apple SWBO-101 [2]   1
Rarities LP (US, 1980) – Capitol SHAL 12060 [1]   21
Anthology 3 CD (1996) – Apple 8 34451 2 [3]   4/1
The Beatles Deluxe CD (2018) – Apple 0602567571957 [4] [5]   4/6

=== NOTES ===

♪ Ringo's first composition, begun in 1962/63.
♪ The edit removed a repeated first verse after the false ending.
♪ The orchestral introduction became the track 'A Beginning'.

Dream
[Mercer]

Lead vocals, **George**. Early silent colour footage of the Beatles in 1962 shows George singing this song. It was recorded by Cliff Richard in 1961 and released on an EP of the same name.

Dream Baby
[Walker]

Paul – lead vocals, bass
John – backing vocals, rhythm guitar
George – backing vocals, lead guitar
Pete Best – drums

BBC and other performances

7 March 1962 – 8 March 1962 edition of *Here We Go*

═══ NOTES ═══

♪ A UK and US top 5 hit for Roy Orbison, it
was never released by the Beatles.
♪ A hit for Glen Campbell in 1971.
♪ One of only two titles recorded for the
BBC that are unreleased, the other being
'A Picture Of You'.

Drive My Car

[Lennon-McCartney]

Paul – lead vocals, bass, lead guitar
John – harmony vocals, piano, tambourine
George – harmony vocals, guitar
Ringo – drums, cowbell

Studio recording and mixing

13 October 1965 – Studio Two – Rubber Soul session 2 out of 15

Takes 1–4
Overdubs onto take 4

25 October 1965 – Studio Two control room

RM1 [1] – mono mix from take 4

26 October 1965 – Studio Two control room

RS1 [2] – stereo mix from take 4

13 May 1966 – Capitol

[3] – mastering of mono mix from [2]

1987 – EMI

[4] – stereo mix from take 4

2004–06 – EMI

[5] – stereo mix from take 4, in medley with 'What You're Doing' take 19 and 'The Word'
take 3: includes samples from 'Savoy Truffle' (saxophones); 'Taxman' (guitar); 'Lucy In
The Sky With Diamonds' (organ); 'Helter Skelter' (vocals); possibly handclaps from 'And
Your Bird Can Sing'

Releases   *UK/US peak*

Rubber Soul LP (1965) – Parlophone PMC 1267 [1], PCS 3075 [2]	1
Nowhere Man EP (1966) – Parlophone GEP 8952 [1]	4
"Yesterday" … And Today LP (US, 1966) – Capitol T 2553 [3], ST 2553 [2]	1

'Michelle' / 'Drive My Car' single (1966) – Parlophone DP 564 **[1]**   –
The Beatles 1962–1966 LP (1973) – Apple PCSP 717 **[2]**   3
The Beatles 1962–1966 LP (US, 1973)– Apple SKBO 3403 **[2]**   3
Rock 'n' Roll Music LP (1976) – Parlophone PCSP 719 / Capitol SKBO 11537 **[2]**   11/2
Rubber Soul CD (1987) – EMI CDP 7 46440 2 **[4]**   60
The Beatles 1962–1966 CD (1993) – EMI CDP 7 97036 2 **[4]**   4
Love CD (2006) – Apple 0946 3 80790 2 6 **[5]**   3/4

═══════════════════ **NOTES** ═══════════════════

♪ The 13 October session was the first to run past midnight.
♪ The guitar intro includes a 9/8 bar.

Eight Days A Week

[Lennon-McCartney]

John – lead vocals, acoustic guitar
Paul – harmony vocals, bass
George – harmony vocals, lead guitar
Ringo – drums

Studio recording and mixing

6 October 1964 – Studio Two – Beatles For Sale session 5 out of 8
Takes 1–6
Overdubs onto take 6 – vocals, handclaps > takes 7–13

18 October 1964 – Studio Two – Beatles For Sale session 7 out of 8
Takes 14–15, edit pieces for intro and outro

27 October 1964 – Studio Two control room
RM2, RM3 **[1]** – mono mixes from takes 13, 15, edited
RS1, RS2 **[2]** – stereo mixes from takes 13, 15, edited

1993 – EMI
[3] – stereo mix from takes 13, 15, edited

1995 – EMI
[4] – mono mix from edits of takes 1, 2, 4
[5] – mono mix from take 5

Releases   *UK/US peak*

Beatles For Sale LP (1964) – Parlophone PMC 1240 **[1]**, PCS 3062 **[2]**   1
Beatles For Sale EP (1965) – Parlophone GEP 8931 **[1]**   1
Beatles VI LP (US, 1965) – Capitol T 2358 **[1]**, ST 2358 **[2]**   1
'Eight Days A Week' / 'I Don't Want To Spoil The Party' single (US, 1965) – Capitol 5371 **[1]**   1
The Beatles 1962–1966 LP (1973) – Apple PCSP 717 **[2]**   3

The Beatles 1962–1966 LP (US, 1973)– Apple SKBO 3403 [2]	3
20 Greatest Hits LP (US, 1982) – Capitol SV-12245 [2]	50
The Beatles 1962–1966 CD (1993) – EMI CDP 7 97036 2 [3]	3
Anthology 1 CD (1995) – Apple 8 34445 2 [4] [5]	2/1
1+ CD/DVD (2015) – Apple 6205 47567727 [3]	5/6

NOTES

♪ The first significant experiment on a song's arrangement in the studio.
♪ John sings lead on what is essentially Paul's song.
♪ The first of three US-only singles to reach #1 in the *Billboard* charts.

Eleanor Rigby

[Lennon-McCartney]

Paul – lead vocals
John – harmony and backing vocals
George – harmony and backing vocals
Session musicians – four violins, two violas, two cellos

Studio recording and mixing

***28 April 1966** – Studio Two – Revolver session 15 out of 33*
Takes 1–14 – strings
Tape reduction of take 14 > take 15

***29 April 1966** – Studio Three – Revolver session 16 out of 33*
Overdubs onto take 15 – vocals

***6 June 1966** – Studio Three – Revolver session 27 out of 33*
Overdubs onto take 15 – vocals

***22 June 1966** – Studio Three control room*
RM5 [1] – mono mix from take 15
RS1 [2] – stereo mix from take 15

***1995** – EMI*
[3] – stereo mix from take 14

***1999** – EMI*
[4] – stereo mix from takes 14, 15

***2004–06** – EMI*
[5] – stereo mix from take 15, in medley with 'Julia' take 15: includes samples from 'A Day In The Life' (orchestra); possibly also samples from 'Strawberry Fields Forever'

Releases   *UK/US peak*

Release	UK/US peak
Revolver LP (1966) – Parlophone PMC 7009 [1], PCS 7009 [2]	1
Revolver LP (US, 1966) – Capitol T 2576 [1], ST 2576 [2]	1
'Eleanor Rigby' / 'Yellow Submarine' single (1966) – Parlophone R 5493 [1]	1
'Eleanor Rigby' / 'Yellow Submarine' single (US, 1966) – Capitol 5715 [1]	11
A Collection Of Beatles Oldies LP (1966) – Parlophone PMC 7016 [1], PCS 7016 [2]	7
The Beatles 1962–1966 LP (1973) – Apple PCSP 717 [2]	3
The Beatles 1962–1966 LP (US, 1973)– Apple SKBO 3403 [2]	3
20 Greatest Hits LP (1982) – Parlophone PCTC 260 [2]	10
Anthology 2 CD (1996) – Apple 8 34448 2 [3]	1/1
Yellow Submarine Songtrack CD (1999) – Apple 5 21481 2 [4]	8/15
Love CD (2006) – Apple 0946 3 80790 2 6 [5]	3/4
1+ CD/DVD (2015) – Apple 6205 47567727 [4]	5/6

═══ NOTES ═══

♪ The first track with no Beatles instruments.
♪ The strings were mixed down to a single track, and so are centred in [2], used for the *1* CD in 2000 – [4] has stereo strings and centred vocals.
♪ Won Paul the Grammy for Best Contemporary Pop Vocal Performance.

The End

[Lennon-McCartney]

Paul – lead vocals, bass, guitar solo, piano
John – harmony and backing vocals, guitar and guitar solo
George – harmony and backing vocals, guitar and guitar solo
Ringo – drums
Session musicians – twelve violins, four violas, four cellos, double bass, four horns, three trumpets, trombone, bass trombone

Studio recording and mixing

23 July 1969 – Studio Three – Abbey Road session 26 out of 42
Takes 1–7
Overdubs onto take 7 – piano, drums, guitar

5 August 1969 – Studio Two – Abbey Road session 35 out of 42
Overdubs onto take 7 – vocals

7 August 1969 – Studio Two – Abbey Road session 37 out of 42
Overdubs onto take 7 – vocals, guitar

8 August 1969 – Studio Two – Abbey Road session 38 out of 42
Overdubs onto take 7 – drums, bass

15 August 1969 – *Studio One* – *Abbey Road session 40 out of 42*
Overdubs onto take 7 – orchestra

18 August 1969 – *Studio Two* – *Abbey Road session 41 out of 42*
Overdubs onto take 7 – piano

21 August 1969 – *Studio Two control room*
RS4 [1] – stereo mix from take 7

1996 – *EMI*
[2] – stereo mix from take 7

Releases   *UK/US peak*

	UK/US peak
Abbey Road LP (1969) – Apple PCS 7088 [1]	1
Abbey Road LP (US, 1969) – Apple SO 383 [1]	1
Anthology 3 CD (1996) – Apple 8 34451 2 [2]	4/1
Tomorrow Never Knows (2012) – iTunes [2]	44/24

===== **NOTES** =====

♪ George, Paul and John play successive guitar solos.
♪ The only Beatles track featuring a drum solo.

Every Little Thing

[Lennon-McCartney]

John – lead vocals, lead guitar
Paul – harmony vocals, bass, piano
George – acoustic guitar
Ringo – drums, timpani

Studio recording and mixing

29 September 1964 – *Studio Two* – *Beatles For Sale session 3 out of 8*
Takes 1–4

30 September 1964 – *Studio Two* – *Beatles For Sale session 4 out of 8*
Takes 5–9
Overdubs onto take 9 – guitar, piano, timpani

27 October 1964 – *Studio Two control room*
RM1 [1] – mono mix from take 9
RS1 [2] – stereo mix from take 9

Releases   *UK/US peak*

	UK/US peak
Beatles For Sale LP (1964) – Parlophone PMC 1240 [1], PCS 3062 [2]	1
Beatles VI LP (US, 1965) – Capitol T 2358 [1], ST 2358 [2]	1

NOTES

♪ The first Lennon-McCartney song with a repeated coda.
♪ John takes the lead vocal, though the song was written by Paul.

Everybody's Got Something To Hide Except Me And My Monkey

[Lennon-McCartney]

John – lead vocals, rhythm guitar
Paul – backing vocals, bass, hand-bell, chocalho
George – backing vocals, lead guitar
Ringo – drums

Studio recording and mixing

May 1968 – Kinfauns, Esher
Demo recording

26 June 1968 – Studio Two – White Album session 13 out of 81
Unnumbered rehearsals

27 June 1968 – Studio Two – White Album session 14 out of 81
Takes 1–6
Tape reduction of take 6 > takes 7, 8
Overdubs onto take 8 – guitar, percussion

1 July 1968 – Studio Two – White Album session 16 out of 81
Overdubs onto take 8 – bass
Tape reduction of take 8 > takes 9, 10
Overdubs onto take 10 – vocals

23 July 1968 – Studio Two – White Album session 31 out of 81
Overdubs onto take 10 – vocals
Tape reduction of take 10 > takes 11, 12
Overdubs onto take 12 – vocals, handclaps

12 October 1968 – Studio Two control room
RM1 **[1]** – mono mix from take 12
RS1 **[2]** – stereo mix from take 12

2018 – EMI
[3] – stereo mix from demo
[4] – stereo mix from unnumbered rehearsal
[5] – stereo mix from take 12

Releases

	UK/US peak
The Beatles LP (1968) – Apple PMC 7067–7068 [1], PCS 7067–7068 [2]	1
The Beatles LP (US, 1968) – Apple SWBO-101 [2]	1
The Beatles Deluxe CD (2018) – Apple 0602567571957 [3] [4] [5]	4/6

═ NOTES ═

♪ Contains phrases used by Maharishi, such as "come on is such a joy".
♪ The title refers to a contemporary drawing of Yoko as a monkey perched on John's shoulder.
♪ Covered by Fats Domino who released it as a single in 1969.

Everybody's Trying To Be My Baby

[Perkins]

George – lead vocals, lead guitar
Paul – backing vocals, bass
John – acoustic guitar, tambourine
Ringo – drums

Studio recording and mixing

18 October 1964 – Studio Two – Beatles For Sale session 7 out of 8
Take 1
Overdubs onto take 1 – vocals, tambourine

21 October 1964 – Room 65
RM1 [1] – mono mix from take 1

4 November 1964 – Studio Two control room
RS1 [2] – stereo mix from take 1

BBC and other performances

December 1962 [3] – Star-Club, Hamburg (live)
24 May 1963 – 4 June 1963 edition of *Pop Go The Beatles*
31 March 1964 – 4 April 1964 edition of *Saturday Club*
17 November 1964 [4] – 26 November 1964 edition of *Top Gear*, repeated on 26 December 1964 edition of *Saturday Club*
26 May 1965 – 7 June 1965 edition of *The Beatles Invite You To Take A Ticket To Ride*
20 June 1965 – *Les Beatles* (Europe 1 TV, France, live)
15 August 1965 [5] – *The Beatles At Shea Stadium* (live, not broadcast)
30 August 1965 [6] – Hollywood Bowl (live)

Releases	UK/US peak
Beatles For Sale LP (1964) – Parlophone PMC 1240 [1], PCS 3062 [2]	1
Beatles '65 LP (US, 1964) – Capitol T 2228 [1], ST 2228 [2]	1
4 – By The Beatles EP (US, 1965) – Capitol R 5365 [1]	68
Rock 'n' Roll Music LP (1976) – Parlophone PCSP 719 / Capitol SKBO 11537 [2]	11/2
Live! At The Star-Club In Hamburg, Germany; 1962 LP (1977) – Lingasong LNL 1 / Lingasong LS 2 7001 [3]	–
Live At The BBC CD (1994) – Apple 8 31796 2 [4]	1/3
Anthology 2 CD (1996) – Apple 8 34448 2 [5]	1/1
Live At The Hollywood Bowl CD (2016) – Apple 6025 57054972 [6]	3/7

NOTES

♪ Appropriated by Carl Perkins from a similar song by Rex Griffin.
♪ Performed live in 1961–62, and again in 1964–65
♪ The first use of the repeat echo technique.

Falling In Love Again (Can't Help It)

[Holländer-Lerner]

Paul – lead vocals, bass
John – rhythm guitar
George – lead guitar
Ringo – drums

BBC and other performances

December 1962 [1] – Star-Club, Hamburg (live)

Releases	UK/US peak
Live! At The Star-Club In Hamburg, Germany; 1962 LP (1977) – Lingasong LNL 1 / Lingasong LS 2 7001 [1]	–

NOTES

♪ The German song by Friedrich Holländer was given English lyrics by Romanian-born Sammy Lerner.
♪ Originally performed by Marlene Dietrich in *The Blue Angel*.
♪ Part of the Beatles' set 1961–62.

Fixing A Hole

[Lennon-McCartney]

Paul – lead and backing vocals, guitar, possibly harpsichord
John – backing vocals, possibly bass
George – backing vocals, lead guitar
Ringo – drums, maracas

Studio recording and mixing

9 February 1967 – Regent Sound – Sgt Pepper session 26 out of 56
Takes 1–3
Overdubs onto take 2 – vocals, guitar

21 February 1967 – Studio Two – Sgt Pepper session 31 out of 56
Tape reduction of take 2 > new take 3
Overdubs onto new take 3 – vocals

21 February 1967 – Studio Two control room
RM3, RM6 [1] – mono mixes from new take 3, edited

7 April 1967 – Studio Two control room
RS1 [2] – stereo mix from new take 3

2016/17 – EMI
[3] – stereo mix from take 1
[4] – stereo mix from original take 3
[5] – stereo mix from new take 3

Releases .... *UK/US peak*

Sgt Pepper's Lonely Hearts Club Band LP (1967) – Parlophone PMC 7027 [1], PCS 7027 [2] 1
Sgt Pepper's Lonely Hearts Club Band LP (US, 1967) – Capitol MAS 2653 [1], SMAS 2653 [2] 1
Sgt Pepper's Lonely Hearts Club Band Deluxe CD (2017) – Apple 0602557455328 [1] [3] [4] [5] 1/3

═══ NOTES ═══

♪ The first session was the only one made by the Beatles at Regent Sound studios – and was also the first time they used non-EMI studio.
♪ Recorded as "live", including the bass, possibly played by John.

Flying

[Lennon-McCartney-Harrison-Starkey]

John – scat vocals, organs, Mellotron
Paul – scat vocals, bass, guitar
George – scat vocals, guitar
Ringo – scat vocals, drums, percussion

Studio recording and mixing

8 September 1967 – Studio Three – Magical Mystery Tour session 15 out of 30
Takes 1–6
Overdubs onto take 6 – organ
Tape reduction of take 6 > takes 7, 8
Overdubs onto take 8 – Mellotron, vocals

28 September 1967 – Studio Two – Magical Mystery Tour session 20 out of 30
Overdubs onto take 8 – Mellotron, guitar, percussion
Effects takes 1–5 – tape loops and effects
Overdub onto take 8 – effects take 5

28 September 1967 – Studio Two control room
RM6 [1] – mono mix from take 8

7 November 1967 – Studio Two control room
RS1 [2] – stereo mix from take 8

Releases   UK/US peak

Magical Mystery Tour EP (1967) – Parlophone MMT-1 [1], SMMT-1 [2]   2
Magical Mystery Tour LP (US, 1967) – Capitol MAL 2835 [1], SMAL 2835 [2]   1

═══════ **NOTES** ═══════

♪ The original 9½-minute recording was called
  'Aerial Tour Instrumental' after its role in
  Magical Mystery Tour.
♪ The Beatles' first instrumental release, though
  '12-Bar Original' had been recorded nearly two
  years earlier.
♪ The first core release credited to all four
  Beatles, to be followed by 'Dig It'.

The Fool On The Hill

[Lennon-McCartney]

Paul – lead vocals, piano, recorder, bass
John – harmonica
George – acoustic guitar, harmonica
Ringo – drums, maracas, finger cymbals
George Martin – possibly celeste
Session musicians – three flutes

Studio recording and mixing

6 September 1967 – Studio Two – Magical Mystery Tour session 13 out of 30
Demo take 1

6 September 1967 – *Studio Two control room*
[1] – mono mix from demo take 1

25 September 1967 – *Studio Two – Magical Mystery Tour session 17 out of 30*
Takes 1–3
Tape reduction of take 3 > take 4
Overdubs onto take 4 – recorder, drums, vocals

26 September 1967 – *Studio Two – Magical Mystery Tour session 18 out of 30*
Remake take 5
Overdubs onto take 5 – piano, celeste, percussion, recorder
Tape reduction of take 5 > take 6
Overdubs onto take 6

27 September 1967 – *Studio Two – Magical Mystery Tour session 19 out of 30*
Overdubs onto take 6 – vocals, recorder, harmonicas, tape loop

20 October 1967 – *Studio Three – Magical Mystery Tour session 26 out of 30*
Take 7 – flutes
Take 7 flown into take 6

25 October 1967 – *Studio Two control room*
RM12 [2] – mono mix from take 6, edited

1 November 1967 – *Studio Three control room*
RS5 [3] – stereo mix from take 6, edited

1995 –EMI
[4] – stereo mix from take 4

2004–06 – EMI
[5] – stereo mix from take 6: includes samples from 'Mother Nature's Son' (vocals, brass); 'Maxwell's Silver Hammer' (drums); possibly 'Sea Of Time' (sitar), 'Dear Prudence' (piano)

Releases

	UK/US peak
Magical Mystery Tour EP (1967) – Parlophone MMT-1 [2], SMMT-1 [3]	2
Magical Mystery Tour LP (US, 1967) – Capitol MAL 2835 [2], SMAL 2835 [3]	1
The Beatles Ballads LP (1980) – Parlophone PCS 7214 [3]	17
Anthology 2 CD (1996) – Apple 8 34448 2 [1] [4]	1/1
Love (2006) – iTunes [5]	–

─══════**NOTES**══════─

♪ The *Magical Mystery Tour* segment was filmed outside Nice, France.
♪ Paul forgot his passport on the trip, but reasoned with the officials that they knew who he was, so why did he need a passport.
♪ The demo features Paul and a piano.

Fools Like Me

[Clement-Muddux]

Lead vocals, **Paul**. Performed by the Beatles throughout the first three Hamburg seasons. Originally recorded by Jerry Lee Lewis (and His Pumping Piano), released in 1958 on the B side of 'High School Confidential', it made #11 on *Billboard*.

For No One

[Lennon-McCartney]

Paul – lead vocals, piano, clavichord, bass
Ringo – hi-hat, cymbals, tambourine, maracas
Alan Civil – French horn

Studio recording and mixing

9 May 1966 – Studio Two – Revolver session 19 out of 33
Takes 1–10
Overdubs onto take 10 – clavichord, cymbals, maracas

16 May 1966 – Studio Two – Revolver session 20 out of 33
Overdubs onto take 10 – vocals
Tape reduction of take 10 > takes 13, 14

19 May 1966 – Studio Three – Revolver session 22 out of 33
Overdubs onto take 14 – horn, bass, tambourine

21 June 1966 – Studio Three control room
RM8 [1] – mono mix from take 14
RS1 [2] – stereo mix from take 14

Releases	UK/US peak
Revolver LP (1966) – Parlophone PMC 7009 [1], PCS 7009 [2]	1
Revolver LP (US, 1966) – Capitol T 2576 [1], ST 2576 [2]	1
The Beatles Ballads LP (1980) – Parlophone PCS 7214 [2]	17

=**NOTES**=

♪ Originally called 'Why Did It Die?', written on a skiing holiday in Klosters.
♪ The clavichord had recently been bought by George Martin for £110.
♪ Paul's vocal was sped up by about a semitone on playback.

For You Blue

[Harrison]

George – lead vocals, acoustic guitar
John – steel guitar
Paul – piano
Ringo – drums

Studio recording and mixing

8 January 1969 – Twickenham Studios – Let It Be rehearsal session
Take 8.18 of 'Too Bad About Sorrows' (spoken intro)

25 January 1969 – Apple Studio – Let It Be session 5 out of 17
Takes 25.20, 25.23, 25.24 [1, edited], 25.25

8 January 1970 – Olympic Studios – Let It Be session 16 out of 17
Overdubs onto take 25.25 – vocals

25 March 1970 – Room 4
RS1, RS5 – stereo mix from take 25.25, RS1 (the body of the song) and RS5 (the introduction) edited together

30 March 1970 – Studio Two control room
[2] – edit of take 8.18 onto RS1 and RS5

1996 – EMI
[3] – stereo mix from take 25.25, without vocal overdub

2003 – EMI
[4] – stereo mix from take 25.25

Releases

	UK/US peak
Let It Be LP (1970) – Apple PXS1, PCS 7096 [2]	1
Let It Be LP (US, 1970) – Apple AR 34001 [2]	1
'The Long And Winding Road' / 'For You Blue' single (US, 1970) – Apple 2832 [2]	–
Let It Be movie (1970) [1]	
Anthology 3 CD (1996) – Apple 8 34451 2 [3]	4/1
Let It Be... Naked CD (2003) – Apple 24359 57142 [4]	7/5

NOTES

♪ Of all the Beatles' songs recorded for *Let It Be*, only 'For You Blue' was tackled on just one day, all recordings taking place within one hour.
♪ George re-recorded his vocal at Olympic Studios on 8 January 1970 – in what was to be his last session as a Beatle.

Free As A Bird

[Lennon-McCartney-Harrison-Starkey]

John – lead vocals, piano
Paul – lead and harmony vocals, bass, acoustic guitar, piano, synthesiser
George – harmony vocals, electric and acoustic guitar, ukulele
Ringo – harmony vocals, drums

Studio recording and mixing

c. 1977 – Dakota Apartments, New York
Basic recording – vocals, piano

February 1994 – Mill Studio, Sussex
Overdubs onto edit of basic recording – vocals, bass, guitars, drums, piano, synthesiser, ukulele

1995 – EMI
[1] – stereo mix

2015 – EMI
[2] – stereo mix

Releases

	UK/US peak
'Free As A Bird' single (1995) – Apple 8 82587 2 [1]	2/6
Anthology 1 CD (1995) – Apple 8 34445 2 [1]	2/1
1+ CD/DVD (2015) – Apple 6205 47567727 [2]	5/6

NOTES

♪ Based on a mono cassette recording from 1977 of John's voice and piano.
♪ The demo was cut into short sections and fit to a mechanical drum track. Paul, George and Ringo then dubbed on their new parts.
♪ The *1+* mix includes a different take of part of George's vocal, and John's "turned out nice again" at the end played forwards not backwards.

Freight Train

[Cotten]

Lead vocals, **John**. A skiffle number performed by the Quarry Men prior to the Hamburg period. A version by Chas McDevitt Skiffle Group featuring Nancy Whiskey reached #5 in the UK, while Rusty Draper reached #6 on *Billboard*, both in 1957.

From Me To You

[McCartney-Lennon]

John – lead vocals, rhythm guitar, harmonica
Paul – lead and harmony vocals, bass
George – harmony vocals, lead guitar
Ringo – drums

Studio recording and mixing

5 March 1963 – Studio Two – Please Please Me session 7 out of 8

Takes 1–7
Takes 8–10, edit pieces 1–3 – harmonica
Takes 11–13, edit pieces 4–6 – vocals

14 March 1963 – Studio Two control room

Edit of takes 12, 8, 9, 10
RM1 [1] – mono mix from edit of takes 12, 8, 9, 10; take 8 flown in
RS1 [2] – stereo mix from edit of takes 12, 8, 9, 10

2013 – EMI

[3] – stereo mix from takes 1, 2
[4] – stereo mix from take 5

BBC and other performances

1 April 1963 – 22 April 1963 edition of *Side By Side*
1 April 1963 – 13 May 1963 edition of *Side By Side*
3 April 1963 – 7 April 1963 edition of *Easy Beat*
13 April 1963 – 16 April 1963 edition of *The 625 Show* (BBC TV)
18 April 1963 – *Swinging Sound '63* (live)
16 May 1963 – *Pops And Lenny* (TV, live)
21 May 1963 [5] – 25 May 1963 edition of *Saturday Club*
21 May 1963 – 3 June 1963 edition of *Steppin' Out*
24 May 1963 – 4 June 1963 edition of *Pop Go The Beatles*
1 June 1963 – 18 June 1963 edition of *Pop Go The Beatles*
4 April 1963 – 24 June 1963 edition of *Side By Side*
19 June 1963 – 23 June 1963 edition of *Easy Beat*
24 June 1963 – 29 June 1963 edition of *Saturday Club*
3 July 1963 – 4 July 1963 edition of *The Beat Show*
1 August 1963 – 3 September 1963 edition of *Pop Go The Beatles*
3 September 1963 – 17 September 1963 edition of *Pop Go The Beatles*
13 October 1963 – *Sunday Night At The London Palladium* (ATV, live)
16 October 1963 [6] – 20 October 1963 edition of *Easy Beat*
24 October 1963 [7] – Karlaplansstudion, Stockholm (live)
4 November 1963 [8] – *Royal Variety Performance* broadcast on 10 November
    1963 (ATV)

7 December 1963 – *It's The Beatles* broadcast the same day (BBC TV)
16 February 1964 **[9]** – *The Ed Sullivan Show* (CBS TV, live)
19 April 1964 – *Around The Beatles*, mimed performance recorded on 28 April
and broadcast on 6 May 1964 (Rediffusion TV)

Releases   *UK/US peak*

'From Me To You' / 'Thank You Girl' single (1963) – Parlophone R 5015 **[1]**	1
'From Me To You' / 'Thank You Girl' single (US, 1963) – Vee Jay VJ 522 **[1]**	116
The Beatles' Hits EP (1963) – Parlophone GEP 8880 **[1]**	1
'Please Please Me' / 'From Me To You' single (US, 1964) – Vee Jay VJ 581 **[1]**	41
'Please Please Me' / 'From Me To You' single (US, 1965) – Capitol Starline 6063 **[1]**	–
A Collection Of Beatles Oldies LP (1966) – Parlophone PMC 7016 **[1]**, PCS 7016 **[2]**	7
The Beatles 1962–1966 LP (1973) – Apple PCSP 717 **[2]**	3
The Beatles 1962–1966 LP (US, 1973)– Apple SKBO 3403 **[2]**	3
20 Greatest Hits LP (1982) – Parlophone PCTC 260 **[2]**	10
Past Masters 1 CD (1988) – EMI CDP 7 90043 2 **[1]**	49/–
The Beatles 1962–1966 CD (1993) – EMI CDP 7 97036 2 **[1]**	3
Anthology 1 CD (1995) – Apple 8 34445 2 **[7]**	2/1
The Four Historic Ed Sullivan Shows DVD (2003) – EREDV 372 **[9]**	
Past Masters CD (2009) – EMI CDP 2 43807 2 **[2]**	31
On Air – Live At The BBC Volume 2 CD (2013) – Apple 6025 37491698 **[6]**	12/7
The Beatles Bootleg Recordings 1963 (2013) – iTunes **[3] [4] [5]**	–
1+ CD/DVD (2015) – Apple 6205 47567727 **[8]**	5/6

===== **NOTES** =====

♪ The first Beatles single to top all the UK charts.
♪ The US single only reached #41, never charting on the Capitol label.
♪ The first Lennon-McCartney song to enter the *Billboard* chart when covered by Del Shannon. It reached #77.
♪ Performed in concert until 1964.

From Us To You

[Lennon-McCartney]

John – lead vocals, rhythm guitar
Paul – lead and harmony vocals, bass
George – lead guitar
Ringo – drums

BBC and other performances

18 December 1963 – 26 December 1963 edition of *From Us To You*
28 February 1964 – 30 March 1964, 18 May 1964 and 3 August 1964 editions of *From Us To You*

1994 – *EMI*
[1] – mono mix from 28 February 1964 version

Releases   *UK/US peak*

Live At The BBC CD (1994) – Apple 8 31796 2 [1]   1/3

═ NOTES ═

♪ The 26 December 1963 and 3 August 1964 shows were
  entitled *The Beatles Say From Us To You*, and the other
  two *From Us To You Say The Beatles*.
♪ Separate versions were used to open and close show –
  the closing version was slightly longer.

Get Back

[Lennon-McCartney]

Paul – lead vocals, bass
John – harmony vocals, lead guitar
George – rhythm guitar
Ringo – drums
Billy Preston – electric piano

Studio recording and mixing

January 1969 – *Apple Studio*
Spoken introduction

27 January 1969 – *Apple Studio – Let It Be session 7 out of 17*
Take 27.6 – body of song

28 January 1969 – *Apple Studio – Let It Be session 8 out of 17*
Take 28.1 [1] – coda

30 January 1969 – *Apple rooftop – Let It Be session 9 out of 17*
Take 30.2 [2] – first proper rooftop version
Take 30.13 [3] – final rooftop version
Spoken coda

7 April 1969 – *Olympic Sound*
RM5 [4] – mono mix from edit of take 27.6, take 28.1
RS1 [5] – stereo mix from edit of take 27.6, take 28.1

26 March 1970 – *Room 4*
RS3 [6] – stereo mix from edit of spoken introduction, take 27.6, spoken coda

1996 – *EMI*
[7] – stereo mix from take 30.13

2003 – EMI

[8] – stereo mix from take 27.6

2004–06 – EMI

[9] – stereo mix from take 27.6: includes samples from 'Hello, Goodbye', 'Come Together' (vocals); 'A Hard Day's Night' (opening chord); 'The End' (guitars, drums); Shea Stadium crowd noise; 'Sgt Pepper's Lonely Hearts Club Band' (percussion); 'A Day In The Life' (orchestra); also possibly vocals from 'I Am The Walrus'

2015 – EMI

[10] – stereo mix from edit of take 27.6, take 28.1

Releases   UK/US peak

'Get Back' / 'Don't Let Me Down' single (1969) – Apple R 5777 [4]	1
'Get Back' / 'Don't Let Me Down' single (US, 1969) – Apple 2490 [5]	1
Let It Be LP (1970) – Apple PXS1, PCS 7096 [6]	1
Let It Be LP (US, 1970) – Apple AR 34001 [6]	1
Let It Be movie (1970) [1] [2] [3]	
The Beatles 1967–1970 LP (1973) – Apple PCSP 718 [5]	2
The Beatles 1967–1970 LP (US, 1973) – Apple SKBO 3404 [5]	1
Rock 'n' Roll Music LP (1976) – Parlophone PCSP 719 / Capitol SKBO 11537 [6]	11/2
Reel Music LP (1982) – Parlophone PCS 7218 / Capitol SV-12199 [6]	–/19
20 Greatest Hits LP (1982) – Parlophone PCTC 260 / Capitol SV-12245 [5]	10/50
Past Masters 2 CD (1988) – EMI CDP 7 90044 2 [5]	46/–
Anthology 3 CD (1996) – Apple 8 34451 2 [7]	4/1
Let It Be… Naked CD (2003) – Apple 24359 57142 [8]	7/5
Love CD (2006) – Apple 0946 3 80790 2 6 [9]	3/4
1+ CD/DVD (2015) – Apple 6205 47567727 [10] [10, without coda]	5/6

=== NOTES ===

♪ The coda for the single was recorded 28 January; the coda for the LP was recorded 30 January.
♪ The date of recording of the introductory speech is unknown.
♪ The single is credited to The Beatles with Billy Preston.
♪ The only Beatles single to enter the UK charts at #1.

Getting Better

[Lennon-McCartney]

Paul – lead vocals, bass
John – harmony and backing vocals, guitar
George – harmony and backing vocals, guitar, tamboura
Ringo – drums, bongos
George Martin – piano, possibly electric piano

Studio recording and mixing

9 March 1967 – Studio Two – Sgt Pepper session 41 out of 56
Takes 1–7
Overdubs onto take 7 – drums
Tape reduction of take 7 > takes 8–12

10 March 1967 – Studio Two – Sgt Pepper session 42 out of 56
Overdubs onto take 12 – tamboura, bass, drums

21 March 1967 – Studio Two – Sgt Pepper session 47 out of 56
Tape reduction of take 12 > takes 13, 14
Overdubs onto take 14 – vocals

23 March 1967 – Studio Two – Sgt Pepper session 49 out of 56
Overdubs onto take 14 – vocals
Tape reduction of take 14 > take 15
Overdubs onto take 15 – bongos, piano, guitar, handclaps

23 March 1967 – Studio Two control room
RM3 [1] – mono mix from take 15

17 April 1967 – Studio Two control room
RS1 [2] – stereo mix from take 15

2016/17 – EMI
[3] – stereo mix from take 1
[4] – stereo mix from take 12
[5] – stereo mix from take 15

Releases   *UK/US peak*

Sgt Pepper's Lonely Hearts Club Band LP (1967) – Parlophone PMC 7027 [1], PCS 7027 [2]	1
Sgt Pepper's Lonely Hearts Club Band LP (US, 1967) – Capitol MAS 2653 [1], SMAS 2653 [2]	1
Sgt Pepper's Lonely Hearts Club Band Deluxe CD (2017) – Apple 0602557455328 [1] [3] [4] [5]	1/3

=== NOTES ===

♪ Based on a phrase often used by Jimmy Nicol on the 1964 world tour.
♪ John accidentally took LSD during the 21 March overdub session.
♪ The electric piano – a Pianet – was possibly played by Paul.

Girl

[Lennon-McCartney]

John – lead vocals, acoustic guitar
Paul – harmony and backing vocals, bass
George – harmony and backing vocals, acoustic guitar
Ringo – drums

Studio recording and mixing

11 November 1965 – Studio Two – Rubber Soul session 15 out of 15
Takes 1–2
Overdubs onto take 2 – vocals, guitar

15 November 1965 – Studio One control room
RM1 [1] – mono mix from take 2
RS1 [2] – stereo mix from take 2

28 September 1977 – EMI
[3] – stereo mix from take 2

1987 – EMI
[4] – stereo mix from take 2

2004–06 – EMI
[5] – stereo mix from take 2: includes samples from 'And I Love Her' (guitar); 'Being For The Benefit Of Mr Kite!' (drums); also possibly sitar from 'Within You Without You'

Releases   *UK/US peak*

Rubber Soul LP (1965) – Parlophone PMC 1267 [1], PCS 3075 [2]	1
Rubber Soul LP (US, 1965) – Capitol T 2442 [1], ST 2442 [2]	1
The Beatles 1962–1966 LP (1973) – Apple PCSP 717 [2]	3
The Beatles 1962–1966 LP (US, 1973)– Apple SKBO 3403 [2]	3
Love Songs LP (1977) – Parlophone PCSP 721 / Capitol SKBL 11711 [3]	7/24
Rubber Soul CD (1987) – EMI CDP 7 46440 2 [4]	60
The Beatles 1962–1966 CD (1993) – EMI CDP 7 97036 2 [4]	3
Love (2006) – iTunes [5]	–

=== NOTES ===

♪ Capitol planned to release 'Girl' / 'You're Going To Lose That Girl' in 1977 to promote *Love Songs*, but the release was cancelled.

Glad All Over

[Bennett-Tepper-Schroeder]

George – lead vocals, lead guitar
John – rhythm guitar
Paul – bass
Ringo – drums

BBC and other performances

16 July 1963 [1] – 20 August 1963 edition of *Pop Go The Beatles*
30 July 1963 [2] – 24 August 1963 edition of *Saturday Club*

Releases *UK/US peak*

Live At The BBC CD (1994) – Apple 8 31796 2 **[1]**   1/3
On Air – Live At The BBC Volume 2 CD (2013) – Apple 6025 37491698 **[2]**   12/7

```
╔══════════ NOTES ══════════╗
║                                          ║
║  ♪ Carl Perkins' third British single,   ║
║     released in 1958 – in the US it was   ║
║     backed with 'Lend Me Your Comb'.     ║
║  ♪ Played live by the Beatles from 1960.  ║
║                                          ║
╚══════════════════════════╝
```

Glass Onion

[Lennon-McCartney]

John – lead vocals, acoustic guitar
Paul – bass, piano, recorder
George – lead guitar
Ringo – drums, tambourine
Chris Thomas – recorder
Session musicians – four violins, two violas, two cellos

Studio recording and mixing

May 1968 – Kinfauns, Esher
Demo recording

11 September 1968 – Studio Two – White Album session 58 out of 81
Takes 1–34

12 September 1968 – Studio Two – White Album session 59 out of 81
Overdubs onto take 33 – vocals, tambourine

13 September 1968 – Studio Two – White Album session 60 out of 81
Overdubs onto take 33 – drums, piano

16 September 1968 – Studio Two – White Album session 61 out of 81
Overdubs onto take 33 – recorder, Mellotron (mixed out)

26 September 1968 – Studio Two control room
Unnumbered take – sound effects, edited onto take 33

26 September 1968 – Studio Two control room
RM2 **[1]** – mono mix from take 33

10 October 1968 – Studio Two – White Album session 78 out of 81
Overdubs onto take 33 – strings

10 October 1968 – Studio Two control room
RS2 **[2]** – stereo mix from take 33

RM11 [3] – mono mix from take 33

1996 – EMI

[4] – stereo mix from demo

2004–06 – EMI

[5] – stereo mix from take 33: includes samples from 'Hello, Goodbye', 'Strawberry Fields Forever', 'I Am The Walrus' (vocals); 'Penny Lane' (piccolo); 'A Day In The Life' (orchestra); 'Magical Mystery Tour' (trumpets); 'Only A Northern Song' (effects); 'Sgt Pepper's Lonely Hearts Club Band (Reprise)' (drums); also possibly guitar from 'Things We Said Today'

2018 – EMI

[6] – stereo mix from demo
[7] – stereo mix from take 10
[8] – stereo mix from take 33

Releases   *UK/US peak*

	UK/US peak
The Beatles LP (1968) – Apple PMC 7067–7068 [3], PCS 7067–7068 [2]	1
The Beatles LP (US, 1968) – Apple SWBO-101 [2]	1
Anthology 3 CD (1996) – Apple 8 34451 2 [4] [1]	4/1
Love CD (2006) – Apple 0946 3 80790 2 6 [5]	3/4
The Beatles Deluxe CD (2018) – Apple 0602567571957 [6] [7] [8]	4/6

=== **NOTES** ===

♪ The first of a series of four tracks produced by Chris Thomas – George Martin was also not present for the orchestral recording in October.
♪ [1] includes the tape of effects compiled by John on 26 September.

Golden Slumbers / Carry That Weight

[Lennon-McCartney]

Paul – lead and chant vocals, rhythm guitar, piano
John – possibly chant vocals
George – harmony and chant vocals, six-string bass, lead guitar
Ringo – chant vocals, drums, possibly timpani
Session musicians – twelve violins, four violas, four cellos, double bass, four horns, three trumpets, trombone, bass trombone

Studio recording and mixing

2 July 1969 – Studio Two – Abbey Road session 12 out of 42

Takes 1–15

3 July 1969 – Studio Two – Abbey Road session 13 out of 42

Edit of takes 13, 15 > take 13

Overdubs onto take 13 – guitar, vocals, drums
Tape reduction of take 13 > takes 16, 17

4 July 1969 – Studio Two – Abbey Road session 14 out of 42
Overdubs onto take 17

30 July 1969 – Studio Three – Abbey Road session 31 out of 42
Overdubs onto take 17 – vocals

31 July 1969 – Studio Two – Abbey Road session 32 out of 42
Overdubs onto take 17 – drums, timpani, vocals

15 August 1969 – Studio One – Abbey Road session 40 out of 42
Overdubs onto take 17 – orchestra

18 August 1969 – Studio Two control room
RS2 [1] – stereo mix from take 17

Releases
UK/US peak

Abbey Road LP (1969) – Apple PCS 7088 [1]	1
Abbey Road LP (US, 1969) – Apple SO 383 [1]	1

=**NOTES**=

♪ Based on a song from a 17th-century play by Thomas Dekker.
♪ Unlike the other *Abbey Road* song pairs, these were written as one
    song – Paul played them as such during the 7 January *Get Back* session.

Good Day Sunshine

[Lennon-McCartney]

Paul – lead vocals, bass, piano
John – harmony vocals
George – harmony vocals
Ringo – drums
George Martin – piano

Studio recording and mixing

8 June 1966 – Studio Two – Revolver session 28 out of 33
Takes 1–3
Overdubs onto take 1 – vocals

9 June 1966 – Studio Two – Revolver session 29 out of 33
Overdubs onto take 1 – drums, piano, handclaps, vocals

22 June 1966 – Studio Three control room
RM2 [1] – mono mix from take 1 (actually RM7, wrongly labelled)
RS1 [2] – stereo mix from take 1

Releases   *UK/US peak*

Revolver LP (1966) – Parlophone PMC 7009 [1], PCS 7009 [2]   1
Revolver LP (US, 1966) – Capitol T 2576 [1], ST 2576 [2]   1

```
┌─────────────────── NOTES ───────────────────┐
│  ♪ The song's introduction features 3/4 and 5/4 │
│    time signatures.                              │
│  ♪ Originally called 'A Good Day's Sunshine',    │
│    Paul said it was "influenced by the Lovin'    │
│    Spoonful".                                    │
│  ♪ Released as a single by the Tremeloes in      │
│    1966, just after Brian Poole left the group.  │
└──────────────────────────────────────────────┘
```

Good Golly Miss Molly

[Marascalco-Blackwell]

Lead vocals, **Paul**. Performed by the Beatles throughout the first two Hamburg seasons. Originally recorded by Little Richard, released in January 1958 it got to #4 on *Billboard* and #8 in the UK. It was written by John Marascalco and Little Richard's producer, Robert "Bumps" Blackwell.

Good Morning Good Morning

[Lennon-McCartney]

John – lead vocals, rhythm guitar
Paul – harmony and backing vocals, lead guitar, bass
George – harmony and backing vocals, lead guitar
Ringo – drums, tambourine
Session musicians – two tenor saxophones, baritone saxophone, two trombones, French horn

Studio recording and mixing

8 February 1967 – Studio Two – Sgt Pepper session 25 out of 56
Takes 1–8

16 February 1967 – Studio Three – Sgt Pepper session 28 out of 56
Overdubs onto take 8 – vocals, bass
Tape reduction of take 8 > takes 9, 10

13 March 1967 – Studio Two – Sgt Pepper session 43 out of 56
Overdubs onto take 10 – brass

28 March 1967 – Studio Two – Sgt Pepper session 50 out of 56
Overdubs onto take 10 – vocals
Tape reduction of take 10 > take 11

Overdubs onto take 11 – guitar, vocals
Edit of animal noise effects

29 March 1967 – Studio Two – Sgt Pepper session 51 out of 56
Further edit of animal noise effects
Overdubs onto take 11 – animal noise effects

6 April 1967 – Studio Two control room
RS5 [1] – stereo mix from take 11

19 April 1967 – Studio Two control room
RM23 [2] – mono mix from take 11

1995 – EMI
[3] – stereo mix from take 8

2016/17 – EMI
[4] – stereo mix from take 1
[5] – stereo mix from take 8
[6] – stereo mix from take 11

Releases   _UK/US peak_

Sgt Pepper's Lonely Hearts Club Band LP (1967) – Parlophone PMC 7027 [2], PCS 7027 [1]	1
Sgt Pepper's Lonely Hearts Club Band LP (US, 1967) – Capitol MAS 2653 [2], SMAS 2653 [1]	1
Anthology 2 CD (1996) – Apple 8 34448 2 [3]	1/1
Sgt Pepper's Lonely Hearts Club Band Deluxe CD (2017) – Apple 0602557455328 [2] [4] [5] [6]	1/3

=== **NOTES** ===

♪ The brass is played by members of former support act
  Sounds Inc., their only appearance on a Beatles recording.
♪ Rhythmically, the most irregular of any Beatles songs.

Good Night

[Lennon-McCartney]

Ringo – lead vocals
George Martin – possibly celeste
Mike Sammes singers – backing vocals
Session musicians – twelve violins, three violas, three cellos, harp, three flutes, clarinet,
    horn, vibraphone, double bass

Studio recording and mixing

28 June 1968 – Studio Two – White Album session 15 out of 81
Unnumbered rehearsals
Takes 1–5

2 July 1968 *– Studio Two – White Album session 17 out of 81*
Overdubs onto take 5 – vocals > takes 6–15

22 July 1968 *– Studio One – White Album session 30 out of 81*
Rehearsal takes 16–22
Remake takes 23–34
Overdubs onto take 34 – choir, vocals

11 October 1968 *– Studio Two control room*
RM2 [1] – mono mix from take 34
RS1 [2] – stereo mix from take 34

1996 *– EMI*
[3] – stereo mix from unnumbered rehearsal, take 34

2018 *– EMI*
[4] – stereo mix from unnumbered rehearsal
[5] – stereo mix from take 10
[6] – stereo mix from take 22
[7] – stereo mix from take 34

Releases	*UK/US peak*
The Beatles LP (1968) – Apple PMC 7067–7068 [1], PCS 7067–7068 [2]	1
The Beatles LP (US, 1968) – Apple SWBO-101 [2]	1
Anthology 3 CD (1996) – Apple 8 34451 2 [3]	4/1
The Beatles Deluxe CD (2018) – Apple 0602567571957 [4] [5] [6] [7]	4/6

═══ **NOTES** ═══

♪ The rehearsal takes feature a spoken intro along the lines of "it's time you little toddlers were in bed – I'm having no more messing …".
♪ Just Ringo, with an orchestra, the Mike Sammes Singers and possibly George Martin on celeste.
♪ The high D in the intro is not a theremin or other electronic instrument but a soprano voice.

Got To Get You Into My Life

[Lennon-McCartney]

Paul – lead vocals, bass
John – possibly rhythm guitar
George – lead guitar
Ringo – drums, percussion
George Martin – possibly organ
Session musicians – three trumpets, two tenor saxophones

Studio recording and mixing

7 April 1966 – Studio Three – Revolver session 2 out of 33
Takes 1–5

8 April 1966 – Studio Two – Revolver session 3 out of 33
Takes 6–8
Overdubs onto take 8 – bass, vocals

11 April 1966 – Studio Two – Revolver session 4 out of 33
Overdubs onto take 8 – guitar

18 May 1966 – Studio Two – Revolver session 21 out of 33
Overdubs onto take 8 – guitar, brass
Tape reduction of take 8 > takes 9–11
Overdubs onto take 9 – vocals, guitar, tambourine, organ

17 June 1966 – Studio Two – Revolver session 32 out of 33
Overdubs onto take 9 – guitar

17 June 1966 – Studio Two control room
RM7 – mono mix from take 9

20 June 1966 – Studio One control room
Tape copy of RM7 with overdub from take 8 > RM8 [1]

22 June 1966 – Studio Three control room
RS1 [2] – stereo mix from take 9

1995 – EMI
[3] – mono mix from take 5

Releases   *UK/US peak*

	UK/US peak
Revolver LP (1966) – Parlophone PMC 7009 [1], PCS 7009 [2]	1
Revolver LP (US, 1966) – Capitol T 2576 [1], ST 2576 [2]	1
Rock 'n' Roll Music LP (1976) – Parlophone PCSP 719 / Capitol SKBO 11537 [2]	11/2
'Got To Get You Into My Life' / 'Helter Skelter' (US, 1976) – Capitol 4274 [2]	7
Anthology 2 CD (1996) – Apple 8 34448 2 [3]	1/1

NOTES

♪ Recorded over a 10-week period.
♪ The tape copy of RM7 was made in order to beef up the sound of the brass – it was not done for the stereo mix.
♪ The US single was released to promote the LP *Rock 'n' Roll Music*.

Hallelujah, I Love Her So

[Charles]

Paul – vocals (1960), acoustic guitar (1960), bass (1962)
John – acoustic guitar (1960), rhythm guitar (1962)
George – lead guitar (1962)
Ringo – drums (1962)
Stuart Sutcliffe – bass (1960)
Horst Fascher – vocals (1962)

BBC and other performances

June 1960 – amateur recording made at the McCartney home, Liverpool
December 1962 [1] – Star-Club, Hamburg (live)

1995 – EMI
[2] – 1960 recording edited and reprocessed from source tape

Releases   *UK/US peak*

Live! At The Star-Club In Hamburg, Germany; 1962 LP (1977) – Lingasong LNL 1 /
   Lingasong LS 2 7001 [1]   –
Anthology 1 CD (1995) – Apple 8 34445 2 [2]   2/1

═ NOTES ═

> ♪ A #5 hit on the *Billboard* R&B charts for Ray Charles
>   in 1955, covered by Eddie Cochran in 1959.
> ♪ Performed by the Beatles 1960–62, with Paul
>   usually on vocals.
> ♪ The Star-Club recording has Horst Fascher on
>   vocals.

Happiness Is A Warm Gun

[Lennon-McCartney]

John – lead vocals, lead guitar, possibly organ
Paul – backing vocals, bass, possibly piano
George – backing vocals, lead guitar
Ringo – drums, tambourine
Possibly tuba

May 1968 – Kinfauns, Esher
Demo recording

Studio recording and mixing

May 1968 – Kinfauns, Esher
Demo recording

23 September 1968 – *Studio Two – White Album session 66 out of 81*
Takes 1–45

24 September 1968 – *Studio Two – White Album session 67 out of 81*
Takes 46–70

25 September 1968 – *Studio Two – White Album session 68 out of 81*
Edit of takes 53, 65 > take 65
Overdubs onto take 65 – vocals, organ, piano, tuba, drum, tambourine, bass

26 September 1968 – *Studio Two control room*
RM12 [1] – mono mix from take 65

15 October 1968 – *Studio Two control room*
RS4 [2] – stereo mix from take 65

1996 – *EMI*
[3] – mono mix from demo

2018 – *EMI*
[4] – stereo mix from demo
[5] – stereo mix from take 19
[6] – stereo mix from take 65

Releases	UK/US peak
The Beatles LP (1968) – Apple PMC 7067–7068 [1], PCS 7067–7068 [2]	1
The Beatles LP (US, 1968) – Apple SWBO-101 [2]	1
Anthology 3 CD (1996) – Apple 8 34451 2 [3]	4/1
The Beatles Deluxe CD (2018) – Apple 0602567571957 [4] [5] [6]	4/6

=== NOTES ===

♪ The title comes from an article in
American Rifleman magazine, written
shortly after the assassination of Robert
Kennedy.
♪ 70 takes were needed to perfect the
rhythm track …
♪ … possibly because the song contains
sections in 4/4, 6/4, 5/4, 3/8, and 6/16.

Happy Birthday Dear Saturday Club

[Hill-Hill]

John – vocals, rhythm guitar
Paul – vocals, bass
George – vocals, lead guitar
Ringo – drums

BBC and other performances

7 September 1963 [1] – 5 October 1963 edition of *Saturday Club*

Releases   *UK/US peak*

On Air – Live At The BBC Volume 2 CD (2013) – Apple 6025 37491698 [1]   12/7

═══ NOTES ═══

♪ Recorded to mark the fifth birthday of *Saturday Club*, first
broadcast on the BBC Light Programme on 4 October 1958.

A Hard Day's Night

[Lennon-McCartney]

John – lead vocals, rhythm guitars
Paul – lead and harmony vocals, bass
George – harmony vocals, lead guitar
Ringo – drums, cowbell
George Martin – piano
Norman Smith – possibly bongos

Studio recording and mixing

16 April 1964 – Studio Two – A Hard Day's Night session 7 out of 12
Takes 1–9
Overdubs onto take 9 – vocals, bongos, drums, guitar, piano

23 April 1964 – Studio Two control room
RM10 [1] – mono mix from take 9

9 June 1964 – Studio Three control room
[2] –mono mix from take 9, edited for extended outro

22 June 1964 – Studio Two control room
RS1 [3] – stereo mix from take 9

1964 – United Artists
[4] – panned mono mix made from [1]

1993 – EMI
[5] – stereo mix from take 1

1995 – EMI
[6] – mono mix from take 1

BBC and other performances

14 July 1964 [7] – 16 July 1964 edition of *Top Gear*

17 July 1964 – 3 August 1964 edition of *From Us To You*
19 July 1964 – *Blackpool Night Out* (Associated British Corp. TV, live)
20 June 1965 **[8]** – *Les Beatles* (Europe 1 TV, France, live)
15 August 1965 – *The Beatles At Shea Stadium* (live), broadcast by BBC TV on
    1 March 1966
30 August 1965 **[9]** – Hollywood Bowl (live)

Releases   *UK/US peak*

A Hard Day's Night LP (1964) – Parlophone PMC 1230 [1], PCS 3058 [3]	1
A Hard Day's Night LP (US, 1964) – United Artists UAL 3366 [1], UAS 6366 [4]	1
A Hard Day's Night movie (1964) [2]	
'A Hard Day's Night' / 'Things We Said Today' single (1964) – Parlophone R 5160 [1]	1
'A Hard Day's Night' / 'I Should Have Known Better' single (US, 1964) – Capitol 5222 [1]	1
Extracts From The Film 'A Hard Day's Night' EP (1964) – Parlophone GEP 8920 [1]	1
A Collection Of Beatles Oldies LP (1966) – Parlophone PMC 7016 [1], PCS 7016 [3]	7
The Beatles 1962–1966 LP (1973) – Apple PCSP 717 [3]	3
The Beatles 1962–1966 LP (US, 1973) – Apple SKBO 3403 [1]	3
The Beatles At The Hollywood Bowl LP (1977) – Parlophone EMTV 4 / Capitol SMAS 11638 [9]	1/2
Reel Music LP (1982) – Parlophone PCS 7218 / Capitol SV-12199 [3]	–/19
20 Greatest Hits LP (1982) – Parlophone PCTC 260 / Capitol SV-12245 [3]	10/50
The Beatles 1962–1966 CD (1993) – EMI CDP 7 97036 2 [5]	3
Anthology 1 CD (1995) – Apple 8 34445 2 [6]	2/1
Live At The BBC CD (1994) – Apple 8 31796 2 [7]	1/3
1+ CD/DVD (2015) – Apple 6205 47567727 [8]	5/6
Live At The Hollywood Bowl CD (2016) – Apple 6025 57054972 [9]	3/7

=== **NOTES** ===

♪ Simultaneously #1 in both
  single and LP charts in both
  the UK and US.
♪ Mix [2] was also used by United
  Artists for the 1968 cassette
  and the 1970 8-track tape
  versions.
♪ Performed live until 1965.
♪ George Martin was nominated
  for an Oscar for best adapted
  score for the movie.

Hello, Goodbye

[Lennon-McCartney]

Paul – lead and backing vocals, bass, piano, bongos, conga drum
John – backing vocals, lead guitar, organ

George – backing vocals, lead guitar, possibly tambourine
Ringo – drums, possibly maracas
Session musicians – two violas

Studio recording and mixing

2 October 1967 – Studio Two – Magical Mystery Tour session 22 out of 30
Takes 1–14
Overdubs onto take 14 – percussion
Tape reduction of take 14 > takes 15, 16

19 October 1967 – Studio One – Magical Mystery Tour session 25 out of 30
Overdubs onto take 16 – guitar, vocals
Tape reduction of take 16 > take 17

20 October 1967 – Studio Three – Magical Mystery Tour session 26 out of 30
Overdubs onto take 17 – violas

25 October 1967 – Studio Two – Magical Mystery Tour session 27 out of 30
Tape reduction of take 17 > takes 18–21
Overdubs onto take 21 – bass

1 November 1967 – Room 53
Possible tape reduction of take 21 > takes 22–25

2 November 1967 – Studio Three – Magical Mystery Tour session 28 out of 30
Overdubs onto take 22 – bass

2 November 1967 – Studio Three control room
RM6 [1] – mono mix from take 22

6 November 1967 – Studio Three control room
RS2 [2] – stereo mix from take 22

1995 – EMI
[3] – stereo mix from take 16

2015 – EMI
[4] – stereo mix from take 22

Releases   *UK/US peak*

	UK/US peak
'Hello, Goodbye' / 'I Am The Walrus' single (1967) – Parlophone R 5655 [1]	1
'Hello, Goodbye' / 'I Am The Walrus' single (US, 1967) – Capitol 2056 [1]	1
Magical Mystery Tour LP (US, 1967) – Capitol MAL 2835 [1], SMAL 2835 [2]	1
The Beatles 1967–1970 LP (1973) – Apple PCSP 718 [2]	2
The Beatles 1967–1970 LP (US, 1973) – Apple SKBO 3404 [1]	1
20 Greatest Hits LP (1982) – Parlophone PCTC 260 / Capitol SV-12245 [2]	10/50
The Beatles 1967–1970 CD (1993) – EMI CDP 7 97039 2 [2]	4
Anthology 2 CD (1996) – Apple 8 34448 2 [3]	1/1

1+ CD/DVD (2015) – Apple 6205 47567727 [4]   5/6

========= **NOTES** =========

♪ A promotional film was made on 10 November 1967.
♪ The track's finale appears over the final credits of the *Magical Mystery Tour* movie.

Hello Little Girl

[Lennon-McCartney]

John – lead vocals, rhythm guitar
Paul – harmony and backing vocals, bass
George – lead guitar
Pete Best – drums

Studio recording and mixing

1 January 1962 – Decca Studios

Studio test recorded in mono [1]

BBC and other performances

7 March 1962 – 8 March 1962 edition of *Here We Go* (not broadcast)

Releases   *UK/US peak*

Anthology 1 CD (1995) – Apple 8 34445 2 [1]   2/1

========= **NOTES** =========

♪ John's third composition, written in 1957.
♪ A rehearsal was recorded at Paul's house in Forthlin Road in June 1960.
♪ Played in concert by the Quarry Men/Beatles until 1962.
♪ One of four songs played at an audition for the BBC in Manchester on 8 February 1962.
♪ A cover by the Fourmost reached #9 in October 1963.

Help!

[Lennon-McCartney]

John – lead vocals, acoustic guitar
Paul – harmony and backing vocals, bass
George – harmony and backing vocals, lead guitar
Ringo – drums, tambourine

Studio recording and mixing

13 April 1965 – Studio Two – Help! session 8 out of 13
Takes 1–9
Overdubs onto take 9 – vocals, guitar, tambourine > takes 10–12

18 April 1965 – Room 65
Mono or twin-track mix from take 12

24 May 1965 – CTS Studios – Help! session 10 out of 13
Overdubs onto take 12 – vocals (replacing tambourine) > unnumbered take

18 June 1965 – Studio Two control room
RM4 [1] – mono mix from edit of take 12 and unnumbered take
RS2 [2] – stereo mix from take 12

1965 – Capitol
[3] – mono mix from [2]

1987 – EMI
[4] – stereo mix from take 12

2004–06 – EMI
[5] – stereo mix from take 12

BBC and other performances

1 August 1965 [6] – *Blackpool Night Out* (Associated British Corp. TV, live)
29 August 1965 [7] – Hollywood Bowl (live)
14 August 1965 [8] – *The Ed Sullivan Show* broadcast on 12 September 1965
   (CBS TV)
15 August 1965 – *The Beatles At Shea Stadium* (live), broadcast by BBC TV on
   1 March 1966

Releases   *UK/US peak*

Help! LP (1965) – Parlophone PMC 1255 [1], PCS 3071 [2]	1
Help! LP (US, 1965) – Capitol MAS 2386 [3], SMAS 2386 [2]	1
'Help!' / 'I'm Down' single (1965) – Parlophone R 5305 [1]	1
'Help!' / 'I'm Down' single (US, 1965) – Capitol 5476 [1]	1
Help! movie (1965) [1]	
A Collection Of Beatles Oldies LP (1966) – Parlophone PMC 7016 [1], PCS 7016 [2]	7
The Beatles 1962–1966 LP (1973) – Apple PCSP 717 [2]	3
The Beatles 1962–1966 LP (US, 1973)– Apple SKBO 3403 [2]	3
The Beatles At The Hollywood Bowl LP (1977) – Parlophone EMTV 4 / Capitol SMAS 11638 [7]	1/2
Rarities LP (US, 1980) – Capitol SHAL 12060 [1]	21
Reel Music LP (1982) – Parlophone PCS 7218 / Capitol SV-12199 [2]	–/19
20 Greatest Hits LP (1982) – Parlophone PCTC 260 / Capitol SV-12245 [2]	10/50
Help! CD (1987) – EMI CDP 7 46439 2 [4]	61

The Beatles 1962–1966 CD (1993) – EMI CDP 7 97036 2 [4]	3
Anthology 2 CD (1996) – Apple 8 34448 2 [6]	1/1
The Four Historic Ed Sullivan Shows DVD (2003) – EREDV 372 [8]	
Love CD (2006) – Apple 0946 3 80790 2 6 [5]	3/4
1+ CD/DVD (2015) – Apple 6205 47567727 [4]	5/6
Live At The Hollywood Bowl CD (2016) – Apple 6025 57054972 [7]	3/7

=== **NOTES** ===

♪ Performed in concert in 1965.
♪ A promotional film was made on 23 November 1965.
♪ Winner of the Ivor Novello award for the highest sales of 1965.
♪ The movie mix is possibly from 18 April.
♪ The edit of take 12 for RM4 was for the introduction only.

Helter Skelter

[Lennon-McCartney]

Paul – lead vocals, guitar
John – backing vocals, bass, tenor saxophone, piano
George – backing vocals, guitar
Ringo – drums
Mal Evans – trumpet

Studio recording and mixing

18 July 1968 – Studio Two – White Album session 28 out of 81
Takes 1–3

9 September 1968 – Studio Two – White Album session 56 out of 81
Remake takes 4–21

10 September 1968 – Studio Two – White Album session 57 out of 81
Overdubs onto take 21 – vocals, guitar, drums, piano, saxophone, trumpet

17 September 1968 – Studio Two control room
RM1 [1] – mono mix from take 21

12 October 1968 – Studio Two control room
RS5 [2] – stereo mix from take 21

1996 – EMI
[3] – mono mix from take 2

2018 – EMI
[4] – stereo mix from take 2
[5] – stereo mix from take 17
[6] – stereo mix from take 21

See 'Being For The Benefit Of Mr Kite!' **[5]** for *Love* CD info.

Releases
UK/US peak

The Beatles LP (1968) – Apple PMC 7067–7068 **[1]**, PCS 7067–7068 **[2]**	1
The Beatles LP (US, 1968) – Apple SWBO-101 **[2]**	1
Rock 'n' Roll Music LP (1976) – Parlophone PCSP 719 / Capitol SKBO 11537 **[2]**	11/2
'Got To Get You Into My Life' / 'Helter Skelter' (US, 1976) – Capitol 4274 **[2]**	–
Rarities LP (US, 1980) – Capitol SHAL 12060 **[1]**	21
Anthology 3 CD (1996) – Apple 8 34451 2 **[3]**	4/1
Tomorrow Never Knows (2012) – iTunes **[2]**	44/24
The Beatles Deluxe CD (2018) – Apple 0602567571957 **[4] [5] [6]**	4/6

NOTES

♪ The 9 September session marked the debut of Chris Thomas as producer, standing in for a holidaying George Martin.
♪ The mono version is nearly a minute shorter than the stereo.
♪ A 27-minute rehearsal take – the longest the Beatles recorded – remains unreleased.

Her Majesty
[Lennon-McCartney]

Paul – lead vocals, acoustic guitar

Studio recording and mixing

2 July 1969 – Studio Two – Abbey Road session 12 out of 42
Takes 1–3

30 July 1969 – Studio Two control room
RS1 **[1]** – stereo mix from take 3

Releases
UK/US peak

Abbey Road LP (1969) – Apple PCS 7088 **[1]**	1
Abbey Road LP (US, 1969) – Apple SO 383 **[1]**	1

NOTES

♪ Not listed on the LP sleeve.
♪ Originally intended to appear between 'Mean Mr Mustard' and 'Polythene Pam', but was physically cut out of an early tape mix.
♪ The final chord was sacrificed in the cut.

Here Comes The Sun

[Harrison]

George – lead and harmony vocals, acoustic guitar, harmonium, Moog synthesiser
Paul – harmony vocals, bass
Ringo – drums
Session musicians – four violas, four cellos, double bass, two clarinets, two alto flutes, two flutes, two piccolos

Studio recording and mixing

7 July 1969 – Studio Two – Abbey Road session 15 out of 42
Takes 1–13
Overdubs onto take 13 – guitar

8 July 1969 – Studio Two – Abbey Road session 16 out of 42
Overdubs onto take 13 – vocals, guitar, drums
Tape reduction of take 13 > takes 14, 15

16 July 1969 – Studio Three – Abbey Road session 21 out of 42
Overdubs onto take 15 – vocals, handclaps, harmonium

6 August 1969 – Studio Three – Abbey Road session 36 out of 42
Overdubs onto take 15 – guitar

11 August 1969 – Studio Two – Abbey Road session 39 out of 42
Overdubs onto take 15 – guitar

15 August 1969 – Studio One – Abbey Road session 40 out of 42
Overdubs onto take 15 – orchestra

19 August 1969 – Studio Two – Abbey Road session 42 out of 42
Overdubs onto take 15 – Moog

19 August 1969 – Studio Two control room
RS1 [1] – stereo mix from take 15

2004–06 – EMI
[2] – stereo mix from take 1, in medley with 'The Inner Light' take 6: includes samples from 'Within You Without You' (Indian instruments); 'Oh! Darling' (bass); 'I Want You (She's So Heavy)' (bass)

Releases   *UK/US peak*

Abbey Road LP (1969) – Apple PCS 7088 [1]	1
Abbey Road LP (US, 1969) – Apple SO 383 [1]	1
The Beatles 1967–1970 LP (1973) – Apple PCSP 718 [1]	2
The Beatles 1967–1970 LP (US, 1973) – Apple SKBO 3404 [1]	1
The Beatles Ballads LP (1980) – Parlophone PCS 7214 [1]	17
Love CD (2006) – Apple 0946 3 80790 2 6 [2]	3/4

╔═══════════════ **NOTES** ═══════════════╗

♪ John does not appear on the recording.
♪ Although never released as a single, it charted
as a download in 2010 and 2012, peaking at #58.

╚══════════════════════════════════════╝

Here, There And Everywhere

[Lennon-McCartney]

Paul – lead vocals, acoustic guitar, bass
John – backing vocals
George – backing vocals, lead guitar
Ringo – drums

Studio recording and mixing

14 June 1966 – Studio Two – Revolver session 30 out of 33
Takes 1–4
Overdubs onto take 4 – vocals

16 June 1966 – Studio Two – Revolver session 31 out of 33
Takes 5–13
Overdubs onto take 13 – vocals, bass
Tape reduction of take 13 > take 14
Overdubs onto take 14 – vocals

17 June 1966 – Studio Two – Revolver session 32 out of 33
Overdubs onto take 14 – vocals, guitar

21 June 1966 – Studio Three control room
RM3 [1] – mono mix from take 14
RS2 [2] – stereo mix from take 14

1995 – EMI
[3] – stereo mix from takes 7, 13

Releases   *UK/US peak*

Revolver LP (1966) – Parlophone PMC 7009 [1], PCS 7009 [2]	1
Revolver LP (US, 1966) – Capitol T 2576 [1], ST 2576 [2]	1
Love Songs LP (1977) – Parlophone PCSP 721 / Capitol SKBL 11711 [2]	7/24
The Beatles Ballads LP (1980) – Parlophone PCS 7214 [2]	17
'Real Love' single (1996) – Apple 8 82646 2 [3]	4/11

╔═══════════════ **NOTES** ═══════════════╗

♪ The introduction features 9/8 and 7/8 time signatures.

╚══════════════════════════════════════╝

Hey! Ba-Ba-Re-Bop

[Hampton-Hamner]

Lead vocals, **Paul**. Played by the Beatles around 1960–62. It was originally recorded by Lionel Hampton in 1946 and covered by Tony Sheridan and the Big Six in 1965.

Hey! Baby

[Cobb-Channel]

Lead vocals, **Paul**. Part of the Beatles' set in 1962, and one of the first songs to feature John's harmonica. Bruce Channel reached #1 on *Billboard* and #2 in the UK in 1962.

Hey Bulldog

[Lennon-McCartney]

John – lead vocals, piano, possibly guitar
Paul – harmony vocals, bass, tambourine
George – lead guitar
Ringo – drums

Studio recording and mixing

11 February 1968 – Studio Three – Yellow Submarine session 15 out of 15
Takes 1–10
Overdubs onto take 10 – fuzz bass, drums, guitar, vocals

11 February 1968 – Studio Three control room
RM2 [1] – mono mix from take 10

29 October 1968 – Studio Two control room
RS3 [2] – stereo mix from take 10

25 November 1968 – EMI
[3] – mono mix from [2]

1999 – EMI
[4] – stereo mix from take 10

2015 – EMI
[5] – stereo mix from take 10

Releases   UK/US peak

Yellow Submarine movie (1968) [1]	
Yellow Submarine LP (1969) – Apple PMC 7070 [3], PCS 7070 [2]	3
Yellow Submarine LP (US, 1969) – Apple SW 153 [2]	2
Rock 'n' Roll Music LP (1976) – Parlophone PCSP 719 / Capitol SKBO 11537 [2]	11/2
Yellow Submarine Songtrack CD (1999) – Apple 5 21481 2 [4]	8/15
Mono Masters CD (2009) – Apple 6 849582 4 [1]	–

Tomorrow Never Knows (2012) – iTunes **[4]**   44/24
1+ CD/DVD (2015) – Apple 6205 47567727 **[5]**   5/6

> ═══════ **NOTES** ═══════
>
> ♪ Cut from the film after the premiere, but
>   reinstated in later releases.
> ♪ The studio recording was filmed to promote
>   'Lady Madonna'.

Hey, Good Lookin'

[Porter-Williams]

The song was played by the Beatles around 1960–62 with **George** singing lead. Based on
a Cole Porter song, it was recorded by Hank Williams in 1951.

Hey Jude

[Lennon-McCartney]

Paul – lead vocals, piano, bass
John – harmony and backing vocals, acoustic guitar
George – harmony and backing vocals, lead guitar
Ringo – harmony and backing vocals, drums, tambourine
Session musicians – ten violins, three violas, three cellos, two string basses, two flutes,
contra bassoon, bassoon, two clarinets, contra bass clarinet, four trumpets, four
trombones, two horns, percussion

Studio recording and mixing

***29 July 1968** – Studio Two – White Album session 34 out of 81*
Takes 1–6

***30 July 1968** – Studio Two – White Album session 35 out of 81*
Takes 7–23
Tape reduction of take 23 > takes 24, 25

***31 July 1968** – Trident Studios – White Album session 36 out of 81*
Remake takes 1–4
Overdubs onto remake take 1

***1 August 1968** – Trident Studios – White Album session 37 out of 81*
Overdubs onto remake take 1 – bass, vocals, orchestra

***8 August 1968** – Studio Two control room*
RM4 **[1]** – mono mix from remake take 1

***5 December 1969** – Studio Two control room*
RS21 **[2]** – stereo mix from remake take 1

1996 – EMI

[3] – stereo mix from take 2 (29 July 1968)

2004–06 – EMI

[4] – stereo mix from take 1: includes samples from 'Magical Mystery Tour' (drums)

2018 – EMI

[5] – stereo mix from take 1 (29 July 1968)

BBC and other performances

30 July 1968 – *Music!* (National Music Council of Great Britain documentary)
4 September 1968 [6] [7] – Twickenham Film Studios, broadcast on 8 September
      1968 edition of *Frost on Sunday* (London Weekend Television)

Releases

	UK/US peak
'Hey Jude' / 'Revolution' single (1968) – Apple R 5722 [1]	1
'Hey Jude' / 'Revolution' single (1968) – Parlophone DP 570 [1]	–
'Hey Jude' / 'Revolution' single (US, 1968) – Apple 2276 [1]	1
Hey Jude LP (US, 1970) – Apple SW 385 [2]	2
The Beatles 1967–1970 LP (1973) – Apple PCSP 718 [2]	2
The Beatles 1967–1970 LP (US, 1973) – Apple SKBO 3404 [2]	1
The Beatles Ballads LP (1980) – Parlophone PCS 7214 [2]	17
20 Greatest Hits LP (1982) – Parlophone PCTC 260 [2]	10
20 Greatest Hits LP (US, 1982) – Capitol SV-12245 [2, edited]	50
Past Masters 2 CD (1988) – EMI CDP 7 90044 2 [2]	46/–
Anthology 3 CD (1996) – Apple 8 34451 2 [3]	4/1
Love CD (2006) – Apple 0946 3 80790 2 6 [4]	3/4
1+ CD/DVD (2015) – Apple 6205 47567727 [6] [7]	5/6
The Beatles Deluxe CD (2018) – Apple 0602567571957 [5]	4/6

═══ **NOTES** ═══

- ♪ The *Frost on Sunday* performances feature Paul singing live to a remixed backing track.
- ♪ The first eight-track recording, made during the first recording session at Trident.
- ♪ Spent nine weeks at #1 in the *Billboard* charts.
- ♪ Also reached #12 in 1976 and #52 in 1988, and #40 in 2010 as a download.

High School Confidential

[Hargrave-Lewis]

Lead vocals, **Paul**. Performed by the Quarry Men and Beatles until 1961. Originally recorded in 1958 by Jerry Lee Lewis as the title song for the film *High School Confidential*. It reached #21 on *Billboard* and #12 in the UK.

The Hippy Hippy Shake

[Romero]

Paul – lead vocals, bass
John – rhythm guitar
George – lead guitar
Ringo – drums

BBC and other performances

December 1962 **[1]** – Star-Club, Hamburg (live)
16 March 1963 – *Saturday Club* (live)
24 May 1963 **[2]** – 4 June 1963 edition of *Pop Go The Beatles*
10 July 1963 **[3]** – 30 July 1963 edition of *Pop Go The Beatles*
3 September 1963 **[4]** – 10 September 1963 edition of *Pop Go The Beatles*
7 January 1964 – 15 February 1964 edition of *Saturday Club*

Releases   *UK/US peak*

Live! At The Star-Club In Hamburg, Germany; 1962 LP (1977) – Lingasong LNL 1 /
  Lingasong LS 2 7001 **[1]**   –
Live At The BBC CD (1994) – Apple 8 31796 2 **[3]**   1/3
On Air – Live At The BBC Volume 2 CD (2013) – Apple 6025 37491698 **[4]**   12/7
The Beatles Bootleg Recordings 1963 (2013) – iTunes **[2]**   –

NOTES

> ♪ Released by Chan Romero in 1959, and a hit for the
>   Swinging Blue Jeans in 1964.
> ♪ Picked up by Paul after being played by the Cavern
>   DJ Bob Wooler.
> ♪ Played through on the second day of the *Let It Be*
>   sessions in 1969.

Hold Me Tight

[Lennon-McCartney]

Paul – lead vocals, bass
John – harmony vocals, rhythm guitar
George – harmony vocals, lead guitar
Ringo – drums

Studio recording and mixing

11 February 1963 – Studio Two – Please Please Me session 5 out of 8
Takes 1–9
Edit pieces takes 10–13

12 September 1963 – *Studio Two – With The Beatles session 5 out of 9*
Remake takes 20–24
Overdubs onto take 24 – handclaps, vocals > takes 25–29

30 September 1963 – *Studio Two control room*
Edit of takes 26, 29

23 October 1963 – *Studio Two control room*
RM29 [1] – mono mix from edit of takes 26, 29

29 October 1963 – *Studio Two control room*
RS29 [2] – stereo mix from edit of takes 26, 29

19 December 1963 – *Capitol*
[3] – mastering of stereo mix from [2]
[4] – mastering of mono mix from [3]

2013 – *EMI*
[5] – stereo mix from take 21

Releases

	UK/US peak
With The Beatles LP (1963) – Parlophone PMC 1206 [1], PCS 3045 [2]	1
Meet The Beatles! LP (US, 1964) – Capitol T 2047 [4], ST 2047 [3]	1
The Beatles Bootleg Recordings 1963 (2013) – iTunes [5]	–

=== NOTES ===

♪ Originally recorded during the *Please Please Me* session on 11 February, re-recorded for inclusion on *With The Beatles*.
♪ One of the first Lennon-McCartney songs that the group played live (between 1961 and 1963), but never recorded for BBC radio.

Honey Don't

[Perkins]

Ringo – lead vocals, drums
John – acoustic rhythm guitar, tambourine
Paul – bass
George – lead guitar

Studio recording and mixing

26 October 1965 – *Studio Two – Beatles For Sale session 8 out of 8*
Takes 1–5

27 October 1965 – *Studio Two control room*
RM1 [1] – mono mix from take 5
RS1 [2] – stereo mix from take 5

BBC and other performances

1 August 1963 [3] – 3 September 1963 edition of *Pop Go The Beatles*
1 May 1964 – 18 May 1964 edition of *From Us To You*
17 November 1964 [4] – 26 November 1964 edition of *Top Gear*
26 May 1965 – 7 June 1965 edition of *The Beatles Invite You To Take A Ticket To Ride*

Releases	UK/US peak
Beatles For Sale LP (1964) – Parlophone PMC 1240 [1], PCS 3062 [2]	1
Beatles '65 LP (US, 1964) – Capitol T 2228 [1], ST 2228 [2]	1
4 – By The Beatles EP (US, 1965) – Capitol R 5365 [1]	68
Live At The BBC CD (1994) – Apple 8 31796 2 [3]	1/3
On Air – Live At The BBC Volume 2 CD (2013) – Apple 6025 37491698 [4]	12/7

NOTES

♪ Released by Carl Perkins in January 1956 on the B-side of 'Blue Suede Shoes'.
♪ Played live by the Beatles until 1965, with John singing lead until 1964.

Honey Pie

[Lennon-McCartney]

Paul – lead vocals, piano
John – guitar
George – bass
Ringo – drums
Session musicians – five saxophones, two clarinets

Studio recording and mixing

May 1968 – *Kinfauns, Esher*
Demo recording

1 October 1968 – *Trident Studios – White Album session 70 out of 81*
Take 1

2 October 1968 – *Trident Studios – White Album session 71 out of 81*
Overdubs onto take 1 – vocals, guitar

4 October 1968 – Trident Studios – White Album session 73 out of 81
Overdubs onto take 1 – brass, woodwind

5 October 1968 – Trident Studios
RM1 – mono mix from take 1
RS1 – stereo mix from take 1

7 October 1968 – Studio Two control room
Tape copying RM1 [1]
Tape copying RS1 [2]

1996 – EMI
[3] – stereo mix from demo, edited

2018 – EMI
[4] – stereo mix from demo
[5] – stereo mix from take 1, without vocals
[6] – stereo mix from take 1

Releases   *UK/US peak*

The Beatles LP (1968) – Apple PMC 7067–7068 [1], PCS 7067–7068 [2]	1
The Beatles LP (US, 1968) – Apple SWBO-101 [2]	1
Anthology 3 CD (1996) – Apple 8 34451 2 [3]	4/1
The Beatles Deluxe CD (2018) – Apple 0602567571957 [4] [5] [6]	4/6

NOTES

♪ Overdubs for 'Martha My Dear' were also recorded on 4 October, though using different musicians.
♪ The tape copying was to correct equalisation incompatibility between Trident's American NAB system and EMI's European CCIR system.
♪ The *Anthology 3* track was edited to nearly half the length of the full demo.

The Honeymoon Song

[Theodorakis-Sansom]

Paul – lead vocals, bass
John – rhythm guitar
George – lead guitar
Ringo – drums

BBC and other performances

16 July 1963 [1] – 6 August 1963 edition of *Pop Go The Beatles*

Releases .... *UK/US peak*

Live At The BBC CD (1994) – Apple 8 31796 2 **[1]**   1/3

```
╔══════════════════ NOTES ══════════════════╗
║ ♪ From the 1959 Michael Powell film Honeymoon, ║
║   performed by Marino Marini and his Quartet.   ║
╚═══════════════════════════════════════════╝
```

Honky Tonk Blues

[Williams]

Played by the Quarry Men/Beatles until the end of the Hamburg shows, with **John** singing lead. It was recorded by Hank Williams in 1952.

Hot As Sun

[McCartney]

An instrumental, most likely played by the Quarry Men until around 1959. Paul released a version recorded live in Glasgow in 1979 as a bonus track on the 2011 remaster of his *McCartney* album.

Hound Dog

[Leiber-Stoller]

Lead vocals, **John**. The song was played by the Quarry Men/Beatles from 1957 until 1961. It was a US #1 and UK #2 for Elvis Presley in 1956.

How Do You Do It

[Murray]

John – lead vocals, rhythm guitar
Paul – harmony vocals, bass
George – backing vocals, lead guitar
Ringo – drums

Studio recording and mixing

4 September 1962 – Studio Two – Please Please Me session 2 out of 8
Unknown take numbers
Overdubs onto take 2 – vocals

21 October 1964 – Studio Two control room
[1] – mono mix from take 2

1984 – AIR Studios
[2] – edit of [1]

Releases

	UK/US peak
Anthology 1 CD (1995) – Apple 8 34445 2 **[2]**	2/1

= NOTES =

♪ Originally offered by composer Mitch Murray for Adam Faith to record.

♪ Rejected by the Beatles for their debut single, Gerry and the Pacemakers took the song to #1 in April 1963.

♪ Performed live for a short time in 1963.

♪ The edit was to replace the first "I'd do it to you" line at the end with a copy of the "but I haven't a clue" line from earlier in the song.

Hully Gully

[Smith-Goldsmith]

Lead vocals, **John**. Played by the Beatles from 1960 to 1962. '(Baby) Hully Gully' was written by Fred Sledge Smith and Clifford Goldsmith. A version by the Olympics crept into the *Billboard* top 100 in 1960. It appears on the LP *Beach Boys Party!* from 1965.

I Am The Walrus

[Lennon-McCartney]

John – lead vocals, electric piano
Paul – backing vocals, bass, tambourine
George – backing vocals, lead guitar
Ringo – drums
Mike Sammes Singers – eight male and eight female backing vocalists
Session musicians – eight violins, four cellos, contra bass clarinet, three horns

Studio recording and mixing

5 September 1967 – Studio One – Magical Mystery Tour session 12 out of 30

Takes 1–16
Overdubs onto take 16 – Mellotron

6 September 1967 – Studio Two – Magical Mystery Tour session 13 out of 30

Tape reduction of take 16 > take 17
Overdubs onto take 17 – bass, drums, vocals

27 September 1967 – Studios One and Two – Magical Mystery Tour session 19 out of 30

Tape reduction of take 17 > takes 18–24
Overdubs onto takes 18–24 – orchestra
Tape reduction of take 20 > take 25
Overdubs onto take 25 – choir

28 September 1967 *– Studio Two control room*
Tape reduction of take 25 as overdub onto take 17

29 September 1967 *– Studio Two control room*
RM10 – mono mix from take 17
RM22 – mono mix from take 17, with live radio feed
Edit of RM10, RM22 > RM23

6 November 1967 *– Studio Three control room*
RS1–RS7 – stereo mixes from take 17, RM22
[1] – edit of RS6, RS7

7 November 1967 *– Studio One control room*
[2] – tape copying of edit of RM23

15 November 1967 *– Studio Two control room*
[3] – edit of RM23

17 November 1967 *– Room 53*
RS25 – stereo mix from take 17
[4] – edit of RS25, RS7

1967 *– Capitol*
[5] – edit of [2] to match UK single
[6] – edit of [1] to match length of [2]

1980 *– Capitol*
[7] – edit of [1] with mock stereo edit of [2]

1995 *– EMI*
[8] – stereo mix from take 16

c. 1999 *– EMI*
[9] – stereo mix from take 25 with speech from archive

2004–06 *– EMI*
[10] – stereo mix from take 25 with speech from archive: includes George Martin's count-in from take 20 and other unspecified samples

Releases · *UK/US peak*

'Hello, Goodbye' / 'I Am The Walrus' single (1967) – Parlophone R 5655 [3]	1
'Hello, Goodbye' / 'I Am The Walrus' single (US, 1967) – Capitol 2056 [2]	56
Magical Mystery Tour EP (1967) – Parlophone MMT-1 [3], SMMT-1 [4]	2
Magical Mystery Tour LP (US, 1967) – Capitol MAL 2835 [5], SMAL 2835 [6]	1
The Beatles 1967–1970 LP (1973) – Apple PCSP 718 [4]	2
The Beatles 1967–1970 LP (US, 1973) – Apple SKBO 3404 [6]	1
Rarities LP (US, 1980) – Capitol SHAL 12060 [7]	21
Reel Music LP (1982) – Parlophone PCS 7218 / Capitol SV-12199 [4]	–/19
The Beatles 1967–1970 CD (1993) – EMI CDP 7 97039 2 [4]	4

Anthology 2 CD (1996) – Apple 8 34448 2 **[8]**   1/1
Anthology DVD (2003) – Apple 4 92969 9 **[9]**
Love CD (2006) – Apple 0946 3 80790 2 6 **[10]**   3/4

NOTES

♪ The first song to be recorded following the death of Brian Epstein.

♪ Simultaneously #1 and #2 in the UK singles chart in January 1968, as a B-side and an EP track.

♪ [1], [4] and [7] have a 6-beat intro and [2] has extra bar after "I'm crying".

♪ [9] is full stereo throughout – the problem of the original radio feed of *King Lear* being locked into the mono version was solved by using a copy of the play from the BBC archive and faking the radio interference.

I Call Your Name

[Lennon-McCartney]

John – lead vocals, rhythm guitar
Paul – bass
George – lead guitar
Ringo – drums, cowbell

Studio recording and mixing

1 March 1964 – Studio Two – A Hard Day's Night session 5 out of 12
Takes 1–7
Overdubs onto take 7 – vocals, cowbell

4 March 1964 – Studio Three control room
RM1 **[1]** – mono mix from take 7

10 March 1964 – Studio Two control room
RS1 **[2]** – stereo mix from take 7

4 June 1964 – Studio Two control room
RM1, RM2 **[3]** – mono mixes from takes 5, 7, edited

22 June 1964 – Studio One control room
RS1, RS3 **[4]** – stereo mixes from takes 5, 7, edited

BBC and other performances

31 March 1964 – 4 April 1964 edition of *Saturday Club*

Releases	UK/US peak
Long Tall Sally EP (1964) – Parlophone GEP 8913 [3]	1
The Beatles' Second Album LP (US, 1964) – Capitol T 2080 [1], ST 2080 [2]	1
The Beatles' Second Album EP (US, 1964) – Capitol SXA 2080 [2]	–
Rock 'n' Roll Music LP (1976) – Parlophone PCSP 719 / Capitol SKBO 11537 [4]	11/2
Rarities LP (1978) – Parlophone PCM 1001, PSLP 261 [3]	71
Past Masters 1 CD (1988) – EMI CDP 7 90043 2 [4]	49/–

═ NOTES ═

♪ Written by John around 1958.
♪ The song had already been recorded the previous year
  by Billy J Kramer and the Dakotas, released as the B-side
  to 'Bad To Me'.
♪ The 4 March mix was possibly made the previous day.

I Don't Care If The Sun Don't Shine

[David]

Lead vocals, **Paul**. On the earliest known (partial) set list written by Paul in mid-1960.
Released by Elvis Presley in 1954 as the B-side to 'Good Rockin' Tonight'.

I Don't Want To Spoil The Party

[Lennon-McCartney]

John – lead and harmony vocals, acoustic guitar
George – harmony and backing vocals, lead guitar
Paul – lead and backing vocals, bass
Ringo – drums, tambourine

Studio recording and mixing

29 September 1964 – Studio Two – Beatles For Sale session 3 out of 8
Takes 1–19
Overdubs onto take 19 – vocals, tambourine

26 October 1964 – Studio Two control room
RM1 [1] – mono mix from take 19

4 November 1964 – Studio Two control room
RS1 [2] – stereo mix from take 19

Releases	UK/US peak
Beatles For Sale LP (1964) – Parlophone PMC 1240 [1], PCS 3062 [2]	1
Beatles VI LP (US, 1965) – Capitol T 2358 [1], ST 2358 [2]	1
Beatles For Sale (No. 2) EP (1965) – Parlophone GEP 8938 [1]	5

'Eight Days A Week'/'I Don't Want To Spoil The Party' single (US, 1965) – Capitol 5371 [1]   39

```
┌────────────────── NOTES ──────────────────┐
│  ♪ Allegedly written for Ringo to sing.     │
│  ♪ Only five of the 19 takes were           │
│    complete run throughs.                   │
│  ♪ Take 19 is written as "Take 9" on the    │
│    tape box.                                │
└─────────────────────────────────────────────┘
```

I Fancy Me Chances

[Lennon-McCartney]

Written in 1958, this is a comedy song that was still being performed by **John** and **Paul** as late as 1962. They revisited it during the *Let It Be* sessions on 24 January 1969.

I Feel Fine

[Lennon-McCartney]

John – lead vocals, lead/rhythm guitar
Paul – harmony/backing vocals, bass
George – harmony/backing vocals, lead/rhythm guitar
Ringo – drums

Studio recording and mixing

18 October 1964 – Studio Two – Beatles For Sale session 7 out of 8
Takes 1–9
Overdubs onto take 9 – vocals, guitar

21 October 1964 – Studio Two control room
RM3 [1] – mono mix from take 9
RM4 [2] – mono mix from take 9

4 November 1964 – Studio Two control room
RS1 [3] – stereo mix from take 9

9 November 1964 – Capitol
[4] – mastering of mock stereo from [2]

BBC and other performances

17 November 1964 [5] – 26 November 1964 edition of *Top Gear,* repeated on 26
    December 1964 edition of *Saturday Club*
17 November 1964 [6] – as [5] before double-tracking of the vocals
11 April 1965 – *NME 1964-65 Annual Poll-Winners' Concert*
20 June 1965 – *Les Beatles* (Europe 1 TV, France, live)
1 August 1965 [7] – *Blackpool Night Out* (Associated British Corp. TV, live)

14 August 1965 **[8]** – *The Ed Sullivan Show* broadcast on 12 September 1965 (CBS TV)

15 August 1965 – *The Beatles At Shea Stadium* (live), broadcast by BBC TV on 1 March 1966

24 June 1966 – *Die Beatles* broadcast on 5 July 1966 (ZDF TV, Germany)

Releases	UK/US peak
'I Feel Fine' / 'She's A Woman' single (1964) – Parlophone R 5200 **[1]**	1
'I Feel Fine' / 'She's A Woman' single (US, 1964) – Capitol 5327 **[2]**	1
Beatles '65 LP (US, 1964) – Capitol T 2228 **[2]**, ST 2228 **[4]**	1
The Beatles' Million Sellers EP (1965) – Parlophone GEP 8946 **[1]**	1
A Collection Of Beatles Oldies LP (1966) – Parlophone PMC 7016 **[1]**, PCS 7016 **[3,** trimmed]	7
The Beatles 1962–1966 LP (1973) – Apple PCSP 717 **[3]**	3
The Beatles 1962–1966 LP (US, 1973)– Apple SKBO 3403 **[2]**	3
20 Greatest Hits LP (1982) – Parlophone PCTC 260 / Capitol SV-12245 **[3]**	10/50
Past Masters 1 CD (1988) – EMI CDP 7 90043 2 **[3,** trimmed]	49/–
The Beatles 1962–1966 CD (1993) – EMI CDP 7 97036 2 **[3,** trimmed]	3
Live At The BBC CD (1994) – Apple 8 31796 2 **[5]**	1/3
Anthology 2 CD (1996) – Apple 8 34448 2 **[7]**	1/1
The Four Historic Ed Sullivan Shows DVD (2003) – EREDV 372 **[8]**	
On Air – Live At The BBC Volume 2 CD (2013) – Apple 6025 37491698 **[6]**	12/7
1+ CD/DVD (2015) – Apple 6205 47567727 **[3,** trimmed]	5/6

═══════════ **NOTES** ═══════════

♪ The promotional film made on 23 November 1965 appears on *1+*.
♪ Performed in concert until 1966.
♪ The first of three riffs to be based on Bobby Parker's 'Watch Your Step'.
♪ The "trimmed" version omits whispering at the start of the recording.

I Feel So Bad

[Willis]

Lead vocals, **Paul**. Played by Beatles from 1961–62. It was the B-side of Elvis Presley's 1961 hit 'Wild In The Country'.

I Forgot To Remember To Forget

[Kesler-Feathers]

George – lead vocals, lead guitar
John – rhythm guitar
Paul – bass
Ringo – drums

BBC and other performances

1 May 1964 **[1]** – 18 May 1964 edition of *From Us To You*

Releases

UK/US peak

Live At The BBC CD (1994) – Apple 8 31796 2 **[1]**   1/3

═══ NOTES ═══

♪ Elvis Presley single from 1955, the follow-up to 'Baby Let's Play House'.

I Got A Woman

[Charles-Richard]

John – lead vocals, rhythm guitar
Paul – bass
George – lead guitar
Ringo – drums

BBC and other performances

16 July 1963 **[1]** – 13 August 1963 edition of *Pop Go The Beatles*
31 March 1964 **[2]** – 4 April 1964 edition of *Saturday Club*

Releases

UK/US peak

Live At The BBC CD (1994) – Apple 8 31796 2 **[1]**   1/3
On Air – Live At The BBC Volume 2 CD (2013) – Apple 6025 37491698 **[2]**   12/7

═══ NOTES ═══

♪ A Ray Charles song from 1954, his first R&B #1, which
was covered by Elvis Presley on his debut LP.

I Got To Find My Baby

[Berry]

John – lead vocals, rhythm guitar
Paul – bass
George – lead guitar
Ringo – drums

BBC and other performances

1 June 1963 **[1]** – 11 June 1963 edition of *Pop Go The Beatles*
24 June 1963 **[2]** – 29 June 1963 edition of *Saturday Club*

Releases *UK/US peak*

Live At The BBC CD (1994) – Apple 8 31796 2 **[1]** 1/3
The Beatles Bootleg Recordings 1963 (2013) – iTunes **[2]** –

═══════════ **NOTES** ═══════════

♪ A Chuck Berry single from 1960.
♪ Written by "Doctor" Peter Clayton in 1941, but Berry claimed ownership.

I Just Don't Understand

[Wilkin-Westberry]

John – lead vocals, rhythm guitar
Paul – backing vocals, bass
George – backing vocals, lead guitar
Ringo – drums

BBC and other performances

16 July 1963 **[1]** – 20 August 1963 edition of *Pop Go The Beatles*

Releases *UK/US peak*

Live At The BBC CD (1994) – Apple 8 31796 2 **[1]** 1/3

═══════════ **NOTES** ═══════════

♪ Ann-Margret single from 1961, which reached #17 on the *Billboard* chart.

I Lost My Little Girl

[McCartney]

Lead vocals, **Paul**. Written by Paul in 1957 and played by the Quarry Men until around 1959. An unreleased version was performed on 24 January 1969 during the *Let It Be* sessions, with John singing lead. Paul recorded a version that was released on *Unplugged* in 1991.

I Me Mine

[Harrison]

George – lead vocals, acoustic guitar, lead guitar
Paul – harmony vocals, bass, organ, electric piano, acoustic guitar
Ringo – drums
Session musicians – eighteen violins, four violas, four cellos; possibly fourteen-voice female choir, three trumpets, three trombones, harp

Studio recording and mixing

8 January 1969 – Twickenham Film Studios – Let It Be rehearsal session
Takes 8.1, 8.63, 8.81, 8.82 [1, edited]

3 January 1970 – Studio Two – Let It Be session 14 out of 17
Takes 1–16
Overdubs onto take 16 – electric piano, guitar, vocals, organ

1 April 1970 – Studio One – Let It Be session 17 out of 17
Tape reduction of extended edit of take 16 > takes 17, 18
Overdubs onto take 18 – orchestra, choir

2 April 1970 – Studio Two control room
RS11, 12 [2] – stereo mixes from take 18, edited

1996 – EMI
[3] – stereo mix from take 16

2003 – EMI
[4] – stereo mix from extended edit of take 16

Releases   *UK/US peak*

Let It Be LP (1970) – Apple PXS1, PCS 7096 [2]	1
Let It Be LP (US, 1970) – Apple AR 34001 [2]	1
Let It Be movie (1970) [1]	
Anthology 3 CD (1996) – Apple 8 34451 2 [3]	4/1
Let It Be... Naked CD (2003) – Apple 24359 57142 [4]	7/5

NOTES

♪ Recorded while John was on holiday, a recording was needed as the song was to be included in the movie.
♪ Only Ringo was present on 1 April, the last Beatles recording session.

I Need You

[Harrison]

George – lead vocals, lead and acoustic guitar
John – backing and harmony vocals, drums
Paul – backing and harmony vocals, bass
Ringo – percussion

Studio recording and mixing

15 February 1965 – Studio Two – Help! session 1 out of 13
Takes 1–5
Overdubs onto take 5 – vocals

16 February 1965 – Studio Two – Help! session 2 out of 13
Overdubs onto take 5 – vocals, cowbell, tone-pedal guitar

18 February 1965 – Studio Two control room
RM1 [1] – mono mix from take 5

23 February 1965 – Studio Two control room
RS1 [2] – stereo mix from take 5

1965 – Capitol
[3] – mono mix from [2]

1987 – EMI
[4] – stereo mix from take 5

Releases   *UK/US peak*

Help! LP (1965) – Parlophone PMC 1255 [1], PCS 3071 [2]	1
Help! LP (US, 1965) – Capitol MAS 2386 [3], SMAS 2386 [2]	1
Love Songs LP (1977) – Parlophone PCSP 721 / Capitol SKBL 11711 [2]	7/24
Help! CD (1987) – EMI CDP 7 46439 2 [4]	61

=== NOTES ===

♪ The recording features Ringo slapping the back of an acoustic guitar.
♪ George uses a foot-controlled volume control pedal for the first time.

I Remember You
[Mercer-Schertzinger]

Paul – lead vocals, bass
John – rhythm guitar, harmonica
George – lead guitar
Ringo – drums

BBC and other performances

December 1962 [1] – Star-Club, Hamburg (live)

Releases   *UK/US peak*

Live! At The Star-Club In Hamburg, Germany; 1962 LP (1977) – Lingasong LNL 1 /
   Lingasong LS 2 7001 [1]   –

=== NOTES ===

♪ Published in 1941 by Victor Schertinger and Johnny Mercer.
♪ Frank Ifield spent 7 weeks at #1 in the UK in 1962.

I Saw Her Standing There

[McCartney-Lennon]

Paul – lead vocals, bass
John – harmony vocals, rhythm guitar
George – lead guitar
Ringo – drums

Studio recording and mixing

11 February 1963 – Studio Two – Please Please Me session 5 out of 8
Takes 1–9
Overdubs onto take 1 – handclaps > takes 10–12

25 February 1963 – Studio One control room
[1] – mono mix from edit of takes 9, 12
[2] – stereo mix from edit of takes 9, 12

19 December 1963 – Capitol
[3] – mastering of stereo mix from [2]
[4] – mastering of mono mix from [3]

1976 – Capitol
[5] – stereo mix from edit of takes 9, 12

1995 – EMI
[6] – stereo mix from take 9

2013 – EMI
[7] – stereo mix from take 7

BBC and other performances

December 1962 [8] – Star-Club, Hamburg (live)
6 March 1963 – 12 March 1963 edition of *Here We Go* (not broadcast)
16 March 1963 [9] – *Saturday Club* (live)
1 April 1963 – 22 April 1963 edition of *Side By Side*
21 May 1963 – 25 May 1963 edition of *Saturday Club*
21 May 1963 – 3 June 1963 edition of *Steppin' Out*
17 June 1963 – 25 June 1963 edition of *Pop Go The Beatles*
17 July 1963 – 21 July 1963 edition of *Easy Beat*
27 August 1963 – *The Mersey Sound* broadcast on 9 October 1963 (BBC TV)
3 September 1963 [10] – 24 September 1963 edition of *Pop Go The Beatles*
7 September 1963 [11] – 5 October 1963 edition of *Saturday Club*
16 October 1963 [12] – 20 October 1963 edition of *Easy Beat*
24 October 1963 [13] – Karlaplansstudion, Stockholm (live)
30 October 1963 – *Drop In* broadcast on 3 November 1963 (Sveriges TV)
7 December 1963 – *It's The Beatles* broadcast the same day (BBC TV)

18 December 1963 – 26 December 1963 edition of *From Us To You*
9 February 1964 **[14]** – *The Ed Sullivan Show* (CBS TV, live)
16 February 1964 **[15]** – *The Ed Sullivan Show* (CBS TV, live)
1 May 1964 – 18 May 1964 edition of *From Us To You*
17 June 1964 – *The Beatles Sing For Shell* broadcast on 1 July 1964 (Channel 9
    TV, Australia)

Releases   *UK/US peak*

Please Please Me LP (1963) – Parlophone PMC 1202 [1], PCS 3042 [2]	1
The Beatles (No. 1) EP (1963) – Parlophone GEP 8883 [1]	2
'I Want To Hold Your Hand' / 'I Saw Her Standing There' single (US, 1963) – Capitol 5112 [4]	14
Introducing... The Beatles LP (US, 1963) – Vee Jay VJLP 1062 [1], VJSR 1062 [2]	2
Meet The Beatles! LP (US, 1964) – Capitol T 2047 [4], ST 2047 [3]	1
Rock 'n' Roll Music LP (1976) – Parlophone PCSP 719 [2]	11
Rock 'n' Roll Music LP (US, 1976) – Capitol SKBO 11537 [5]	2
Live! At The Star-Club In Hamburg, Germany; 1962 LP (1977) – Lingasong LNL 1 [8]	–
Live At The BBC CD (1994) – Apple 8 31796 2 [12]	1/3
Anthology 1 CD (1995) – Apple 8 34445 2 [13]	2/1
'Free As A Bird' single (1995) – Apple 8 82587 2 [6]	2/6
The Four Historic Ed Sullivan Shows DVD (2003) – EREDV 372 [14] [15]	
On Air – Live At The BBC Volume 2 CD (2013) – Apple 6025 37491698 [11]	12/7
The Beatles Bootleg Recordings 1963 (2013) – iTunes [7] [9] [10]	–

═══ **NOTES** ═══

♪ Appears on a rehearsal tape recorded at the Cavern in late 1962.
♪ The first of three songs to have count-ins edited on (here from take 9).
♪ *The Mersey Sound* recording is an instrumental version used as
    incidental music.
♪ Played live until 1964.
♪ Released as a single in South Africa in 1964 as 'Just Seventeen (I Saw Her
    Standing There)', backed with 'Roll Over Beethoven'.

I Should Have Known Better

[Lennon-McCartney]

John – lead vocals, rhythm guitar, harmonica
Paul – bass
George – lead guitar
Ringo – drums

Studio recording and mixing

25 February 1964 – Studio Two – A Hard Day's Night session 2 out of 12
Takes 1–3

26 February 1964 – Studio Two – A Hard Day's Night session 3 out of 12
Remake takes 1–22 or 4–22
Overdubs onto take 22 – harmonica, guitar

3 March 1964 – Studio One control room
RM1 [1] – mono mix from take 22, edited

22 June 1964 – Studio Two control room
RS1 [2] – stereo mix from take 22

1964 – United Artists
[3] – panned mono mix made from [1]

1982 – Capitol
[4] – editing of [2] to match [1]

BBC and other performances

17 July 1964 – 3 August 1964 edition of *From Us To You*

Releases	UK/US peak
A Hard Day's Night LP (1964) – Parlophone PMC 1230 [1], PCS 3058 [2]	1
A Hard Day's Night LP (US, 1964) – United Artists UAL 3366 [1], UAS 6366 [3]	1
Extracts From The Film 'A Hard Day's Night' EP (1964) – Parlophone GEP 8920 [1]	1
'A Hard Day's Night' / 'I Should Have Known Better' single (US, 1964) – Capitol 5222 [1]	53
Hey Jude LP (US, 1970) – Apple SW 385 [2]	2
'Yesterday' / 'I Should Have Known Better' single (1976) – Parlophone R 6103 [1]	8
Reel Music LP (1982) – Parlophone PCS 7218 [2]	–
Reel Music LP (US, 1982) – Capitol SV-12199 [4]	19

NOTES

♪ The last song to feature John's harmonica.
♪ Played in concert until 1964.
♪ The editing is to fix a drop in the fourth bar of the harmonica intro – the mono uses a copy of the third bar and the stereo a copy of the second bar.
♪ Mark Lewisohn says that the remake consisted of takes 4–22, John Barrett's notes say they were takes 1–22.

I Wanna Be Your Man

[Lennon-McCartney]

Ringo – lead vocals, drums, maracas
Paul – harmony vocals, bass
John – harmony vocals, rhythm guitar

George – lead guitar
George Martin – Hammond organ

Studio recording and mixing

11 September 1963 – Studio Two – With The Beatles session 4 out of 9
Take 1

12 September 1963 – Studio Two – With The Beatles session 5 out of 9
Takes 2–7

30 September 1963 – Studio Two – With The Beatles session 6 out of 9
Overdubs onto take 7 – organ > takes 8–13

3 October 1963 – Studio Two – With The Beatles session 7 out of 9
Overdubs onto take 8[?] – maracas, vocals > takes 14–15

23 October 1963 – Studio Two – With The Beatles session 9 out of 9
Overdubs onto take 15 – tambourine, possibly organ > take 16

23 October 1963 – Studio Two control room
RM16 [1] – mono mix from take 16

29 October 1963 – Studio Two control room
RS16 [2] – stereo mix from take 16

19 December 1963 – Capitol
[3] – mastering of stereo mix from [2]
[4] – mastering of mono mix from [3]

1976 – Capitol
[5] – stereo mix from take 16

BBC and other performances

7 January 1964 – 15 February 1964 edition of *Saturday Club*
28 February 1964 [6] – 30 March 1964 edition of *From Us To You*
19 April 1964 [7] – *Around The Beatles*, mimed performance recorded on 28
    April and broadcast on 6 May 1964 (Rediffusion TV)
20 June 1965 – *Les Beatles* (Europe 1 TV, France, live)

Releases   UK/US peak

	UK/US peak
With The Beatles LP (1963) – Parlophone PMC 1206 [1], PCS 3045 [2]	1
Meet The Beatles! LP (US, 1964) – Capitol T 2047 [4], ST 2047 [3]	1
Meet The Beatles! EP (US, 1964)– Capitol SXA 2047 [3]	–
Rock 'n' Roll Music LP (1976) – Parlophone PCSP 719 [2]	11
Rock 'n' Roll Music LP (US, 1976) – Capitol SKBO 11537 [5]	2
Live At The BBC CD (1994) – Apple 8 31796 2 [6]	1/3
Anthology 1 CD (1995) – Apple 8 34445 2 [7]	2/1

╔═══════ **NOTES** ═══════╗

♪ The last time that a twin-track recording was used.
♪ The first appearance of a (Hammond) organ on a Beatles track.
♪ Played live until the Beatles stopped touring in 1966.
♪ Recorded by the Rolling Stones, getting to #12 in the UK, their first top twenty hit.

╚═══════════════════════╝

I Want To Hold Your Hand

[Lennon-McCartney]

John – lead vocals, rhythm guitar
Paul – lead vocals, bass
George – backing vocals, lead guitar
Ringo – drums

Studio recording and mixing

17 October 1963 – Studio Two – With The Beatles session 8 out of 9
Takes 1–17
Overdubs onto take 17 – guitar, handclaps

21 October 1963 – Studio Two control room
RM1 [1] – mono mix from take 17
RS17 [2] – stereo mix from take 17

19 December 1963 – Capitol
[3] – mastering of mock stereo from [1]

8 June 1965 – Studio One control room
RS2 [4] – stereo mix from take 17

7 November 1966 – Studio Two control room
RS1 [5] – stereo mix from take 17

1973 – Capitol
[6] – mock stereo from [1]

2004–06 – EMI
[7] – stereo mix from take 17 and [14]: includes introduction to 'Twist And Shout' from Hollywood Bowl

BBC and other performances

2 December 1963 [8] – *The Morecambe And Wise Show* broadcast on 18 April 1964 (ATV)

7 December 1963 – *It's The Beatles* broadcast the same day (BBC TV)

17 December 1963 **[9]** – 21 December 1963 edition of *Saturday Club*

18 December 1963 **[10]** – 26 December 1963 edition of *From Us To You*

7 January 1963 – 15 February 1964 edition of *Saturday Club*

12 January 1964 – *Sunday Night At The London Palladium* (ATV, live)

9 February 1964 **[11]** – *The Ed Sullivan Show* (CBS TV, live)

9 February 1964 **[12]** – *The Ed Sullivan Show* broadcast on 23 February 1964 (CBS TV)

16 February 1964 **[13]** – *The Ed Sullivan Show* (CBS TV, live)

19 April 1964 – *Around The Beatles*, mimed performance recorded on 28 April and broadcast on 6 May 1964 (Rediffusion TV)

23 August 1964 **[14]** – Hollywood Bowl (live)

Releases   *UK/US peak*

Release	Peak
'I Want To Hold Your Hand' / 'This Boy' single (1963) – Parlophone R 5084 **[1]**	1
'I Want To Hold Your Hand' / 'I Saw Her Standing There' single (US, 1963) – Capitol 5112 **[1]**	1
Meet The Beatles! LP (US, 1964) – Capitol T 2047 **[1]**, ST 2047 **[3]**	1
The Beatles' Greatest LP (Germany, 1965) – Odeon SMO 83 991 **[4]**	–
The Beatles' Million Sellers EP (1965) – Parlophone GEP 8946 **[1]**	1
A Collection Of Beatles Oldies LP (1966) – Parlophone PMC 7016 **[1]**, PCS 7016 **[5]**	7
The Beatles 1962–1966 LP (1973) – Apple PCSP 717 **[5]**	3
The Beatles 1962–1966 LP (US, 1973) – Apple SKBO 3403 **[6]**	3
'I Want To Hold Your Hand' / 'This Boy' single (Australia, 1976 reissue) – Parlophone A 8103 **[2]**	–
20 Greatest Hits LP (1982) – Parlophone PCTC 260 / Capitol SV-12245 **[5]**	10/50
Past Masters 1 CD (1988) – EMI CDP 7 90043 2 **[5]**	49/–
The Beatles 1962–1966 CD (1993) – EMI CDP 7 97036 2 **[5]**	3
Anthology 1 CD (1995) – Apple 8 34445 2 **[8]**	2/1
The Four Historic Ed Sullivan Shows DVD (2003) – EREDV 372 **[11] [12] [13]**	
Love CD (2006) – Apple 0946 3 80790 2 6 **[7]**	3/4
On Air – Live At The BBC Volume 2 CD (2013) – Apple 6025 37491698 **[10]**	12/7
The Beatles Bootleg Recordings 1963 (2013) – iTunes **[9]**	–
1+ CD/DVD (2015) – Apple 6205 47567727 **[2]**	5/6
Live At The Hollywood Bowl CD (2016) – Apple 6025 57054972 **[14]**	3/7

═ NOTES ═

♪ The first release that was recorded on four-track tape.

♪ The single had advance sales of over 1,000,000.

♪ The first of three songs that put the Beatles at #1 in the US for 14 consecutive weeks.

♪ Played by the Beatles in concert until 1964.

♪ RS17 was George Martin's first stereo mix from a 4-track tape – it has vocals hard right with nothing centred, as he had done with twin-track recordings.

I Want To Tell You

[Harrison]

George – lead vocals, lead guitar
Paul – harmony vocals, bass, piano, possibly guitar
John – harmony vocals, tambourine
Ringo – drums, maracas

Studio recording and mixing

2 June 1966 – Studio Two – Revolver session 25 out of 33

Takes 1–5
Overdubs onto take 3 – vocals, percussion, piano
Tape reduction of take 3 > take 4
Overdubs onto take 4 – handclaps

3 June 1966 – Studio Two – Revolver session 26 out of 33

Overdubs onto take 4 – bass

3 June 1966 – Studio Two control room

RM1 [1] – mono mix from take 4

21 June 1966 – Studio Three control room

RS2 [2] – stereo mix from take 4

Releases | UK/US peak

Revolver LP (1966) – Parlophone PMC 7009 [1], PCS 7009 [2]   1
Revolver LP (US, 1966) – Capitol T 2576 [1], ST 2576 [2]   1

> **═ NOTES ═**
>
> ♪ George's "invented" E7/F chord was
> re-used on 'When We Was Fab'.

I Want You (She's So Heavy)

[Lennon-McCartney]

John – lead vocals, lead guitars, organ, Moog synthesiser/white noise generator
Paul – backing vocals, bass, possibly organ
George – backing vocals, lead guitars
Ringo – drums, congas
Billy Preston – organ

Studio recording and mixing

22 February 1969 – Trident Studios – Abbey Road session 1 out of 42

Takes 1–35

23 February 1969 – *Trident Studios*

Edit of takes 9, 20, 32 > Trident master

18 April 1969 – *Studio Two – Abbey Road session 4 out of 42*

Overdubs onto Trident master – guitar
Tape reduction of Trident master > take 1
Overdubs onto take 1 – guitar

20 April 1969 – *Studio Three – Abbey Road session 5 out of 42*

Overdubs onto take 1 – organ, congas

8 August 1969 – *Studio Two – Abbey Road session 38 out of 42*

Overdubs onto Trident master – Moog, drums

11 August 1969 – *Studio Two – Abbey Road session 39 out of 42*

Overdubs onto take 1 – vocals
Tapy copying of take 1 and editing into Trident master

20 August 1969 – *Studio Three control room*

RS8 – stereo mix from take 1
RS10 – stereo mix from Trident master
[1] – edit of take 1 and Trident master mixes

See 'Being For The Benefit Of Mr Kite!' [5] for *Love* CD info.

Releases

	UK/US peak
Abbey Road LP (1969) – Apple PCS 7088 [1]	1
Abbey Road LP (US, 1969) – Apple SO 383 [1]	1

═══ NOTES ═══

♪ The first session for the LP *Abbey Road*, held at Trident Studios.
♪ Sessions spanned nearly six months.
♪ The abrupt ending comes from a direct splice of the tape.
♪ The track's mixing session on 20 August marked the last time that all four Beatles were together in the studio.

I Will

[Lennon-McCartney]

Paul – lead vocals, harmony vocals, scat bass, acoustic guitars
John – skulls, maracas
Ringo – drums

Studio recording and mixing

16 September 1968 – Studio Two – White Album session 61 out of 81
Takes 1–67
Four- to eight-track tape copying of take 65 > take 68

17 September 1968 – Studio Two – White Album session 62 out of 81
Overdubs onto take 68 – vocals, guitar, maracas

26 September 1968 – Studio Two control room
RM2 [1] – mono mix from take 68

14 October 1968 – Studio Two control room
RS1 [2] – stereo mix from take 68

1996 – EMI
[3] – stereo mix from take 1

2018 – EMI
[4] – stereo mix from take 13
[5] – stereo mix from take 29
[6] – stereo mix from take 68

Releases

	UK/US peak
The Beatles LP (1968) – Apple PMC 7067–7068 [1], PCS 7067–7068 [2]	1
The Beatles LP (US, 1968) – Apple SWBO-101 [2]	1
Love Songs LP (1977) – Parlophone PCSP 721 / Capitol SKBL 11711 [2]	7/24
Anthology 3 CD (1996) – Apple 8 34451 2 [3]	4/1
The Beatles Deluxe CD (2018) – Apple 0602567571957 [4] [5] [6]	4/6

=== **NOTES** ===

♪ 67 takes were recorded in over eight hours, without George.

I Will Always Be In Love With You

[Green-Ruby-Stept]

Lead vocals, **John**. Performed by the Beatles in 1960–61, and recorded at Paul's house in June 1960. Supposedly based on a version by Fats Domino, but even though he recorded the song in 1958, it seems to have been first released in 1961.

I Wonder If I Care As Much

[Everly]

Lead vocals, **John** and **Paul**. Performed by the Quarry Men/Beatles around 1959–61. Released by the Everly Brothers in 1957 as the B-side to 'Bye Bye Love'.

I'll Be Back

[Lennon-McCartney]

John – lead vocals, acoustic rhythm guitar
Paul – harmony vocals, bass
George – possibly harmony vocals, acoustic lead guitar
Ringo – drums, bongos, percussion

Studio recording and mixing

1 June 1964 – Studio Two – A Hard Day's Night session 9 out of 12
Takes 1–16
Overdubs onto take 16 – vocals, guitar

22 June 1964 – Studio Two control room
RM2 [1] – mono mix from take 16
RM3 [2] – mono mix from take 16
RS1 [3] – stereo mix from take 16

1994 – EMI
[4] – mono mix from take 3

1995 – EMI
[5] – mono mix from take 2

Releases   *UK/US peak*

A Hard Day's Night LP (1964) – Parlophone PMC 1230 [1], PCS 3058 [3]	1
Beatles '65 LP (US, 1964) – Capitol T 2228 [2], ST 2228 [3]	1
Love Songs LP (1977) – Parlophone PCSP 721 / Capitol SKBL 11711 [3]	7/24
Anthology 1 CD (1995) – Apple 8 34445 2 [5] [4]	2/1

NOTES

♪ The first session with Ken Scott as
tape operator.

I'll Be On My Way

[Lennon-McCartney]

John – lead vocals, rhythm guitar
Paul – lead and harmony vocals, bass
George – lead guitar
Ringo – drums

BBC and other performances

4 April 1963 [1] – 24 June 1963 edition of *Side By Side*

Releases_____ *UK/US peak*

Live At The BBC CD (1994) – Apple 8 31796 2 [1]   1/3

NOTES

♪ The only recording by the Beatles of this song, written by Paul in 1959.
♪ The only Lennon-McCartney song recorded for the BBC that was not released by the Beatles.
♪ Played in concert in 1961–62.
♪ The B-side of Billy J Kramer's 'Do You Want To Know A Secret'.

I'll Cry Instead

[Lennon-McCartney]

John – lead vocals, rhythm guitar, tambourine
Paul – bass
George – lead guitar
Ringo – drums

Studio recording and mixing

1 June 1964 – Studio Two – A Hard Day's Night session 9 out of 12

Takes 1–6 (section A)
Takes 7–8 (section B)

4 June 1964 – Studio Two control room

RM1 [1] – mono mix from takes 6, 8 (shorter edit)
RM1 [2] – mono mix from takes 6, 8 (full edit)

22 June 1964 – Studio Two control room

RS1 [3] – stereo mix from takes 6, 8 (shorter edit)

Releases_____ *UK/US peak*

A Hard Day's Night LP (1964) – Parlophone PMC 1230 [1], PCS 3058 [3]	1
A Hard Day's Night LP (US, 1964) – United Artists UAL 3366 [2], UAS 6366 [2]	1
Extracts From The Album 'A Hard Day's Night' EP (1964) – Parlophone GEP 8924 [1]	7
'I'll Cry Instead' / 'I'm Happy Just To Dance With You' single (US, 1964) – Capitol 5234 [2]	25
Something New LP (US, 1964) – Capitol T 2108 [2], ST 2108 [3]	2
Something New EP (US, 1964) – Capitol SXA 2108 [3]	–

NOTES

♪ The US mono version has an extra verse.
♪ The United Artists sleeve and labels list the song as 'I Cry Instead'.
♪ The US single label states "From the United Artists Picture 'A Hard Day's Night'", although the song was not in the film.

I'll Follow The Sun

[Lennon-McCartney]

Paul – lead vocals, acoustic guitar
John – harmony vocals, rhythm guitar
George – lead guitar
Ringo – percussion

Studio recording and mixing

18 October 1964 – Studio Two – Beatles For Sale session 7 out of 8
Takes 1–8

21 October 1964 – Room 65
RM1 [1] – mono mix from take 8

4 November 1964 – Studio Two control room
RS1 [2] – stereo mix from take 8

BBC and other performances

17 November 1964 [3] – 26 November 1964 edition of *Top Gear*

Releases   *UK/US peak*

	UK/US peak
Beatles For Sale LP (1964) – Parlophone PMC 1240 [1], PCS 3062 [2]	1
Beatles '65 LP (US, 1964) – Capitol T 2228 [1], ST 2228 [2]	1
Beatles For Sale (No. 2) EP (1965) – Parlophone GEP 8938 [1]	5
Love Songs LP (1977) – Parlophone PCSP 721 / Capitol SKBL 11711 [2]	7/24
'Baby It's You' single (1995) – Apple 8 82073 2 [3]	7/67
On Air – Live At The BBC Volume 2 CD (2013) – Apple 6025 37491698 [3]	12/7

NOTES

- ♪ Written by Paul and played by the Quarry Men probably as early as 1959.
- ♪ A version was recorded at Paul's house in June 1960.
- ♪ Played live by the Quarry Men/Beatles until 1961.

I'll Get You

[Lennon-McCartney]

John – lead and harmony vocals, rhythm guitar, harmonica
Paul – lead and harmony vocals, bass
George – harmony vocals
Ringo – drums

Studio recording and mixing

1 July 1963 – Studio Two – With The Beatles session 1 out of 9
Unknown take numbers
Overdubs onto unknown take number – harmonica

4 July 1963 – Studio Two control room
RM1 [1] – mono mix from unknown take number

17 March 1964 – Capitol
[2] – mastering of mock stereo mix from [1]
[3] – mastering of mono mix from [1]

BBC and other performances

16 July 1963 – 13 August 1963 edition of *Pop Go The Beatles*
30 July 1963 – 24 August 1963 edition of *Saturday Club*
1 August 1963 – 3 September 1963 edition of *Pop Go The Beatles*
3 September 1963 [4] – 10 September 1963 edition of *Pop Go The Beatles*
7 September 1963 [5] – 5 October 1963 edition of *Saturday Club*
13 October 1963 [6] – *Sunday Night At The London Palladium* (ATV, live)

Releases   UK/US peak

	UK/US peak
'She Loves You' / 'I'll Get You' single (1963) – Parlophone R 5055 [1]	1
'She Loves You' / 'I'll Get You' single (US, 1963) – Swan 4152 [1]	–
'Sie Liebt Dich' / 'I'll Get You' single (US, 1964) – Swan 4182 [1]	–
The Beatles' Second Album LP (US, 1964) – Capitol T 2080 [3], ST 2080 [2]	1
Rarities LP (1978) – Parlophone PCM 1001, PSLP 261 [1]	71
Past Masters 1 CD (1988) – EMI CDP 7 90043 2 [1]	49/–
Anthology 1 CD (1995) – Apple 8 34445 2 [6]	2/1
On Air – Live At The BBC Volume 2 CD (2013) – Apple 6025 37491698 [5]	12/7
The Beatles Bootleg Recordings 1963 (2013) – iTunes [4]	–

=== **NOTES** ===

♪ The last track only available in mono, until 'You Know My
  Name (Look Up The Number)'.
♪ Released by Swan as the B-side to both 'She Loves You' and
  'Sie Liebt Dich'.

I'll Never Let You Go (Little Darling)

[Wakely]

Lead vocals, **John** and **Paul**. Part of the Beatles' set 1960–62. On the earliest surviving
(partial) set list, from mid-1960. Released as a single by Elvis Presley in 1956 (with 'I'm
Gonna Sit Right Down And Cry (Over You)' on the B-side), and on his LP *Elvis Presley*.

I'm A Loser

[Lennon-McCartney]

John – lead vocals, acoustic guitar, harmonica
Paul – backing vocals, bass
George – lead guitar
Ringo – drums, tambourine

Studio recording and mixing

14 August 1964 – Studio Two – Beatles For Sale session 2 out of 8
Takes 1–8
Overdubs onto take 8 – guitar, tambourine, vocals, harmonica

26 October 1964 – Studio Two control room
RM2 [1] – mono mix from take 8

4 November 1964 – Studio Two control room
RS1 [2] – stereo mix from take 8

BBC and other performances

3 October 1964 – *Shindig* broadcast on 7 October 1964 (American
 Broadcasting Co. TV)
17 November 1964 [3] – 26 November 1964 edition of *Top Gear*, repeated on 26
 December 1964 edition of *Saturday Club*
26 May 1965 – 7 June 1965 edition of *The Beatles Invite You To Take A Ticket
 To Ride*
20 June 1965 – *Les Beatles* (Europe 1 TV, France, live)

Releases

	UK/US peak
Beatles For Sale LP (1964) – Parlophone PMC 1240 [1], PCS 3062 [2]	1
Beatles '65 LP (US, 1964) – Capitol T 2228 [1], ST 2228 [2]	1
Beatles For Sale EP (1965) – Parlophone GEP 8931 [1]	1
4 – By The Beatles EP (US, 1965) – Capitol R 5365 [1]	68
Live At The BBC CD (1994) – Apple 8 31796 2 [3]	1/3

―――――― **NOTES** ――――――

♪ Played live until 1965.
♪ The first "ad libitum" introduction.
♪ An early batch of stereo Parlophone labels gave the title as "I'm
 A Losser", and credited 'Eight Days A Week' to Northern SSongs.
♪ The *Shindig* recording took place in London, and was not
 screened in the UK.
♪ The *Les Beatles* show was a live broadcast of their evening
 performance at Palais des Sports hall in Paris.

I'm Down

[Lennon-McCartney]

Paul – lead vocals, bass
John – backing vocals, rhythm guitar, organ
George – backing vocals, lead guitar
Ringo – drums, bongos

Studio recording and mixing

14 June 1965 – Studio Two – Help! session 11 out of 13
Takes 1–7
Overdubs onto take 7 – organ, bongos, guitar, vocals

18 June 1965 – Studio Two control room
RM1 [1] – mono mix from take 7

28 April 1976 – EMI
RS1 [2] – stereo mix from take 7

1995 – EMI
[3] – stereo mix from take 1

BBC and other performances

1 August 1965 – *Blackpool Night Out* (Associated British Corp. TV, live)
14 August 1965 [4] – *The Ed Sullivan Show* broadcast on 12 September 1965
   (CBS TV)
15 August 1965 – *The Beatles At Shea Stadium* (live), broadcast by BBC TV on
   1 March 1966
24 June 1966 – *Die Beatles* broadcast on 5 July 1966 (ZDF TV, Germany)

Releases   *UK/US peak*

'Help!' / 'I'm Down' single (1965) – Parlophone R 5305 [1]	1
'Help!' / 'I'm Down' single (US, 1965) – Capitol 5476 [1]	101
Rock 'n' Roll Music LP (1976) – Parlophone PCSP 719 / Capitol SKBO 11537 [2]	11/2
Rarities LP (1978) – Parlophone PCM 1001, PSLP 261 [1]	71
Past Masters 1 CD (1988) – EMI CDP 7 90043 2 [2]	49/–
Anthology 2 CD (1996) – Apple 8 34448 2 [3]	1/1
The Four Historic Ed Sullivan Shows DVD (2003) – EREDV 372 [4]	
Tomorrow Never Knows (2012) – iTunes [2]	44/24

=== NOTES ===

♪ The recording was completed immediately before taping 'Yesterday'.
♪ Played live until 1966.
♪ The first LP – and therefore the first stereo – release was in 1976.

I'm Gonna Sit Right Down And Cry (Over You)

[Thomas-Biggs]

John – lead vocals, rhythm guitar
Paul – lead and harmony vocals, bass
George – lead guitar
Ringo – drums

BBC and other performances

December 1962 **[1]** – Star-Club, Hamburg (live)
16 July 1963 **[2]** – 6 August 1963 edition of *Pop Go The Beatles*

Releases
UK/US peak

Live! At The Star-Club In Hamburg, Germany; 1962 LP (US, 1977) – Lingasong LS 2 7001 **[1]** –
Live At The BBC CD (1994) – Apple 8 31796 2 **[2]** 1/3

NOTES

♪ Released on Elvis Presley's eponymous debut LP in March 1956, having been recorded less than two months earlier.

I'm Happy Just To Dance With You

[Lennon-McCartney]

George – lead vocals, lead guitar
John – harmony and backing vocals, rhythm guitar
Paul – harmony and backing vocals, bass
Ringo – drums, bongo

Studio recording and mixing

1 March 1964 – Studio Two – A Hard Day's Night session 5 out of 12
Takes 1–4
Overdubs onto take 4 – vocals, tom tom

3 March 1964 – Studio One control room
RM1 **[1]** – mono mix from take 4

22 June 1964 – Studio One control room
RS1 **[2]** – stereo mix from take 4

BBC and other performances

17 July 1964 – 3 August 1964 edition of *From Us To You*

Releases | UK/US peak

Release	
A Hard Day's Night LP (1964) – Parlophone PMC 1230 [1], PCS 3058 [2]	1
A Hard Day's Night LP (US, 1964) – United Artists UAL 3366 [1], UAS 6366 [1]	1
Something New LP (US, 1964) – Capitol T 2108 [1], ST 2108 [2]	2
'I'll Cry Instead' / 'I'm Happy Just To Dance With You' single (US, 1964) – Capitol 5234 [1]	95
'The Beatles' Movie Medley' / 'I'm Happy Just To Dance With You' single (1982) – Parlophone R 6055 [1]	10
'The Beatles' Movie Medley' / 'I'm Happy Just To Dance With You' single (US, 1982) – Capitol B 5107 [1]	–

===== NOTES =====

♪ The first song to be recorded on a Sunday.
♪ Played in concert in 1964.
♪ 'The Beatles' Movie Medley' single was released to promote the *Reel Music* LP; it reached #12 in the US; the B-side was originally intended to be collage of interviews entitled 'Fab Four On Film'.
♪ Possibly remixed for the 1982 release.
♪ Released in India in 1964 as 'I Am Happy Just To Dance With You'.

I'm Henery The Eighth I Am

[Murray-Weston]

Lead vocals, **George**. Played by the Beatles until 1962. It was released by Joe Brown in 1961.

I'm In Love

[Lennon-McCartney]

John – lead vocals, piano
Paul – backing vocals

Studio recording and mixing

1963 – unknown location
[1] – demo version

Releases | UK/US peak

Release	
The Beatles Bootleg Recordings 1963 (2013) – iTunes [1]	–

===== NOTES =====

♪ Recorded by the Fourmost in 1963, the follow-up to 'Hello Little Girl', it reached #17 in the UK charts.

I'm Looking Through You

[Lennon-McCartney]

Paul – lead vocals, bass, acoustic guitar, possibly lead guitar
John – harmony vocals, acoustic guitar
George – tambourine, possibly lead guitar
Ringo – drums, organ, percussion

Studio recording and mixing

24 October 1965 – Studio Two – Rubber Soul session 8 out of 15
Take 1
Overdubs onto take 1 – handclaps, maracas, organ

6 November 1965 – Studio Two – Rubber Soul session 12 out of 15
Remake takes 2–3

10 November 1965 – Studio Two – Rubber Soul session 14 out of 15
Second remake take 4

11 November 1965 – Studio Two – Rubber Soul session 15 out of 15
Overdubs onto take 4 – vocals, percussion, guitar, organ

15 November 1965 – Studio One control room
RM1 [1] – mono mix from take 4
RS1 [2] – stereo mix from take 4

1985 – EMI
[3] – stereo mix from take 4

1987 – EMI
[4] – stereo mix from take 1

Releases   *UK/US peak*

	UK/US peak
Rubber Soul LP (1965) – Parlophone PMC 1267 [1], PCS 3075 [2]	1
Rubber Soul LP (US, 1965) – Capitol T 2442 [1], ST 2442 [2, untrimmed]	1
Rubber Soul CD (1987) – EMI CDP 7 46440 2 [3]	60
Anthology 2 CD (1996) – Apple 8 34448 2 [4]	1/1

=== NOTES ===

♪ Ringo plays organ, probably for
   the only time on a Beatles record.
♪ The untrimmed version on the
   US *Rubber Soul* includes two false
   starts.
♪ The title track from a Portuguese
   EP from 1966.

I'm Only Sleeping

[Lennon-McCartney]

John – lead vocals, acoustic guitar
Paul – harmony and backing vocals, bass
George – harmony and backing vocals, lead guitar
Ringo – drums

Studio recording and mixing

27 April 1966 – Studio Three – Revolver session 14 out of 33
Rehearsal [1]
Takes 1–11 [2]

29 April 1966 – Studio Three – Revolver session 16 out of 33
Overdubs onto take 11 – vocals

5 May 1966 – Studio Three – Revolver session 17 out of 33
Overdubs onto take 11 – backwards guitar

6 May 1966 – Studio Two – Revolver session 18 out of 33
Overdubs onto take 11 – vocals
Tape reduction of take 11 > takes 12, 13

12 May 1966 – Studio Three control room
RM5 [3] – mono mix from take 13

13 May 1966 – Capitol
[4] – mastering of mock stereo mix from [3]

20 May 1966 – Studio One control room
RS1 [5] – stereo mix from take 13
RS2 [6] – stereo mix from take 13

6 June 1966 – Studio Three control room
RM6 [7] – mono mix from take 13

Releases   UK/US peak

Revolver LP (1966) – Parlophone PMC 7009 [7], PCS 7009 [6]	1
"Yesterday" … And Today LP (US, 1966) – Capitol T 2553 [3], ST 2553 [4] [5]	1
Rarities LP (US, 1980) – Capitol SHAL 12060 [6]	21
Anthology 2 CD (1996) – Apple 8 34448 2 [1] [2]	1/1

=== NOTES ===

♪ The four US/UK mono/stereo versions all have different guitar mixes.
♪ The two *Anthology* versions were recorded in mono.

I'm So Tired

John – lead vocals, guitars, organ
Paul – harmony vocals, bass, electric piano
George – lead guitar
Ringo – drums

Studio recording and mixing

May 1968 – Kinfauns, Esher

Demo recording

8 October 1968 – Studio Two – White Album session 76 out of 81

Takes 1–14
Overdubs onto take 14 – vocals, piano, organ, guitar, drums

15 October 1968 – Studio Two control room

RS5 [1] – stereo mix from take 14
RM3 [2] – mono mix from take 14

1996 – EMI

[3] – stereo edit from takes 3, 6, 9

2018 – EMI

[4] – stereo mix from demo
[5] – stereo mix from take 7
[6] – stereo mix from take 14
[7] – stereo mix from take 14

Releases

	UK/US peak
The Beatles LP (1968) – Apple PMC 7067–7068 [2], PCS 7067–7068 [1]	1
The Beatles LP (US, 1968) – Apple SWBO-101 [1]	1
Anthology 3 CD (1996) – Apple 8 34451 2 [3]	4/1
The Beatles Deluxe CD (2018) – Apple 0602567571957 [4] [5] [6] [7]	4/6

=== NOTES ===

♪ Mix [7] contains elements that were mixed out of [1] and [4].
♪ The first of two of John's White Album songs started and finished in one and the same session, which ended at 8am.

I'm Talking About You

[Berry]

John – lead vocals, rhythm guitar
Paul – bass

George – lead guitar
Ringo – drums

BBC and other performances

December 1962 **[1]** – Star-Club, Hamburg (live)
16 March 1963 **[2]** – *Saturday Club* (live)

Releases   *UK/US peak*

Live! At The Star-Club In Hamburg, Germany; 1962 LP (1977) – Lingasong LNL 1 /
   Lingasong LS 2 7001 **[1]**   –
On Air – Live At The BBC Volume 2 CD (2013) – Apple 6025 37491698 **[2]**   12/7

NOTES

♪ Chuck Berry single, released in
   the UK in September 1961.
♪ John's cold and another
   engagement on 11 March meant
   the BBC session could not
   be pre-recorded and so was
   performed live.
♪ Paul stole the bass line ("exactly
   the same notes") for 'I Saw Her
   Standing There'.

I've Got A Feeling

[Lennon-McCartney]

Paul – lead vocals, bass
John – lead and harmony vocals, rhythm guitar
George – lead guitar
Ringo – drums
Billy Preston – electric piano

Studio recording and mixing

8 January 1969 – Twickenham Film Studios – Let It Be rehearsal session
Takes 8.15 **[1]**

9 January 1969 – Twickenham Film Studios – Let It Be rehearsal session
Takes 9.32 **[2]**

22 January 1969 – Apple Studio – Let It Be rehearsal session
Rehearsal

30 January 1969 – Apple rooftop – Let It Be session 9 out of 17
Takes 30.4 **[3]**, 30.9

23 March 1970 – Room 4
[4] – stereo mix from take 30.4

1996 – EMI
[5] – stereo mix from rehearsal

2003 – EMI
[6] – stereo mix from edit of takes 30.4, 30.9

Releases UK/US peak

Let It Be LP (1970) – Apple PXS1, PCS 7096 [4]	1
Let It Be LP (US, 1970) – Apple AR 34001 [4]	1
Let It Be movie (1970) [1, 2, edited] [3]	
Anthology 3 CD (1996) – Apple 8 34451 2 [5]	4/1
Let It Be… Naked CD (2003) – Apple 24359 57142 [6]	7/5
Tomorrow Never Knows (2012) – iTunes [6]	44/24

═══ NOTES ═══

♪ All *Let It Be* versions are taken from the rooftop performance.
♪ The rehearsal recording date is listed (probably wrongly) as 23 January in the *Anthology 3* liner notes.

I've Just Seen A Face

[Lennon-McCartney]

Paul – lead vocals, acoustic guitar
John – acoustic guitar
George – acoustic guitar
Ringo – brushes, maracas

Studio recording and mixing

14 June 1965 – Studio Two – Help! session 11 out of 13
Takes 1–6
Overdubs onto take 6 – guitar, maracas, vocals

18 June 1965 – Studio Two control room
RM1 [1] – mono mix from take 6
RS1 [2] – stereo mix from take 6

1987 – EMI
[3] – stereo mix from take 6

Releases   *UK/US peak*

Help! LP (1965) – Parlophone PMC 1255 [1], PCS 3071 [2]   1
Rubber Soul LP (US, 1965) – Capitol T 2442 [1], ST 2442 [2]   1
Help! CD (1987) – EMI CDP 7 46439 2 [3]   61

NOTES

♪ Recorded immediately before 'I'm Down' and 'Yesterday'.
♪ An all-acoustic recording – three acoustic guitars, snare drum and maracas.

If I Fell

[Lennon-McCartney]

John – lead and harmony vocals, acoustic guitar
Paul – harmony vocals, bass
George – lead guitar
Ringo – drums

Studio recording and mixing

27 February 1964 – Studio Two – A Hard Day's Night session 4 out of 12
Takes 1–15
Overdubs onto take 15 – vocals, guitar

3 March 1964 – Studio One control room
RM1 [1] – mono mix from take 15

22 June 1964 – Studio One control room
RS1 [2] – stereo mix from take 15

1964 – United Artists
[3] – panned mono mix made from [1]

BBC and other performances

14 July 1964 [4] – 16 July 1964 edition of *Top Gear*
17 July 1964 – 3 August 1964 edition of *From Us To You*
19 July 1964 – *Blackpool Night Out* (Associated British Corp. TV, live)

Releases   *UK/US peak*

A Hard Day's Night LP (1964) – Parlophone PMC 1230 [1], PCS 3058 [2]   1
A Hard Day's Night LP (US, 1964) – United Artists UAL 3366 [1], UAS 6366 [3]   1
Extracts From The Film 'A Hard Day's Night' EP (1964) – Parlophone GEP 8920 [1]   1
Something New LP (US, 1964) – Capitol T 2108 [1], ST 2108 [2]   2
Something New EP (US, 1964) – Capitol SXA 2108 [2]   –

'If I Fell' / 'Tell Me Why' single (1964) – Parlophone DP 562 **[1]**   –
'And I Love Her' / 'If I Fell' single (US, 1964) – Capitol 5235 **[1]**   53
Love Songs LP (1977) – Parlophone PCSP 721 / Capitol SKBL 11711 **[2]**   7/24
On Air – Live At The BBC Volume 2 CD (2013) – Apple 6025 37491698 **[4]**   12/7

NOTES

♪ Played live in 1964.
♪ DP 562 was the first Parlophone single release for export only.

If I Needed Someone

[Harrison]

George – lead vocals, lead guitar
John – harmony vocals, rhythm guitar
Paul – harmony vocals, bass
Ringo – drums, tambourine
George Martin – harmonium

Studio recording and mixing

16 October 1965 – Studio Two – Rubber Soul session 3 out of 15
Take 1

18 October 1965 – Studio Two – Rubber Soul session 4 out of 15
Overdubs onto take 1 – vocals, tambourine, guitar

25 October 1965 – Studio Two control room
RM1 **[1]** – mono mix from take 1

26 October 1965 – Studio Two control room
RS1 **[2]** – stereo mix from take 1

1987 – EMI
[3] – stereo mix from take 1

Releases   *UK/US peak*

Rubber Soul LP (1965) – Parlophone PMC 1267 **[1]**, PCS 3075 **[2]**   1
"Yesterday" … And Today LP (US, 1966) – Capitol T 2553 **[1]**, ST 2553 **[2]**   1
Rubber Soul CD (1987) – EMI CDP 7 46440 2 **[3]**   60

NOTES

♪ Performed in concert until 1966.
♪ A cover version by the Hollies reached #20
   in January 1966.

If You Gotta Make A Fool Of Somebody

[Clark]

Lead vocals, **Paul**. Part of the Beatles' set in 1962. It was the only hit for James Ray, reaching #22 on *Billboard* in 1962.

If You've Got Trouble

[Lennon-McCartney]

Ringo – lead vocals, drums
John – rhythm guitar
Paul – bass
George – lead guitar

Studio recording and mixing

18 February 1965 – Studio Two – Help! session 4 out of 13
Take 1
Overdubs onto take 1 – vocals, guitar

1995 – EMI
[1] – stereo mix from take 1

Releases   *UK/US peak*

Anthology 2 CD (1996) – Apple 8 34448 2 [1]   1/1

NOTES

♪ Intended to be Ringo's vocal contribution to *Help!* – 'Act Naturally' was used instead.
♪ John's hand-written lyrics sold for $38,000 in 2003.

In My Life

[Lennon-McCartney]

John – lead vocals, rhythm guitar
Paul – harmony and backing vocals, bass
George – harmony and backing vocals, lead guitar
Ringo – drums, tambourine
George Martin – piano

Studio recording and mixing

18 October 1965 – Studio Two – Rubber Soul session 4 out of 15
Takes 1–3
Overdubs onto take 3 – guitar (not used), tambourine, vocals

22 October 1965 – *Studio Two – Rubber Soul session 7 out of 15*

Overdubs onto take 3 – piano

25 October 1965 – *Studio Two control room*

RM1 [1] – mono mix from take 3

26 October 1965 – *Studio Two control room*

RS1 [2] – stereo mix from take 3

1987 – *EMI*

[3] – stereo mix from take 3

Releases   UK/US peak

Rubber Soul LP (1965) – Parlophone PMC 1267 [1], PCS 3075 [2]	1
Rubber Soul LP (US, 1965) – Capitol T 2442 [1], ST 2442 [2]	1
The Beatles 1962–1966 LP (1973) – Apple PCSP 717 [2]	3
The Beatles 1962–1966 LP (US, 1973) – Apple SKBO 3403 [2]	3
Love Songs LP (1977) – Parlophone PCSP 721 / Capitol SKBL 11711 [2]	7/24
Rubber Soul CD (1987) – EMI CDP 7 46440 2 [3]	60
The Beatles 1962–1966 CD (1993) – EMI CDP 7 97036 2 [3]	3

=== NOTES ===

♪ A double-speed piano technique was used for the middle eight.

♪ Authorship of the melody was claimed by both John and Paul.

♪ The original lyrics, which include a reference to Penny Lane, have been donated to the British Library.

In Spite Of All The Danger

[McCartney-Harrison]

John – lead vocals, guitar
Paul – harmony and backing vocals, guitar
George – harmony and backing vocals, guitar
John Lowe – piano
Colin Hanton – drums

BBC and other performances

1958 – Phillips Sound Recording Service, Liverpool

1995 – *EMI*

[1] – edited and reprocessed from source tape

Releases_____*UK/US peak*

Anthology 1 CD (1995) – Apple 8 34445 2 [1]   2/1

```
═════════ NOTES ═════════
```
♪ Along with 'That'll Be The Day', the first recording
   by the Beatles, as the Quarry Men, in 1958.
♪ Played live by the Quarry Men until about 1959.

The Inner Light

[Harrison]

George – lead vocals
Paul – harmony vocals
Session musicians – shehnai, sarod, tabla, pakhavaj, flutes, harmonium; possibly also sitar, sur-bahar, santir, taar shehnai

Studio recording and mixing

12 January 1968 – EMI Studios, Bombay – White Album session 1 out of 81
Takes 1–5

6 February 1968 – Studio One – White Album session 3 out of 81
Two- to four-track tape copying take 5 > take 6
Overdubs onto take 6 – shehnai (possibly on 8 February), vocals

8 February 1968 – Studio Two – Let It Be session 3 out of 17
Overdubs onto take 6 – vocals

8 February 1968 – Studio Two control room
RM4 [1] – mono mix from take 6, with edit piece

27 January 1970 – Studio Two control room
RS1 [2] – stereo mix from take 6

2018 – EMI
[3] – stereo mix from take 6, without vocals

See 'Here Comes The Sun' [2] for *Love* CD info.

Releases_____*UK/US peak*

'Lady Madonna' / 'The Inner Light' single (1968) – Parlophone R 5675 [1]	1
'Lady Madonna' / 'The Inner Light' single (US, 1968) – Capitol 2138 [1]	96
Rarities LP (1978) – Parlophone PCM 1001, PSLP 261 [1]	71
Rarities LP (US, 1980) – Capitol SHAL 12060 [1]	21
The Beatles EP (1981) – Parlophone SGE 1 [2]	
Past Masters 2 CD (1988) – EMI CDP 7 90044 2 [2]	46/–

The Beatles Deluxe CD (2018) – Apple 0602567571957 **[3]**   4/6

```
═══════════ NOTES ═══════════
♪ The last of George's Indian songs.
♪ The stereo version was finally released in 1981.
♪ The mono/stereo shehnai introductions are
  different – an edit piece was possibly overlooked
  for the stereo mix.
```

It Won't Be Long

[Lennon-McCartney]

John – lead vocals, rhythm guitar
Paul – backing vocals, bass
George – backing vocals, lead guitar
Ringo – drums

Studio recording and mixing

30 July 1963 – Studio Two – With The Beatles session 3 out of 9
Takes 1–10
Overdubs onto take 7 – vocals, guitar > takes 11–17
Edit piece (ending) takes 18–23

21 August 1963 – Studio Three control room
RM17/21 **[1]** – mono mix from edit of takes 17, 21

29 October 1963 – Studio Three control room
RS17 **[2]** – stereo mix from take 17

19 December 1963 – Capitol
[3] – mastering of stereo mix from **[2]**
[4] – mastering of mono mix from **[3]**

Releases   *UK/US peak*

With The Beatles LP (1963) – Parlophone PMC 1206 **[1]**, PCS 3045 **[2]**	1
Meet The Beatles! LP (US, 1964) – Capitol T 2047 **[4]**, ST 2047 **[3]**	1
Meet The Beatles! EP (US, 1964)– Capitol SXA 2047 **[3]**	–

```
═══════════ NOTES ═══════════
♪ Chronologically, the earliest of the Beatles' songs
  that was never played for the BBC.
♪ The edit piece of the ending was not used for the
  stereo version.
```

It's All Too Much

[Harrison]

George – lead vocals, organ, lead guitar
John – harmony vocals, lead guitar
Paul – harmony vocals, bass
Ringo – drums
Session musicians – four trumpets, bass clarinet, contrabass clarinet

Studio recording and mixing

25 May 1967 – De Lane Lea Studios – Yellow Submarine session 6 out of 15
Takes 1–4

31 May 1967 – De Lane Lea Studios – Yellow Submarine session 7 out of 15
Tape reduction of take 4 > takes 1, 2
Overdubs onto take 2 – percussion, vocals, handclaps

2 June 1967 – De Lane Lea Studios – Yellow Submarine session 8 out of 15
Overdubs onto take 2 – brass, woodwind

12 October 1967 – De Lane Lea Studios
RM1 [1] – mono mix from take 2

16 October 1968 – Studio Two control room
Tape copying take 2 > take 196
RM1 [2] – mono mix from take 196
RS1 [3] – stereo mix from take 196

25 November 1968 – EMI
[4] – mono mix from [3]

1999 – EMI
[5] – stereo mix from takes 4, 196

Releases *UK/US peak*

Yellow Submarine movie (1968) [1]	
Yellow Submarine LP (1969) – Apple PMC 7070 [4], PCS 7070 [3]	3
Yellow Submarine LP (US, 1969) – Apple SW 153 [3]	2
Yellow Submarine Songtrack CD (1999) – Apple 5 21481 2 [5]	8/15
Mono Masters CD (2009) – Apple 6 849582 4 [2]	–
Tomorrow Never Knows (2012) – iTunes [5]	44/24

=**NOTES**=

♪ Recorded at De Lane Lea, the only release recorded there.
♪ The original recording was around 8½ minutes long.

It's Only Love

[Lennon-McCartney]

John – lead vocals, acoustic guitars
Paul – bass
George – lead guitar
Ringo – drums, tambourine

Studio recording and mixing

15 June 1965 – Studio Two – Help! session 12 out of 13
Takes 1–6
Overdubs onto take 6 – guitar, tambourine, vocals

18 June 1965 – Studio Two control room
RM1 [1] – mono mix from take 6
RS1 [2] – stereo mix from take 6

1987 – EMI
[3] – stereo mix from take 6

1995 – EMI
[4] – stereo mix from take 2

Releases   *UK/US peak*

Help! LP (1965) – Parlophone PMC 1255 [1], PCS 3071 [2]	1
Rubber Soul LP (US, 1965) – Capitol T 2442 [1], ST 2442 [2]	1
Yesterday EP (1966) – Parlophone GEP 8948 [1]	1
Love Songs LP (1977) – Parlophone PCSP 721 / Capitol SKBL 11711 [2]	7/24
Help! CD (1987) – EMI CDP 7 46439 2 [3]	61
Anthology 2 CD (1996) – Apple 8 34448 2 [4]	1/1

NOTES

♪ Unusually, technical problems regarding a double-tracking vocal dropout and the tambourine part were corrected for the 1987 CD release.

Jessie's Dream

[McCartney-Starkey-Harrison-Lennon]

Mellotron, tape effects

Studio recording and mixing

October 1967 – unknown location
[1] – unknown takes

Releases *UK/US peak*

Magical Mystery Tour movie (1967) **[1]**   –

```
╔══════════ NOTES ══════════╗
║  ♪ A track of amateurish   ║
║    vamping and electronic  ║
║    sounds made to accompany║
║    Auntie Jessie's dream   ║
║    sequence in the movie.  ║
╚════════════════════════════╝
```

Johnny B Goode

[Berry]

John – lead vocals, rhythm guitar
Paul – bass
George – lead guitar
Ringo – drums

BBC and other performances

7 January 1964 **[1]** – 15 February 1964 edition of *Saturday Club*

Releases *UK/US peak*

Live At The BBC CD (1994) – Apple 8 31796 2 **[1]**   1/3

```
╔══════════ NOTES ══════════╗
║  ♪ Chuck Berry's US top ten hit from 1958.        ║
║  ♪ Played by the Beatles until 1961.              ║
║  ♪ Voted #1 guitar song of all time by Rolling    ║
║    Stone in 2008.                                 ║
╚═══════════════════════════════════════════════════╝
```

Julia

[Lennon-McCartney]

John – lead vocals, acoustic guitar

Studio recording and mixing

May 1968 – Kinfauns, Esher
Demo recording

13 October 1968 – Studio Two – White Album session 80 out of 81
Unnumbered rehearsals
Takes 1–3
Overdubs onto take 3 – vocals, guitar

13 October 1968 – Studio Two control room
RM1 [1] – mono mix from take 3
RS1 [2] – stereo mix from take 3

1996 – EMI
[3] – stereo mix from take 2

2018 – EMI
[4] – stereo mix from demo
[5] – stereo mix from unnumbered rehearsals
[6] – stereo mix from take 3

See 'Eleanor Rigby' [5] for *Love* CD info.

Releases   *UK/US peak*

The Beatles LP (1968) – Apple PMC 7067–7068 [1], PCS 7067–7068 [2]	1
The Beatles LP (US, 1968) – Apple SWBO-101 [2]	1
'Ob-La-Di, Ob-La-Da' / 'Julia' (US, 1976) – Capitol 4347 [2]	–
Anthology 3 CD (1996) – Apple 8 34451 2 [3]	4/1
The Beatles Deluxe CD (2018) – Apple 0602567571957 [4] [5] [6]	4/6

NOTES

♪ The only Beatles song with just John, recorded and mixed in one session.
♪ The song is as much about Yoko as it is about John's mother Julia.
♪ The double-tracked demo version is longer than the released track, with verses being repeated.

Junk

[McCartney]

Paul – lead vocals, acoustic guitar
John – possibly backing vocals

Studio recording and mixing

May 1968 – Kinfauns, Esher
Demo recording

1996 – EMI
[1] – stereo mix from demo

2018 – EMI
[2] – stereo mix from demo

Releases

	UK/US peak
Anthology 3 CD (1996) – Apple 8 34451 2 [1]	4/1
The Beatles Deluxe CD (2018) – Apple 0602567571957 [2]	4/6

═ NOTES ═

♪ Written by Paul while in India, with the original title 'Jubilee'.
♪ Not recorded by the Beatles, but released on Paul's 1970 *McCartney* LP.

Just Because

[Robin-Shelton-Shelton]

Lead vocals, **Paul**. Played by the Beatles until 1961. Recorded by Elvis Presley for his debut LP. John recorded a different song of the same name, written by Lloyd Price, for his 1975 *Rock 'n' Roll* LP.

Kansas City / Hey, Hey, Hey, Hey

[Leiber-Stoller/Penniman]

Paul – lead vocals, bass, possibly piano
John – backing vocals, rhythm guitar
George – backing vocals, lead guitar
Ringo – backing vocals, drums

Studio recording and mixing

18 October 1964 – Studio Two – Beatles For Sale session 7 out of 8
Takes 1–2
Overdubs onto take 2 – vocals

26 October 1964 – Studio Two control room
RM1 [1] – mono mix from take 1
RS1 [2] – stereo mix from take 1

1995 – EMI
[3] – stereo mix from take 2

BBC and other performances

22 August 1962 – *Know The North* (Granada TV, unbroadcast)
December 1962 [4] – Star-Club, Hamburg (live)
16 July 1963 [5] – 6 August 1963 edition of *Pop Go The Beatles*
1 May 1964 – 18 May 1964 edition of *From Us To You*
17 July 1964 – 3 August 1964 edition of *From Us To You*
3 October 1964 – *Shindig* broadcast on 7 October 1964 (American
    Broadcasting Co. TV)

25 November 1964 **[6]** – 26 December 1964 edition of *Saturday Club*

Releases UK/US peak

Beatles For Sale LP (1964) – Parlophone PMC 1240 [1], PCS 3062 [2]	1
Beatles VI LP (US, 1965) – Capitol T 2358 [1], ST 2358 [2]	1
'Kansas City/Hey, Hey, Hey, Hey' / 'Boys' single (US, 1965) – Capitol Starline 6066 [1]	–
Rock 'n' Roll Music LP (1976) – Parlophone PCSP 719 / Capitol SKBO 11537 [2]	11/2
Live! At The Star-Club In Hamburg, Germany; 1962 LP (1977) – Lingasong LNL 1 / Lingasong LS 2 7001 [4]	–
Anthology 1 CD (1995) – Apple 8 34445 2 [3]	2/1
Live At The BBC CD (1994) – Apple 8 31796 2 [5]	1/3
On Air – Live At The BBC Volume 2 CD (2013) – Apple 6025 37491698 [6]	12/7

═══ NOTES ═══

♪ Little Richard originally merged Leiber and Stoller's 'Kansas City' with his own 'Hey, Hey, Hey, Hey' in 1958.

♪ Rarely performed in concert, but an exception was made for a one-off concert in Kansas City in 1964.

Kansas City / Miss Ann / Lawdy Miss Clawdy

[Leiber-Stoller/Penniman-Johnson/Price]

Paul – lead and backing vocals, bass,
John – lead and backing vocals, guitar
George – backing vocals, guitar
Ringo – drums

Studio recording and mixing

26 January 1969 – Apple Studio – Let It Be session 6 out of 17
Take 26.30 [1]

Releases UK/US peak

Let It Be movie (1970) [1]

═══ NOTES ═══

♪ A medley of rock 'n' roll songs originally recorded by Wilbert Harrison in 1959, Little Richard in 1957 and Elvis Presley in 1956.

♪ 'Miss Ann' and 'Lawdy Miss Clawdy', sung by Paul, were played by the group until 1961–62.

Keep Your Hands Off My Baby

[Goffin-King]

John – lead vocals, rhythm guitar
Paul – backing vocals, bass
George – backing vocals, lead guitar
Ringo – drums

BBC and other performances

22 January 1963 [1] – 26 January 1963 edition of *Saturday Club*

Releases   *UK/US peak*

Live At The BBC CD (1994) – Apple 8 31796 2 [1]   1/3

═══ NOTES ═══

♪ A Gerry Goffin–Carole King
song that was a US and UK
hit for Little Eva at the time
of this recording.
♪ Part of the Beatles' live set in
1963.

Komm, Gib Mir Deine Hand

[Lennon-McCartney]

John – lead vocals, rhythm guitar
Paul – lead vocals, bass
George – backing vocals, lead guitar
Ringo – drums

Studio recording and mixing

29 January 1964 – EMI Pathé Studios, Paris – A Hard Day's Night session 1 out of 12
Takes 1–11 – vocals overdubbed onto original backing track
Overdubs onto edit of takes 5, 7 – handclaps,

29 January 1964 – EMI Pathé Studios, Paris
[1] – mono mix from edit of takes 5, 7

10 March 1964 – Studio Two control room
[2] – mono mix from edit of takes 5, 7

12 March 1964 – Studio Three control room
[3] – stereo mix from edit of takes 5, 7

1988 – EMI
[4] – mono mix from [3]

Releases *UK/US peak*

'Komm, Gib Mir Deine Hand' / 'Sie Liebt Dich' single (Germany, 1964) – Odeon O 22671 [1]	–
Something New LP (US, 1964) – Capitol T 2108 [2], ST 2108 [3]	2
Something New LP (Germany, 1964) – Odeon STO 83 756 [2]	–
Rarities LP (1978) – Parlophone PCM 1001, PSLP 261 [3]	71
Past Masters 1 CD (1988) – EMI CDP 7 90043 2 [4]	49/–
Past Masters CD (2009) – EMI CDP 2 43807 2 [3]	31

=== NOTES ===

♪ The release of the Odeon single in February means that an undocumented mono mix must have been made in Paris.

♪ The *Past Masters 1* release may alternatively be a collapsed version of [3].

Lady Madonna

[Lennon-McCartney]

Paul – lead vocals, piano, bass, possibly tambourine
John – harmony and backing vocals, lead guitar
George – harmony and backing vocals, lead guitar
Ringo – drums
Session musicians – two baritone saxophones, two tenor saxophones

Studio recording and mixing

3 February 1968 – *Studio Three* – *White Album session 2 out of 81*

Takes 1–3
Overdubs onto take 3 – bass, guitar, drums, vocals

6 February 1968 – *Studio One* – *White Album session 3 out of 81*

Tape reduction of take 3 > take 4
Overdubs onto take 4 – vocals, piano, tambourine, handclaps > take 5
Overdubs onto take 5 – brass, vocals

15 February 1968 – *Studio Three control room*

Take 3 lead vocal flown in to replace lead vocal on take 5
RM10 [1] – mono mix from take 5

2 December 1969 – *Studio Two control room*

RS1 [2] – stereo mix from take 5

1995 – *EMI*

[3] – stereo mix from takes 3, 4

2004–06 – *EMI*

[4] – stereo mix from take 5: includes samples from 'I Want You (She's So Heavy)' (organ); 'Hey Bulldog' (percussion, guitar); 'While My Guitar Gently Weeps' (guitar);

'Don't Let Me Down' (vocals); also possibly 'Why Don't We Do It In The Road' (drums) and 'Ob-La-Di, Ob-La Da' (percussion)

2015 – EMI

[5] – stereo mix from takes 4, 5

2018 – EMI

[6] – stereo mix from take 2, piano and drums

[7] – stereo mix from take 3, backing vocals

Releases   UK/US peak

'Lady Madonna' / 'The Inner Light' single (1968) – Parlophone R 5675 [1]	1
'Lady Madonna' / 'The Inner Light' single (US, 1968) – Capitol 2138 [1]	4
Hey Jude LP (US, 1970) – Apple SW 385 [2]	2
The Beatles 1967–1970 LP (1973) – Apple PCSP 718 [2]	2
The Beatles 1967–1970 LP (US, 1973) – Apple SKBO 3404 [2]	1
20 Greatest Hits LP (1982) – Parlophone PCTC 260 [2]	10
Past Masters 2 CD (1988) – EMI CDP 7 90044 2 [2]	46/–
Anthology 2 CD (1996) – Apple 8 34448 2 [3]	1/1
Love CD (2006) – Apple 0946 3 80790 2 6 [4]	3/4
1+ CD/DVD (2015) – Apple 6205 47567727 [5]	5/6
The Beatles Deluxe CD (2018) – Apple 0602567571957 [6] [7]	4/6

═══ NOTES ═══

♪ Failed to make #1 in the US.

♪ No John composition featured on either side of single.

♪ A promotional film was made on 11 February 1968, while the group were recording 'Hey Bulldog'.

Lawdy Miss Clawdy
see 'Kansas City/Miss Ann/Lawdy Miss Clawdy'

Leave My Kitten Alone
[John-Turner-McDougal]

John – lead vocals, rhythm guitar
Paul – bass, piano
George – lead guitar
Ringo – drums, tambourine

Studio recording and mixing

14 August 1964 – Studio Two – Beatles For Sale session 2 out of 8
Takes 1–5

Overdubs onto take 5 – vocals, tambourine, piano, guitar

1984 – AIR Studios

[1] – mock stereo mix from take 5

c. 2003 – EMI

[2] – stereo mix from take 5

Releases UK/US peak

Anthology 1 CD (1995) – Apple 8 34445 2 [1]	2/1
Anthology DVD (2003) – Apple 4 92969 9 [2]	2/1

NOTES

♪ A Little Willie John single from 1959.
♪ Played in concert in 1961–62.
♪ The 1984 mix was originally for the aborted *Sessions* LP – some sources say the *Anthology 1* track is a new mix from 1994.

Lend Me Your Comb

[Twomey-Wise-Weisman]

John – lead and harmony vocals, rhythm guitar
Paul – lead and harmony vocals, bass
George – harmony vocals, lead guitar
Ringo – drums

BBC and other performances

December 1962 [1] – Star-Club, Hamburg (live)
2 July 1963 [2] – 16 July 1963 edition of *Pop Go The Beatles*

Releases UK/US peak

Live! At The Star-Club In Hamburg, Germany; 1962 LP (1977) – Lingasong LNL 1 / Lingasong LS 2 7001 [1]	–
Anthology 1 CD (1995) – Apple 8 34445 2 [2]	2/1
On Air – Live At The BBC Volume 2 CD (2013) – Apple 6025 37491698 [2]	12/7

NOTES

♪ Originally released in 1957 as the B-side to Carl Perkins' single 'Glad All Over'.
♪ The only BBC recording to appear on any of the *Anthology* CDs.
♪ Played live until 1963.

Let It Be

[Lennon-McCartney]

Paul – lead and backing vocals, piano, bass, maracas
John – backing vocals
George – backing vocals, lead guitar
Ringo – drums
Billy Preston – organ, possibly electric piano
Linda McCartney – possibly backing vocals
Session musicians – two trumpets, one or two trombones, tenor and possibly baritone saxophones, cellos

Studio recording and mixing

5 September 1968 – Apple Studio – White Album session 54 out of 81
Rehearsal

25 January 1969 – Apple Studio – Let It Be session 5 out of 17
Rehearsal

31 January 1969 – Apple Studio – Let It Be session 10 out of 17
Takes 31.37, 31.38, 31.39 [1]

30 April 1969 – Studio Three – Let It Be session 12 out of 17
Overdubs onto take 31.38 – guitar

4 January 1970 – Studio Two – Let It Be session 15 out of 17
Overdubs onto take 31.38 – bass, brass
Tape reduction of take 31.38 with overdubs – brass > takes 28–30
Overdubs onto take 30 – vocals, guitar, drums, maracas, cellos

8 January 1970 – Olympic Studios
[2] – stereo mix from take 30 (with 30 April 1969 guitar solo)

26 March 1970 – Studio Two control room
RS1 [3] – stereo mix from take 30 (with 4 January 1970 guitar solo), edited

1996 – EMI
[4] – stereo mix from rehearsal (25 January 1969)

2003 – EMI
[5] – stereo mix from take 31.38 (with 31 January 1969 guitar solo)

2018 – EMI
[6] – stereo mix from rehearsal (5 September 1968)

Releases   *UK/US peak*

	UK/US peak
'Let It Be' / 'You Know My Name (Look Up The Number)' single (1970) – Apple R 5833 [2]	2
'Let It Be' / 'You Know My Name (Look Up The Number)' single (1970) – Parlophone P-R 5833 [2]	–
'Let It Be' / 'You Know My Name (Look Up The Number)' single (US, 1970) – Apple 2764 [2]	1

Let It Be LP (1970) – Apple PXS1, PCS 7096 [3]   1
Let It Be LP (US, 1970) – Apple AR 34001 [3]   1
Let It Be movie (1970) [1]
The Beatles 1967–1970 LP (1973) – Apple PCSP 718 [2]   2
The Beatles 1967–1970 LP (US, 1973) – Apple SKBO 3404 [2]   1
The Beatles Ballads LP (1980) – Parlophone PCS 7214 [3]   17
Reel Music LP (1982) – Parlophone PCS 7218 / Capitol SV-12199 [3]   –/19
20 Greatest Hits LP (US, 1982) – Capitol SV-12245 [2]   50
Past Masters 2 CD (1988) – EMI CDP 7 90044 2 [2]   46/–
Anthology 3 CD (1996) – Apple 8 34451 2 [4]   4/1
Let It Be… Naked CD (2003) – Apple 24359 57142 [5]   7/5
1+ CD/DVD (2015) – Apple 6205 47567727 [2]   5/6
The Beatles Deluxe CD (2018) – Apple 0602567571957 [6]   4/6

NOTES

♪ Takes 31.38 and 31.39, the last two recordings of the entire month-long project, were used for release on record and film respectively.
♪ Paul, George & Ringo were together for the last time as the Beatles at the session on 4 January 1970.
♪ Apart from minor cosmetic surgery, such as removing a popped "p" in the "whisper words …", the *1+* track is more of a remaster than a remix.

Like Dreamers Do

[Lennon-McCartney]

Paul – lead vocals, bass
John – rhythm guitar
George – lead guitar
Pete Best – drums

Studio recording and mixing

1 January 1962 – Decca Studios
Studio test recorded in mono [1]

Releases   *UK/US peak*

Anthology 1 CD (1995) – Apple 8 34445 2 [1]   2/1

NOTES

♪ Written by Paul before 1959 and played live until 1962.
♪ One of four songs auditioned for the BBC on 8 February 1962.
♪ Recorded by the Applejacks in 1964, reaching #20 in the UK charts.

Little Child

[Lennon-McCartney]

John – lead and harmony vocals, harmonica
Paul – possibly backing vocals, bass
George – possibly guitar
Ringo – drums
George Martin – possibly piano

Studio recording and mixing

11 September 1963 – Studio Three – With The Beatles session 4 out of 9
Takes 1–2

12 September 1963 – Studio Two – With The Beatles session 5 out of 9
Takes 3–13
Overdubs onto take 13 – harmonica, piano > takes 14–18
Edit of takes 15, 18

3 October 1963 – Studio Two – With The Beatles session 7 out of 9
Overdubs onto edit of takes 15, 18 – vocals > takes 19–21

23 October 1964 – Studio Two control room
RM21 [1] – mono mix from take 21

29 October 1964 – Studio Three control room
RS21 [2] – stereo mix from take 21

19 December 1963 – Capitol
[3] – mastering of stereo mix from [2]
[4] – mastering of mono mix from [3]

Releases
UK/US peak

With The Beatles LP (1963) – Parlophone PMC 1206 [1], PCS 3045 [2]	1
Meet The Beatles! LP (US, 1964) – Capitol T 2047 [4], ST 2047 [3]	1

=**NOTES**=

♪ The first Beatles recording in Abbey Road's Studio Three.
♪ Possibly no guitars appear on the final recording.

Little Queenie

[Berry]

Paul – lead vocals, bass
John – rhythm guitar

George – lead guitar
Ringo – drums

BBC and other performances

December 1962 **[1]** – Star-Club, Hamburg (live)

Releases   *UK/US peak*

Live! At The Star-Club In Hamburg, Germany; 1962 LP (1977) – Lingasong LNL 1 /
   Lingasong LS 2 7001 **[1]**   –

NOTES

♪ 1959 Chuck Berry single release with 'Almost Grown',
   which was also part of the Beatles' live set.
♪ Played live by the Quarry Men/Beatles until 1963.

Lonesome Tears In My Eyes

[Burnette-Burnette-Burlison-Mortimer]

John – lead vocals, rhythm guitar
Paul – bass
George – lead guitar
Ringo – drums

BBC and other performances

10 July 1963 **[1]** – 23 July 1963 edition of *Pop Go The Beatles*

Releases   *UK/US peak*

Live At The BBC CD (1994) – Apple 8 31796 2 **[1]**   1/3

NOTES

♪ Released by Johnny Burnette and his Rock 'n' Roll Trio in 1957.

The Long And Winding Road

[Lennon-McCartney]

Paul – lead vocals, piano
John – bass
George – acoustic guitar
Ringo – drums
Billy Preston – Hammond organ
Session musicians – eighteen violins, four violas, four cellos, three trumpets, three
   trombones, two guitars, harp, fourteen-voice choir

Studio recording and mixing

26 January 1969 – Apple Studio – Let It Be session 6 out of 17
Takes 26.38, 26.39 [1, edited]
Take [26.91]

31 January 1969 – Apple Studio – Let It Be session 10 out of 17
Take 31.22 [2]

1 April 1970 – Studio One – Let It Be session 17 out of 17
Tape reduction of take [26.91] > takes 17–19
Overdubs onto take 18 – orchestra, choir

2 April 1970 – Room 4
RS10, 13 [3] – stereo mixes from take 18, edited

1996 – EMI
[4] – stereo mix from take [26.91]

2003 – EMI
[5] – stereo mix from take 31.22

Releases

	UK/US peak
Let It Be LP (1970) – Apple PXS1, PCS 7096 [3]	1
Let It Be LP (US, 1970) – Apple AR 34001 [3]	1
Let It Be movie (1970) [1] [2]	
'The Long And Winding Road' / 'For You Blue' single (US, 1970) – Apple 2832 [3]	1
The Beatles 1967–1970 LP (1973) – Apple PCSP 718 [3]	2
The Beatles 1967–1970 LP (US, 1973) – Apple SKBO 3404 [3]	1
Love Songs LP (1977) – Parlophone PCSP 721 / Capitol SKBL 11711 [3]	7/24
The Beatles Ballads LP (1980) – Parlophone PCS 7214 [3]	17
Reel Music LP (1982) – Parlophone PCS 7218 / Capitol SV-12199 [3]	–/19
20 Greatest Hits LP (US, 1982) – Capitol SV-12245 [3]	50
Anthology 3 CD (1996) – Apple 8 34451 2 [4]	4/1
Let It Be… Naked CD (2003) – Apple 24359 57142 [5]	7/5
1+ CD/DVD (2015) – Apple 6205 47567727 [3]	5/6

═ NOTES ═

♪ The first US-only single to reach #1 since 'Yesterday'.
♪ Spector's "interference" was cited in Paul's bid to disband the group.
♪ Take [26.91] was unlisted in the original Sulpy & Schweighardt book, this number is from the 2007 edition.

Long Long Long

[Harrison]

George – lead vocals, acoustic guitar
Paul – harmony vocals, bass, organ
Ringo – drums
Chris Thomas – piano

Studio recording and mixing

7 October 1968 – Studio Two – White Album session 75 out of 81
Takes 1–67
Overdubs onto take 67 – drums

8 October 1968 – Studio Two – White Album session 76 out of 81
Overdubs onto take 67 – guitar, vocals, bass

9 October 1968 – Studio Two – White Album session 77 out of 81
Overdubs onto take 67 – vocals, piano

10 October 1968 – Studio Two control room
RS4 **[1]** – stereo mix from take 67

14 October 1968 – Studio Two control room
RM3 **[2]** – mono mix from take 67

2018 – EMI
[3] – stereo mix from take 44
[4] – stereo mix from take 67

Releases .... *UK/US peak*

The Beatles LP (1968) – Apple PMC 7067–7068 **[2]**, PCS 7067–7068 **[1]**	1
The Beatles LP (US, 1968) – Apple SWBO-101 **[1]**	1
The Beatles Deluxe CD (2018) – Apple 0602567571957 **[3] [4]**	4/6

NOTES

♪ 67 takes were recorded in a 16½-hour session.

Long Tall Sally

[Johnson-Penniman-Blackwell]

Paul – lead vocals, bass
John – rhythm guitar
George – lead guitar
Ringo – drums
George Martin – piano

Studio recording and mixing

1 March 1964 – Studio Two – A Hard Day's Night session 5 out of 12
Take 1

10 March 1964 – Studio Two control room
RS1 [1] – stereo mix from take 1
RM1 [2] – mono mix from take 1

4 June 1964 – Studio Two control room
RM1 #2 [3] – mono mix from take 1

22 June 1964 – Studio One control room
RS1 #2 [4] – stereo mix from take 1

June 1964 – Capitol Canada
[5] – mono mix from [1]

BBC and other performances

December 1962 [6] – Star-Club, Hamburg (live)
1 April 1963 [7] – 13 May 1963 edition of *Side By Side*
21 May 1963 – 25 May 1963 edition of *Saturday Club*
16 July 1963 [8] – 13 August 1963 edition of *Pop Go The Beatles*
30 July 1963 – 24 August 1963 edition of *Saturday Club*
30 October 1963 – *Drop In* broadcast on 3 November 1963 (Sveriges TV)
31 March 1964 – 4 April 1964 edition of *Saturday Club*
19 April 1964 [9] – *Around The Beatles*, mimed performance recorded on 28
    April and broadcast on 6 May 1964 (Rediffusion TV)
26 April 1964 – *NME 1963-64 Annual Poll-Winners' Concert*
17 June 1964 – *The Beatles Sing For Shell* broadcast on 1 July 1964 (Channel 9
    TV, Australia)
14 July 1964 [10] – 16 July 1964 edition of *Top Gear*
17 July 1964 – 3 August 1964 edition of *From Us To You*
19 July 1964 – *Blackpool Night Out* (Associated British Corp. TV, live)
23 August 1964 [11] – Hollywood Bowl (live)
11 April 1965 – *NME 1964-65 Annual Poll-Winners' Concert*
20 June 1965 – *Les Beatles* (Europe 1 TV, France, live)

Releases   *UK/US peak*

Long Tall Sally EP (1964) – Parlophone GEP 8913 [3]	1
The Beatles' Second Album LP (US, 1964) – Capitol T 2080 [2], ST 2080 [1]	1
Long Tall Sally LP (Canada, 1964) – Capitol T 6063 [5], ST 6063 [1]	–
The Beatles' Second Album EP (US, 1964) – Capitol SXA 2080 [1]	–
Rock 'n' Roll Music LP (1976) – Parlophone PCSP 719 / Capitol SKBO 11537 [4]	11/2
The Beatles At The Hollywood Bowl LP (1977) – Parlophone EMTV 4 / Capitol SMAS 11638 [11]	1/2

Live! At The Star-Club In Hamburg, Germany; 1962 LP (1977) – Lingasong LNL 1 /
    Lingasong LS 2 7001 **[6]**   –
Rarities LP (1978) – Parlophone PCM 1001, PSLP 261 **[3]**   71
Past Masters 1 CD (1988) – EMI CDP 7 90043 2 **[4]**   49/–
Live At The BBC CD (1994) – Apple 8 31796 2 **[8]**   1/3
Anthology 1 CD (1995) – Apple 8 34445 2 **[9]**   2/1
On Air – Live At The BBC Volume 2 CD (2013) – Apple 6025 37491698 **[10]**   12/7
The Beatles Bootleg Recordings 1963 (2013) – iTunes **[7]**   –
Live At The Hollywood Bowl CD (2016) – Apple 6025 57054972 **[11]**   3/7

NOTES

♪ Little Richard reached #6 in the US and #3 in the UK in early 1956.
♪ Performed by the Quarry Men in 1957, and the last song performed at the Beatles' last concert in 1966.

Los Paranoias

[Lennon-McCartney-Harrison-Starkey]

Paul – lead vocals, acoustic guitar
John – skulls
Ringo – percussion

Studio recording and mixing

16 September 1968 – Studio Two – White Album session 61 out of 81
Studio jam from take 35 of 'I Will'

1996 – EMI
[1] – stereo mix from studio jam

2018 – EMI
[2] – stereo mix from studio jam

Releases   UK/US peak

Anthology 3 CD (1996) – Apple 8 34451 2 [1]   4/1
The Beatles Deluxe CD (2018) – Apple 0602567571957 [2]   4/6

NOTES

♪ Released on *Anthology 3* jointly with 'Step Inside Love'.

Love Me Do

[Lennon-McCartney]

John – lead and harmony vocals, harmonica, guitar
Paul – lead and harmony vocals, bass
George – harmony vocals, guitar
Pete Best – drums (6 June)
Andy White – drums (11 September)
Ringo – drums (all other dates)

Studio recording and mixing

6 June 1962 – Studio Two or Three – Please Please Me session 1 out of 8
Unknown take numbers

6 June 1962 – Studio Two or Three control room
[1] – mono mix from unknown take number

4 September 1962 – Studio Two – Please Please Me session 2 out of 8
Takes 1–15+
Overdubs onto unknown 4 September take number – vocals, handclaps

4 September 1962 – Studio Two control room
[2] – mono mix from unknown 4 September take number

11 September 1962 – Studio Two – Please Please Me session 3 out of 8
Remake takes 1–18

11 September 1962 – Studio Two control room
[3] – mono mix from take 18

25 February 1963 – Studio One control room
[4] – mock stereo mix from [3]

1965 – Capitol
[5] – mono mix from [4]

1978 – EMI
[6] – mono mix from transfer of single [2]

BBC and other performances

17 October 1962 – *People And Places* (Granada TV, live)
25 October 1962 – 26 October 1962 edition of *Here We Go*
29 October 1962 – 2 November 1962 edition of *People And Places* (Granada TV)
17 December 1962 – *People And Places* (Granada TV, live)
27 November 1962 – 4 December 1962 edition of *The Talent Spot*
22 January 1963 [7] – 26 January 1963 edition of *Saturday Club*
20 February 1963 – *Parade Of The Pops* (live)
24 May 1963 – 11 June 1963 edition of *Pop Go The Beatles*

4 April 1963 – 24 June 1963 edition of *Side By Side*
10 July 1963 [8] – 23 July 1963 edition of *Pop Go The Beatles*
27 August 1963 – *The Mersey Sound* broadcast on 9 October 1963 (BBC TV)
2 September 1963 [9] – 10 September 1963 edition of *Pop Go The Beatles*
16 October 1963 [10] – 20 October 1963 edition of *Easy Beat*
19 April 1964 – *Around The Beatles*, mimed performance recorded on 28 April
    and broadcast on 6 May 1964 (Rediffusion TV)

Releases   UK/US peak

'Love Me Do' / 'P.S. I Love You' single (1962) – Parlophone 45-R 4949 [2] [3]	17
Please Please Me LP (1963) – Parlophone PMC 1202 [3], PCS 3042 [4]	1
Introducing… The Beatles LP (US, 1963) – Vee Jay VJLP 1062 [3], VJSR 1062 [4]	2
The Beatles' Hits EP (1963) – Parlophone GEP 8880 [3]	1
'Love Me Do' / 'P.S. I Love You' single (US, 1964) – Tollie 9008 [3]	1
The Early Beatles LP (US, 1965) – Capitol T 2309 [5], ST 2309 [4]	43
'Love Me Do' / 'P.S. I Love You' single (US, 1965) – Capitol Starline 6062 [3]	–
The Beatles 1962–1966 LP (1973) – Apple PCSP 717 [4]	3
The Beatles 1962–1966 LP (US, 1973)– Apple SKBO 3403 [4]	3
Rarities LP (US, 1980) – Capitol SHAL 12060 [6]	21
20 Greatest Hits LP (1982) – Parlophone PCTC 260 / Capitol SV-12245 [4]	10/50
Past Masters 1 CD (1988) – EMI CDP 7 90043 2 [2]	49/–
The Beatles 1962–1966 CD (1993) – EMI CDP 7 97036 2 [3]	3
Live At The BBC CD (1994) – Apple 8 31796 2 [8]	1/3
Anthology 1 CD (1995) – Apple 8 34445 2 [1]	2/1
The Beatles Bootleg Recordings 1963 (2013) – iTunes [7] [9] [10]	–
1+ CD/DVD (2015) – Apple 6205 47567727 [3]	5/6

NOTES

♪ Three versions were recorded at the group's first three visits to Abbey Road studios, each with a different drummer.
♪ Played live until 1963.
♪ The performance recorded for *The Mersey Sound* was (partially) broadcast with the studio recording dubbed on.

Love Me Tender

[Matson-Presley]

Part of the Beatles' set 1960–61, with **Stuart Sutcliffe** singing lead. It was a US #1 and UK #11 for Elvis Presley in 1956. Based on the song 'Aura Lee' which was written by George Poulton, with new words by Ken Darby (credited under the name of his wife, Vera Matson) and Elvis.

Love Of The Loved

[Lennon-McCartney]

Paul – lead vocals, bass
John – rhythm guitar
George – lead guitar
Pete Best – drums

Studio recording and mixing

1 January 1962 – Decca Studios
Studio test recorded in mono

═══════NOTES═══════

♪ Written in 1959 by Paul, though John claimed joint ownership.
♪ Recorded by Cilla Black in 1963, but never released by the Beatles.

Love You To

[Harrison]

George – lead vocals, guitars, possibly sitar
Paul – possibly bass
Ringo – tambourine
Session musicians – tabla, sitar, tamboura

Studio recording and mixing

11 April 1966 – Studio Two – Revolver session 4 out of 33
Takes 1–6
Overdubs onto take 6 – sitar, tabla, bass, guitar

13 April 1966 – Studio Three – Revolver session 5 out of 33
Tape reduction take 6 > take 7
Overdubs onto take 7 – tambourine, vocals

13 April 1966 – Studio Three control room
RM1–RM3 – mono mixes from take 7
Edit of RM1–RM3[?]

25 April 1966 – Room 65
Edit piece (introduction) mixed for mono and stereo

16 May 1966 – Studio Two control room
[1] – copying RM3 plus edit piece > RM5

21 June 1966 – Studio Three control room
RS1–RS3 – stereo mixes from take 7 plus edit piece

[2] – edit of RS1–RS3

1999 – EMI

[3] – stereo mix from takes 6, 7 plus edit piece

Releases   *UK/US peak*

Revolver LP (1966) – Parlophone PMC 7009 [1], PCS 7009 [2]	1
Revolver LP (US, 1966) – Capitol T 2576 [1], ST 2576 [2]	1
Yellow Submarine Songtrack CD (1999) – Apple 5 21481 2 [3]	8/15

═══NOTES═══

♪ George's original title for the song was 'Granny Smith'.
♪ Paul's backing vocals were removed during the mix, so he may not appear on the released recording – if so, this is a first for a Beatles track.

Lovely Rita

[Lennon-McCartney]

Paul – lead vocals, bass, piano, comb and paper
John – harmony and backing vocals, acoustic guitar, comb and paper
George – harmony vocals, acoustic guitar, comb and paper
Ringo – drums, comb and paper
George Martin – piano

Studio recording and mixing

23 February 1967 – Studio Two – Sgt Pepper session 33 out of 56
Takes 1–8
Tape reduction of take 8 > take 9
Overdubs onto take 9 – bass

24 February 1967 – Studio Two – Sgt Pepper session 34 out of 56
Overdubs onto take 9 – vocals
Tape reduction of take 9 > takes 10, 11

7 March 1967 – Studio Two – Sgt Pepper session 40 out of 56
Overdubs onto take 11 – vocals, effects

21 March 1967 – Studio Two – Sgt Pepper session 47 out of 56
Overdubs onto take 11 – piano

21 March 1967 – Studio Two control room
RM1–RM15 – mono mixes from take 11
[1] – edit of RM11, RM14

17 April 1967 – Studio Two control room
RS2 [2] – stereo mix from take 11

2016/17 – EMI
[3] – stereo mix from take 9
[4] – stereo mix from take 11

Releases   *UK/US peak*

	UK/US peak
Sgt Pepper's Lonely Hearts Club Band LP (1967) – Parlophone PMC 7027 [1], PCS 7027 [2]	1
Sgt Pepper's Lonely Hearts Club Band LP (US, 1967) – Capitol MAS 2653 [1], SMAS 2653 [2]	1
Sgt Pepper's Lonely Hearts Club Band Deluxe CD (2017) – Apple 0602557455328 [1] [3] [4]	1/3

═══ NOTES ═══

♪ The wobbly piano sound was achieved using strips of sticky tape placed on tape capstan.
♪ *Not* based on an encounter with a traffic warden called Meta.

Lucille

[Collins-Penniman]

Paul – lead vocals, bass
John – rhythm guitar
George – lead guitar
Ringo – drums

BBC and other performances

3 September 1963 [1] – 17 September 1963 edition of *Pop Go The Beatles*
7 September 1963 [2] – 5 October 1963 edition of *Saturday Club*

Releases   *UK/US peak*

	UK/US peak
Live At The BBC CD (1994) – Apple 8 31796 2 [2]	1/3
On Air – Live At The BBC Volume 2 CD (2013) – Apple 6025 37491698 [1]	12/7

═══ NOTES ═══

♪ A Little Richard single released in 1957. It peaked at #21 in the US and #10 in the UK.
♪ Played live by the Quarry Men/Beatles until 1962.

Lucy In The Sky With Diamonds

[Lennon-McCartney]

John – lead vocals
Paul – harmony vocals, bass, organ

George – electric and acoustic guitars, tamboura
Ringo – drums, maracas

Studio recording and mixing

28 February 1967 – Studio Two – Sgt Pepper session 35 out of 56
Rehearsal

1 March 1967 – Studio Two – Sgt Pepper session 36 out of 56
Takes 1–7
Overdubs onto take 7 – tamboura
Tape reduction of take 7 > take 8

2 March 1967 – Studio Two – Sgt Pepper session 37 out of 56
Overdubs onto take 8 – vocals, bass, guitar

3 March 1967 – Studio Two control room
RM4 [1] – mono mix from take 8

7 April 1967 – Studio Two control room
RS5 [2] – stereo mix from take 8

1 November 1967 – Room 53
RM11 [3] – mono mix from take 8

1995 – EMI
[4] – stereo mix from takes 6, 8

1999 – EMI
[5] – stereo mix from take 8

2004–06 – EMI
[6] – stereo mix from take 8: includes samples from 'Baby You're A Rich Man' (clavioline); 'Sgt Pepper's Lonely Hearts Club Band' (horns); 'Tomorrow Never Knows' (effects); 'Old Brown Shoe' (organ); 'Your Mother Should Know', 'Magical Mystery Tour' (vocals)

2016/17 – EMI
[7] – stereo mix from take 1
[8] – stereo mix from take 5
[9] – stereo mix from take 8

Releases   UK/US peak

	UK/US peak
Sgt Pepper's Lonely Hearts Club Band LP (1967) – Parlophone PMC 7027 [1], PCS 7027 [2]	1
Sgt Pepper's Lonely Hearts Club Band LP (US, 1967) – Capitol MAS 2653 [1], SMAS 2653 [2]	1
Yellow Submarine movie (1968) [3]	
The Beatles 1967–1970 LP (1973) – Apple PCSP 718 [2]	2
The Beatles 1967–1970 LP (US, 1973) – Apple SKBO 3404 [2]	1
Anthology 2 CD (1996) – Apple 8 34448 2 [4]	1/1
Yellow Submarine Songtrack CD (1999) – Apple 5 21481 2 [5]	8/15

Love CD (2006) – Apple 0946 3 80790 2 6 [6]   3/4
Sgt Pepper's Lonely Hearts Club Band Deluxe CD (2017) – Apple 0602557455328 [1] [3] [7] [8] [9]   1/3

NOTES

♪ The rehearsal took up all of the 28 February session.
♪ A US #1 and UK top ten hit for Elton John in 1974,
  featuring John on guitar and vocals, playing under the
  name of Dr Winston O'Boogie.
♪ RM11 was believed wiped, but turned up during
  research for the 2017 remaster of *Sgt Pepper*.

Maggie Mae

[Trad. arr. Lennon-McCartney-Harrison-Starkey]

John – lead vocals, acoustic guitar
Paul – lead and backing vocals, acoustic guitar
George – lead guitar
Ringo – drums
Billy Preston – possibly electric piano

Studio recording and mixing

24 January 1969 – Apple Studio – Let It Be session 4 out of 17

Take 24.41

26 March 1970 – Studio Two control room

[1] – stereo mix from take 24.41

Releases   *UK/US peak*

Let It Be LP (1970) – Apple PXS1, PCS 7096 [1]   1
Let It Be LP (US, 1970) – Apple AR 34001 [1]   1

NOTES

♪ The last non-original
  song to be recorded,
  and the first since
  'Bad Boy' in 1965.

Magical Mystery Tour

[Lennon-McCartney]

Paul – lead vocals, bass, piano, possibly celeste, percussion
John – harmony and backing vocals, acoustic guitar, percussion

George – harmony and backing vocals, lead guitar, percussion
Ringo – drums, tambourine
Mal Evans, Neil Aspinall – percussion
Session musicians – four trumpets

Studio recording and mixing

25 April 1967 – Studio Three – Magical Mystery Tour session 1 out of 30
Tape loop of coach noise
Takes 1–3
Tape reduction of take 3 > takes 4–8

26 April 1967 – Studio Three – Magical Mystery Tour session 2 out of 30
Overdubs onto take 8 – bass, percussion, vocals
Tape reduction of take 8 > take 9

27 April 1967 – Studio Three – Magical Mystery Tour session 3 out of 30
Overdubs onto take 9 – vocals

3 May 1967 – Studio Three – Magical Mystery Tour session 4 out of 30
Overdubs onto take 9 – brass, celeste

4 May 1967 – Studio Three control room
RM7 [1] – mono mix from take 9

6 November 1967 – Studio Three control room
RS1–RS4 – stereo mixes from take 9

7 November 1967 – Studio One control room
Tape reduction of RS4 with overdubs – vocals, sound effects > RS5–RS6
Tape reduction of RM7 with overdubs – vocals, sound effects > RM8–RM10
Tape copying of RM10 [2] and RS4 [3]

Releases   UK/US peak

Magical Mystery Tour movie (1967) [1]	
Magical Mystery Tour EP (1967) – Parlophone MMT-1 [2], SMMT-1 [3]	2
Magical Mystery Tour LP (US, 1967) – Capitol MAL 2835 [2], SMAL 2835 [3]	1
The Beatles 1967–1970 LP (1973) – Apple PCSP 718 [3]	2
The Beatles 1967–1970 LP (US, 1973) – Apple SKBO 3404 [3]	1
Reel Music LP (1982) – Parlophone PCS 7218 / Capitol SV-12199 [3]	–/19

=== NOTES ===

♪ The film version has John calling
the introductory "roll up", which was
replaced with Paul's supplication on
all current CD & DVD releases.

Mailman, Bring Me No More Blues

[Roberts-Katz-Clayton]

John – lead vocals, rhythm guitar
Paul – bass
George – harmony vocals, lead guitar
Ringo – drums

Studio recording and mixing

29 January 1969 – Apple Studio – Let It Be rehearsal session
Take 29.11

1984 – AIR Studios
[1] – stereo mix from take 29.11, edited

Releases   *UK/US peak*

Anthology 3 CD (1996) – Apple 8 34451 2 [1]   4/1

=== **NOTES** ===

♪ The B-side of Buddy Holly's 'Words Of Love'
  from 1957.
♪ The recording was edited to rearrange the
  verses and instrumental passages.

Mama Said

[Dixon-Denson]

Lead vocals, **Paul**. Part of the Beatles' set in 1961–62. It was a #4 *Billboard* hit for the Shirelles in 1961.

Martha My Dear

[Lennon-McCartney]

Paul – lead vocals, piano, bass
George – guitar
Ringo – drums
Session musicians – four violins, two violas, two cellos, three trumpets, horn, trombone, tuba, flügelhorn

Studio recording and mixing

4 October 1968 – Trident Studios – White Album session 73 out of 81
Take 1
Overdubs onto take 1 – strings, brass, vocals, handclaps

5 October 1968 – Trident Studios – White Album session 74 out of 81
Overdubs onto take 1 – guitar, bass
RM1 – mono mix from take 1
RS1 – stereo mix from take 1

7 October 1968 – Studio Two control room
Tape copying RM1 [1]
Tape copying RS1 [2]

2018 – EMI
[3] – stereo mix from take 1
[4] – stereo mix from take 1 (vocals, drums, guitar, piano)

Releases

	UK/US peak
The Beatles LP (1968) – Apple PMC 7067–7068 [1], PCS 7067–7068 [2]	1
The Beatles LP (US, 1968) – Apple SWBO-101 [2]	1
The Beatles Deluxe CD (2018) – Apple 0602567571957 [3] [4]	4/6

NOTES

♪ Like 'Honey Pie', the song was recorded and mixed at Trident Studios.
♪ Martha was Paul's sheepdog.

Matchbox

[Perkins]

Ringo – lead vocals, drums
John – rhythm guitar
Paul – bass
George – lead guitar
George Martin – piano

Studio recording and mixing

1 June 1964 – Studio Two – A Hard Day's Night session 9 out of 12
Takes 1–5
Overdubs onto take 5 – vocals, guitar

4 June 1964 – Studio Two control room
RM1 [1] – mono mix from take 5

22 June 1964 – Studio One control room
RS1 [2] – stereo mix from take 5

BBC and other performances

December 1962 [3] – Star-Club, Hamburg (live)

10 July 1963 [4] – 30 July 1963 edition of *Pop Go The Beatles*
1 May 1964 – 18 May 1964 edition of *From Us To You*

Releases   UK/US peak

Long Tall Sally EP (1964) – Parlophone GEP 8913 [1]	1
Something New LP (US, 1964) – Capitol T 2108 [1], ST 2108 [2]	2
Something New EP (US, 1964) – Capitol SXA 2108 [2]	–
'Matchbox' / 'Slow Down' single (US, 1964) – Capitol 5255 [1]	17
Rock 'n' Roll Music LP (1976) – Parlophone PCSP 719 / Capitol SKBO 11537 [2]	11/2
Live! At The Star-Club In Hamburg, Germany; 1962 LP (1977) – Lingasong LNL 1 / Lingasong LS 2 7001 [3]	–
Rarities LP (1978) – Parlophone PCM 1001, PSLP 261 [1]	71
Past Masters 1 CD (1988) – EMI CDP 7 90043 2 [2]	49/–
Live At The BBC CD (1994) – Apple 8 31796 2 [4]	1/3

─────── **NOTES** ───────

♪ A Carl Perkins single from 1957, inspired by Blind Lemon Jefferson's 1927 'Match Box Blues'.
♪ Recorded with Carl Perkins present in the studio.
♪ There are differences in the vocal and guitar between mono and stereo.
♪ At 1'37", the shortest track to be released as a single.
♪ An excerpt appears on a tape recorded at Paul's house in June 1960, with John singing lead.
♪ Played live by the Beatles until 1962.

Maxwell's Silver Hammer

[Lennon-McCartney]

Paul – lead vocals, piano, guitars, Moog synthesiser
George – backing and harmony vocals, lead guitar, six-string bass
Ringo – backing and harmony vocals, drums, anvil
George Martin – Hammond organ

Studio recording and mixing

3 January 1969 – *Twickenham Film Studios – Let It Be rehearsal session*
Take 3.97 [1]

7 January 1969 – *Twickenham Film Studios – Let It Be rehearsal session*
Takes 7.46, 7.58 [2, edited]

9 July 1969 – *Studio Two – Abbey Road session 17 out of 42*
Takes 1–21
Overdubs onto take 21 – guitar

10 July 1969 – Studio Two – Abbey Road session 18 out of 42
Overdubs onto take 21 – piano, organ, anvil, guitar, vocals

11 July 1969 – Studio Two – Abbey Road session 19 out of 42
Overdubs onto take 21 – guitar, vocals

6 August 1969 – Room 43 – Abbey Road session 36 out of 42
Tape reduction of take 21 with overdubs – Moog > takes 22–27

12 August 1969 – Studio Two control room
RS27–RS36 – stereo mixes from take 27

14 August 1969 – Studio Two control room
RS37 – stereo mix from edit piece
[3] – edit of RS34, RS37

1996 – EMI
[4] – stereo mix from take 5

Releases _____ *UK/US peak*

Abbey Road LP (1969) – Apple PCS 7088 [3]	1
Abbey Road LP (US, 1969) – Apple SO 383 [3]	1
Let It Be movie (1970) [1, 2, edited]	
Anthology 3 CD (1996) – Apple 8 34451 2 [4]	4/1

========= **NOTES** =========

♪ George plays bass, and John does not appear on the recording.
♪ Rather than use a keyboard, Paul played the Moog by sliding his finger along an endless ribbon, feeling out the notes.
♪ Rehearsals of the track feature in the *Let It Be* film.

Maybellene

[Berry]

Lead vocals, **John**. The song was played by the Quarry Men/Beatles until 1961. It was Chuck Berry's first single release, reaching #5 in the US in 1955.

Mean Woman Blues

[Demetrius]

Lead vocals, **Paul**. Part of the Quarry Men/Beatles' set from 1957 to 1962. On the earliest known (partial) Beatles set list from mid-1960. Recorded by Elvis Presley and Jerry Lee Lewis in 1957, and later a hit for Roy Orbison in 1963.

Memphis, Tennessee

[Berry]

John – lead vocals, rhythm guitar
Paul – bass
George – lead guitar
Pete Best – drums (1962)
Ringo – drums (1963)

Studio recording and mixing

1 January 1962 – Decca Studios
Studio test recorded in mono

BBC and other performances

7 March 1962 – 8 March 1962 edition of *Here We Go*
1 June 1963 – 18 June 1963 edition of *Pop Go The Beatles*
24 June 1963 – 29 June 1963 edition of *Saturday Club*
10 July 1963 [1] – 30 July 1963 edition of *Pop Go The Beatles*
7 September 1963 [2] – 5 October 1963 edition of *Saturday Club*

Releases

	UK/US peak
Live At The BBC CD (1994) – Apple 8 31796 2 [1]	1/3
On Air – Live At The BBC Volume 2 CD (2013) – Apple 6025 37491698 [2]	12/7

=**NOTES**=

♪ The B-side to Chuck Berry's 'Back In The USA', which got to #37 in the US, while 'Memphis, Tennessee' itself got to #6 in the UK in 1963.
♪ One of four songs played at an audition for the BBC in Manchester on 8 February 1962 and recorded for the group's first ever BBC session.

Michelle

[Lennon-McCartney]

Paul – lead vocals, acoustic guitar, guitar, bass
John – backing vocals, acoustic guitar
George – backing vocals, guitar
Ringo – drums

Studio recording and mixing

3 November 1965 – Studio Two – Rubber Soul session 10 out of 15
Take 1
Tape reduction of take 1 > take 2
Overdubs onto take 2 – vocals, guitar, bass

9 November 1965 – Room 65
RM1 [1] – mono mix from take 2
RS1 [2] – stereo mix from take 2

15 November 1965 – Studio One control room
RM2 [3] – mono mix from take 2

1987 – EMI
[4] – stereo mix from take 2

Releases	UK/US peak
Rubber Soul LP (1965) – Parlophone PMC 1267 [3], PCS 3075 [2]	1
Rubber Soul LP (US, 1965) – Capitol T 2442 [1], ST 2442 [2]	1
A Collection Of Beatles Oldies LP (1966) – Parlophone PMC 7016 [3], PCS 7016 [2]	7
Nowhere Man EP (1966) – Parlophone GEP 8952 [3]	4
'Michelle' / 'Drive My Car' single (1966) – Parlophone DP 564 [1]	–
The Beatles 1962–1966 LP (1973) – Apple PCSP 717 [2]	3
The Beatles 1962–1966 LP (US, 1973) – Apple SKBO 3403 [2]	3
Love Songs LP (1977) – Parlophone PCSP 721 / Capitol SKBL 11711 [2]	7/24
The Beatles Ballads LP (1980) – Parlophone PCS 7214 [2]	17
Rubber Soul CD (1987) – EMI CDP 7 46440 2 [4]	60
The Beatles 1962–1966 CD (1993) – EMI CDP 7 97036 2 [4]	3

=== NOTES ===

♪ The first time that a four-track recording was mixed down to free up a track on the tape.
♪ Won the Grammy Award for Song of the Year.
♪ Covered by the Overlanders, reaching #1 in January 1966.
♪ The Parlophone DP single was for export only.

Midnight Special

[Trad.]

Performed by the Quarry Men/Beatles at the Casbah in 1958 and until 1960. Played through during the *Let It Be* sessions on 3 January 1969. Released by Lonnie Donegan in 1956 (reissued in 1958).

Misery

[McCartney-Lennon]

John – lead vocals, rhythm guitar
Paul – lead and harmony vocals, bass
George – lead guitar
Ringo – drums
George Martin – piano

Studio recording and mixing

11 February 1963 – Studio Two – Please Please Me session 5 out of 8
Takes 1–11

20 February 1963 – Studio One – Please Please Me session 6 out of 8
Overdubs onto take 11 – piano > takes 12–16

25 February 1963 – Studio One control room
[1] – mono mix from take 16
[2] – stereo mix from take 16

1980 – Capitol
[3] – stereo mix from [2]

2013 – EMI
[4] – stereo mix from take 1
[5] – stereo mix from take 7

BBC and other performances

6 March 1963 [6] – 12 March 1963 edition of *Here We Go*
16 March 1963 – *Saturday Club* (live)
21 March 1963 – 28 March 1963 edition of *On The Scene*
3 April 1963 – 7 April 1963 edition of *Easy Beat*
1 April 1963 – 22 April 1963 edition of *Side By Side*
24 May 1963 – 4 June 1963 edition of *Pop Go The Beatles*
3 September 1963 – 17 September 1963 edition of *Pop Go The Beatles*

Releases

	UK/US peak
Please Please Me LP (1963) – Parlophone PMC 1202 [1], PCS 3042 [2]	1
Introducing… The Beatles LP (US, 1963) – Vee Jay VJLP 1062 [1], VJSR 1062 [2]	2
The Beatles (No. 1) EP (1963) – Parlophone GEP 8883 [1]	2
Souvenir Of Their Visit To America EP (US, 1964) – Vee Jay VJEP 1903 [1]	–
'Roll Over Beethoven' / 'Misery' single (US, 1965) – Capitol Starline 6065 [1]	–
Rarities LP (US, 1980) – Capitol SHAL 12060 [3]	21
On Air – Live At The BBC Volume 2 CD (2013) – Apple 6025 37491698 [6]	12/7
The Beatles Bootleg Recordings 1963 (2013) – iTunes [4] [5]	–

Miss Ann

see 'Kansas City/Miss Ann/Lawdy Miss Clawdy'

Money (That's What I Want)

[Bradford-Gordy]

John – lead vocals, rhythm guitar
Paul – backing vocals, bass
George – backing vocals, lead guitar
Pete Best – drums (1962)
Ringo – drums (1963)
George Martin – piano

Studio recording and mixing

1 January 1962 – Decca Studios
Studio test recorded in mono

18 July 1963 – Studio Two – With The Beatles session 2 out of 9
Takes 1–5
Tape reduction of take 5 with overdubs – handclaps, vocals[?] > takes 6–7

30 July 1963 – Studio Two – With The Beatles session 3 out of 9
Tape reduction of take 7 with edit pieces > takes 8–14

21 August 1963 – Studio Three control room
RM7 – mono mix from edit of takes 6, 7 with piano overdub

30 September 1963 – Studio Two – With The Beatles session 6 out of 9
Overdubs onto take 7 [1] – piano

30 October 1963 – Studio Three control room
RS7 [2] – stereo mix from take 7 with piano overdub

17 March 1964 – Capitol
[3] – mastering of stereo mix from [2]
[4] – mastering of mono mix from [1]

1976 – Capitol
[5] – stereo mix from take 7

2013 – EMI
[6] – mono mix from take 7 with no piano overdub

BBC and other performances

21 May 1963 – 25 May 1963 edition of *Saturday Club*
1 June 1963 [7] – 18 June 1963 edition of *Pop Go The Beatles*
24 June 1963 – 29 June 1963 edition of *Saturday Club*
1 August 1963 – 3 September 1963 edition of *Pop Go The Beatles*
24 October 1963 [8] – Karlaplansstudion, Stockholm (live)
7 December 1963 – *It's The Beatles* broadcast the same day (BBC TV)
18 December 1963 [9] – 26 December 1963 edition of *From Us To You*
7 January 1964 – 15 February 1964 edition of *Saturday Club*
12 January 1964 – *Sunday Night At The London Palladium* (ATV, live)

Releases   *UK/US peak*

With The Beatles LP (1963) – Parlophone PMC 1206 [1], PCS 3045 [2]	1
With The Beatles LP (Germany, 1963) – Odeon O 83 991 [1], Odeon STO 83 568 [2]	–
The Beatles' Second Album LP (US, 1964) – Capitol T 2080 [4], ST 2080 [3]	1
The Beatles' Second Album EP (US, 1964) – Capitol SXA 2080 [3]	–
All My Loving EP (1964) – Parlophone GEP 8891 [1]	1
Rock 'n' Roll Music LP (1976) – Parlophone PCSP 719 [2]	11
Rock 'n' Roll Music LP (US, 1976) – Capitol SKBO 11537 [5]	2
Anthology 1 CD (1995) – Apple 8 34445 2 [8]	2/1
On Air – Live At The BBC Volume 2 CD (2013) – Apple 6025 37491698 [9]	12/7
The Beatles Bootleg Recordings 1963 (2013) – iTunes [6] [7]	–

=== NOTES ===

♪ The 1960 original by Barrett Strong was the first hit on the Tamla label.
♪ Uses a double twin-track recording technique.
♪ The first recording with sessions that spanned over a month.
♪ Played in concert until 1964.

Moonlight Bay

[Madden-Wenrich]

John, Paul, George, Eric Morecambe, Ernie Wise – vocals
Ringo – drums
Kenny Powell – piano

BBC and other performances

2 December 1963 [1] – *The Morecambe And Wise Show* broadcast on 18 April 1964 (ATV)

Releases .... *UK/US peak*

Anthology 1 CD (1995) – Apple 8 34445 2 [1]   2/1

┌─────────────── **NOTES** ───────────────┐

♪ The song was first published in 1912.
♪ It was a top 5 hit in May 1952 for Doris Day,
   taken from her film *On Moonlight Bay*.
♪ The group sing a short spoof of the chorus
   with Morecambe and Wise at the end of
   the show.

└──┘

Movin' 'n' Groovin'

[Hazlewood-Eddy]

Duane Eddy instrumental from 1957 that appears on a tape recorded at Paul's house in June 1960.

Mother Nature's Son

[Lennon-McCartney]

Paul – lead vocals, acoustic guitars, drums, percussion
Session musicians – two trumpets, two trombones

Studio recording and mixing

May 1968 – Kinfauns, Esher
Demo recording

9 August 1968 – Studio Two – White Album session 40 out of 81
Takes 1–24

20 August 1968 – Studio Two – White Album session 46 out of 81
Overdubs onto take 24 – brass
Tape reduction of take 24 > take 26
Overdubs onto take 26 – vocals, percussion, guitar

12 October 1968 – Studio Two control room
RM2 [1] – mono mix from take 26
RS2 [2] – stereo mix from take 26

1996 – EMI
[3] – stereo mix from take 2

2018 – EMI
[4] – stereo mix from demo
[5] – stereo mix from take 15
[6] – stereo mix from take 26

Releases *UK/US peak*

	UK/US peak
The Beatles LP (1968) – Apple PMC 7067–7068 **[1]**, PCS 7067–7068 **[2]**	1
The Beatles LP (US, 1968) – Apple SWBO-101 **[2]**	1
Anthology 3 CD (1996) – Apple 8 34451 2 **[3]**	4/1
The Beatles Deluxe CD (2018) – Apple 0602567571957 **[4] [5] [6]**	4/6

═══ NOTES ═══

♪ Another solo recording by Paul, with two trumpets and two trombones.
♪ The percussive sound is Paul tapping on the cover of a hardback copy of *The Song Of Haiwatha*.

Mr Moonlight

[Johnson]

John – lead vocals, acoustic guitar
Paul – backing vocals, bass, Hammond organ
George – backing vocals, lead guitar, African drum
Ringo – percussion

Studio recording and mixing

14 August 1964 – Studio Two – Beatles For Sale session 2 out of 8
Takes 1–4

18 October 1964 – Studio Two – Beatles For Sale session 7 out of 8
Takes 5–8
Overdubs onto take 8 – organ, percussion

27 October 1964 – Studio Two control room
RM1 – mono mix from take 4
RM2 – mono mix from take 8
[1] – edit of RM1, RM2

27 October 1964 or 4 November 1964 – Studio Two control room
RS1 – stereo mix from take 4
RS2 – stereo mix from take 8
[2] – edit of RS1, RS2

1995 – EMI
[3] – mono mix from takes 1, 4

BBC and other performances

December 1962 **[4]** – Star-Club, Hamburg (live)

Releases UK/US peak

Beatles For Sale LP (1964) – Parlophone PMC 1240 [1], PCS 3062 [2] 1
Beatles '65 LP (US, 1964) – Capitol T 2228 [1], ST 2228 [2] 1
4 – By The Beatles EP (US, 1965) – Capitol R 5365 [1] 68
Live! At The Star-Club In Hamburg, Germany; 1962 LP (1977) – Lingasong LNL 1 /
　　Lingasong LS 2 7001 [4] –
Anthology 1 CD (1995) – Apple 8 34445 2 [3] 2/1

NOTES

♪ An obscure B-side by Dr Feelgood and the Interns from 1962.
♪ Played live by the Beatles until 1963.
♪ Ringo plays a "horn-shaped conga".
♪ The opening "Mister Moonlight" on *Anthology 1* is from
　take 1, rest of the song is from take 4.

My Bonnie

[Trad. arr. Sheridan]

Tony Sheridan – lead vocals, lead guitar
John – backing vocals, rhythm guitar
Paul – backing vocals, bass
George – backing vocals, guitar
Pete Best – drums

Studio recording and mixing

22 June 1961 – Friedrich-Eberts-Halle, Hamburg
Unknown take numbers

22 June 1961 – Polydor, Hamburg
[1] – stereo mix from unknown take number (English intro)
Stereo mix from unknown take number (German intro)

1961 – Polydor, Hamburg
[2] – mono mix from [1]
[3] – mono mix from stereo mix with German intro

1995 – EMI
[4] – stereo mix from [1]

Releases UK/US peak

'My Bonnie' / 'The Saints (When The Saints Go Marching In)' single (Germany, 1961)
　– Polydor NH 24673 [3] –
'My Bonnie' / 'The Saints (When The Saints Go Marching In)' single (1962) –
　Polydor NH 66833 [2] –

'My Bonnie' / 'The Saints (When The Saints Go Marching In)' single (US, 1962) –
    Decca 31382 [2]   –
'My Bonnie (My Bonnie Lies Over The Ocean)' / 'The Saints (When The Saints Go Marching In)'
    single (US, 1964) – MGM K13213 [2, intro removed]   26
Beatles First LP (1967) – Polydor 236 201 [1, intro removed]   –
The Early Tapes Of The Beatles CD (1985) – Polydor 823701-2 [1]   –
Anthology 1 CD (1995) – Apple 8 34445 2 [4]   2/1

===== NOTES =====

♪ The Beatles back Tony Sheridan on both sides of the
   single.
♪ The recording was produced by Bert Kaempfert.
♪ *Beatles First* has a mono label, but the disc is stereo.
♪ Polydor NH 24673 has subtitle 'Mein Herz ist bei dir nur'.

New Orleans

[Guida-Royster]

Played by the Beatles in 1961–62, with **John** and any of the others grabbing a solo. It was
released by Gary US Bonds (as simply US Bonds) in 1960, reaching #6 on *Billboard*.

The Night Before

[Lennon-McCartney]

Paul – lead vocals, bass, lead guitar
John – backing vocals, electric piano
George – backing vocals, lead guitar
Ringo – drums, percussion

Studio recording and mixing

17 February 1965 – Studio Two – Help! session 3 out of 13
Takes 1–2
Overdubs onto take 2 – vocals, guitar, maracas

18 February 1965 – Studio Two control room
RM1 [1] – mono mix from take 2

23 February 1965 – Studio Two control room
RS1 [2] – stereo mix from take 2

1965 – Capitol
[3] – mono mix from [2]

1987 – EMI
[4] – stereo mix from take 2

BBC and other performances

26 May 1965 – 7 June 1965 edition of *The Beatles Invite You To Take A Ticket To Ride*

Releases   *UK/US peak*

Help! LP (1965) – Parlophone PMC 1255 [1], PCS 3071 [2]	1
Help! LP (US, 1965) – Capitol MAS 2386 [3], SMAS 2386 [2]	1
Rock 'n' Roll Music LP (1976) – Parlophone PCSP 719 / Capitol SKBO 11537 [2]	11/2
Help! CD (1987) – EMI CDP 7 46439 2 [4]	61

═══════ **NOTES** ═══════

♪ Chronologically, the last Lennon-McCartney song to be performed for the BBC.

No Reply

[Lennon-McCartney]

John – lead vocals, acoustic guitar
Paul – harmony vocals, bass
George – acoustic guitar
Ringo – drums
George Martin – piano

Studio recording and mixing

3 June 1964 – Studio Two – A Hard Day's Night session 11 out of 12
Demo recording

30 September 1964 – Studio Two – Beatles For Sale session 4 out of 8
Takes 1–8

16 October 1964 – Studio One control room
RM2 [1] – mono mix from take 8

4 November 1964 – Studio Two control room
RS1 [2] – stereo mix from take 8

1995 – EMI
[3] – mono mix from demo
[4] – mono mix from take 2

Releases   *UK/US peak*

Beatles For Sale LP (1964) – Parlophone PMC 1240 [1], PCS 3062 [2]	1
Beatles For Sale EP (1965) – Parlophone GEP 8931 [1]	1

Beatles '65 LP (US, 1964) – Capitol T 2228 [1], ST 2228 [2]   1
Anthology 1 CD (1995) – Apple 8 34445 2 [3] [4]   2/1

---NOTES---

♪ The demo was recorded for Epstein stablemate Tommy Quickly
   to record, but he reportedly turned it down.
♪ The first song in which John sets out to tell a story.

Nobody's Child

[Foree-Coben]

Tony Sheridan – lead vocals, lead guitar
John – rhythm guitar
Paul – bass
George – guitar
Pete Best – drums

Studio recording and mixing

22 June 1961 – Friedrich-Eberts-Halle, Hamburg
Unknown take numbers

23 June 1961 – Polydor, Hamburg
[1] – stereo mix from unknown take number

1964 – Atlantic Studios, USA
[2] – mono mix from edit of [1]

Releases   *UK/US peak*

'Ain't She Sweet' / 'Nobody's Child' single (US, 1964) – Atco 45-6308 [2]   –
Beatles First LP (1967) – Polydor 236 201 [1]   –
The Early Tapes Of The Beatles CD (1985) – Polydor 823701-2 [1]   –

---NOTES---

♪ Recorded by Lonnie Donegan on his debut 10" LP *Showcase*.
♪ The Beatles backing Tony Sheridan, produced by Bert Kaempfert.

Norwegian Wood (This Bird Has Flown)

[Lennon-McCartney]

John – lead vocals, acoustic guitar
Paul – harmony vocals, bass
George – 12-string acoustic guitar, sitar
Ringo – tambourine, bass drum, crash cymbal

Studio recording and mixing

12 October 1965 – Studio Two – Rubber Soul session 1 out of 15
Take 1
Overdubs onto take 1 – vocals, sitar, tambourine, maracas

21 October 1965 – Studio Two – Rubber Soul session 6 out of 15
Remake takes 2–4
Overdubs onto take 4 – sitar, tambourine

25 October 1965 – Studio Two control room
RM1 [1] – mono mix from take 4

26 October 1965 – Studio Two control room
RS1 [2] – stereo mix from take 4

Unknown date – EMI
[3] – stereo mix from take 4

1987 – EMI
[4] – stereo mix from take 4

1995 – EMI
[5] – stereo mix from take 1

Releases

	UK/US peak
Rubber Soul LP (1965) – Parlophone PMC 1267 [1], PCS 3075 [2]	1
Rubber Soul LP (US, 1965) – Capitol T 2442 [1], ST 2442 [2]	1
The Beatles 1962–1966 LP (1973) – Apple PCSP 717 [2]	3
The Beatles 1962–1966 LP (US, 1973) – Apple SKBO 3403 [2]	3
Love Songs LP (1977) – Parlophone PCSP 721 / Capitol SKBL 11711 [3]	7/24
The Beatles Ballads LP (1980) – Parlophone PCS 7214 [3]	17
Rubber Soul CD (1987) – EMI CDP 7 46440 2 [4]	60
The Beatles 1962–1966 CD (1993) – EMI CDP 7 97036 2 [4]	3
Anthology 2 CD (1996) – Apple 8 34448 2 [5]	1/1

===== NOTES =====

♪ Written by John about an affair he was having at the time.
♪ Reputedly the first sitar on a pop record.

Not A Second Time

[Lennon-McCartney]

John – lead vocals, acoustic guitar
Paul – bass
George – possibly acoustic guitar

Ringo – drums
George Martin – piano

Studio recording and mixing

11 September 1963 – Studio Two – With The Beatles session 4 out of 9
Takes 1–5
Overdubs onto take 5 – vocals, piano > takes 6–9

30 September 1963 – Studio Two control room
RM9 [1] – mono mix from take 9

29 October 1963 – Studio Two control room
RS9 [2] – stereo mix from take 9

19 December 1963 – Capitol
[3] – mastering of stereo mix from [2]
[4] – mastering of mono mix from [3]

Releases   *UK/US peak*

With The Beatles LP (1963) – Parlophone PMC 1206 [1], PCS 3045 [2]	1
With The Beatles LP (Germany, 1963) – Odeon O 83 991 [1], Odeon STO 83 568 [2]	–
Meet The Beatles! LP (US, 1964) – Capitol T 2047 [4], ST 2047 [3]	1

═══ NOTES ═══

♪ The first Beatles song significantly in a minor key.
♪ The first piano solo on a Beatles recording, played by George Martin.

Not Guilty

[Harrison]

George – lead vocals, guitar
John – harpsichord
Paul – bass
Ringo – drums

Studio recording and mixing

May 1968 – Kinfauns, Esher
Demo recording

7 August 1968 – Studio Two – White Album session 38 out of 81
Takes 1–46

8 August 1968 – Studio Two – White Album session 39 out of 81
Takes 47–97

Tape reduction of take 97 > takes 98–101

9 August 1968 – *Studio Two* – *White Album session 40 out of 81*
Tape reduction of take 97 > take 102
Overdubs onto take 102 – drums, guitar, bass

12 August 1968 – *Studio Two* – *White Album session 41 out of 81*
Overdubs onto take 102 – vocals

1984 – *AIR Studios*
[1] – stereo mix from take 102, edited

2018 – *EMI*
[2] – stereo mix from demo
[3] – stereo mix from take 102

Releases   UK/US peak

Anthology 3 CD (1996) – Apple 8 34451 2 [1]   4/1
The Beatles Deluxe CD (2018) – Apple 0602567571957 [2] [3]   4/6

NOTES

♪ The *Anthology 3* version
   is heavily edited and
   treated with flanging.
♪ George re-recorded
   the song in 1978 and
   released it on his 1979
   George Harrison LP.

Nothin' Shakin'

[Fontaine-Calacrai-Lampert-Gluck]

George – lead vocals, guitar
John – rhythm guitar
Paul – bass,
Ringo – drums

BBC and other performances

December 1962 [1] – Star-Club, Hamburg (live)
10 July 1963 [2] – 23 July 1963 edition of *Pop Go The Beatles*

Releases   UK/US peak

Live! At The Star-Club In Hamburg, Germany; 1962 LP (1977) – Lingasong LNL 1 /
   Lingasong LS 2 7001 [1]   –
Live At The BBC CD (1994) – Apple 8 31796 2 [2]   1/3

========= NOTES =========

♪ A single from 1958 by Eddie Fontaine, who appeared in the movie *The Girl Can't Help It* with Jayne Mansfield.

Nowhere Man

[Lennon-McCartney]

John – lead vocals, acoustic guitar, possibly lead guitar
Paul – harmony and backing vocals, bass
George – harmony and backing vocals, lead guitar
Ringo – drums

Studio recording and mixing

21 October 1965 – Studio Two – Rubber Soul session 6 out of 15
Takes 1–2
Overdubs onto take 2 – vocals

22 October 1965 – Studio Two – Rubber Soul session 7 out of 15
Remake takes 3–5
Overdubs onto take 4 – vocals, guitar

25 October 1965 – Studio Two control room
RM1 [1] – mono mix from take 4

26 October 1965 – Studio Two control room
RS1 [2] – stereo mix from take 4

1987 – EMI
[3] – stereo mix from take 4

1999 – EMI
[4] – stereo mix from take 4

BBC and other performances

24 June 1966 – *Die Beatles* broadcast on 5 July 1966 (ZDF TV, Germany)

Releases

	UK/US peak
Rubber Soul LP (1965) – Parlophone PMC 1267 [1], PCS 3075 [2]	1
"Yesterday" ... And Today LP (US, 1966) – Capitol T 2553 [1], ST 2553 [2]	1
Nowhere Man EP (1966) – Parlophone GEP 8952 [1]	4
'Nowhere Man' / 'What Goes On' single (US, 1966) – Capitol 5587 [1]	3
The Beatles 1962–1966 LP (1973) – Apple PCSP 717 [2]	3
The Beatles 1962–1966 LP (US, 1973)– Apple SKBO 3403 [2]	3
The Beatles Ballads LP (1980) – Parlophone PCS 7214 [2]	17
Rubber Soul CD (1987) – EMI CDP 7 46440 2 [3]	60

The Beatles 1962–1966 CD (1993) – EMI CDP 7 97036 2 **[3]**   3
Yellow Submarine Songtrack CD (1999) – Apple 5 21481 2 **[4]**   8/15

NOTES

♪ The first harmonised a capella introduction.
♪ Played live by the Beatles until 1966.
♪ John's handwritten lyrics were sold at
  auction for $455,000 at Christie's in New
  York in 2003.

Ob-La-Di, Ob-La-Da

[Lennon-McCartney]

Paul – lead vocals, bass, possibly drums
John – backing vocals, piano
George – backing vocals, acoustic guitar
Ringo – possibly drums, percussion
Session musicians – three saxophones

Studio recording and mixing

May 1968 – Kinfauns, Esher
Demo recording

3 July 1968 – Studio Two – White Album session 18 out of 81
Takes 1–7
Overdubs onto take 7 – vocals, guitar
Overdubs onto take 4 – guitar

4 July 1968 – Studio Two – White Album session 19 out of 81
Overdubs onto take 4 – vocals
Tape reduction take 4 > take 5
Overdubs onto take 5 – vocals

5 July 1968 – Studio Two – White Album session 20 out of 81
Overdubs onto take 5 – saxophones, bongos, piccolo, guitar

8 July 1968 – Studio Two – White Album session 21 out of 81
Remake takes 1–12
Tape reduction take 12 > take 13
Overdubs onto take 13 – vocals, percussion

9 July 1968 – Studio Three – White Album session 22 out of 81
Re-remake takes 20–21
Overdubs onto take 13 – vocals, drums
Tape reduction take 13 > take 22
Overdubs onto take 22 – vocals, handclaps

11 July 1968 – Studio Three – White Album session 24 out of 81
Overdubs onto take 22 – saxophones, piano
Tape reduction take 22 > takes 23, 24
Overdubs onto take 23 – bass

15 July 1968 – Studio Two – White Album session 26 out of 81
Overdubs onto take 23 – vocals

12 October 1968 – Studio Two control room
RS4 [1] – stereo mix from take 23
RM10 [2] – mono mix from take 23

1996 – EMI
[3] – stereo mix from take 5 (5 July)

2018 – EMI
[4] – stereo mix from demo
[5] – stereo mix from take 3
[6] – stereo mix from take 23

Releases

	UK/US peak
The Beatles LP (1968) – Apple PMC 7067–7068 [2], PCS 7067–7068 [1]	1
The Beatles LP (US, 1968) – Apple SWBO-101 [1]	1
The Beatles 1967–1970 LP (1973) – Apple PCSP 718 [1]	2
The Beatles 1967–1970 LP (US, 1973) – Apple SKBO 3404 [1]	1
'Ob-La-Di, Ob-La-Da' / 'Julia' (US, 1976) – Capitol 4347 [1]	49
Anthology 3 CD (1996) – Apple 8 34451 2 [3]	4/1
The Beatles Deluxe CD (2018) – Apple 0602567571957 [4] [5] [6]	4/6

NOTES

♪ Remade twice – the first time a recording by
  recruited musicians was rejected.
♪ A UK #1 for Marmalade in January 1969.

Octopus's Garden

[Starkey]

Ringo – lead vocals, drums, percussion
Paul – harmony and backing vocals, piano, bass
John – guitar
George – harmony and backing vocals, lead guitar, synthesiser

Studio recording and mixing

26 January 1969 – Apple Studio – Let It Be session 6 out of 17
Takes 26.7, 26.9 [1, edited]

26 April 1969 – Studio Two – Abbey Road session 6 out of 42
Takes 1–32
Overdubs onto take 32 – piano

29 April 1969 – Studio Three – Abbey Road session 7 out of 42
Overdubs onto take 32 – vocals

17 July 1969 – Studio Two – Abbey Road session 22 out of 42
Overdubs onto take 32 – vocals, piano, effects

18 July 1969 – Studio Three – Abbey Road session 23 out of 42
Overdubs onto take 32 – vocals, percussion

18 July 1969 – Studio Two control room
RM7 – mono mix from take 32
RS14 [2] – stereo mix from take 32

1996 – EMI
[3] – stereo mix from take 2

2004–06 – EMI
[4] – stereo mix from take 32, fades into 'Sun King' take 35: includes samples from 'Goodnight' (orchestra); 'Yellow Submarine' (sound effects); 'Lovely Rita', 'Polythene Pam' (drums); 'Helter Skelter' (guitar)

Releases

	UK/US peak
Abbey Road LP (1969) – Apple PCS 7088 [2]	1
Abbey Road LP (US, 1969) – Apple SO 383 [2]	1
Let It Be movie (1970) [1]	
The Beatles 1967–1970 LP (1973) – Apple PCSP 718 [2]	2
The Beatles 1967–1970 LP (US, 1973) – Apple SKBO 3404 [2]	1
Anthology 3 CD (1996) – Apple 8 34451 2 [3]	4/1
Love CD (2006) – Apple 0946 3 80790 2 6 [4]	3/4

═══════ NOTES ═══════

♪ Billed as 'In An Octopus's Garden (Or I Would Like To Live Up A Tree)' in an NME interview with Ringo on 29 March.
♪ The only *Abbey Road* track mixed for mono, although this was unused.

Oh! Darling

[Lennon-McCartney]

Paul – lead vocals, piano, guitar
John – backing vocals, bass
George – backing vocals, guitar
Ringo – drums

Studio recording and mixing

6 January 1969 – *Twickenham Film Studios* – *Let It Be rehearsal session*
Take 6.1 [1]

27 January 1969 – *Apple Studio* – *Let It Be session 7 out of 17*
Rehearsal

20 April 1969 – *Studio Three* – *Abbey Road session 5 out of 42*
Takes 1–26
Overdubs onto take 26 – organ

26 April 1969 – *Studio Two* – *Abbey Road session 6 out of 42*
Overdubs onto take 26 – vocals

17 July 1969 – *Studio Three* – *Abbey Road session 22 out of 42*
Overdubs onto take 16 – vocals

18 July 1969 – *Studio Three* – *Abbey Road session 23 out of 42*
Overdubs onto take 26 – vocals

22 July 1969 – *Studio Three* – *Abbey Road session 25 out of 42*
Overdubs onto take 26 – vocals

23 July 1969 – *Studio Three* – *Abbey Road session 26 out of 42*
Overdubs onto take 26 – vocals

8 August 1969 – *Studio Three* – *Abbey Road session 38 out of 42*
Overdubs onto take 26 – guitar, tambourine

11 August 1969 – *Studio Two* – *Abbey Road session 39 out of 42*
Overdubs onto take 26 – vocals

12 August 1969 – *Studio Two control room*
RS9 [2] – stereo mix from take 26

1996 – *EMI*
[3] – stereo mix from rehearsal

Releases   *UK/US peak*

Abbey Road LP (1969) – Apple PCS 7088 [2]	1
Abbey Road LP (US, 1969) – Apple SO 383 [2]	1
Let It Be movie (1970) [1]	
Anthology 3 CD (1996) – Apple 8 34451 2 [3]	4/1

=====NOTES=====

♪ The 6 January recording is a brief run-through by Paul on the piano.
♪ The 11 August session was John's last recording on Beatles track.

Old Brown Shoe

[Harrison]

George – lead vocals, guitars, Hammond organ
Paul – harmony vocals, piano, bass
John – harmony vocals, possibly Hammond organ
Ringo – drums

Studio recording and mixing

25 February 1969 – unknown studio – Abbey Road rehearsal session
Demo takes 1–2
Overdubs onto demo take 2 – guitar

16 April 1969 – Studio Three – Abbey Road session 3 out of 42
Demo take 1
Takes 1–4
Overdubs onto take 4 – bass, guitar, vocals

18 April 1969 – Studio Three – Abbey Road session 4 out of 42
Overdubs onto take 4 – organ, guitar

18 April 1969 – Studio Three control room
RS23 [1] – stereo mix from take 4

1996 – EMI
[2] – stereo mix from demo take 2

Releases   *UK/US peak*

'The Ballad Of John And Yoko' / 'Old Brown Shoe' single (1969) – Apple R 5786 [1]	1
'The Ballad Of John And Yoko' / 'Old Brown Shoe' single (US, 1969) – Apple 2531 [1]	–
Hey Jude LP (US, 1970) – Apple SW 385 [1]	2
The Beatles 1967–1970 LP (1973) – Apple PCSP 718 [1]	2
The Beatles 1967–1970 LP (US, 1973) – Apple SKBO 3404 [1]	1
Past Masters 2 CD (1988) – EMI CDP 7 90044 2 [1]	46/–
Anthology 3 CD (1996) – Apple 8 34451 2 [2]	4/1

=== NOTES ===

♪ Uses a Challen Jangle Box piano.
♪ The first Capitol B-side not to make the *Billboard* top 100.

One After 909

[Lennon-McCartney]

John – lead vocals, rhythm guitar
Paul – harmony vocals, bass

George – lead guitar
Ringo – drums
Billy Preston – electric piano

Studio recording and mixing

5 March 1963 – Studio Two – Please Please Me session 7 out of 8
Takes 1–4
Edit piece take 5

9 January 1969 – Twickenham Film Studios – Let It Be rehearsal session
Takes 9.36, 9.37, 9.38 [1]

30 January 1969 – Apple rooftop – Let It Be session 9 out of 17
Take 30.6

23 March 1970 – Room 4
RS3 [2] – stereo mix from take 30.6

1995 – EMI
[3] – mono mix from takes 3–5 (in sequence)
[4] – mono mix from edit of takes 4, 5

2002 – EMI
[5] – stereo mix from take 30.6

2013 – EMI
[6] – stereo mix from takes 1, 2

Releases   *UK/US peak*

Let It Be LP (1970) – Apple PXS1, PCS 7096 [2]	1
Let It Be LP (US, 1970) – Apple AR 34001 [2]	1
Let It Be movie (1970) [1] [2]	
Anthology 1 CD (1995) – Apple 8 34445 2 [3] [4]	2/1
Let It Be… Naked CD (2003) – Apple 24359 57142 [5]	7/5
The Beatles Bootleg Recordings 1963 (2013) – iTunes [6]	–

```
━━━━━━━━━━━━ NOTES ━━━━━━━━━━━━
```

♪ Written in the Quarry Men days, first
  recorded in 1963, released in 1970.
♪ Two versions were also recorded
  at Paul's house in June 1960, and a
  further version on a rehearsal tape
  recorded at the Cavern in December
  1962.
♪ Played live by the Quarry Men/Beatles
  until 1962.

Only A Northern Song

[Harrison]

George – lead vocals, organ
Paul – bass, trumpet
John – possibly piano
Ringo – drums
Glockenspiel, tambourine, taped effects

Studio recording and mixing

13 February 1967 – Studio Two – Yellow Submarine session 1 out of 15
Takes 1–9

14 February 1967 – Studio Two – Yellow Submarine session 2 out of 15
Tape reduction of take 3 > takes 10–12
Overdubs onto take 12 – vocals

20 April 1967 – Studio Two – Yellow Submarine session 3 out of 15
Overdubs onto take 3 – bass, trumpet, glockenspiel
Overdubs onto take 11 – vocals, taped effects

21 April 1967 – Studio Two control room
RM6 [1] – mono mix from takes 3, 11

29 October 1968 – Studio Two control room
RS1 [2] – mock stereo mix from RM6

25 November 1968 – EMI
[3] – mono mix from [2]

1995 – EMI
[4] – stereo mix from takes 3, 12

1999 – EMI
[5] – stereo mix from takes 3, 11

Releases
	UK/US peak
Yellow Submarine movie (1968) [1]	
Yellow Submarine LP (1969) – Apple PMC 7070 [3], PCS 7070 [2]	3
Yellow Submarine LP (US, 1969) – Apple SW 153 [2]	2
Anthology 2 CD (1996) – Apple 8 34448 2 [4]	1/1
Yellow Submarine Songtrack CD (1999) – Apple 5 21481 2 [5]	8/15
Mono Masters CD (2009) – Apple 6 849582 4 [1]	–

♪ NOTES

♪ Nearly two years between the start of recording and the track's release.

Ooh! My Soul

[Penniman]

Paul – lead vocals, bass
John – rhythm guitar
George – lead guitar
Ringo – drums

BBC and other performances

1 August 1963 [1] – 27 August 1963 edition of *Pop Go The Beatles*

Releases   *UK/US peak*

Live At The BBC CD (1994) – Apple 8 31796 2 [1]   1/3

NOTES

- ♪ A minor hit for Little Richard in 1958.
- ♪ The only BBC release to run into following broadcast track, including the linking speech track.
- ♪ Part of the Beatles' set until 1963.

Open (Your Lovin' Arms)

[Knox]

Lead vocals, **George**. Part of the Beatles' repertoire in 1962. It was a Buddy Knox B-side (to 'Chi-Hua-Hua') from 1962.

Over The Rainbow

[Arlen-Harburg]

Lead vocals, **Paul**. Part of the Beatles' set until 1962, based on the version by Gene Vincent from 1959.

P.S. I Love You

[Lennon-McCartney]

Paul – lead vocals, bass
John – harmony vocals, guitar
George – harmony vocals, guitar
Pete Best – drums (6 June)
Ringo – drums (6 September and BBC dates), maracas (11 September)
Andy White – drums (11 September)

Studio recording and mixing

6 June 1962 – Studio Two or Three – Please Please Me session 1 out of 8
Unknown take numbers

11 September 1962 – Studio Two – Please Please Me session 3 out of 8
Takes 1–10

11 September 1962 – Studio Two control room
[1] – mono mix from take 10

25 February 1963 – Studio One control room
[2] – mock stereo mix from take 10

1965 – Capitol
[3] – mono mix from [2]

BBC and other performances

25 October 1962 – 26 October 1962 edition of *Here We Go*
27 November 1962 – 4 December 1962 edition of *The Talent Spot*
17 June 1963 [4] – 25 June 1963 edition of *Pop Go The Beatles*

Releases   *UK/US peak*

'Love Me Do' / 'P.S. I Love You' single (1962) – Parlophone 45-R 4949 [1]	17
Please Please Me LP (1963) – Parlophone PMC 1202 [1], PCS 3042 [2]	1
Introducing… The Beatles LP (US, 1963) – Vee Jay VJLP 1062 [1], VJSR 1062 [2]	2
All My Loving EP (1964) – Parlophone GEP 8891 [1]	1
'Love Me Do' / 'P.S. I Love You' single (US, 1964) – Tollie 9008 [1]	10
The Early Beatles LP (US, 1965) – Capitol T 2309 [3], ST 2309 [2]	43
'Love Me Do' / 'P.S. I Love You' single (US, 1965) – Capitol Starline 6062 [1]	–
Love Songs LP (1977) – Parlophone PCSP 721 / Capitol SKBL 11711 [2]	7/24
Live At The BBC CD (1994) – Apple 8 31796 2 [4]	1/3

═══ NOTES ═══

♪ With Ringo on maracas, and session player Andy White on drums.
♪ Played live in 1962–63.
♪ The Tollie single B-side made the top ten in the US in 1964, the only non-Capitol B-side to do so.

Pantomime: Everywhere It's Christmas
[Lennon-McCartney-Harrison-Starkey]

John, Paul, George, Ringo – vocals, piano, percussion, effects

Studio recording and mixing

25 November 1966 – Dick James' home studio
Unknown takes – Christmas message for fan club members

2 December 1966 – Room 53
[1] – edit of unknown takes

Releases

From Then To You LP (1970) – Apple LYN 2153/2154 [1]   –

=== NOTES ===

♪ The fourth Christmas flexidisc and the first to be produced by George Martin.
♪ Recorded between sessions for 'Strawberry Fields Forever'.
♪ Features a series of songs and sketches, with Paul on piano.

Paperback Writer

[Lennon-McCartney]

Paul – lead vocals, lead guitar, bass
John – harmony and backing vocals, rhythm guitar
George – harmony and backing vocals, tambourine
Ringo – drums

Studio recording and mixing

13 April 1966 – Studio Three – Revolver session 5 out of 33
Takes 1–2
Overdubs onto take 2 – vocals

14 April 1966 – Studio Three – Revolver session 6 out of 33
Overdubs onto take 2 – bass, guitar, vocals

14 April 1966 – Studio Two control room
RM2 [1] – mono mix from take 2

31 October 1966 – Studio Two control room
RS3 [2] – stereo mix from take 2
[3] – stereo mix [2] with channels reversed

2015 – EMI
[4] – stereo mix from take 2

Releases

'Paperback Writer' / 'Rain' single (1966) – Parlophone R 5452 [1]   1
'Paperback Writer' / 'Rain' single (US, 1966) – Capitol 5651 [1]   1

A Collection Of Beatles Oldies LP (1966) – Parlophone PMC 7016 [1], PCS 7016 [2]   7
Hey Jude LP (US, 1970) – Apple SW 385 [3]   2
The Beatles 1962–1966 LP (1973) – Apple PCSP 717 [2]   3
The Beatles 1962–1966 LP (US, 1973)– Apple SKBO 3403 [3]   3
20 Greatest Hits LP (1982) – Parlophone PCTC 260 / Capitol SV-12245 [2]   10/50
Past Masters 2 CD (1988) – EMI CDP 7 90044 2 [2]   46/–
The Beatles 1962–1966 CD (1993) – EMI CDP 7 97036 2 [2]   3
Tomorrow Never Knows (2012) – iTunes [2]   44/24
1+ CD/DVD (2015) – Apple 6205 47567727 [4]   5/6

NOTES

♪ Two promotional films were made on 19–20 May 1966.
♪ The disc was cut using Automatic Transient Overload Control to boost the bass.
♪ Played live on the 1966 tour.

Peaches And Cream

[Williams]

Lead vocals, **John**. Played by the Beatles around 1960–61. It was recorded by Larry Williams in 1958.

Peggy Sue

[Holly-Allison-Petty]

Lead vocals, **John**. Performed by the Quarry Men and Beatles until 1962. In 1957, Buddy Holly reached #3 on *Billboard* and #6 in the UK, where it was his first hit. Appears on John's *Rock 'n' Roll* LP from 1975.

Penny Lane

[Lennon-McCartney]

Paul – lead vocals, piano, bass, harmonium, tambourine
John – backing vocals, piano, rhythm guitar, congas
George – backing vocals, lead guitar
Ringo – drums, possibly tubular bells
George Martin – piano
David Mason – piccolo trumpet
Session musicians – four flutes, two trumpets, two piccolos, flügelhorn (9 January); two trumpets, two oboes, two cor anglais, double bass (12 January)

Studio recording and mixing

29 December 1966 – Studio Two – Sgt Pepper session 11 out of 56
Takes 1–6 (piano only)

Overdubs onto take 6 – piano, tambourine, harmonium, effects

30 December 1966 – *Studio Two – Sgt Pepper session 12 out of 56*
Tape reduction of take 6 > take 7
Overdubs onto take 7 – vocals

4 January 1967 – *Studio Two – Sgt Pepper session 13 out of 56*
Overdubs onto take 7 – piano, guitar, vocals

5 January 1967 – *Studio Two – Sgt Pepper session 14 out of 56*
Overdubs onto take 7 – vocals

6 January 1967 – *Studio Two – Sgt Pepper session 15 out of 56*
Tape reduction of take 7 > take 8
Overdubs onto take 8 – bass, guitar, drums
Tape reduction of take 8 > take 9
Overdubs onto take 9 – piano, handclaps, vocals

9 January 1967 – *Studio Two – Sgt Pepper session 16 out of 56*
Overdubs onto take 9 – brass, woodwind

10 January 1967 – *Studio Three – Sgt Pepper session 17 out of 56*
Overdubs onto take 9 – vocals, tubular bells, effects

12 January 1967 – *Studio Three – Sgt Pepper session 18 out of 56*
Overdubs onto take 9 – brass, woodwind, double bass

17 January 1967 – *Studio Two – Sgt Pepper session 19 out of 56*
Overdubs onto take 9 – piccolo trumpet

17 January 1967 – *Studio Two control room*
RM11 [1] – mono mix from take 9

25 January 1967 – *Studio One control room*
RM14 [2] – mono mix from take 9

1967 – *Capitol*
[3] – mock stereo mix from [2]

30 September 1971 – *AIR Studios*
[4] – stereo mix from take 9

c.1972 – *Capitol*
[5] – mock stereo mix from [2]

1980 – *Capitol*
[6] – stereo mix from [1] and [4]

1995 – *EMI*
[7] – stereo mix from takes 6–9

2015 – EMI
[8] – stereo mix from take 9

2016/17 – EMI
[9] – stereo mix from take 6
[10] – stereo mix from vocal overdubs onto take 7
[11] – stereo mix from takes 6–9

Releases   *UK/US peak*

'Strawberry Fields Forever' / 'Penny Lane' single (1967) – Parlophone R 5570 [2]	2
'Strawberry Fields Forever' / 'Penny Lane' single (US, 1967) – Capitol 5810 [1] [2]	1
Magical Mystery Tour LP (US, 1967) – Capitol MAL 2835 [2], SMAL 2835 [3]	1
Magical Mystery Tour LP (Germany, 1971) – Hör Zu SHZE 327 / Apple 1C 072-04449 [4]	–
The Beatles 1967–1970 LP (1973) – Apple PCSP 718 [4]	2
The Beatles 1967–1970 LP (US, 1973) – Apple SKBO 3404 [5]	1
Rarities LP (US, 1980) – Capitol SHAL 12060 [6]	21
20 Greatest Hits LP (US, 1982) – Capitol SV-12245 [4]	50
Magical Mystery Tour CD (1987) – EMI CDP 7 48062 2 [4]	52
The Beatles 1967–1970 CD (1993) – EMI CDP 7 97039 2 [4]	4
Anthology 2 CD (1996) – Apple 8 34448 2 [7]	1/1
1+ CD/DVD (2015) – Apple 6205 47567727 [8]	5/6
Sgt Pepper's Lonely Hearts Club Band Deluxe CD (2017) – Apple 0602557455328 [1] [2] [9] [10] [11]	1/3

NOTES

♪ A promotional film was made in Stratford, London and Knole Park, Sevenoaks on 5 and 7 February 1967.

♪ Stalled at #2 in the UK behind Englebert Humperdinck's 'Release Me', which became the biggest selling single of 1967.

♪ The subject of a leader article in *The Times* on 1 April 1967.

♪ The remix for the deluxe *Sgt Pepper* was possible as a supposedly lost 4-track of piano, harmonium and drums was discovered – 'Strawberry Fields Forever' uses the *1+* mix.

Peppermint Twist

[Schroeder-Gold]

Briefly part of the Beatles' set in 1962, with **Pete Best** singing lead. A US #1 for Joey Dee and the Starliters in 1961.

A Picture Of You

[Beveridge-Oakman]

George – lead vocals, lead guitar
John – backing vocals, rhythm guitar
Paul – backing vocals, bass
Pete Best – drums

BBC and other performances

11 June 1962 – 15 June 1962 edition of *Here We Go*

═ NOTES ═

♪ A UK #2 hit for Joe Brown in 1962 – it was actually the B-side of 'A Lay-About's Lament' but 'A Picture Of You' became the hit. Like 'Please Please Me', it reached #1 on all but the "official" charts.
♪ One of only two titles recorded for the BBC that have not yet been released, the other being 'Dream Baby'.
♪ Performed in concert by the Beatles in 1962.

Piggies

[Harrison]

George – lead vocals, guitar
John – harmony vocals
Paul – bass, harmony vocals
Ringo – tambourine, bass drum
Chris Thomas – harpsichord
Session musicians – four violins, two violas, two cellos

Studio recording and mixing

May 1968 – Kinfauns, Esher
Demo recording

19 September 1968 – Studio One and Two – White Album session 64 out of 81
Takes 1–11

20 September 1968 – Studio Two – White Album session 65 out of 81
Four- to eight-track tape copying of take 11 > take 12
Overdubs onto take 12 – vocals, effects

10 October 1968 – Studio Two – White Album session 78 out of 81
Overdubs onto take 12 – strings

11 October 1968 – Studio Two control room
RM4 [1] – mono mix from take 12
RS3 [2] – stereo mix from take 12

1996 – EMI
[3] – stereo mix from demo

2018 – EMI
[4] – stereo mix from demo
[5] – stereo mix from take 12 (without vocals)
[6] – stereo mix from take 12

Releases
UK/US peak

The Beatles LP (1968) – Apple PMC 7067–7068 [1], PCS 7067–7068 [2]	1
The Beatles LP (US, 1968) – Apple SWBO-101 [2]	1
Anthology 3 CD (1996) – Apple 8 34451 2 [3]	4/1
The Beatles Deluxe CD (2018) – Apple 0602567571957 [4] [5] [6]	4/6

═══════ **NOTES** ═══════

♪ The "one more time" at the end of the track is edited on from speech at the beginning of the take.
♪ Sound effects were added before mixing, apart from the end grunts.

Pinwheel Twist

[Lennon-McCartney]

Written by Paul in 1962, and performed that year, on occasion with **Pete Best** singing lead and Paul on drums. Inspired by 'Peppermint Twist'.

Please Mister Postman

[Dobbins-Garrett-Holland-Bateman-Gorman]

John – lead vocals, rhythm guitar
Paul – backing vocals, bass
George – backing vocals, lead guitar
Pete Best – drums (7 March 1962)
Ringo – drums

Studio recording and mixing

30 July 1963 – Studio Two – With The Beatles session 3 out of 9
Takes 1–2
Overdubs onto take 2 – vocals > take 3
Takes 4–7
Overdubs onto take 7 – vocals, handclaps > take 9

21 August 1963 – *Studio Two control room*
RM9 [1] – mono mix from take 9

29 October 1963 – *Studio Two control room*
RS9 [2] – stereo mix from take 9

17 March 1964 – *Capitol*
[3] – mastering of stereo mix from [2]
[4] – mastering of mono mix from [2]

BBC and other performances

7 March 1962 – 8 March 1962 edition of *Here We Go*
10 July 1963 [5] – 30 July 1963 edition of *Pop Go The Beatles*
28 February 1964 – 30 March 1964 edition of *From Us To You*

Releases

	UK/US peak
With The Beatles LP (1963) – Parlophone PMC 1206 [1], PCS 3045 [2]	1
With The Beatles LP (Germany, 1963) – Odeon O 83 991 [1], Odeon STO 83 568 [2]	–
'Roll Over Beethoven' / 'Please Mister Postman' single (Canada, 1963) Capitol 72133 [1]	–
The Beatles' Second Album LP (US, 1964) – Capitol T 2080 [4], ST 2080 [3]	1
The Beatles' Second Album EP (US, 1964) – Capitol SXA 2080 [3]	–
Four By The Beatles EP (US, 1964)– Capitol EAP 1-2121 [3]	92
Live At The BBC CD (1994) – Apple 8 31796 2 [5]	1/3

```
============ NOTES ============

 ♪ The first of three Tamla
   tracks to feature on
   With The Beatles.
 ♪ Performed by the Beatles
   on their first radio
   broadcast in March 1962.
```

Please Please Me

[McCartney-Lennon]

John – lead vocals, rhythm guitar, harmonica
Paul – harmony and backing vocals, bass
George – harmony and backing vocals, lead guitar
Ringo – drums (26 November)
Andy White – drums (11 September)

Studio recording and mixing

11 September 1962 – *Studio Two* – *Please Please Me session 3 out of 8*
Unknown take numbers

26 November 1962 – *Studio Two* – *Please Please Me session 4 out of 8*
Remake takes 1–15
Overdubs onto take 15 – harmonica > takes 16–18

30 November 1962 – *Studio Two control room*
[1] – mono mix from edit of unknown remake take numbers

25 February 1963 – *Studio One control room*
[2] – stereo mix from edit of remake takes 16–18

1965 – *Capitol*
[3] – stereo mix from [2]
[4] – mono mix from [3]

1995 – *EMI*
[5] – mono mix from unknown 11 September take number

BBC and other performances

16 January 1963 – 25 January 1963 edition of *Here We Go*
22 January 1963 – 26 January 1963 edition of *Saturday Club*
22 January 1963 – 29 January 1963 edition of *The Talent Spot*
20 February 1963 – *Parade Of The Pops* (live)
6 March 1963 [6] – 12 March 1963 edition of *Here We Go*
16 March 1963 – *Saturday Club* (live)
21 March 1963 – 28 March 1963 edition of *On The Scene*
1 April 1963 – 22 April 1963 edition of *Side By Side*
3 April 1963 – 7 April 1963 edition of *Easy Beat*
13 April 1963 – 16 April 1963 edition of *The 625 Show* (BBC TV)
16 May 1963 – *Pops And Lenny* (TV, live)
21 May 1963 – 3 June 1963 edition of *Steppin' Out*
16 July 1963 [7] – 13 August 1963 edition of *Pop Go The Beatles*
16 October 1963 [8] – 20 October 1963 edition of *Easy Beat*
9 February 1964 [9] – *The Ed Sullivan Show* broadcast on 23 February 1964
    (CBS TV)
19 April 1964 – *Around The Beatles*, mimed performance recorded on 28 April
    and broadcast on 6 May 1964 (Rediffusion TV)

Releases   *UK/US peak*

	UK/US peak
'Please Please Me' / 'Ask Me Why' single (1963) – Parlophone 45-R 4983 [1]	2
Please Please Me LP (1963) – Parlophone PMC 1202 [1], PCS 3042 [2]	1
The Beatles' Hits EP (1963) – Parlophone GEP 8880 [1]	1
Introducing... The Beatles LP (US, 1963) – Vee Jay VJLP 1062 [1], VJSR 1062 [2]	2
'Please Please Me' / 'Ask Me Why' single (US, 1963) – Vee Jay VJ 498 [1]	–
'Please Please Me' / 'From Me To You' single (US, 1964) – Vee Jay VJ 581 [1]	3
The Early Beatles LP (US, 1965) – Capitol T 2309 [4], ST 2309 [3]	43

'Please Please Me' / 'From Me To You' single (US, 1965) – Capitol Starline 6063 [4]	–
The Beatles 1962–1966 LP (1973) – Apple PCSP 717 [2]	3
The Beatles 1962–1966 LP (US, 1973)– Apple SKBO 3403 [3]	3
The Beatles 1962–1966 CD (1993) – EMI CDP 7 97036 2 [1]	3
Anthology 1 CD (1995) – Apple 8 34445 2 [5]	2/1
The Four Historic Ed Sullivan Shows DVD (2003) – EREDV 372 [9]	
On Air – Live At The BBC Volume 2 CD (2013) – Apple 6025 37491698 [7]	12/7
The Beatles Bootleg Recordings 1963 (2013) – iTunes [6] [8]	–
1+ CD/DVD (2015) – Apple 6205 47567727 [9]	5/6

NOTES

- ♪ Different vocal takes were used for the mono/ stereo versions.
- ♪ The first UK #1 single, topping five of the six national charts, though on the "official" charts it only reached #2.
- ♪ The group mimed to the song on their first national TV appearance, on *Thank Your Lucky Stars*, broadcast on 19 January 1963.
- ♪ Played in concert until 1964.

Polythene Pam / She Came In Through The Bathroom Window

[Lennon-McCartney]

John – lead vocals, backing vocals, acoustic guitar, maracas
Paul – lead vocals, backing vocals, bass, guitar, piano, electric piano
George – backing vocals, guitar, tambourine
Ringo – drums, cowbell

Studio recording and mixing

May 1968 – Kinfauns, Esher
Demo recording ('Polythene Pam')

22 January 1969 – Apple Studio – Let It Be rehearsal session
Rehearsal ('She Came In Through The Bathroom Window')

25 July 1969 – Studio Two – Abbey Road session 28 out of 42
Takes 1–39
Overdubs onto take 39 – vocals, bass, drums

28 July 1969 – Studio Three – Abbey Road session 29 out of 42
Overdubs onto take 39 – vocals, guitar, percussion, piano, electric piano
Tape reduction of take 39 > take 40

30 July 1969 – Studio Three – Abbey Road session 31 out of 42
Overdubs onto take 40 – vocals, guitar, percussion

14 August 1969 – Studio Two control room
RS32 [1] – stereo mix from take 40

1996 – EMI
[2] – stereo mix from demo
[3] – stereo mix from rehearsal

2018 – EMI
[4] – stereo mix from demo

Releases_____UK/US peak

Abbey Road LP (1969) – Apple PCS 7088 [1]	1
Abbey Road LP (US, 1969) – Apple SO 383 [1]	1
Anthology 3 CD (1996) – Apple 8 34451 2 [2] [3]	4/1
The Beatles Deluxe CD (2018) – Apple 0602567571957 [4]	4/6

=====NOTES=====

♪ The last track combining separate songs of John and Paul.
♪ According to the *Beatles Book* of November 1968, 'Polythene Pam'
just missed out on appearing on the White Album.

Pop Go The Beatles

[Trad. arr. Patrick]

John – harmonica
George – lead guitar
Paul – bass
Ringo – drums

BBC and other performances_____

24 May 1963 – used for all 15 editions of *Pop Go The Beatles*

=====NOTES=====

♪ Instrumental opening and closing themes for
the show.

Putting On The Style

[Trad.-Cazden]

Lead vocals, **John**. Played by the Quarry Men at St Peter's Church fete when John met
Paul on 6 July 1957. An unofficial recording exists of the performance. Lonnie Donegan
was at #1 in the UK charts with the song at the time.

Rain

[Lennon-McCartney]

John – lead vocals, rhythm guitar
Paul – harmony and backing vocals, lead guitar, bass
George – harmony and backing vocals
Ringo – drums, tambourine

Studio recording and mixing

14 April 1966 – Studio Three – Revolver session 6 out of 33
Takes 1–5
Overdubs onto take 5 – vocals

16 April 1966 – Studio Two – Revolver session 7 out of 33
Overdubs onto take 5 – bass, vocals, tambourine
Tape reduction of take 5 > take 6
Overdubs onto take 6 – backward vocals > takes 7, 8

16 April 1966 – Studio Two control room
RM3 [1] – mono mix from take 7

2 December 1969 – Studio Two control room
RS1 [2] – stereo mix from take 7

Releases UK/US peak

'Paperback Writer' / 'Rain' single (1966) – Parlophone R 5452 [1]	1
'Paperback Writer' / 'Rain' single (US, 1966) – Capitol 5651 [1]	23
Hey Jude LP (US, 1970) – Apple SW 385 [2]	2
Rarities LP (1978) – Parlophone PCM 1001, PSLP 261 [1]	71
Past Masters 2 CD (1988) – EMI CDP 7 90044 2 [2]	46/–

NOTES

♪ The first use of automatic double-tracking on the vocals, and first use of backward vocal.
♪ The backwards vocal is isolated from a different take.
♪ Two promotional films were made on 19–20 May 1966.

Ramrod

[Casey]

Played by the Quarry Men/Beatles until 1960. A Duane Eddy instrumental from 1957, it appears on the tape recorded at Paul's house in June 1960.

Ready Teddy

[Marascalco-Blackwell]

Lead vocals, **John**. Played by the Quarry Men/Beatles until around 1961. Released in 1956 by Little Richard on the B-side of 'Rip It Up'. Appears on John's 1975 *Rock 'n' Roll* LP.

Real Love

[Lennon]

John – lead vocals, piano
Paul – backing vocals, bass, guitar, piano, synthesiser, percussion
George – backing vocals, guitars, harmonium, percussion
Ringo – backing vocals, drums, percussion
Jeff Lynne – backing vocals, guitar

Studio recording and mixing

c. 1979 – Dakota Apartments, New York
Basic recording – vocals, piano

6–7 February and 15–16 May 1995 – Mill Studio, Sussex
Overdubs onto edit of basic recording

1995 – EMI
[1] – stereo mix

2015 – EMI
[2] – stereo mix

Releases | UK/US peak

	UK/US peak
'Real Love' single (1996) – Apple 8 82646 2 [1]	4/11
Anthology 2 CD (1996) – Apple 8 34448 2 [1]	1/1
1+ CD/DVD (2015) – Apple 6205 47567727 [2]	5/6

NOTES

♪ The source tape, taken from a cassette, plays back faster than the basic recording.
♪ John considered the song for opening side 2 of *Double Fantasy*.
♪ Produced by Jeff Lynne.
♪ The *1+* version has some guitar and drum parts that were deleted for the original release.

Red Hot

[Emerson]

Lead vocals, **John**. Played by the Beatles until 1962. It was part of the tape that produced *Live! At The Star-Club In Hamburg, Germany; 1962*, but the performance was incomplete and so was never released. Recorded by Ronnie Hawkins in 1959.

Red Sails In The Sunset

[Kennedy-Williams]

Paul – lead vocals, bass
John – rhythm guitar
George – lead guitar
Ringo – drums

BBC and other performances

December 1962 [1] – Star-Club, Hamburg (live)

Releases   *UK/US peak*

Live! At The Star-Club In Hamburg, Germany; 1962 LP (1977) – Lingasong LNL 1 /
    Lingasong LS 2 7001 [1]   –

> === NOTES ===
>
> ♪ Hit versions were recorded
>   by Nat King Cole in 1951,
>   the Platters in 1960 and
>   Fats Domino in 1963.
> ♪ John's father Alf would sing
>   this in the ship's bars when a
>   merchant seaman.

Reminiscing

[Curtis]

George – lead vocals, lead guitar
John – rhythm guitar
Paul – bass
Ringo – drums

BBC and other performances

December 1962 [1] – Star-Club, Hamburg (live)

Releases   *UK/US peak*

Live! At The Star-Club In Hamburg, Germany; 1962 LP (1977) – Lingasong LNL 1 [1]   –

┌──────────────── **NOTES** ────────────────┐

♪ Credited writer King Curtis was a sax player for the
Coasters and Buddy Holly – the song was written
by Buddy Holly, but he gave the credit to Curtis for
flying in to record the track.

♪ Holly's version of 'Reminiscing' was in the top 30 in
the week that 'Love Me Do' entered the charts.

└──┘

Revolution

[Lennon-McCartney]

John – lead vocals, lead guitar
Paul – bass, organ
George – lead guitar
Ringo – drums
Nicky Hopkins – electric piano

Studio recording and mixing

10 July 1968 – Studio Three – White Album session 23 out of 81

Takes 1–10
Overdubs onto take 10 – guitar, handclaps
Tape reduction of take 10 > takes 11–13
Overdubs onto take 13 – vocals
Tape reduction of take 13 > takes 14–15

11 July 1968 – Studio Three – White Album session 24 out of 81

Overdubs onto take 15
Tape reduction of take 15 > take 16
Overdubs onto take 16 – electric piano, guitar, bass

12 July 1968 – Studio Two – White Album session 25 out of 81

Overdubs onto take 16 – bass

15 July 1968 – Studio Two control room

RM21 [1] – mono mix from take 16

5 December 1969 – Studio Two control room

RS1 [2] – stereo mix from take 16

2004–06 – EMI

[3] – stereo mix from take 16

2018 – EMI

[4] – stereo mix from unnumbered rehearsal
[5] – stereo mix from take 10
[6] – stereo mix from take 16

BBC and other performances

4 September 1968 [7] – Twickenham Film Studios, broadcast on 19 September 1968 edition of Top of the Pops (BBC) and 13 October 1968 edition of *The Smothers Brothers Comedy Hour* (CBS TV)

Releases	UK/US peak
'Hey Jude' / 'Revolution' single (1968) – Apple R 5722 [1]	1
'Hey Jude' / 'Revolution' single (1968) – Parlophone DP 570 [1]	–
'Hey Jude' / 'Revolution' single (US, 1968) – Apple 2276 [1]	12
Hey Jude LP (US, 1970) – Apple SW 385 [2]	2
The Beatles 1967–1970 LP (1973) – Apple PCSP 718 [2]	2
The Beatles 1967–1970 LP (US, 1973) – Apple SKBO 3404 [2]	1
Rock 'n' Roll Music LP (1976) – Parlophone PCSP 719 / Capitol SKBO 11537 [2]	11/2
Past Masters 2 CD (1988) – EMI CDP 7 90044 2 [2]	46/–
Love CD (2006) – Apple 0946 3 80790 2 6 [3]	3/4
Tomorrow Never Knows (2012) – iTunes [2]	44/24
1+ CD/DVD (2015) – Apple 6205 47567727 [7]	5/6
The Beatles Deluxe CD (2018) – Apple 0602567571957 [4] [5] [6]	4/6

═ NOTES ═

♪ The 4 September 1968 performance featured John singing live to a remixed backing track with Paul and George providing 'Revolution 1' doo-wop backing vocals.
♪ The guitar distortion is due to the signal being fed directly into the recording console.
♪ The highest US placing for a B-side since 'She's A Woman' in 1964.

Revolution 1

[Lennon-McCartney]

John – lead vocals, acoustic and lead guitars
Paul – backing vocals, bass, piano, organ
George – backing vocals, lead guitar
Ringo – drums
Session musicians – two trumpets, four trombones

Studio recording and mixing

May 1968 – Kinfauns, Esher

Demo recording

30 May 1968 – Studio Two – White Album session 4 out of 81

Takes 1–18

31 May 1968 – Studio Three – White Album session 5 out of 81
Overdubs onto take 18 – vocals, bass
Tape reduction of take 18 > take 19
Overdubs onto take 19 – vocals

4 June 1968 – Studio Three – White Album session 6 out of 81
Overdubs onto take 19 – vocals
Tape loops takes 1–2
Tape reduction of take 19 > take 20
Overdubs onto take 20 – drums, guitar, organ

21 June 1968 – Studio Two – White Album session 12 out of 81
Overdubs onto take 20 – brass
Tape reduction of take 20 > takes 21, 22
Overdubs onto take 22 – guitar

25 June 1968 – Studio Two control room
RS12 [1] – stereo mix from take 22, edited
RM1 [2] – mono mix from [1]

2018 – EMI
[3] – stereo mix from demo
[4] – stereo mix from take 18
[5] – stereo mix from take 22, edited

Releases   *UK/US peak*

The Beatles LP (1968) – Apple PMC 7067–7068 [2], PCS 7067–7068 [1]	1
The Beatles LP (US, 1968) – Apple SWBO-101 [1]	1
The Beatles Deluxe CD (2018) – Apple 0602567571957 [3] [4] [5]	4/6

=== **NOTES** ===

♪ No mono mix was made, just the left and right channels collapsed.
♪ The edit was made to give the triple beat towards the end of the song.

Revolution 9

[Lennon-McCartney]

Tape effects

Studio recording and mixing

30 May 1968 – Studio Two – White Album session 4 out of 81
Takes 1–18 (of 'Revolution 1')

6 June 1968 – *Studio Two – White Album session 8 out of 81*
Sound effects takes 1–12

10 June 1968 – *Studio Three – White Album session 9 out of 81*
Sound effects takes 1–3

11 June 1968 – *Studio Three – White Album session 10 out of 81*
Sound effects unnumbered takes

20 June 1968 – *Studios One, Two and Three – White Album session 11 out of 81*
Sound effects takes 1–2 compilation with overdubs

21 June 1968 – *Studio Two – White Album session 12 out of 81*
Overdubs onto master – sound effects

21 June 1968 – *Studio Two control room*
RS1–RS2 – stereo mixes from master

25 June 1968 – *Studio Two control room*
[1] – edit of RS2

26 August 1968 – *Studio Two control room*
RM2 [2] – mono mix from [1]

2018 – *EMI*
[3] – stereo mix of edit from master

Releases_____ *UK/US peak*

The Beatles LP (1968) – Apple PMC 7067–7068 **[2]**, PCS 7067–7068 **[1]**   1
The Beatles LP (US, 1968) – Apple SWBO-101 **[1]**   1
The Beatles Deluxe CD (2018) – Apple 0602567571957 **[3]**   4/6

```
════════ NOTES ════════
♪ The longest Beatles track.
♪ Based on the full-length take 18 of
  'Revolution 1'.
♪ Like 'Revolution 1', the mono mix is
  simply a fold-down of the stereo,
  combining the left and right channels.
```

Rip It Up / Shake, Rattle And Roll / Blue Suede Shoes
[Blackwell-Marascalco/Calhoun/Perkins]

John – lead vocals, rhythm guitar
Paul – lead and harmony vocals, bass
George – lead guitar
Ringo – drums
Billy Preston – organ

Studio recording and mixing

26 January 1969 – Apple Studio – Let It Be session 6 out of 17
Takes 26.28, 26.29 [1], and 26.31

1996 – EMI
[2] – stereo mix of edit from takes 26.28, 26.29 and 26.31

Releases
UK/US peak

Let It Be movie (1970) [1]
Anthology 3 CD (1996) – Apple 8 34451 2 [2]   4/1

=== NOTES ===

♪ A medley of Little Richard, Bill Haley and Elvis Presley
   songs.
♪ The three songs are heavily edited and were not
   recorded as a medley – although the first two were
   played together, 'Blue Suede Shoes' was recorded
   shortly afterwards and does not appear in the film.
♪ 'Rip It Up' appears on John's *Rock 'n' Roll* LP.

Road Runner
[McDaniel]

Lead vocals, **John**. Played by the Beatles in concert from 1961–62. It was part of the *Live!
At The Star-Club In Hamburg, Germany; 1962* tape, but the performance was incomplete.
The song was originally recorded by Bo Diddley in September 1959 and reached #20
in the *Billboard* R&B charts. The Rolling Stones recorded the song in 1963, but did not
release it.

Rock And Roll Music
[Berry]

John – lead vocals, rhythm guitar, piano
Paul – bass, piano
George – possibly acoustic guitar
Ringo – drums
George Martin – piano

Studio recording and mixing

18 October 1964 – Studio Two – Beatles For Sale session 7 out of 8
Take 1
Overdubs onto take 1 – piano, drums

26 October 1964 – Studio Two control room
RM1 [1] – mono mix from take 1

4 November 1964 – *Studio Two control room*
RS1 [2] – stereo mix from take 1

BBC and other performances

25 November 1964 [3] – 26 December 1964 edition of *Saturday Club*
20 June 1965 – *Les Beatles* (Europe 1 TV, France, live)
24 June 1966 – *Die Beatles* broadcast on 5 July 1966 (ZDF TV, Germany)
30 June 1966 [4] – Nippon Budokan Hall, Tokyo (live)

Releases   *UK/US peak*

Beatles For Sale LP (1964) – Parlophone PMC 1240 [1], PCS 3062 [2]	1
Beatles For Sale EP (1965) – Parlophone GEP 8931 [1]	1
Beatles '65 LP (US, 1964) – Capitol T 2228 [1], ST 2228 [2]	1
Rock 'n' Roll Music LP (1976) – Parlophone PCSP 719 / Capitol SKBO 11537 [2]	11/2
Anthology 2 CD (1996) – Apple 8 34448 2 [4]	1/1
Live At The BBC CD (1994) – Apple 8 31796 2 [3]	1/3

=== NOTES ===

♪ Chuck Berry's original reached #8 in the *Billboard* charts in 1957.
♪ John, Paul and George Martin "on one piano".
♪ Played live by the Quarry Men/Beatles between 1959 and 1966.

Rocky Raccoon

[Lennon-McCartney]

Paul – lead vocals, acoustic guitar
John – backing vocals, harmonica, harmonium, bass
George – backing vocals, bass
Ringo – drums
George Martin – piano, possibly harmonium

Studio recording and mixing

May 1968 – *Kinfauns, Esher*
Demo recording

15 August 1968 – *Studio Two – White Album session 44 out of 81*
Takes 1–9
Overdubs onto take 9 – bass, harmonium, drums
Tape reduction of take 9 > take 10
Overdubs onto take 10 – harmonica, piano, harmonium, vocals

15 August 1968 – *Studio Two control room*
RM1 [1] – mono mix from take 10

10 October 1968 – Studio Two control room
RS1 [2] – stereo mix from take 10

1996 – EMI
[3] – stereo mix from take 8

2018 – EMI
[4] – stereo mix from demo
[5] – stereo mix from take 8
[6] – stereo mix from take 10

Releases   *UK/US peak*

The Beatles LP (1968) – Apple PMC 7067–7068 [1], PCS 7067–7068 [2]	1
The Beatles LP (US, 1968) – Apple SWBO-101 [2]	1
Anthology 3 CD (1996) – Apple 8 34451 2 [3]	4/1
The Beatles Deluxe CD (2018) – Apple 0602567571957 [4] [5] [6]	4/6

NOTES

♪ Consists of just 4½ chords, which were also used in the chorus of 'Can't Buy Me Love', repeated over and over.

Roll Over Beethoven

[Berry]

George – lead vocals, lead guitar
John – rhythm guitar
Paul – bass
Ringo – drums

Studio recording and mixing

30 July 1963 – Studio Two – With The Beatles session 3 out of 9
Takes 1–5
Overdubs onto take 5 – guitar, handclaps, vocals > takes 6–7
Edit piece take 8 (final guitar chord)

21 August 1963 – Studio Two control room
RM7/8 [1] – mono mix from edit of takes 7, 8

29 October 1963 – Studio Two control room
RS7/8 [2] – stereo mix from edit of takes 7, 8

1964 – Capitol
[3] – stereo mix from [2]
[4] – mono mix from [2]

1976 – Capitol

[5] – stereo mix from edit of takes 7, 8

BBC and other performances

December 1962 **[6]** – Star-Club, Hamburg (live)
21 May 1963 – 3 June 1963 edition of *Steppin' Out*
24 June 1963 **[7]** – 29 June 1963 edition of *Saturday Club*
1 August 1963 **[8]** – 3 September 1963 edition of *Pop Go The Beatles*
24 October 1963 **[9]** – Karlaplansstudion, Stockholm (live)
7 December 1963 – *It's The Beatles* broadcast the same day (BBC TV)
17 December 1963 **[10]** – 21 December 1963 edition of *Saturday Club*
18 December 1963 **[11]** – 26 December 1963 edition of *From Us To You*
7 January 1964 – 15 February 1964 edition of *Saturday Club*
28 February 1964 **[12]** – 30 March 1964 edition of *From Us To You*
19 April 1964 – *Around The Beatles*, mimed performance recorded on 28 April
   and broadcast on 6 May 1964 (Rediffusion TV)
17 June 1964 – *The Beatles Sing For Shell* broadcast on 1 July 1964 (Channel 9
   TV, Australia)
23 August 1964 **[13]** – Hollywood Bowl (live)

Releases   *UK/US peak*

With The Beatles LP (1963) – Parlophone PMC 1206 [1], PCS 3045 [2]	1
With The Beatles LP (Germany, 1963) – Odeon O 83 991 [1], Odeon STO 83 568 [2]	–
'Roll Over Beethoven' / 'Please Mister Postman' single (Canada, 1963) Capitol 72133 [1]	68
The Beatles' Second Album LP (US, 1964) – Capitol T 2080 [4], ST 2080 [3]	1
Four By The Beatles EP (US, 1964) – Capitol EAP 1-2121 [4]	92
'Roll Over Beethoven' / 'Misery' single (US, 1965) – Capitol Starline 6065 [4]	–
Rock 'n' Roll Music LP (1976) – Parlophone PCSP 719 [2]	11
Rock 'n' Roll Music LP (US, 1976) – Capitol SKBO 11537 [5]	2
The Beatles At The Hollywood Bowl LP (1977) – Parlophone EMTV 4 / Capitol SMAS 11638 [13]	1/2
Live! At The Star-Club In Hamburg, Germany; 1962 LP (1977) – Lingasong LNL 1 / Lingasong LS 2 7001 [6]	–
Live At The BBC CD (1994) – Apple 8 31796 2 [12]	1/3
Anthology 1 CD (1995) – Apple 8 34445 2 [9]	2/1
On Air – Live At The BBC Volume 2 CD (2013) – Apple 6025 37491698 [8]	12/7
The Beatles Bootleg Recordings 1963 (2013) – iTunes [7] [10] [11]	–
Live At The Hollywood Bowl CD (2016) – Apple 6025 57054972 [13]	3/7

═══ **NOTES** ═══

♪ A US top 30 hit for Chuck Berry from 1956.
♪ Performed by John in various groups from 1957,
   still part of the Beatles' set in 1964.

Run For Your Life

[Lennon-McCartney]

John – lead vocals, acoustic guitar
Paul – harmony vocals, bass
George – harmony vocals, lead guitar
Ringo – drums, possibly tambourine

Studio recording and mixing

12 October 1965 – Studio Two – Rubber Soul session 1 out of 15
Takes 1–5
Overdubs onto take 5 – guitar, vocals, tambourine

9 November 1965 – Room 65
RM1 [1] – mono mix from take 5

10 November 1965 – Room 65
RS1 [2] – stereo mix from take 5

1987 – EMI
[3] – stereo mix from take 5

Releases

	UK/US peak
Rubber Soul LP (1965) – Parlophone PMC 1267 [1], PCS 3075 [2]	1
Rubber Soul LP (US, 1965) – Capitol T 2442 [1], ST 2442 [2]	1
Rubber Soul CD (1987) – EMI CDP 7 46440 2 [3]	60

═ NOTES ═

♪ The first line is lifted from 'Baby Let's Play House', recorded by Elvis Presley in 1954.
♪ Almost a month lapsed before it was mixed.
♪ The first track to be produced by George Martin as a freelancer working for the newly formed AIR.

Saint Louis Blues

[Handy]

Paul – lead vocals, piano
John – acoustic guitar
Ringo – drums

Studio recording and mixing

30 July 1968 – Studio Two – White Album session 35 out of 81
Studio jam

2018 – EMI
[1] – stereo mix from studio jam

Releases   *UK/US peak*

The Beatles Deluxe CD (2018) – Apple 0602567571957 [1]   4/6

```
┌─────────── NOTES ───────────┐
│  ♪ Written by WC Handy,      │
│    and published in 1914.    │
│  ♪ Recorded by Bessie        │
│    Smith in 1925 with        │
│    Louis Armstrong on        │
│    cornet.                   │
└──────────────────────────────┘
```

The Saints (When The Saints Go Marching In)
[Trad. arr. Sheridan]

Tony Sheridan – lead vocals, lead guitar
John – rhythm guitar
Paul – bass
George – guitar
Pete Best – drums

Studio recording and mixing

22 June 1961 – Friedrich-Eberts-Halle, Hamburg
Unknown take numbers

22 June 1961 – Polydor, Hamburg
[1] – stereo mix from unknown take number

1961 – Polydor, Hamburg
[2] – mono mix from [1]

Releases   *UK/US peak*

'My Bonnie' / 'The Saints (When The Saints Go Marching In)' single (Germany, 1961) –
    Polydor 24673 [2]   –
'My Bonnie' / 'The Saints (When The Saints Go Marching In)' single (1962) –
    Polydor NH 66833 [2]   –
'My Bonnie' / 'The Saints (When The Saints Go Marching In)' single (US, 1962) –
    Decca 31382 [2]   –

'My Bonnie (My Bonnie Lies Over The Ocean)' / 'The Saints (When The Saints Go Marching In)'
single (US, 1964) – MGM K13213 [2]   –
Beatles First LP (1967) – Polydor 236 201 [1]   –
The Early Tapes Of The Beatles CD (1985) – Polydor 823701-2 [1]   –

> **════ NOTES ════**
>
> ♪ Although credited as "traditional", the gospel song was written in 1937 by Luther G Presley and VO Stamps.
> ♪ Fats Domino was one of the first performers to put the song in a rock'n'roll context.
> ♪ The Beatles back Tony Sheridan on both sides of the single, which was produced by Bert Kaempfert.

Save The Last Dance For Me

[Pomus-Shuman]

Lead vocals, **John**. The song was played by the Beatles until 1962. It was also played during the *Let It Be* Sessions in 1969, with one version being slated for the aborted *Get Back* LP. It reached #1 in the US and #2 in the UK for the Drifters in 1960.

Savoy Truffle

[Harrison]

George – lead vocals, lead guitar, possibly tambourine
Paul – bass, possibly bongos, harmony vocals
Ringo – drums
Chris Thomas – electric piano, organ
Session musicians – two baritone saxophones, four tenor saxophones

Studio recording and mixing

3 October 1968 – Trident Studios – White Album session 72 out of 81
Take 1

5 October 1968 – Trident Studios – White Album session 74 out of 81
Overdubs onto take 1 – vocals

11 October 1968 – Studio Two – White Album session 79 out of 81
Overdubs onto take 1 – brass

14 October 1968 – Studio Two – White Album session 81 out of 81
Overdubs onto take 1 – guitar, organ, tambourine, bongos

14 October 1968 – *Studio Two control room*
RM6 [1] – mono mix from take 1
RS2 [2] – stereo mix from take 1

2018 – *EMI*
[3] – stereo mix from take 1, without vocals
[4] – stereo mix from take 1

Releases   *UK/US peak*

	UK/US peak
The Beatles LP (1968) – Apple PMC 7067–7068 [1], PCS 7067–7068 [2]	1
The Beatles LP (US, 1968) – Apple SWBO-101 [2]	1
Tomorrow Never Knows (2012) – iTunes [2]	44/24
The Beatles Deluxe CD (2018) – Apple 0602567571957 [3] [4]	4/6

NOTES

♪ Of the chocolates mentioned, creme tangerine, montelimart, ginger sling, pineapple treat, coffee dessert and savoy truffle itself are from the Mackintosh's Good News selection box.
♪ The recording started at Trident and was completed at Abbey Road.
♪ The brass arrangement is by Chris Thomas.

Searchin'

[Leiber-Stoller]

Paul – lead vocals, bass
John – backing vocals, rhythm guitar
George – backing vocals, lead guitar
Pete Best – drums

Studio recording and mixing

1 January 1962 – *Decca Studios*
Studio test recorded in mono [1]

Releases   *UK/US peak*

	UK/US peak
Anthology 1 CD (1995) – Apple 8 34445 2 [1]	2/1

NOTES

♪ Original by the Coasters topped the *Billboard* R&B charts for 12 weeks in 1958. It was their first UK hit.

September In The Rain

[Warren-Dubin]

Paul – lead vocals, bass
John – rhythm guitar
George – lead guitar
Pete Best – drums

Studio recording and mixing

1 January 1962 – Decca Studios
Studio test recorded in mono

NOTES

♪ Unreleased by the Beatles.
♪ Based on the version by Dinah Washington, a UK top 40 hit in 1961.

Sexy Sadie

[Lennon-McCartney]

John – lead vocals, acoustic guitar, rhythm guitar
Paul – backing vocals, bass, piano, organ
George – backing vocals, lead guitar
Ringo – drums, tambourine

Studio recording and mixing

May 1968 – Kinfauns, Esher
Demo recording

19 July 1968 – Studio Two – White Album session 29 out of 81
Takes 1–21

24 July 1968 – Studio Two – White Album session 32 out of 81
Remake takes 25–47

13 August 1968 – Studio Two – White Album session 42 out of 81
Re-remake takes 100–107
Tape reduction of take 107 > takes 108–111

21 August 1968 – Studio Two – White Album session 47 out of 81
Tape reduction of take 107 > take 112
Overdubs onto take 112 – vocals, tambourine, organ
Tape reduction of take 112 > take 113–115
Overdubs onto take 115 – vocals
Tape reduction of take 115 > take 116–117
Overdubs onto take 117 – bass

21 August 1968 – Studio Two control room

RM5 [1] – mono mix from take 117, edited

14 October 1968 – Studio Two control room

RS3 [2] – stereo mix from take 117, edited

1996 – EMI

[3] – stereo mix from take 6

2018 – EMI

[4] – stereo mix from demo

[5] – stereo mix from take 11

[6] – stereo mix from take 117, edited

Releases   UK/US peak

	UK/US peak
The Beatles LP (1968) – Apple PMC 7067–7068 [1], PCS 7067–7068 [2]	1
The Beatles LP (US, 1968) – Apple SWBO-101 [2]	1
Anthology 3 CD (1996) – Apple 8 34451 2 [3]	4/1
The Beatles Deluxe CD (2018) – Apple 0602567571957 [4] [5] [6]	4/6

NOTES

♪ John's tribute to Maharishi Mahesh Yogi.

♪ An instrumental break of around 40 seconds, just before the final fade, were deleted from the released version.

♪ Unusually for this LP, phasing is used on the backing vocals.

Sgt Pepper's Lonely Hearts Club Band

[Lennon-McCartney]

Paul – lead vocals, bass, guitar
John – lead and harmony vocals
George – harmony vocals, guitar
Ringo – drums
Neil Aspinall, Mal Evans – backing vocals
Session musicians – four French horns

Studio recording and mixing

1 February 1967 – Studio Two – Sgt Pepper session 22 out of 56

Takes 1–9

Overdubs onto take 9 – bass

2 February 1967 – Studio Two – Sgt Pepper session 23 out of 56

Overdubs onto take 9 – vocals

Tape reduction of take 9 > take 10

3 March 1967 – Studio Two – Sgt Pepper session 38 out of 56
Overdubs onto take 10 – brass, guitar

6 March 1967 – Studio Two – Sgt Pepper session 39 out of 56
Overdubs onto take 10 – effects

6 March 1967 – Studio Two control room
RM3 [1] – mono mix from take 10
RS8 [2] – stereo mix from take 10

1999 – EMI
[3] – stereo mix from take 10

2016/17 – EMI
[4] – stereo mix from take 1
[5] – stereo mix from take 9
[6] – stereo mix from take 10

Releases
UK/US peak

Sgt Pepper's Lonely Hearts Club Band LP (1967) – Parlophone PMC 7027 [1], PCS 7027 [2]	1
Sgt Pepper's Lonely Hearts Club Band LP (US, 1967) – Capitol MAS 2653 [1], SMAS 2653 [2]	1
The Beatles 1967–1970 LP (1973) – Apple PCSP 718 [2]	2
The Beatles 1967–1970 LP (US, 1973) – Apple SKBO 3404 [2]	1
'Sgt Pepper's Lonely Hearts Club Band' / 'With A Little Help From My Friends' / 'A Day In The Life' single (1978) – Parlophone R 6022 [2]	63
'Sgt Pepper's Lonely Hearts Club Band' / 'With A Little Help From My Friends' / 'A Day In The Life' single (US, 1978) – Capitol 4612 [2]	71
Yellow Submarine Songtrack CD (1999) – Apple 5 21481 2 [3]	8/15
Sgt Pepper's Lonely Hearts Club Band Deluxe CD (2017) – Apple 0602557455328 [1] [4] [5] [6]	1/3

NOTES
♪ The bass signal was directly injected into the recording console – a first for the group.
♪ The 1978 single was to promote the *Sgt Pepper* film.

Sgt Pepper's Lonely Hearts Club Band (Reprise)
[Lennon-McCartney]

Paul – lead vocals, bass
John – harmony vocals, rhythm guitar
George – harmony vocals, lead guitar
Ringo – harmony vocals, drums, tambourine, maracas
George Martin – organ

Studio recording and mixing

1 April 1967 – Studio One – Sgt Pepper session 54 out of 56
Takes 1–9
Overdubs onto take 9 – vocals, organ, percussion, effects

1 April 1967 – Studio One control room
RM9 [1] – mono mix from take 9

20 April 1967 – Studio Three control room
RS10 [2] – stereo mix from take 9

1996 – EMI
[3] – stereo mix from take 5

2004–06 – EMI
[4] – stereo mix from take 9

2016/17 – EMI
[5] – stereo mix from take 8
[6] – stereo mix from take 9

Releases

	UK/US peak
Sgt Pepper's Lonely Hearts Club Band LP (1967) – Parlophone PMC 7027 [1], PCS 7027 [2]	1
Sgt Pepper's Lonely Hearts Club Band LP (US, 1967) – Capitol MAS 2653 [1], SMAS 2653 [2]	1
Anthology 2 CD (1996) – Apple 8 34448 2 [3]	1/1
Love CD (2006) – Apple 0946 3 80790 2 6 [4]	3/4
Sgt Pepper's Lonely Hearts Club Band Deluxe CD (2017) – Apple 0602557455328 [1] [5] [6]	1/3

=== NOTES ===

♪ The only *Sgt Pepper* track completed within a single session.
♪ Much of the atmosphere of the track comes from it having been recorded in the cavernous Studio One.
♪ The mono version has additional speech from Paul.

Shake, Rattle And Roll
see 'Rip It Up/Shake, Rattle And Roll/Blue Suede Shoes'

Sharing You

[Goffin-King]

Lead vocals, **George**. The song was played by the Beatles in 1962. It was a UK #10 and a *Billboard* #15 for Bobby Vee in 1962.

She Loves You

[Lennon-McCartney]

John – lead vocals, rhythm guitar
Paul – lead/harmony vocals, bass
George – harmony vocals, lead guitar
Ringo – drums

Studio recording and mixing

1 July 1963 – Studio Two – With The Beatles session 1 out of 9
Unknown take numbers

4 July 1963 – Studio Two control room
RM1 [1] – mono mix from unknown take number

17 March 1964 – Capitol
[2] – mastering of mock stereo mix from [1]
[3] – mastering of mono mix from [1]

8 November 1966 – Room 53
RS1 [4] – mock stereo mix from [1]

1973 – Capitol
[5] – mock stereo mix from [1]

1992 – EMI
[6] – mono mix from [1]

BBC and other performances

16 July 1963 – 13 August 1963 edition of *Pop Go The Beatles*
16 July 1963 – 20 August 1963 edition of *Pop Go The Beatles*
30 July 1963 – 24 August 1963 edition of *Saturday Club*
1 August 1963 – 27 August 1963 edition of *Pop Go The Beatles*
27 August 1963 – *The Mersey Sound* broadcast on 9 October 1963 (BBC TV)
3 September 1963 [7] – 10 September 1963 edition of *Pop Go The Beatles*
3 September 1963 [8] – 24 September 1963 edition of *Pop Go The Beatles*
7 September 1963 [9] – 5 October 1963 edition of *Saturday Club*
9 October 1963 – 3 November 1963 edition of *The Ken Dodd Show*
13 October 1963 – *Sunday Night At The London Palladium* (ATV, live)
16 October 1963 [10] – 20 October 1963 edition of *Easy Beat*
30 October 1963 [11] – *Drop In* broadcast on 3 November 1963 (Sveriges TV)
4 November 1963 [12] – *Royal Variety Performance* broadcast on 10 November
    1963 (ATV)
20 November 1963 – *The Beatles Come To Town* (Pathe News)
7 December 1963 – *It's The Beatles* broadcast the same day (BBC TV)
17 December 1963 – 21 December 1963 edition of *Saturday Club*

18 December 1963 [13] – 26 December 1963 edition of *From Us To You*
9 February 1964 [14] – *The Ed Sullivan Show* (CBS TV, live)
16 February 1964 [15] – *The Ed Sullivan Show* (CBS TV, live)
19 April 1964 – *Around The Beatles*, mimed performance recorded on 28 April
    and broadcast on 6 May 1964 (Rediffusion TV)
26 April 1964 – *NME 1963-64 Annual Poll-Winners' Concert*
17 June 1964 – *The Beatles Sing For Shell* broadcast on 1 July 1964 (Channel 9
    TV, Australia)
23 August 1964 [16] – Hollywood Bowl (live)

Releases   *UK/US peak*

'She Loves You' / 'I'll Get You' single (1963) – Parlophone R 5055 [1]	1
'She Loves You' / 'I'll Get You' single (US, 1963) – Swan 4152 [1]	–
The Beatles' Second Album LP (US, 1964) – Capitol T 2080 [3], ST 2080 [2]	1
The Beatles' Million Sellers EP (1965) – Parlophone GEP 8946 [1]	1
A Collection Of Beatles Oldies LP (1966) – Parlophone PMC 7016 [1], PCS 7016 [4]	7
The Beatles 1962–1966 LP (1973) – Apple PCSP 717 [4]	3
The Beatles 1962–1966 LP (US, 1973)– Apple SKBO 3403 [5]	3
The Beatles At The Hollywood Bowl LP (1977) – Parlophone EMTV 4 / Capitol SMAS 11638 [16]	1/2
20 Greatest Hits LP (1982) – Parlophone PCTC 260 / Capitol SV-12245 [4]	10/50
Past Masters 1 CD (1988) – EMI CDP 7 90043 2 [1]	49/–
The Beatles 1962–1966 CD (1993) – EMI CDP 7 97036 2 [6]	3
Anthology 1 CD (1995) – Apple 8 34445 2 [12]	2/1
The Four Historic Ed Sullivan Shows DVD (2003) – EREDV 372 [14] [15]	
On Air – Live At The BBC Volume 2 CD (2013) – Apple 6025 37491698 [9]	12/7
The Beatles Bootleg Recordings 1963 (2013) – iTunes [7] [8] [10] [13]	–
1+ CD/DVD (2015) – Apple 6205 47567727 [11]	5/6
Live At The Hollywood Bowl CD (2016) – Apple 6025 57054972 [16]	3/7

═══ NOTES ═══

♪ Played live until 1964.
♪ Reached #1 in the UK twice, the only record to do so until 1991.
♪ The best selling Beatles single in the UK, with sales of some
   1.9 million.
♪ It was the UK's biggest selling single of all time until overtaken
   by 'Mull Of Kintyre' in 1977.

She Said She Said

[Lennon-McCartney]

John – lead vocals, rhythm guitar, Hammond organ
George – harmony vocals, lead guitar, possibly bass
Ringo – drums, percussion

Studio recording and mixing

21 June 1966 – Studio Two – Revolver session 33 out of 33

Takes 1–3
Overdubs onto take 3 – vocals
Tape reduction of take 3 > take 4
Overdubs onto take 4 – guitar, organ

22 June 1966 – Studio Three control room

RM4 [1] – mono mix from take 4
RS1 [2] – stereo mix from take 4

Releases   *UK/US peak*

Revolver LP (1966) – Parlophone PMC 7009 [1], PCS 7009 [2]	1
Revolver LP (US, 1966) – Capitol T 2576 [1], ST 2576 [2]	1
Tomorrow Never Knows (2012) – iTunes [2]	44/24

═══════════════ **NOTES** ═══════════════

♪ The last track to be recorded for *Revolver*,
   rehearsed and recorded within 9 hours.
♪ Paul does not appear on the recording,
   George plays bass.

She's A Woman

[Lennon-McCartney]

Paul – lead vocals, bass, piano
John – rhythm guitar
George – lead guitar
Ringo – drums, chocalho

Studio recording and mixing

8 October 1964 – Studio Two – Beatles For Sale session 6 out of 8

Takes 1–7
Overdubs onto take 6 – piano, guitar, vocals, percussion

12 October 1964 – Studio Two control room

RM1 [1] – mono mix from take 6
RS1 [2] – stereo mix from take 6

21 October 1964 – Room 65

RM2 [3] – mono mix from take 6

9 November 1964 – Capitol

[4] – mastering of mock stereo from [3]

BBC and other performances

17 November 1964 [5] – 26 November 1964 edition of *Top Gear,* repeated on 26 December 1964 edition of *Saturday Club*

11 April 1965 – *NME 1964–65 Annual Poll-Winners' Concert*

26 May 1965 – 7 June 1965 edition of *The Beatles Invite You To Take A Ticket To Ride*

20 June 1965 – *Les Beatles* (Europe 1 TV, France, live)

15 August 1965 – *The Beatles At Shea Stadium* (live, not broadcast)

30 August 1965 [6] – Hollywood Bowl (live)

24 June 1966 – *Die Beatles* broadcast on 5 July 1966 (ZDF TV, Germany)

30 June 1966 [7] – Nippon Budokan Hall, Tokyo (live)

Releases   UK/US peak

'I Feel Fine' / 'She's A Woman' single (1964) – Parlophone R 5200 [1]	1
'I Feel Fine' / 'She's A Woman' single (US, 1964) – Capitol 5327 [3]	4
Beatles '65 LP (US, 1964) – Capitol T 2228 [3], ST 2228 [4]	1
Greatest Hits Volume 2 LP (Australia, 1967) – Parlophone PCSO 7534 [2]	–
The Beatles At The Hollywood Bowl LP (1977) – Parlophone EMTV 4 / Capitol SMAS 11638 [6]	1/2
Rarities LP (1978) – Parlophone PCM 1001, PSLP 261 [1]	71
The Beatles EP (1981) – Parlophone SGE 1 [2, untrimmed]	
Past Masters 1 CD (1988) – EMI CDP 7 90043 2 [2]	49/–
Anthology 2 CD (1996) – Apple 8 34448 2 [7]	1/1
Live At The BBC CD (1994) – Apple 8 31796 2 [5]	1/3
Live At The Hollywood Bowl CD (2016) – Apple 6025 57054972 [6]	3/7

=== NOTES ===

♪ The first stereo release outside Australia was in December 1981.

♪ #4 peak in the US is the highest position for any Beatles B-side.

♪ The untrimmed stereo version includes a count-in.

♪ Played in concert until 1966.

♪ The only Beatles track chosen by Brian Epstein for *Desert Island Discs.*

She's Leaving Home

[Lennon-McCartney]

Paul – lead vocals
John – backing vocals
Session musicians – four violins, two violas, two cellos, double bass, harp

Studio recording and mixing

17 March 1967 – Studio Two – Sgt Pepper session 45 out of 56

Takes 1–6

20 March 1967 – *Studio Two* – *Sgt Pepper session 46 out of 56*
Tape reduction of take 1 > takes 7–9
Tape reduction of take 6 > take 10
Overdubs onto take 9 – vocals

20 March 1967 – *Studio Two control room*
RM1 [1]– mono mix from take 9
RM6 [2] – mono mix from take 9, edited

17 April 1967 – *Studio Two control room*
RS6 [3] – stereo mix from take 9, edited

2016/17 – *EMI*
[4] – stereo mix from take 1
[5] – stereo mix from take 6
[6] – stereo mix from take 9, edited

Releases _____ *UK/US peak*

Sgt Pepper's Lonely Hearts Club Band LP (1967) – Parlophone PMC 7027 [2], PCS 7027 [3]	1
Sgt Pepper's Lonely Hearts Club Band LP (US, 1967) – Capitol MAS 2653 [2], SMAS 2653 [3]	1
Love Songs LP (1977) – Parlophone PCSP 721 / Capitol SKBL 11711 [3]	7/24
The Beatles Ballads LP (1980) – Parlophone PCS 7214 [3]	17
Sgt Pepper's Lonely Hearts Club Band Deluxe CD (2017) – Apple 0602557455328 [1] [2] [4] [5] [6]	1/3

> ═══ **NOTES** ═══
>
> ♪ Only John and Paul's vocals with
>   a string section and harpist Sheila
>   Bromberg, the first woman to
>   appear on a Beatles recording.
> ♪ The edit removed short cello
>   sections.
> ♪ [1] has ADT added to the harp
>   intro.

The Sheik Of Araby

[Smith-Wheeler-Snyder]

George – lead vocals, lead guitar
John – backing vocals, rhythm guitar
Paul – backing vocals, bass
Pete Best – drums

Studio recording and mixing

1 January 1962 – *Decca Studios*
Studio test recorded in mono [1]

Releases *UK/US peak*

Anthology 1 CD (1995) – Apple 8 34445 2 [1]   2/1

NOTES

♪ According to George, this is based on a version by Joe Brown. Brown had not recorded the song by 1962, so it was probably picked up from a radio performance in 1961.

♪ Performed live in concert from 1961–62.

Sheila

[Roe]

George – lead vocals, lead guitar
John – rhythm guitar
Paul – bass
Ringo – drums

BBC and other performances

25 October 1962 – 26 October 1962 edition of *Here We Go* (not broadcast)
December 1962 [1] – Star-Club, Hamburg (live)

Releases *UK/US peak*

Live! At The Star-Club In Hamburg, Germany; 1962 LP (US, 1977) – Lingasong LS 2 7001 [1]   –

NOTES

♪ A US #1 for Tommy Roe in September 1962, which was originally released in 1960.

Shimmy Like Kate

[Piron-Smith-Goldsmith]

John – lead vocals, rhythm guitar
Paul – lead vocals, bass
George – lead guitar
Ringo – drums

BBC and other performances

December 1962 [1] – Star-Club, Hamburg (live)

Releases   *UK/US peak*

Live! At The Star-Club In Hamburg, Germany; 1962 LP (1977) – Lingasong LNL 1 /
    Lingasong LS 2 7001 [1]   –

NOTES

♪ Based on The Olympics' arrangement of 'I Wish I Could Shimmy
Like My Sister Kate', a song originally published in 1919.

Shirley's Wild Accordion

[Leander-Lennon-McCartney]

Shirley Evans – accordion
Paul – maracas
Ringo – drums
Reg Wale – percussion

Studio recording and mixing

12 October 1967 – Studio Three – Magical Mystery Tour session 24 out of 30
Takes 1–8
Tape reduction of take 8 > takes 9–10
Overdubs onto take 10 – percussion, vocals > takes 11–15

12 October 1967 – Studio Three control room
RM1, RM2, RM3 [1] – mono mixes from takes 10, 7, 14 respectively

Releases   *UK/US peak*

Magical Mystery Tour movie (1967) (cut from final print) [1]

NOTES

♪ The accordionist is Shirley Evans,
whose credits include backing Cliff
Richard in the 1968 Eurovision Song
Contest.
♪ Recorded for *Magical Mystery Tour* but
not used in the final cut.
♪ The recording session was produced
by John, and featured Paul on
maracas, Ringo on drums and Evans'
husband Reg Wale on percussion.

Short Fat Fannie

[Williams]

Lead vocals, **John**. Played by the Quarry Men/Beatles between 1958 and 1961. The first of Larry Williams' two hits, reaching #5 in the US, #21 in the UK in 1957.

A Shot Of Rhythm And Blues

[Thompson]

John – lead vocals, rhythm guitar
Paul – harmony vocals, bass
George – lead guitar
Ringo – drums

BBC and other performances

1 June 1963 [1] – 18 June 1963 edition of *Pop Go The Beatles*
17 July 1963 – 21 July 1963 edition of *Easy Beat*
1 August 1963 [2] – 27 August 1963 edition of *Pop Go The Beatles*

Releases   *UK/US peak*

Live At The BBC CD (1994) – Apple 8 31796 2 [2]   1/3
The Beatles Bootleg Recordings 1963 (2013) – iTunes [1]   –

NOTES

♪ First issued by Arthur Alexander, on the B-side of 'You Better Move On'.
♪ 'You Better Move On' was released in December 1961 in the US, and in March 1962 in the UK while it was in the *Billboard* top 30.

Shout

[Isley-Isley-Isley]

John – lead and backing vocals, rhythm guitar
Paul – lead and backing vocals, bass
George – lead and backing vocals, lead guitar
Ringo – lead and backing vocals, drums

BBC and other performances

19 April 1964 [1] – *Around The Beatles*, mimed performance recorded on 28 April and broadcast on 6 May 1964 (Rediffusion TV)

Releases   *UK/US peak*

Anthology 1 CD (1995) – Apple 8 34445 2 [1]   2/1

Side By Side

[Woods]

John, Paul – vocals
Karl Denver Trio

BBC and other performances

1 April 1963 – used for the three editions of *Side By Side* featuring the Beatles

Sie Liebt Dich

[Lennon-McCartney]

John – lead vocals, rhythm guitar
Paul – lead/harmony vocals, bass
George – harmony vocals, lead guitar
Ringo – drums

Studio recording and mixing

29 January 1964 – EMI Pathé Studios, Paris – A Hard Day's Night session 1 out of 12
Takes 1–13
Overdubs onto take 13 – vocals, handclaps > take 14

10 March 1964 – Studio Two control room
[1] – mono mix from edit of take 14

12 March 1964 – Studio Three control room
[2] – stereo mix from edit of take 14

1964 – EMI
[3] – mono mix from vinyl of [1]

1988 – EMI
[4] – mono mix from [2]

Releases   *UK/US peak*

'Komm, Gib Mir Deine Hand' / 'Sie Liebt Dich' single (Germany, 1964) – Odeon O 22671 [1]   –

'Sie Liebt Dich' / 'I'll Get You' single (US, 1964) – Swan 4182 **[3]**	97
Rarities LP (1978) – Parlophone PCM 1001, PSLP 261 **[2]**	71
Rarities LP (US, 1980) – Capitol SHAL 12060 **[2]**	21
Past Masters 1 CD (1988) – EMI CDP 7 90043 2 **[4]**	49/–
Past Masters CD (2009) – EMI CDP 2 43807 2 **[2]**	31

NOTES

♪ The instrumental backing track is sometimes said to be from the original two-track tape from July 1963, though this had almost certainly been scrapped and this is a new recording.

♪ 'Komm, Gib Mir Deine Hand' / 'Sie Liebt Dich' got to #1 in Germany.

Slow Down

[Williams]

John – lead vocals, lead guitar
Paul – bass
George – rhythm guitar
Ringo – drums
George Martin – piano

Studio recording and mixing

1 June 1964 – Studio Two – A Hard Day's Night session 9 out of 12
Takes 1–6

4 June 1964 – Studio Two – A Hard Day's Night session 12 out of 12
Overdubs onto take 6 – piano

4 June 1964 – Studio Two control room
RM1 **[1]** – mono mix from take 6

22 June 1964 – Studio One control room
RS1 **[2]** – stereo mix from take 6

BBC and other performances

16 July 1963 **[3]** – 20 August 1963 edition of *Pop Go The Beatles*

Releases   UK/US peak

Long Tall Sally EP (1964) – Parlophone GEP 8913 **[1]**	1
Something New LP (US, 1964) – Capitol T 2108 **[1]**, ST 2108 **[2]**	2
Something New EP (US, 1964) – Capitol SXA 2108 **[2]**	–
'Matchbox' / 'Slow Down' single (US, 1964) – Capitol 5255 **[1]**	25
Rock 'n' Roll Music LP (1976) – Parlophone PCSP 719 / Capitol SKBO 11537 **[2]**	11/2

Rarities LP (1978) – Parlophone PCM 1001, PSLP 261 [1]   71
Past Masters 1 CD (1988) – EMI CDP 7 90043 2 [2]   49/–
Live At The BBC CD (1994) – Apple 8 31796 2 [3]   1/3

> ═══ **NOTES** ═══
>
> ♪ The B-side to 'Dizzy Miss Lizzy' from 1958.
> ♪ The first of three covers of Larry Williams songs.
> ♪ The final track on Gerry and the Pacemakers' debut LP, *How Do You Do It?*
> ♪ Played live by the Beatles until 1962.

So How Come (No One Loves Me)

[Bryant-Bryant]

George – lead vocals, lead guitar
John – harmony vocals, rhythm guitar
Paul – harmony vocals, bass
Ringo – drums

BBC and other performances

10 July 1963 [1] – 23 July 1963 edition of *Pop Go The Beatles*

Releases   *UK/US peak*

Live At The BBC CD (1994) – Apple 8 31796 2 [1]   1/3

> ═══ **NOTES** ═══
>
> ♪ From the Everly Brothers' 1961 *A Date With The Everly Brothers* LP.
> ♪ Introduced in concert by George as 'So How Come brackets No One Loves Me brackets'.

Soldier Of Love

[Cason-Moon]

John – lead vocals, rhythm guitar
Paul – harmony and backing vocals, bass
George – harmony and backing vocals, lead guitar
Ringo – drums

BBC and other performances

2 July 1963 [1] – 16 July 1963 edition of *Pop Go The Beatles*

Releases _____ *UK/US peak*

Live At The BBC CD (1994) – Apple 8 31796 2 [1]   1/3

┌─────────────── **NOTES** ───────────────┐

♪ The B-side of Arthur Alexander's 'Where Have You Been (All My Life)', which was his follow-up to 'You Better Move On'.
♪ The full title is 'Soldier Of Love (Lay Down Your Arms)'.

└───┘

Some Days

[Lennon-McCartney]

Lead vocals, **Paul**. Recorded at Paul's house in June 1960 and presumably part of the group's repertoire at the time.

Some Other Guy

[Leiber-Stoller-Barrett]

John – lead vocals, rhythm guitar
Paul – lead vocals, bass
George – lead guitar
Ringo – drums

BBC and other performances _____

22 August 1962 – *Know The North* (Granada TV, unbroadcast)
17 October 1962 – *People And Places* (Granada TV, live)
22 January 1963 [1] – 26 January 1963 edition of *Saturday Club*
22 January 1963 – 29 January 1963 edition of *The Talent Club*
19 June 1963 [2] – 23 June 1963 edition of *Easy Beat*

Releases _____ *UK/US peak*

Live At The BBC CD (1994) – Apple 8 31796 2 [2]   1/3
The Beatles Bootleg Recordings 1963 (2013) – iTunes [1]   –

┌─────────────── **NOTES** ───────────────┐

♪ A single released by Richie Barrett in April 1962 in the US.
♪ The footage shot on 22 August 1962 is the only known audiovisual record of the Beatles playing the Cavern. It was finally broadcast by Granada on 6 November 1963.

└───┘

Something

George – lead vocals, lead guitar
Paul – harmony vocals, bass
John – guitar
Ringo – drums
Billy Preston – piano, organ
Session musicians – twelve violins, four violas, four cellos, double bass

Studio recording and mixing

25 February 1969 – unknown studio – Abbey Road rehearsal session
Demo take 1

16 April 1969 – Studio Three – Abbey Road session 3 out of 42
Takes 1–13

2 May 1969 – Studio Three – Abbey Road session 8 out of 42
Remake takes 1–36

5 May 1969 – Olympic Sound – Abbey Road session 9 out of 42
Overdubs onto take 36 – bass, guitar

11 July 1969 – Studio Two – Abbey Road session 19 out of 42
Overdubs onto take 36 – vocals
Tape reduction of take 36 > take 37

16 July 1969 – Studio Two – Abbey Road session 21 out of 42
Overdubs onto take 36 – vocals, handclaps, percussion
Tape reduction of take 36 > takes 38, 39

15 August 1969 – Studio One – Abbey Road session 40 out of 42
Overdubs onto take 39 – strings

19 August 1969 – Studio Two control room
RS10 [1] – stereo mix from take 39

1996 – EMI
[2] – stereo mix from demo take 1

2004–06 – EMI
[3] – stereo mix from take 39, in medley with 'Blue Jay Way' take 3: includes sample from 'Nowhere Man' (vocals)

Releases   *UK/US peak*

Abbey Road LP (1969) – Apple PCS 7088 [1]	1
Abbey Road LP (US, 1969) – Apple SO 383 [1]	1
'Something' / 'Come Together' single (1969) – Apple R 5814 [1]	4
'Something' / 'Come Together' single (US, 1969) – Apple 2654 [1]	3 (1)

The Beatles 1967–1970 LP (1973) – Apple PCSP 718 [1]	2
The Beatles 1967–1970 LP (US, 1973) – Apple SKBO 3404 [1]	1
Love Songs LP (1977) – Parlophone PCSP 721 / Capitol SKBL 11711 [1]	7/24
The Beatles Ballads LP (1980) – Parlophone PCS 7214 [1]	17
Anthology 3 CD (1996) – Apple 8 34451 2 [2]	4/1
Love CD (2006) – Apple 0946 3 80790 2 6 [3]	3/4
1+ CD/DVD (2015) – Apple 6205 47567727 [1]	5/6

NOTES

♪ The last promotional film for a Beatles single, consisting of separately shot sequences of the Beatle couples.
♪ George's only A-side.
♪ On 29 November, with both sides of the single still high in the charts, *Billboard* stopped their practice of listing the two sides of a single separately, so after 'Something' had peaked at #3 and 'Come Together' at #2, that week they jointly hit #1.

Sour Milk Sea

[Harrison]

George – lead vocals, acoustic guitar

Studio recording and mixing

May 1968 – Kinfauns, Esher
Demo recording

2018 – EMI
[1] – stereo mix from demo

Releases

UK/US peak

The Beatles Deluxe CD (2018) – Apple 0602567571957 [1]	4/6

NOTES

♪ Released by Jackie Lomax in 1968, the third Apple single after 'Hey Jude' and Mary Hopkin's 'Those Were The Days'.

Stand By Me

[King-Leiber-Stoller]

Lead vocals, **John**. The song was performed by the Beatles until 1962. It was a hit for Ben E King in 1961, finally making #1 in the UK in 1987. It appears on John's 1975 *Rock 'n' Roll* LP.

Step Inside Love

[Lennon-McCartney]

Paul – lead vocals, acoustic guitar
John – skulls
Ringo – percussion

Studio recording and mixing

16 September 1968 – Studio Two – White Album session 61 out of 81
Studio jam from take 35 of 'I Will'
1996 – EMI
[1] – stereo mix from studio jam
2018 – EMI
[2] – stereo mix from studio jam

Releases   *UK/US peak*

Anthology 3 CD (1996) – Apple 8 34451 2 [1]   4/1
The Beatles Deluxe CD (2018) – Apple 0602567571957 [2]   4/6

NOTES

♪ Written by Paul in 1967 for Cilla Black's TV series *Cilla*. Her version got to #8 in the UK charts in April 1968.
♪ Released on *Anthology 3* jointly with 'Los Paranoias'.

Strawberry Fields Forever

[Lennon-McCartney]

John – lead and harmony vocals, guitar, piano, bongos
Paul – Mellotron, possibly bass, guitar, bongos
George – guitar, Mellotron, swarmandal, maracas, timpani
Ringo – drums
George Martin – Mellotron
Mal Evans, Neil Aspinall, Terry Doran – percussion
Session musicians – four trumpets, three cellos

Studio recording and mixing

November 1966 – Kenwood, Surrey
Demo recordings

24 November 1966 – Studio Two – Sgt Pepper session 1 out of 56
Take 1
Overdubs onto take 1 – percussion, guitar, vocals

28 November 1966 – Studio Two – Sgt Pepper session 3 out of 56
Takes 2–4 – Mellotron, drums, bass, maracas, guitar

29 November 1966 – Studio Two – Sgt Pepper session 4 out of 56
Takes 5–6
Overdubs onto take 6 – vocals
Tape reduction of take 6 > take 7
Overdubs onto take 7 – piano, bass
RM3 – mono mix from take 7

8 December 1966 – Studio Two – Sgt Pepper session 6 out of 56
Remake takes 9–24
Edit of takes 15, 24

9 December 1966 – Studio Two – Sgt Pepper session 7 out of 56
Tape reduction of edit of takes 15, 24 > take 25
Overdubs onto take 25 – percussion, swardmandal

15 December 1966 – Studio Two – Sgt Pepper session 8 out of 56
Overdubs onto take 25 – trumpets, cellos
Tape reduction of take 25 > take 26
Overdubs onto take 26 – vocals, drums

21 December 1966 – Studio Two – Sgt Pepper session 10 out of 56
Overdubs onto take 26 – vocals, piano

22 December 1966 – Studio Two control room
RM10 – mono mix from take 7
RM11 – mono mix from take 26
Edit of RM10, RM11 > RM12 [1]

29 December 1966 – Studio Three control room
RM13 [2] – mono mix from RM12
RS1 – stereo mix from take 7
RS2, RS4 – stereo mixes from take 26
Edit of RS1, RS2 > RS3
Edit of RS1, RS4 > RS5 [3]

26 October 1971 – AIR Studios
[4] – stereo mix from edit of takes 7, 26

1995 – EMI
[5] – mono mix from edit of demo recordings
[6] – stereo mix from take 1
[7] – mono mix from edit of take 7 and edit piece from take 25

2004–06 – EMI

[8] – stereo mix from demo, takes 1, 7, 26: includes samples from 'Sgt Pepper's Lonely Hearts Club Band' (orchestra and audience noise); 'In My Life' (piano); 'Penny Lane' (trumpet, backing vocals); 'I'm Only Sleeping' (guitar); 'Piggies' (harpsichord and strings); 'Hello, Goodbye' (vocals); possibly 'Hey Bulldog' and 'Baby You're A Rich Man'

2015 – EMI

[9] – stereo mix from edit of takes 7, 26

2016/17 – EMI

[10] – stereo mix from take 1
[11] – stereo mix from take 4
[12] – stereo mix from take 7
[13] – stereo mix from take 26

Releases   UK/US peak

'Strawberry Fields Forever' / 'Penny Lane' single (1967) – Parlophone R 5570 [1]	2
'Strawberry Fields Forever' / 'Penny Lane' single (US, 1967) – Capitol 5810 [2]	8
Magical Mystery Tour LP (US, 1967) – Capitol MAL 2835 [2], SMAL 2835 [3]	1
Magical Mystery Tour LP (Germany, 1971) – Hör Zu SHZE 327 / Apple 1C 072-04449 [4]	–
The Beatles 1967–1970 LP (1973) – Apple PCSP 718 [3]	2
The Beatles 1967–1970 LP (US, 1973) – Apple SKBO 3404 [3]	1
Magical Mystery Tour CD (1987) – EMI CDP 7 48062 2 [4]	52
The Beatles 1967–1970 CD (1993) – EMI CDP 7 97039 2 [4]	4
Anthology 2 CD (1996) – Apple 8 34448 2 [5] [6] [7]	1/1
Love CD (2006) – Apple 0946 3 80790 2 6 [8]	3/4
1+ CD/DVD (2015) – Apple 6205 47567727 [9]	5/6
Sgt Pepper's Lonely Hearts Club Band Deluxe CD (2017) – Apple 0602557455328 [1] [9] [10] [11] [12] [13]	1/3

=== NOTES ===

♪ Famously the result of two takes, in different keys and at different speeds, edited together.
♪ A promotional film was shot in Knole Park, Sevenoaks, on 30–31 January 1967.
♪ The first (of two) double A-side release in the US, but this side has a lower catalogue number.

Stuck On You

[Fisher-Raskin-Hill]

Lead vocals, **Paul**. Part of the Beatles' set around 1960, appears on the group's earliest known set list from mid-1960. A US #1/UK #3 for Elvis Presley in 1960.

Summertime

[Gershwin-Heyward-Gershwin]

John – guitar
Paul – guitar or bass
George – guitar
Ringo – drums
Lu Walters – vocals

Studio recording and mixing

15 October 1960 – Akustik Studio, Hamburg
Demo recording

NOTES

♪ Lu 'Wally' Walters was bassist with the Hurricanes, Ringo's band at the time of recording.
♪ A number of 78s were made, but all seem lost. Only a photograph of the 'Summertime' side remains.
♪ Part of the Beatles' set from 1959–61, with lead vocals by Paul, based on the version by Gene Vincent from 1959.

Sun King / Mean Mr Mustard

[Lennon-McCartney]

John – lead vocals, guitar, maracas
Paul – harmony vocals, bass, harmonium, piano
George – guitar
Ringo – drums, tambourine, bongos
George Martin – organ

Studio recording and mixing

May 1968 – Kinfauns, Esher
Demo recording ('Mean Mr Mustard')

24 July 1969 – Studio Two – Abbey Road session 27 out of 42
Takes 1–35

25 July 1969 – Studio Two – Abbey Road session 28 out of 42
Overdubs onto take 35 – vocals, piano, organ

29 July 1969 – Studio Three – Abbey Road session 30 out of 42
Overdubs onto take 35 – vocals, piano, organ, percussion

14 August 1969 – Studio Two control room
RS22 [1] – stereo mix from take 35

1996 – EMI
[2] – stereo mix from demo ('Mean Mr Mustard')

2004–06 – EMI
[3] – stereo mix from take 35 (backwards) ('Sun King', listed as 'Gnik Nus'): includes sample from 'Within You Without You' (tamboura)

2018 – EMI
[4] – stereo mix from demo

Releases   UK/US peak

Abbey Road LP (1969) – Apple PCS 7088 [1]	1
Abbey Road LP (US, 1969) – Apple SO 383 [1]	1
Anthology 3 CD (1996) – Apple 8 34451 2 [2]	4/1
Love CD (2006) – Apple 0946 3 80790 2 6 [3]	3/4
The Beatles Deluxe CD (2018) – Apple 0602567571957 [4]	4/6

━━━ NOTES ━━━

♪ Both characters feature in the 1978 *Sgt Pepper* movie, played by Alice Cooper and Frankie Howerd respectively.
♪ Based on Fleetwood Mac's 'Albatross'.

Sure To Fall (In Love With You)

[Perkins-Claunch-Cantrell]

Paul – lead vocals, bass
John – harmony vocals, rhythm guitar
George – lead guitar
Pete Best – drums (1962)
Ringo – drums

Studio recording and mixing

1 January 1962 – Decca Studios
Studio test recorded in mono

BBC and other performances

1 June 1963 [1] – 18 June 1963 edition of *Pop Go The Beatles*
3 September 1963 [2] – 24 September 1963 edition of *Pop Go The Beatles*
31 March 1964 – 4 April 1964 edition of *Saturday Club*
1 May 1964 – 18 May 1964 edition of *From Us To You*

Releases

Releases .... *UK/US peak*

Live At The BBC CD (1994) – Apple 8 31796 2 [1]   1/3
On Air – Live At The BBC Volume 2 CD (2013) – Apple 6025 37491698 [2]   12/7

```
━━━━━━━━━━━ NOTES ━━━━━━━━━━━
  ♪ Written in 1956 and included on Carl Perkins' Dance Album,
    released in the UK in 1959.
  ♪ Played live by the Quarry Men/Beatles between 1957 and 1962.
```

Suzy Parker

[Lennon-McCartney-Harrison-Starkey]

John – lead vocals, rhythm guitar
Paul – backing vocals, bass
George – backing vocals, lead guitar
Ringo – drums

Studio recording and mixing

9 January 1969 – Twickenham Film Studios – Let It Be rehearsal session
Take 9.31 [1]

Releases .... *UK/US peak*

Let It Be movie (1970) [1]

```
━━━━━━━━━━━ NOTES ━━━━━━━━━━━
  ♪ Also known as 'Suzy's Parlour'.
  ♪ An impromptu jam that was registered for copyright in 1971.
```

Sweet Georgia Brown

[Pinkard-Casey-Bernie]

Tony Sheridan – lead vocals
John – rhythm guitar
Paul – bass, backing vocals
George – backing vocals
Pete Best – drums
Roy Young – piano

Studio recording and mixing

24 May 1962 – Studio Rahlstedt, Hamburg
Unknown take numbers

7 June 1962 *– Studio Rahlstedt, Hamburg*
Overdubs onto unknown take number – vocals

June 1962 *– Polydor, Hamburg*
[1] – mono mix from unknown take number

Early 1964 *– Hamburg*
Overdubs onto unknown take number – vocals

1964 *– Polydor, Hamburg*
[2] – mono mix from unknown take number
[3] – stereo mix from unknown take number

1964 *– Atlantic Studios, USA*
[4] – mono mix from [2]

Releases   *UK/US peak*

Ya Ya EP (Germany, 1962) – Polydor 21485 [1]   –
'Sweet Georgia Brown' / 'Nobody's Child' single (Germany, 1964) – Polydor 52906 [2]   –
'Sweet Georgia Brown' / 'Take Out Some Insurance On Me Baby' single (US, 1964)
    – Atco 45-6302 [4]   –
Beatles First LP (1967) – Polydor 236 201 [3]   –
The Early Tapes Of The Beatles CD (1985) – Polydor 823701-2 [3]   –

═══ NOTES ═══

♪ A jazz standard from 1925.
♪ 'Swanee River' was also recorded at the session, but the tape has been lost.
♪ The other *Ya Ya* EP tracks do not feature the Beatles.
♪ 'Nobody's Child' on the German single is not the Beatles – according to the label, Tony Sheridan is "accompanying himself on his Guitar".

Sweet Little Sixteen

[Berry]

John – lead vocals, rhythm guitar
Paul – bass
George – lead guitar
Ringo – drums

BBC and other performances

December 1962 [1] – Star-Club, Hamburg (live)

2 July 1963 – 16 July 1963 edition of *Pop Go The Beatles* (not broadcast)
10 July 1963 [2] – 23 July 1963 edition of *Pop Go The Beatles*

Releases _____ *UK/US peak*

Live! At The Star-Club In Hamburg, Germany; 1962 LP (1977) – Lingasong LNL 1 /
    Lingasong LS 2 7001 [1]   –
Live At The BBC CD (1994) – Apple 8 31796 2 [2]   1/3

NOTES

- ♪ Released in 1958, Chuck Berry's biggest hit until 'My Ding-A-Ling'.
- ♪ Played live by the Quarry Men/ Beatles from 1957.
- ♪ Appears on John's 1975 *Rock 'n' Roll* LP.

Take Good Care Of My Baby

[Goffin-King]

George – lead vocals, lead guitar
John – rhythm guitar
Paul – harmony vocals, bass
Pete Best – drums

Studio recording and mixing _____

1 January 1962 – Decca Studios
Studio test recorded in mono

NOTES

- ♪ Unreleased recording from the Decca studio test, sung by George.
- ♪ A version by Bobby Vee reached #1 on the *Billboard* chart in 1961.

Take Out Some Insurance On Me Baby [If You Love Me Baby]

[Trad. arr. Sheridan]

Tony Sheridan – lead vocals, lead guitar
John – rhythm guitar
Paul – bass
George – guitar
Pete Best – drums

Studio recording and mixing

22 June 1961 – Friedrich-Eberts-Halle, Hamburg
Unknown take numbers

24 June 1961 – Polydor, Hamburg
[1] – stereo mix from unknown take number

1964 – Polydor, Hamburg
[2] – mono mix from [1]

1964 – Atlantic Studios, USA
[3] – mono mix from edit of [1]

Releases   *UK/US peak*

'Ain't She Sweet' / 'If You Love Me Baby' single (1964) – Polydor NH 52317 [2]	29
'Sweet Georgia Brown' / 'Take Out Some Insurance On Me Baby' single (US, 1964) – Atco 45-6302 [3]	–
Beatles First LP (1967) – Polydor 236 201 [1]	–
The Early Tapes Of The Beatles CD (1985) – Polydor 823701-2 [1]	–

─── **NOTES** ───

♪ Recorded in 1959 by blues singer Jimmy Reed, and released on Vee Jay.
♪ It's possible that only one take was recorded.
♪ The Beatles backing Tony Sheridan, produced by Bert Kaempfert.

A Taste Of Honey

[Marlow-Scott]

Paul – lead vocals, bass
John – harmony vocals, rhythm guitar
George – harmony vocals, lead guitar
Ringo – drums

Studio recording and mixing

11 February 1963 – Studio Two – Please Please Me session 5 out of 8
Takes 1–5
Overdubs onto take 5 – vocals > takes 6–7

25 February 1963 – Studio One control room
[1] – mono mix from take 7
[2] – stereo mix from take 7

1965 – Capitol
[3] – stereo mix from [2]
[4] – mono mix from [3]

2013 – EMI
[5] – stereo mix from take 6

BBC and other performances

25 October 1962 – 26 October 1962 edition of *Here We Go*
29 October 1962 – 2 November 1962 edition of *People And Places* (Granada TV)
December 1962 [6] – Star-Club, Hamburg (live)
1 April 1963 [7] – 13 May 1963 edition of *Side By Side*
1 June 1963 [8] – 18 June 1963 edition of *Pop Go The Beatles*
17 June 1963 – 25 June 1963 edition of *Pop Go The Beatles* (not broadcast)
19 June 1963 [9] – 23 June 1963 edition of *Easy Beat*
3 July 1963 – 4 July 1963 edition of *The Beat Show*
10 July 1963 [10] – 23 July 1963 edition of *Pop Go The Beatles*
3 September 1963 [11] – 10 September 1963 edition of *Pop Go The Beatles*
3 September 1963 – 17 September 1963 edition of *Pop Go The Beatles* (not broadcast)

Releases   *UK/US peak*

Please Please Me LP (1963) – Parlophone PMC 1202 [1], PCS 3042 [2]   1
Introducing… The Beatles LP (US, 1963) – Vee Jay VJLP 1062 [1], VJSR 1062 [2]   2
Twist And Shout EP (1963) – Parlophone GEP 8882 [1]   1
Souvenir Of Their Visit To America EP (US, 1964) – Vee Jay VJEP 1903 [1]   –
The Early Beatles LP (US, 1965) – Capitol T 2309 [4], ST 2309 [3]   43
Live! At The Star-Club In Hamburg, Germany; 1962 LP (1977) – Lingasong LNL 1 /
    Lingasong LS 2 7001 [6]   –
Live At The BBC CD (1994) – Apple 8 31796 2 [10]   1/3
The Beatles Bootleg Recordings 1963 (2013) – iTunes [5] [7] [8] [9] [11]   –

NOTES
♪ The Star-Club recording has Tony Sheridan on backing vocals.
♪ Based on the 1962 single by Lenny Welch.
♪ Acker Bilk's recording of the song was at its peak of #16 in the UK charts while the Beatles recorded their cover.
♪ The first recording – and the only Beatles cover – in triple time.

Taxman

George – lead vocals, lead guitar
John – backing vocals
Paul – backing vocals, bass, lead guitar
Ringo – drums, tambourine, cowbell

Studio recording and mixing

20 April 1966 – Studio Two – Revolver session 10 out of 33
Takes 1–4

21 April 1966 – Studio Two – Revolver session 11 out of 33
Remake takes 1–11
Overdubs onto take 11 – guitar, tambourine

22 April 1966 – Studio Two – Revolver session 12 out of 33
Tape reduction of take 11 > take 12
Overdubs onto take 12 – cowbell, vocals

16 May 1966 – Studio Two – Revolver session 20 out of 33
Overdubs onto take 12 – vocals

21 June 1966 – Studio Three control room
RM5, RM6 – mono mixes from take 12
[1] – edit of RM5, RM6
RS1, RS2 – stereo mixes from take 12
[2] – edit of RS1, RS2

1995 – EMI
[3] – stereo mix from take 11

Releases   *UK/US peak*

Revolver LP (1966) – Parlophone PMC 7009 [1], PCS 7009 [2]	1
Revolver LP (US, 1966) – Capitol T 2576 [1], ST 2576 [2]	1
Rock 'n' Roll Music LP (1976) – Parlophone PCSP 719 / Capitol SKBO 11537 [2]	11/2
Anthology 2 CD (1996) – Apple 8 34448 2 [3]	1/1

NOTES

- ♪ Politicians Harold Wilson and Edward Heath are first living people mentioned in a Beatles song.
- ♪ The "1, 2, 3, 4" count-in was recorded on 16 May.

Teddy Boy

[McCartney]

Paul – lead vocals, acoustic guitar
John – backing vocals
George – guitar
Ringo – drums

Studio recording and mixing

24 January 1969 – Apple Studios – Let It Be session 4 out of 17
Take 24.22

28 January 1969 – Apple Studios – Let It Be session 8 out of 17
Take 28.25

1996 – EMI
[1] – stereo mix from edit of takes 24.22, 28.25

Releases   UK/US peak

Anthology 3 CD (1996) – Apple 8 34451 2 [1]   4/1

♪ NOTES

♪ Glyn Johns intended the 24 January recording to appear on the aborted *Get Back*, but it was ultimately rejected by Phil Spector for *Let It Be*.
♪ Re-recorded by Paul in December 1969 and January 1970 for his *McCartney* LP.

Tell Me What You See

[Lennon-McCartney]

Paul – lead vocals, bass, electric piano
John – harmony vocals, guitar, tambourine
George – güiro
Ringo – drums, claves

Studio recording and mixing

18 February 1965 – Studio Two – Help! session 4 out of 13
Takes 1–4
Overdubs onto take 4 – electric piano, percussion

20 February 1965 – Studio Two control room
RM1 [1] – mono mix from take 4

23 February 1965 – *Studio Two control room*
RS1 [2] – stereo mix from take 4

1987 – *EMI*
[3] – stereo mix from take 4

Releases
UK/US peak

Help! LP (1965) – Parlophone PMC 1255 [1], PCS 3071 [2]	1
Beatles VI LP (US, 1965) – Capitol T 2358 [1], ST 2358 [2]	1
Love Songs LP (1977) – Parlophone PCSP 721 / Capitol SKBL 11711 [2]	7/24
Help! CD (1987) – EMI CDP 7 46439 2 [3]	61

NOTES

♪ George plays a güiro, a notched gourd, described on the session's tape box as "Latin American percussion".

Tell Me Why

[Lennon-McCartney]

John – lead vocals, rhythm guitar
Paul – harmony vocals, bass
George – harmony vocals, lead guitar
Ringo – drums
George Martin – piano

Studio recording and mixing

27 February 1964 – *Studio Two – A Hard Day's Night session 4 out of 12*
Takes 1–8
Overdubs onto take 8 – piano, vocals

3 March 1964 – *Studio Two control room*
RM1 [1] – mono mix from take 8
[2] – mono mix from take 8

22 June 1964 – *Studio Two control room*
RS1 [3] – stereo mix from take 8

1964 – *United Artists*
[4] – panned mono mix made from [1]

Releases
UK/US peak

A Hard Day's Night LP (1964) – Parlophone PMC 1230 [1], PCS 3058 [3]	1
A Hard Day's Night LP (US, 1964) – United Artists UAL 3366 [1], UAS 6366 [4]	1
A Hard Day's Night movie (1964) [2]	

Something New LP (US, 1964) – Capitol T 2108 [1], ST 2108 [3]   2
Extracts From The Film 'A Hard Day's Night' EP (1964) – Parlophone GEP 8920 [1]   1
Something New EP (US, 1964) – Capitol SXA 2108 [3]   –
'If I Fell' / 'Tell Me Why' single (1964) – Parlophone DP 562 [1]   –

NOTES

♪ The stereo version double-tracks the vocals throughout.
♪ The stereo also has a third vocal punched in during the bridge.
♪ The first song played during the TV performance at the end of the movie.

Thank You Girl

[McCartney-Lennon]

John – lead vocals, rhythm guitar, harmonica
Paul – harmony vocals, bass
George – lead guitar
Ringo – drums

Studio recording and mixing

5 March 1963 – Studio Two – Please Please Me session 7 out of 8
Takes 1–6
Edit pieces takes 7–13

13 March 1963 – Studio Two – Please Please Me session 8 out of 8
Overdubs onto edit of takes 6, 13 – harmonica > takes 14–28
Edit of takes 6, 13, 17, 20, 21, 23 > take 30

13 March 1963 – Studio Two control room
RM1 [1] – mono mix from take 30
RS1 [2] – stereo mix from take 30

17 March 1964 – Capitol
[3] – mastering of stereo mix from [2]
[4] – mastering of mono mix from [2]

2013 – EMI
[5] – stereo mix from take 1
[6] – stereo mix from take 5

BBC and other performances

1 April 1963 – 13 May 1963 edition of *Side By Side*
13 April 1963 – 16 April 1963 edition of *The 625 Show* (BBC TV)

21 May 1963 – 3 June 1963 edition of *Steppin' Out*
19 June 1963 [7] – 23 June 1963 edition of *Easy Beat*

Releases   UK/US peak

'From Me To You' / 'Thank You Girl' single (1963) – Parlophone R 5015 [1]	1
'From Me To You' / 'Thank You Girl' single (US, 1963) – Vee Jay VJ 522 [1]	–
The Beatles' Hits EP (1963) – Parlophone GEP 8880 [1]	1
'Do You Want To Know A Secret' / 'Thank You Girl' single (US, 1964) – Vee Jay VJ 587 [1]	35
The Beatles' Second Album LP (US, 1964) – Capitol T 2080 [4], ST 2080 [3]	1
The Beatles' Second Album EP (US, 1964) – Capitol SXA 2080 [3]	–
'Do You Want To Know A Secret' / 'Thank You Girl' single (US, 1965) – Capitol Starline 6064 [4]	–
Rarities LP (1978) – Parlophone PCM 1001, PSLP 261 [1]	71
Past Masters 1 CD (1988) – EMI CDP 7 90043 2 [1]	49/–
Live At The BBC CD (1994) – Apple 8 31796 2 [7]	1/3
Past Masters CD (2009) – EMI CDP 2 43807 2 [2]	31
The Beatles Bootleg Recordings 1963 (2013) – iTunes [5] [6]	–

NOTES

♪ The stereo version has extra harmonica tags.
♪ It out-performed 'From Me To You' in the *Billboard* chart.
♪ The first true stereo release was in 2009.
♪ Played live in 1963.

That Means A Lot

[Lennon-McCartney]

Paul – lead vocals, piano, bass
John – backing vocals, guitar, maracas
George – backing vocals, guitar, maracas
Ringo – drums

Studio recording and mixing

20 February 1965 – Studio Two – Help! session 6 out of 13
Take 1
Overdubs onto take 1 – bass, tom tom, guitar, vocals, piano, maracas
Tape reduction of take 1 > take 2
Overdubs onto take 2 – vocals, guitar

20 February 1965 – Studio Two control room
RM1 [1] – mono mix from take 1

30 March 1965 – Studio Two – Help! session 7 out of 13
Remake takes 20–24

Releases UK/US peak

Anthology 2 CD (1996) – Apple 8 34448 2 **[1]** 1/1

```
=== NOTES ===
```

♪ Written by John and Paul for the *Help!* movie.
♪ Recorded as a single by PJ Proby, reaching #30 in October 1965.

That'll Be The Day

[Allison-Holly-Petty]

John – lead vocals, rhythm guitar
Paul – harmony and backing vocals, guitar
George – lead guitar
John Lowe – piano
Colin Hanton – drums

BBC and other performances

1958 – Phillips Sound Recording Service, Liverpool

1995 – EMI

[1] – edited and reprocessed from source tape

Releases UK/US peak

Anthology 1 CD (1995) – Apple 8 34445 2 **[1]** 2/1

```
=== NOTES ===
```

♪ A US and UK #1 for the Crickets in 1957.
♪ First ever recording by the Beatles, as the Quarry Men, in 1958.
♪ Played live by the Quarry Men until 1960.

That's All Right (Mama)

[Crudup]

Paul – lead vocals, bass
John – rhythm guitar
George – lead guitar
Ringo – drums

BBC and other performances

2 July 1963 **[1]** – 16 July 1963 edition of *Pop Go The Beatles*

Releases .... *UK/US peak*

Live At The BBC CD (1994) – Apple 8 31796 2 **[1]**   1/3

```
═══════════ NOTES ═══════════
```

> ♪ Written and recorded by Arthur "Big Boy" Crudup
> in 1946.
> ♪ Elvis Presley's first commercial single release, in
> July 1954.

That's When Your Heartaches Begin

[Fisher-Raskin-Hill]

Part of the Quarry Men/Beatles' set until around 1961, and recorded at Paul's house in June 1960 with **John** singing lead. It was on the B-side of Elvis Presley's 'All Shook Up' in 1957. It was one of the first two songs Presley recorded as a demo at Sun Records in 1953.

There's A Place

[McCartney-Lennon]

John – lead and harmony vocals, rhythm guitar, harmonica
Paul – lead and harmony vocals, bass
George – backing vocals, lead guitar
Ringo – drums

Studio recording and mixing

11 February 1963 – Studio Two – Please Please Me session 5 out of 8
Takes 1–10
Overdubs onto take 10 – harmonica > takes 11–13

25 February 1963 – Studio One control room
[1] – mono mix from take 13
[2] – stereo mix from take 13

1980 – Capitol
[3] – stereo mix from [2]

2013 – EMI
[4] – stereo mix from takes 5, 6
[5] – stereo mix from take 8
[6] – stereo mix from take 9

BBC and other performances

2 July 1963 – 16 July 1963 edition of *Pop Go The Beatles*
17 July 1963 – 21 July 1963 edition of *Easy Beat*
1 August 1963 **[7]** – 3 September 1963 edition of *Pop Go The Beatles*

Releases

UK/US peak

Please Please Me LP (1963) – Parlophone PMC 1202 [1], PCS 3042 [2]	1
Introducing… The Beatles LP (US, 1963) – Vee Jay VJLP 1062 [1], VJSR 1062 [2]	2
Twist And Shout EP (1963) – Parlophone GEP 8882 [2]	1
'Twist And Shout' / 'There's A Place' single (US, 1964) – Tollie 9001 [1]	74
'Twist And Shout' / 'There's A Place' single (US, 1965) – Capitol Starline 6061 [1]	–
Rarities LP (US, 1980) – Capitol SHAL 12060 [3]	21
On Air – Live At The BBC Volume 2 CD (2013) – Apple 6025 37491698 [7]	12/7
The Beatles Bootleg Recordings 1963 (2013) – iTunes [4] [5] [6]	–

═══ NOTES ═══

♪ The first song recorded on the 11 February *Please Please Me* session.

♪ Being the first, it required the most takes to perfect – seven complete and three false starts.

♪ Like 'Misery', 'There's A Place' did not appear on a Capitol release until the Starline singles of 1965.

Things We Said Today

[Lennon-McCartney]

Paul – lead vocals, bass
John – acoustic guitar, piano
George – lead guitar
Ringo – drums, tambourine

Studio recording and mixing

2 June 1964 – Studio Two – A Hard Day's Night session 10 out of 12
Takes 1–3

3 June 1964 – Studio Two – A Hard Day's Night session 11 out of 12
Overdubs onto take 3 – vocals, tambourine, piano

9 June 1964 – Studio Two control room
RM1 [1] – mono mix from take 3

22 June 1964 – Studio Two control room
RS1 [2] – stereo mix from take 3

BBC and other performances

14 July 1964 [3] – 16 July 1964 edition of *Top Gear*
17 July 1964 – 3 August 1964 edition of *From Us To You*
19 July 1964 – *Blackpool Night Out* (Associated British Corp. TV, live)
23 August 1964 [4] – Hollywood Bowl (live)

Releases UK/US peak

	UK/US peak
A Hard Day's Night LP (1964) – Parlophone PMC 1230 [1], PCS 3058 [2]	1
Something New LP (US, 1964) – Capitol T 2108 [1], ST 2108 [2]	2
Extracts From The Album 'A Hard Day's Night' EP (1964) – Parlophone GEP 8924 [1]	7
'A Hard Day's Night' / *'Things We Said Today'* single (1964) – Parlophone R 5160 [1]	1
The Beatles At The Hollywood Bowl LP (1977) – Parlophone EMTV 4 / Capitol SMAS 11638 [4]	1/2
Live At The BBC CD (1994) – Apple 8 31796 2 [3]	1/3
Live At The Hollywood Bowl CD (2016) – Apple 6025 57054972 [4]	3/7

NOTES

♪ Written while Paul was on holiday in the Virgin Islands with Jane Asher and Ringo and Maureen.
♪ The song's major–minor change was inspired by 'Besame Mucho'.
♪ John's piano part was removed in the mix, but leakage is audible.

Think For Yourself

[Harrison]

George – lead vocals, rhythm guitar, possibly tambourine
John – harmony vocals, Vox electric organ
Paul – harmony vocals, bass, fuzz bass
Ringo – drums, maracas

Studio recording and mixing

8 November 1965 – Studio Two – Rubber Soul session 13 out of 15
Take 1
Overdubs onto take 1 – fuzz bass, tambourine, maracas, piano, vocals

9 November 1965 – Room 65
RM1 [1] – mono mix from take 1
RS1 [2] – stereo mix from take 1

1987 – EMI
[3] – stereo mix from take 1

1999 – EMI
[4] – stereo mix from take 1

Releases UK/US peak

	UK/US peak
Rubber Soul LP (1965) – Parlophone PMC 1267 [1], PCS 3075 [2]	1
Rubber Soul LP (US, 1965) – Capitol T 2442 [1], ST 2442 [2]	1
Rubber Soul CD (1987) – EMI CDP 7 46440 2 [3]	60

Yellow Submarine Songtrack CD (1999) – Apple 5 21481 2 **[4]**   8/15

```
┌─────── NOTES ───────┐
│  ♪ Paul's bass is played through a  │
│    fuzz box.                        │
│  ♪ John, Paul and George            │
│    practising harmonies was used    │
│    in the Yellow Submarine film.    │
└─────────────────────┘
```

Thinking Of Linking

[Lennon-McCartney]

Lead vocals, **Paul**. One of Paul's earliest compositions, written we he was about 16. It was briefly resuscitated on 29 January 1969 during the *Let It Be* sessions. Paul, George and Ringo later revived it during the filming for *Anthology* in June 1994.

Thirty Days

[Berry]

Part of the Beatles' set until 1961, with **John** singing lead. It was also busked early in the *Let It Be* sessions. A Chuck Berry single from 1955.

This Boy

[McCartney-Lennon]

John – lead vocals, acoustic guitar
Paul – harmony vocals, bass
George – harmony vocals, lead guitar
Ringo – drums

Studio recording and mixing

17 October 1963 – Studio Two – With The Beatles session 8 out of 9
Takes 1–15
Overdubs onto take 15 – vocals, guitar > takes 16–17

21 October 1963 – Studio One control room
RM1, RM2 – mono mixes from edit of takes 15, 17
[1] – edit of RM1 and RM2
RS15 **[2]** – stereo mix from edit of takes 15, 17

19 December 1963 – Capitol
[3] – mastering of mock stereo mix from **[1]**

10 November 1966 – Studio Two control room
RS1–RS2 – stereo mixes from edit of takes 15, 17, edited

28 September 1977 – EMI
[4] – mock stereo mix from [1]

1988 – EMI
[5] – stereo copy (possibly from vinyl) of [2]

1995 – EMI
[6] – edit of takes 12, 13

BBC and other performances

2 December 1963 [7] – *The Morecambe And Wise Show* broadcast on 18 April 1964 (ATV)
7 December 1963 – *It's The Beatles* broadcast the same day (BBC TV)
17 December 1963 [8] – 21 December 1963 edition of *Saturday Club*
12 January 1964 – *Sunday Night At The London Palladium* (ATV, live)
16 February 1964 [9] – *The Ed Sullivan Show* (CBS TV, live)
28 February 1964 – 30 March 1964 edition of *From Us To You*

Releases   *UK/US peak*

'I Want To Hold Your Hand' / 'This Boy' single (1963) – Parlophone R 5084 [1]	1
Meet The Beatles! LP (US, 1964) – Capitol T 2047 [1], ST 2047 [3]	1
Meet The Beatles! EP (US, 1964) – Capitol SXA 2047 [3]	–
Four By The Beatles EP (US, 1964) – Capitol EAP 1-2121 [1]	92
'All My Loving' / 'This Boy' single (Canada, 1976 reissue) – Capitol 72144 [2]	–
'I Want To Hold Your Hand' / 'This Boy' single (Australia, 1976 reissue) – Parlophone A 8103 [2]	–
Love Songs LP (1977) – Parlophone PCSP 721 / Capitol SKBL 11711 [4]	7/24
Rarities LP (1978) – Parlophone PCM 1001, PSLP 261 [1]	71
The Beatles EP (1981) – Parlophone SGE 1 [4]	
Past Masters 1 CD (1988) – EMI CDP 7 90043 2 [5]	49/–
The Beatles EP (CD issue, 1992) – Parlophone SGE 1 [5]	
Anthology 1 CD (1995) – Apple 8 34445 2 [7]	2/1
'Free As A Bird' single (1995) – Apple 8 82587 2 [6]	2/6
The Four Historic Ed Sullivan Shows DVD (2003) – EREDV 372 [9]	
On Air – Live At The BBC Volume 2 CD (2013) – Apple 6025 37491698 [8]	12/7

NOTES

♪ The first Beatles song in 12/8 time.
♪ The 1966 stereo mixes were made in error and unused, and the 1963 mix [2] was lost c. 1976.
♪ According to John Barrett's notes, takes 16 and 17 were regular takes and not overdubs.
♪ 'Ringo's Theme (This Boy)' released as a single in 1964 by United Artists in Canada.

Three Cool Cats

[Leiber-Stoller]

George – lead vocals, lead guitar
John – backing vocals, rhythm guitar
Paul – backing vocals, bass
Pete Best – drums

Studio recording and mixing

1 January 1962 – Decca Studios
Studio test recorded in mono [1]

BBC and other performances

16 January 1963 – 25 January 1963 edition of *Here We Go* (not broadcast)
2 July 1963 – 16 July 1963 edition of *Pop Go The Beatles* (not broadcast)

Releases   *UK/US peak*

Anthology 1 CD (1995) – Apple 8 34445 2 [1]   2/1

╔══════════ NOTES ══════════╗

  ♪ Originally the B-side of the Coasters'
    1959 US #2 hit 'Charlie Brown'.
  ♪ Played live by the Quarry Men/Beatles
    until 1963.

╚═══════════════════════════╝

Thumbin' A Ride

[Leiber-Stoller]

Lead vocals, **Paul**. Part of the Beatles' set until 1962. A single released by the Coasters in January 1961.

Ticket To Ride

[Lennon-McCartney]

John – lead vocals, rhythm guitar
Paul – harmony vocals, bass, lead guitar
George – harmony vocals, rhythm guitar
Ringo – drums, tambourine

Studio recording and mixing

15 February 1965 – Studio Two – Help! session 1 out of 13
Takes 1–2
Overdubs on take 2 – tambourine, guitar, vocals

18 February 1965 – Studio Two control room
RM1 [1] – mono mix from take 2

23 February 1965 – Studio Two control room
RS1 [2] – stereo mix from take 2

15 March 1965 – Studio Two control room
RM2 [3] – mono mix from take 2

1965 – Capitol
[4] – mock stereo mix from [1]

1987 – EMI
[5] – stereo mix from take 2

BBC and other performances

11 April 1965 – *NME 1964-65 Annual Poll-Winners' Concert*
26 May 1965 [6] – 7 June 1965 edition of *The Beatles Invite You To Take A Ticket To Ride*
20 June 1965 – *Les Beatles* (Europe 1 TV, France, live)
1 August 1965 [7] – *Blackpool Night Out* (Associated British Corp. TV, live)
29 August 1965 [8] – Hollywood Bowl (live)
14 August 1965 [9] – *The Ed Sullivan Show* broadcast on 12 September 1965 (CBS TV)
15 August 1965 – *The Beatles At Shea Stadium* (live), broadcast by BBC TV on 1 March 1966

Releases   UK/US peak

Help! LP (1965) – Parlophone PMC 1255 [1], PCS 3071 [2]	1
Help! LP (US, 1965) – Capitol MAS 2386 [1], SMAS 2386 [4]	1
Help! movie (1965) [3]	
'Ticket To Ride'/'Yes It Is' single (1965) – Parlophone R 5265 [1]	1
'Ticket To Ride'/'Yes It Is' single (US, 1965) – Capitol 5407 [1]	1
A Collection Of Beatles Oldies LP (1966) – Parlophone PMC 7016 [1], PCS 7016 [2]	7
The Beatles 1962–1966 LP (1973) – Apple PCSP 717 [2]	3
The Beatles 1962–1966 LP (US, 1973) – Apple SKBO 3403 [1]	3
The Beatles At The Hollywood Bowl LP (1977) – Parlophone EMTV 4 / Capitol SMAS 11638 [8]	1/2
Reel Music LP (1982) – Parlophone PCS 7218 / Capitol SV-12199 [2]	–/19
20 Greatest Hits LP (1982) – Parlophone PCTC 260 / Capitol SV-12245 [2]	10/50
Help! CD (1987) – EMI CDP 7 46439 2 [5]	61
The Beatles 1962–1966 CD (1993) – EMI CDP 7 97036 2 [5]	3
Live At The BBC CD (1994) – Apple 8 31796 2 [6]	1/3
Anthology 2 CD (1996) – Apple 8 34448 2 [7]	1/1
The Four Historic Ed Sullivan Shows DVD (2003) – EREDV 372 [9]	
1+ CD/DVD (2015) – Apple 6205 47567727 [5]	5/6

Live At The Hollywood Bowl CD (2016) – Apple 6025 57054972 **[8]**   3/7

```
┌────────── NOTES ──────────┐
│                           │
```

♪ A promotional film was
  made on 23 November 1965.
♪ The last track to be played
  on the final session for the
  BBC.
♪ Voted the least popular
  track on *Help!* by readers of
  Beatles Book.
♪ A clip from *Top Of The Pops*
  was shown on *Doctor Who*
  on 22 May 1965.

Till There Was You

[Willson]

Paul – lead vocals, bass
John – acoustic rhythm guitar
George – acoustic lead guitar
Pete Best – drums (1 January 1962)
Ringo – bongos

Studio recording and mixing

1 January 1962 – Decca Studios
Studio test recorded in mono

18 July 1963 – Studio Two – With The Beatles session 2 out of 9
Takes 1–3

30 July 1963 – Studio Two – With The Beatles session 3 out of 9
Takes 4–8

21 August 1963 – Studio Three control room
RM8 [1] – mono mix from take 8

29 October 1963 – Studio Three control room
RS8 [2] – stereo mix from take 8

19 December 1963 – Capitol
[3] – mastering of stereo mix from [2]
[4] – mastering of mono mix from [3]

BBC and other performances

December 1962 **[5]** – Star-Club, Hamburg (live)

1 June 1963 **[6]** – 11 June 1963 edition of *Pop Go The Beatles*
24 June 1963 – 29 June 1963 edition of *Saturday Club*
10 July 1963 **[7]** – 30 July 1963 edition of *Pop Go The Beatles*
3 September 1963 – 10 September 1963 edition of *Pop Go The Beatles*
4 November 1963 **[8]** – *Royal Variety Performance* broadcast on 10 November
   1963 (ATV)
7 December 1963 – *It's The Beatles* broadcast the same day (BBC TV)
17 December 1963 **[9]** – 21 December 1963 edition of *Saturday Club*
18 December 1963 **[10]** – 26 December 1963 edition of *From Us To You*
9 February 1964 **[11]** – *The Ed Sullivan Show* (CBS TV, live)
28 February 1964 **[12]** – 30 March 1964 edition of *From Us To You*
17 June 1964 – *The Beatles Sing For Shell* broadcast on 1 July 1964 (Channel 9
   TV, Australia)

Releases	UK/US peak
With The Beatles LP (1963) – Parlophone PMC 1206 [1], PCS 3045 [2]	1
With The Beatles LP (Germany, 1963) – Odeon O 83 991 [1], Odeon STO 83 568 [2]	–
Meet The Beatles! LP (US, 1964) – Capitol T 2047 [4], ST 2047 [3]	1
Live! At The Star-Club In Hamburg, Germany; 1962 LP (US, 1977) – Lingasong LS 2 7001 [5]	–
The Beatles Ballads LP (1980) – Parlophone PCS 7214 [2]	17
Live At The BBC CD (1994) – Apple 8 31796 2 [12]	1/3
Anthology 1 CD (1995) – Apple 8 34445 2 [8]	2/1
The Four Historic Ed Sullivan Shows DVD (2003) – EREDV 372 [11]	
On Air – Live At The BBC Volume 2 CD (2013) – Apple 6025 37491698 [7]	12/7
The Beatles Bootleg Recordings 1963 (2013) – iTunes [6] [9] [10]	–

```
┌────────────── NOTES ──────────────┐
```

♪ From the 1957 play *The Music Man*, based
   on Peggy Lee's 1961 recording.
♪ One of four songs played at an audition
   for the BBC in Manchester on 8 February
   1962, though dropped for their first BBC
   performance on 7 March.
♪ Ringo on bongos – the first time since
   'Love Me Do' he is not on drums.

Tip Of My Tongue

[Lennon-McCartney]

Paul – lead vocals, bass
John – rhythm guitar
George – lead guitar
Ringo – drums

Studio recording and mixing

26 November 1962 – Studio Two – Please Please Me session 4 out of 8
Unknown takes (possibly rehearsal only)

― NOTES ―

♪ Written by Paul, never released by the Beatles.
♪ Released in 1963 by Tommy Quickly backed by the Remo Four.
♪ It was the first Lennon-McCartney single not to chart.

To Know Her Is To Love Her

[Spector]

John – lead vocals, rhythm guitar
Paul – backing vocals, bass
George – backing vocals, lead guitar
Pete Best – drums (1 January 1962)
Ringo – drums

Studio recording and mixing

1 January 1962 – Decca Studios
Studio test recorded in mono

BBC and other performances

December 1962 [1] – Star-Club, Hamburg (live)
16 July 1963 [2] – 6 August 1963 edition of *Pop Go The Beatles*

Releases   *UK/US peak*

Live! At The Star-Club In Hamburg, Germany; 1962 LP (1977) – Lingasong LNL 1 /
    Lingasong LS 2 7001 [1]   –
Live At The BBC CD (1994) – Apple 8 31796 2 [2]   1/3

― NOTES ―

♪ A *Billboard* #1 for the Teddy Bears in December 1958.
♪ The Teddy Bears was formed by Phil Spector, who was also a member of the group.
♪ Appears as a bonus track on the 2004 reissue of John's *Rock 'n' Roll* album.

Tomorrow Never Knows

[Lennon-McCartney]

John – lead vocals, organ
Paul – bass, lead guitar
George – guitars, tamboura
Ringo – drums, tambourine
George Martin – piano

Studio recording and mixing

6 April 1966 – Studio Three – Revolver session 1 out of 33
Takes 1–3

7 April 1966 – Studio Three – Revolver session 2 out of 33
Overdubs onto take 3 – tape loops

22 April 1966 – Studio Two – Revolver session 12 out of 33
Overdubs onto take 3 – guitar, tambourine, piano, organ, vocals

27 April 1966 – Studio Three control room
RM8 [1] – mono mix from take 3

6 June 1966 – Studio Three control room
RM11 [2] – mono mix from take 3

22 June 1966 – Studio Three control room
RS6 [3] – stereo mix from take 3

1995 – EMI
[4] – stereo mix from take 1

See 'Within You Without You' [4] for *Love* CD info.

Releases

	UK/US peak
Revolver LP (1966) – Parlophone PMC 7009 [2] [1], PCS 7009 [3]	1
Revolver LP (US, 1966) – Capitol T 2576 [1], ST 2576 [3]	1
Anthology 2 CD (1996) – Apple 8 34448 2 [4]	1/1
Tomorrow Never Knows (2012) – iTunes [3]	44/24

NOTES

♪ The first backward effect and first use of automatic double-tracking.
♪ [2], with slightly longer outro, appears on early UK pressings.
♪ The first Beatles song to be licensed to a TV show – *Mad Men* producers reportedly paid $250,000 to use it in an episode in 2011.

Too Bad About Sorrows

[Lennon-McCartney]

One of the first songs written by John and Paul, in 1957. Briefly revisited during the *Get Back* sessions, by John on 8 January and Paul on 22 January. Neither could particularly remember the words.

Too Much Monkey Business

[Berry]

John – lead vocals, rhythm guitar
Paul – bass
George – lead guitar
Ringo – drums

BBC and other performances

16 March 1963 – *Saturday Club* (live)
1 June 1963 [1] – 11 June 1963 edition of *Pop Go The Beatles*
4 April 1963 – 24 June 1963 edition of *Side By Side*
3 September 1963 [2] – 10 September 1963 edition of *Pop Go The Beatles*

Releases   *UK/US peak*

Live At The BBC CD (1994) – Apple 8 31796 2 [2]   1/3
The Beatles Bootleg Recordings 1963 (2013) – iTunes [1]   –

=== NOTES ===

♪ Released by Chuck Berry in 1956, the B-side to 'Brown Eyed Handsome Man' – both songs made the *Billboard* R&B top 5.

Tutti Frutti

[Penniman-LaBostrie]

Lead vocals, **Paul**. Part of the Beatles' set until 1962 and appears on the earliest known set list written by Paul in mid-1960. Little Richard's first hit, reaching #17 on *Billboard* in 1956. It opens side 2 of Elvis Presley's eponymous debut LP.

12-Bar Original

[Lennon-McCartney-Harrison-Starkey]

John – rhythm guitar
Paul – bass
George – lead guitar
Ringo – drums
George Martin – harmonium

Studio recording and mixing

4 November 1965 – Studio Two – Rubber Soul session 11 out of 15
Takes 1–2

1995 – EMI
[1] – stereo mix from take 2, edited

Releases

Anthology 2 CD (1996) – Apple 8 34448 2 **[1]**   1/1

```
════════ NOTES ════════

    ♪ Part of a 6½-minute
    instrumental jam, the group's
    first instrumental recording
    since 'Cry For A Shadow'.
```

Twenty Flight Rock

[Cochran Fairchild]

Lead vocals, **Paul**. Part of the Quarry Men/Beatles from 1957 to 1962. John was famously impressed by Paul's ability to play the song when they first met on 6 July 1957. It was played by Eddie Cochran in the 1956 film *The Girl Can't Help It*.

Twist And Shout

[Medley-Russell]

John – lead vocals, rhythm guitar
Paul – backing vocals, bass
George – backing vocals, lead guitar
Ringo – drums

Studio recording and mixing

11 February 1963 – Studio Two – Please Please Me session 5 out of 8
Takes 1–2

25 February 1963 – Studio One control room
[1] – mono mix from take 1
[2] – stereo mix from take 1

1965 – Capitol
[3] – stereo mix from [2]
[4] – mono mix from [3]

1976 – Capitol
[5] – stereo mix from take 1

2015 – EMI
[6] – stereo mix from take 1

BBC and other performances

27 September 1962 – 4 December 1962 edition of *The Talent Spot*
17 December 1962 – *People And Places* (Granada TV, live)
December 1962 [7] – Star-Club, Hamburg (live)
18 April 1963 – *Swinging Sound '63* (live)
21 May 1963 – 3 June 1963 edition of *Steppin' Out* (not broadcast)
17 June 1963 – 25 June 1963 edition of *Pop Go The Beatles*
3 July 1963 – 4 July 1963 edition of *The Beat Show*
16 July 1963 [8] – 6 August 1963 edition of *Pop Go The Beatles*
17 July 1963 – 21 July 1963 edition of *Easy Beat*
30 July 1963 – 24 August 1963 edition of *Saturday Club*
1 August 1963 – 27 August 1963 edition of *Pop Go The Beatles*
14 August 1963 – *Scene at 6.30* broadcast the same day (Granada TV)
27 August 1963 – *The Mersey Sound* broadcast on 9 October 1963 (BBC TV)
3 September 1963 [9] – 24 September 1963 edition of *Pop Go The Beatles*
13 October 1963 – *Sunday Night At The London Palladium* (ATV, live)
30 October 1963 – *Drop In* broadcast on 3 November 1963 (Sveriges TV)
4 November 1963 [10] – *Royal Variety Performance* broadcast on 10 November
     1963 (ATV)
20 November 1963 – *The Beatles Come To Town* (Pathe News)
7 December 1963 – *It's The Beatles* broadcast the same day (BBC TV)
12 January 1964 – *Sunday Night At The London Palladium* (ATV, live)
9 February 1964 [11] – *The Ed Sullivan Show* broadcast on 23 February 1964
     (CBS TV)
19 April 1964 – *Around The Beatles*, mimed performance recorded on 28 April
     and broadcast on 6 May 1964 (Rediffusion TV)
26 April 1964 – *NME 1963–64 Annual Poll-Winners' Concert*
17 June 1964 – *The Beatles Sing For Shell* broadcast on 1 July 1964 (Channel 9
     TV, Australia)
20 June 1965 – *Les Beatles* (Europe 1 TV, France, live)
15 August 1965 – *The Beatles At Shea Stadium* (live), broadcast by BBC TV on
     1 March 1966
30 August 1965 [12] – Hollywood Bowl (live)

Releases   *UK/US peak*

Please Please Me LP (1963) – Parlophone PMC 1202 [1], PCS 3042 [2]	1
Introducing… The Beatles LP (US, 1963) – Vee Jay VJLP 1062 [1], VJSR 1062 [2]	2
Twist And Shout EP (1963) – Parlophone GEP 8882 [1]	1
'Twist And Shout' / 'There's A Place' single (US, 1964) – Tollie 9001 [1]	2
The Early Beatles LP (US, 1965) – Capitol T 2309 [4], ST 2309 [3]	43

'Twist And Shout' / 'There's A Place' single (US, 1965) – Capitol Starline 6061 **[1]**	–
Rock 'n' Roll Music LP (1976) – Parlophone PCSP 719 **[2]**	11
Rock 'n' Roll Music LP (US, 1976) – Capitol SKBO 11537 **[5]**	2
'Back In The U.S.S.R.' / 'Twist And Shout' single (1976) – Parlophone R 6016 **[2]**	19
The Beatles At The Hollywood Bowl LP (1977) – Parlophone EMTV 4 / Capitol SMAS 11638 **[12]**	1/2
Live! At The Star-Club In Hamburg, Germany; 1962 LP (1977) – Lingasong LNL 1 **[7]**	–
Anthology 1 CD (1995) – Apple 8 34445 2 **[8]**	2/1
The Four Historic Ed Sullivan Shows DVD (2003) – EREDV 372 **[11]**	
On Air – Live At The BBC Volume 2 CD (2013) – Apple 6025 37491698 **[10]**	12/7
The Beatles Bootleg Recordings 1963 (2013) – iTunes **[9]**	–
Live At The Hollywood Bowl CD (2016) – Apple 6025 57054972 **[12]**	3/7
1+ CD/DVD (2015) – Apple 6205 47567727 **[6]**	5/6

NOTES

- ♪ Originally called 'Shake It Up, Baby' by the Top Notes, the Isley Brothers' version was a US top 20 hit in 1962 and as a result of the Beatles' cover, the Isleys' version made the UK charts in July 1963.
- ♪ The last song recorded at 11 February session.
- ♪ Spent four weeks at #2 in the US, stuck behind 'Can't Buy Me Love'.
- ♪ *Twist And Shout* was the Beatles' best-selling EP, selling 670,000 copies.
- ♪ As a download, reached #48 in the charts in 2010.
- ♪ The *1+* video is of a mimed performance for Granada's *Scene at 6:30*, recorded on 14 August 1963 and broadcast that evening.

Two Of Us

[Lennon-McCartney]

Paul – lead vocals, acoustic guitar
John – harmony vocals, acoustic guitar
George – guitar
Ringo – drums

Studio recording and mixing

7 January 1969 – Twickenham Film Studios – Let It Be rehearsal session
Take 8.11 **[1]**

9 January 1969 – Twickenham Film Studios – Let It Be rehearsal session
Take 9.23 **[2]**

21 January 1969 – Apple Studio – Let It Be rehearsal session
Take **[22.45]** (spoken intro)

24 January 1969 – *Apple Studio* – *Let It Be session 4 out of 17*
Take 24.32

31 January 1969 – *Apple Studio* – *Let It Be session 10 out of 17*
Take 31.5 [3]

25 March 1970 – *Studio Two control room*
RS2 [4] – stereo mix from take 31.5, take [22.45] edited on

1996 – *EMI*
[5] – stereo mix from take 24.32

2003 – *EMI*
[6] – stereo mix from take 31.5

Releases _____ *UK/US peak*

Let It Be LP (1970) – Apple PXS1, PCS 7096 [4]	1
Let It Be LP (US, 1970) – Apple AR 34001 [4]	1
Let It Be movie (1970) [1] [2] [3]	
Anthology 3 CD (1996) – Apple 8 34451 2 [5]	4/1
Let It Be… Naked CD (2003) – Apple 24359 57142 [6]	7/5

___NOTES___

♪ The only studio recording that is the same in the film and on the LP.
♪ Take [22.45] was originally thought to date from 22 January.
♪ The song was intended to launch the career of Apple group Mortimer.

Wait

[Lennon-McCartney]

John – lead vocals, rhythm guitar, tambourine
Paul – lead and harmony vocals, bass
George – guitar
Ringo – drums, maracas

Studio recording and mixing _____

17 June 1965 – *Studio Two* – *Help! session 13 out of 13*
Takes 1–4

18 June 1965 – *Studio Two control room*
RM1 – mono mix from take 4

11 November 1965 – Studio Two – Rubber Soul session 15 out of 15
Overdubs on take 4 – guitar, tambourine, maracas, vocals

15 November 1965 – Studio One control room
RM2 [1] – mono mix from take 4
RS1 [2] – stereo mix from take 4

1987 – EMI
[3] – stereo mix from take 4

Releases

	UK/US peak
Rubber Soul LP (1965) – Parlophone PMC 1267 [1], PCS 3075 [2]	1
Rubber Soul LP (US, 1965) – Capitol T 2442 [1], ST 2442 [2]	1
Rubber Soul CD (1987) – EMI CDP 7 46440 2 [3]	60

NOTES

♪ The original recording was held off the previous LP.
♪ No stereo version was made after the 18 June mono mix because the decision had evidently been made in the meantime not to include the track on the *Help!* LP.

Watch Your Step

[Parker]

Lead vocals, **John**. Played by the Beatles until 1962. It provided John with inspiration for the riffs for 'I Feel Fine', 'Day Tripper' and 'Paperback Writer'. Released by Bobby Parker in 1961, it peaked at #51 on the *Billboard* chart.

We Can Work It Out

[Lennon-McCartney]

Paul – lead vocals, harmonium, acoustic guitar
John – harmony vocals, acoustic guitar, harmonium, either bass or tambourine
George – possibly harmony vocals, either bass or tambourine
Ringo – drums

Studio recording and mixing

20 October 1965 – Studio Two – Rubber Soul session 5 out of 15
Takes 1–2
Overdubs onto take 2 – guitar, harmonium, bass, tambourine, vocals

29 October 1965 – *Studio Two – Rubber Soul session 9 out of 15*
Overdubs onto take 2 – vocals, harmonium

29 October 1965 – *Studio Two control room*
RM1 [1] – mono mix from take 2

10 November 1965 – *Studio Two control room*
RS1 [2] – stereo mix from take 2

10 November 1966 – *Studio Two control room*
RS2 [3] – stereo mix from take 2

2015 – *EMI*
[4] – stereo mix from take 2

Releases	UK/US peak
'We Can Work It Out' / 'Day Tripper' single (1965) – Parlophone R 5389 [1]	1
'We Can Work It Out' / 'Day Tripper' single (US, 1965) – Capitol 5555 [1]	1
A Collection Of Beatles Oldies LP (1966) – Parlophone PMC 7016 [1], PCS 7016 [3]	7
"Yesterday" ... And Today LP (US, 1966) – Capitol T 2553 [1], ST 2553 [2]	1
The Beatles 1962–1966 LP (1973) – Apple PCSP 717 [3]	3
The Beatles 1962–1966 LP (US, 1973) – Apple SKBO 3403 [2]	3
20 Greatest Hits LP (1982) – Parlophone PCTC 260 / Capitol SV-12245 [3]	10/50
Past Masters 2 CD (1988) – EMI CDP 7 90044 2 [3]	46/–
The Beatles 1962–1966 CD (1993) – EMI CDP 7 97036 2 [3]	3
1+ CD/DVD (2015) – Apple 6205 47567727 [4]	5/6

═ NOTES ═

♪ The US and UK stereo mixes were made exactly one year apart.
♪ A promotional film was made on 23 November 1965.
♪ The first double A-sided single.

Well Darling

[Lennon-McCartney]

Recorded somewhere in Liverpool in early 1960 with **Paul** singing lead. It may not have been part of the group's live set.

What A Crazy World We're Living In

[Klein]

Lead vocals, **George**. Part of the Beatles' set in 1961–62. It was recorded by Joe Brown in 1961.

What Goes On

[Lennon-McCartney-Starkey]

Ringo – lead vocals, drums
John – harmony and backing vocals, rhythm guitar
Paul – harmony and backing vocals, bass
George – lead guitar

Studio recording and mixing

4 November 1965 – Studio Two – Rubber Soul session 11 out of 15
Take 1
Overdubs onto take 1 – guitar, vocals

9 November 1965 – Room 65
RM1 [1] – mono mix from take 1
RS1 [2] – stereo mix from take 1

1987 – EMI
[3] – stereo mix from take 1

Releases UK/US peak

	UK/US peak
Rubber Soul LP (1965) – Parlophone PMC 1267 [1], PCS 3075 [2]	1
"Yesterday" … And Today LP (US, 1966) – Capitol T 2553 [1], ST 2553 [2]	1
'Nowhere Man'/'What Goes On' single (US, 1966) – Capitol 5587 [1]	81
Rubber Soul CD (1987) – EMI CDP 7 46440 2 [3]	60

NOTES

♪ The chorus had been written by John back in 1959.
♪ The group originally planned to record the song on 5 March 1963 for *With The Beatles*.
♪ A demo acetate from 1963 was sold on eBay for £10,200 in 2017.
♪ The first pressing of the Capitol single credits Lennon-McCartney only.

What You're Doing

[Lennon-McCartney]

Paul – lead vocals, bass, possibly piano
John – backing vocals, acoustic guitar
George – backing vocals, lead guitar
Ringo – drums

Studio recording and mixing

29 September 1964 – Studio Two – Beatles For Sale session 3 out of 8
Takes 1–7

30 September 1964 – *Studio Two – Beatles For Sale session 4 out of 8*
Remake takes 8–12

26 October 1964 – *Studio Two – Beatles For Sale session 8 out of 8*
Remake takes 13–19
Overdubs onto take 19 – vocals, guitar, piano

27 October 1964 – *Studio Two control room*
RM1 [1] – mono mix from take 19
RS1 [2] – stereo mix from take 19

See 'Drive My Car' [5] for *Love* CD info.

Releases _____ *UK/US peak*

Beatles For Sale LP (1964) – Parlophone PMC 1240 [1], PCS 3062 [2]	1
Beatles VI LP (US, 1965) – Capitol T 2358 [1], ST 2358 [2]	1

===== NOTES =====

♪ Written in Atlantic City in August 1964.
♪ Twelve takes of the song were recorded before the remake.
♪ This earlier version had a different bridge and two bars' rest before the coda.
♪ The piano is possibly care of George Martin.

What'd I Say

[Charles]

Lead vocals, **Paul**. Part of the Beatles' set from 1960 until mid-1962, versions could last 15 minutes or more. It is on the earliest known Beatles set list written by Paul in mid-1960. *Billboard* #6 in 1959 for Ray Charles. Also recorded by Tony Sheridan and the Beat Brothers, released on the *Beatles First* LP.

What's The New Mary Jane

[Lennon-McCartney]

John – vocals, piano
George – vocals, acoustic guitar
Yoko Ono – vocals
Mal Evans – handbell
Xylophone, effects

Studio recording and mixing

May 1968 – *Kinfauns, Esher*
Demo recording

14 August 1968 – *Studio Two – White Album session 43 out of 81*
Takes 1–4
Overdubs onto take 4 – guitar, vocals, piano, handbell, xylophone, effects
1984 – *AIR Studios*
[1] – stereo mix from take 4
2018 – *EMI*
[2] – stereo mix from demo
[3] – stereo mix from take 1

Releases	UK/US peak
Anthology 3 CD (1996) – Apple 8 34451 2 [1]	4/1
The Beatles Deluxe CD (2018) – Apple 0602567571957 [2] [3]	4/6

NOTES

♪ The mix was originally made for the aborted *Sessions* LP.
♪ When the song was squeezed off the running order of *The Beatles*, John intended 'You Know My Name (Look Up The Number)'/'What's The New Mary Jane' should be a Plastic Ono Band single.
♪ John originally credited Magic Alex with co-writing the song, but later retracted it.

When I Get Home

[Lennon-McCartney]

John – lead and harmony vocals, rhythm guitar
Paul – harmony vocals, bass
George – harmony vocals, rhythm guitar
Ringo – drums
George Martin – possibly piano

Studio recording and mixing

2 June 1964 – *Studio Two – A Hard Day's Night session 10 out of 12*
Takes 1–11

22 June 1964 – *Studio One control room*
RM2 [1] – mono mix from take 11
RM3 [2] – mono mix from take 11
RS1 [3] – stereo mix from take 11

Releases	UK/US peak
A Hard Day's Night LP (1964) – Parlophone PMC 1230 [1], PCS 3058 [3]	1
Something New LP (US, 1964) – Capitol T 2108 [2], ST 2108 [3]	2
Extracts From The Album 'A Hard Day's Night' EP (1964) – Parlophone GEP 8924 [1]	7

♩ NOTES ♩

♪ The piano only appears on the US mono version.
♪ "Till I walk out that door again" is different in the mono UK/US versions.
♪ The last track to be recorded for *A Hard Day's Night*.

When I'm Sixty-Four

[Lennon-McCartney]

Paul – lead and backing vocals, bass, piano
John – backing vocals, possibly guitar
George – backing vocals
Ringo – drums, chimes
Session musicians – two clarinets, bass clarinet

Studio recording and mixing

6 December 1966 – Studio Two – Sgt Pepper session 5 out of 56
Takes 1–2
Overdubs onto take 2 – piano

8 December 1966 – Studio One – Sgt Pepper session 6 out of 56
Overdubs onto take 2 – vocals

20 December 1966 – Studio Two – Sgt Pepper session 9 out of 56
Overdubs onto take 2 – vocals, percussion
Tape reduction of take 2 > takes 3, 4

21 December 1966 – Studio Two – Sgt Pepper session 10 out of 56
Overdubs onto take 4 – clarinets

30 December 1966 – Studio Two control room
RM8 [1] – mono mix from take 4

17 April 1967 – Studio Two control room
RS1 [2] – stereo mix from take 4

1999 – EMI
[3] – stereo mix from take 4

2016/17 – EMI
[4] – stereo mix from take 2
[5] – stereo mix from take 4

Releases
UK/US peak

Sgt Pepper's Lonely Hearts Club Band LP (1967) – Parlophone PMC 7027 [1], PCS 7027 [2]	1
Sgt Pepper's Lonely Hearts Club Band LP (US, 1967) – Capitol MAS 2653 [1], SMAS 2653 [2]	1
Yellow Submarine Songtrack CD (1999) – Apple 5 21481 2 [3]	8/15
Sgt Pepper's Lonely Hearts Club Band Deluxe CD (2017) – Apple 0602557455328 [1] [4] [5]	1/3

NOTES

♪ Probably already written by Paul in 1956.
♪ The first recording by the Beatles in Studio One.
♪ Played live by the Beatles between 1960 and 1962.

Where Have You Been (All My Life)
[Mann-Weil]

John – lead vocals, rhythm guitar
Paul – bass
George – lead guitar
Ringo – drums

BBC and other performances

December 1962 [1] – Star-Club, Hamburg (live)

Releases
UK/US peak

Live! At The Star-Club In Hamburg, Germany; 1962 LP (US, 1977) – Lingasong LS 2 7001 [1]	–

NOTES

♪ Released by Arthur Alexander in 1962 with 'Soldier Of Love'
on the B-side, it reached #58 in the *Billboard* Hot 100.

While My Guitar Gently Weeps
[Harrison]

George – lead vocals, acoustic guitar, Hammond organ
Paul – harmony vocals, piano, organ
John – guitar, bass
Ringo – drums, tambourine
Eric Clapton – lead guitar
Session musicians – eight violins, three violas, three cellos, one string bass (*Love* version)

Studio recording and mixing

May 1968 – Kinfauns, Esher
Demo recording

25 July 1968 – *Studio Two* – *White Album session 33 out of 81*
Takes 1–2
Overdubs onto take 1 – organ

16 August 1968 – *Studio Two* – *White Album session 45 out of 81*
Remake takes 1–14
Tape reduction take 14 > take 15

3 September 1968 – *Studio Two* – *White Album session 53 out of 81*
Four- to eight-track tape copying of take 15 > take 16
Overdubs onto take 16 – backwards guitar

5 September 1968 – *Studio Two* – *White Album session 54 out of 81*
Overdubs onto take 16 – vocals, maracas, drums, guitar
Remake takes 17–44

6 September 1968 – *Studio Two* – *White Album session 55 out of 81*
Overdubs onto take 25 – guitar, fuzz bass, organ, percussion, vocals

14 October 1968 – *Studio Two control room*
RM11 [1] – mono mix from take 25
RS12 [2] – stereo mix from take 25

1984 – *AIR Studios*
[3] – stereo mix from take 1 (25 July)

April 2006 – *AIR Studios*
Overdubs onto take 1 (25 July) – strings

2006 – *EMI*
[4] – stereo mix from take 1

2018 – *EMI*
[5] – stereo mix from demo
[6] – stereo mix from take 2 (25 July)
[7] – stereo mix from take 25
[8] – stereo mix from take 27

Releases

	UK/US peak
The Beatles LP (1968) – Apple PMC 7067–7068 [1], PCS 7067–7068 [2]	1
The Beatles LP (US, 1968) – Apple SWBO-101 [2]	1
The Beatles 1967–1970 LP (1973) – Apple PCSP 718 [2]	2
The Beatles 1967–1970 LP (US, 1973) – Apple SKBO 3404 [2]	1
Anthology 3 CD (1996) – Apple 8 34451 2 [3]	4/1
Love CD (2006) – Apple 0946 3 80790 2 6 [4]	3/4
The Beatles Deluxe CD (2018) – Apple 0602567571957 [5] [6] [7] [8]	4/6

NOTES

♪ The first Abbey Road eight-track recording.
♪ The first song to be published by George's Harrisongs Ltd.
♪ The only of George's songs on the LP with an instrumental contribution from John.
♪ George's hand-written lyrics were auctioned for $300,000 in 2007.

Whole Lotta Shakin' Goin' On

[Williams-Hall]

Lead vocals, **Paul**. Part of the Quarry Men/Beatles' set from the Casbah in 1958 until around 1962. On the earliest known (partial) set list written by Paul in mid-1960. *Billboard* #3 and UK #8 in 1957 for Jerry Lee Lewis.

Why (Can't You Love Me Again)

[Crompton-Sheridan]

Tony Sheridan – lead vocals, lead guitar
John – backing vocals, rhythm guitar
Paul – backing vocals, bass
George – backing vocals, guitar
Pete Best – drums

Studio recording and mixing

22 June 1961 – Friedrich-Eberts-Halle, Hamburg
Unknown take numbers

22 June 1961 – Polydor, Hamburg
[1] – stereo mix from unknown take number

1961 – Polydor, Hamburg
[2] – mono mix from [1]

Releases   *UK/US peak*

'Cry For A Shadow' / 'Why (Can't You Love Me Again)' single (1964) – Polydor NH 52275 [2]	–
'Why' / 'Cry For A Shadow' single (US, 1964) – MGM K13227 [2]	–
Beatles First LP (1967) – Polydor 236 201 [1]	–
The Early Tapes Of The Beatles CD (1985) – Polydor 823701-2 [1]	–

NOTES

♪ Written by Tony Sheridan and Bill Crompton in the late 1950s.

Why Don't We Do It In The Road

[Lennon-McCartney]

Paul – lead vocals, guitars, piano, bass, drums
Ringo – drums

Studio recording and mixing

9 October 1968 – Studio One – White Album session 77 out of 81

Takes 1–5
Overdubs onto take 5 – piano, percussion

10 October 1968 – Studio Three – White Album session 78 out of 81

Overdubs onto take 5 – vocals, handclaps, bass, drums
Tape reduction of take 5 > take 6
Overdubs onto take 6 – guitar

16 October 1968 – unspecified control room

RM1 [1] – mono mix from take 6
RS1 [2] – stereo mix from take 6

1996 – EMI

[3] – stereo mix from take 4

2018 – EMI

[4] – stereo mix from take 5 (without overdubs)
[5] – stereo mix from take 6

Releases
	UK/US peak
The Beatles LP (1968) – Apple PMC 7067–7068 [1], PCS 7067–7068 [2]	1
The Beatles LP (US, 1968) – Apple SWBO-101 [2]	1
Anthology 3 CD (1996) – Apple 8 34451 2 [3]	4/1
The Beatles Deluxe CD (2018) – Apple 0602567571957 [4] [5]	4/6

═══ NOTES ═══

♪ Inspired by Paul seeing monkeys mating in the road while in India.
♪ The percussive introduction comes from the thumping of the back of the guitar.
♪ The title on the LP sleeve has a question mark.
♪ The last White Album track to be mixed, at a 24-hour session determining the running order.

Wild Cat

[Schroeder-Gold]

Part of the Beatles' set until around 1961, two versions were recorded at Paul's house in June 1960 with **Paul** singing lead. Recorded by Gene Vincent in 1959, making the UK charts in January 1960.

Wild Honey Pie

[Lennon-McCartney]

Paul – lead vocals, guitars, drums, possibly harpsichord, possibly bass

Studio recording and mixing

20 August 1968 – Studio Two – White Album session 46 out of 81
Take 1

20 August 1968 – Studio Two control room
RM6 [1] – mono mix from take 1

13 October 1968 – Studio Two control room
RS2 [2] – stereo mix from take 1

2018 – EMI
[3] – stereo mix from take 1

Releases | UK/US peak

The Beatles LP (1968) – Apple PMC 7067–7068 [1], PCS 7067–7068 [2]	1
The Beatles LP (US, 1968) – Apple SWBO-101 [2]	1
The Beatles Deluxe CD (2018) – Apple 0602567571957 [3]	4/6

=====NOTES=====

> ♪ Recorded while George was on holiday in Greece, and after John and Ringo had gone home having worked on 'Yer Blues' in Studio Three.
> ♪ Apparently included on the White Album on the insistence of Pattie Harrison.

Wild In The Country

[Peretti-Creatore-Weiss]

Part of the Beatles' set until early 1962, one of the few songs performed with **Pete Best** singing lead. The title track from the 1961 Elvis Presley film, it reached #4 in the UK and #26 in the US (as the B-side of 'I Feel So Bad').

Will You Love Me Tomorrow

[Goffin-King]

Lead vocals, **John**. Played by the Beatles until 1962. A US #1 and UK #4 for the Shirelles in 1961.

Winston's Walk

[Lennon-McCartney]

An instrumental, probably played by the Quarry Men before 1960. A version is rumoured to be on the 1960 tape recorded at Paul's house.

With A Little Help From My Friends

[Lennon-McCartney]

Ringo – lead vocals, drums, percussion
Paul – harmony and backing vocals, bass, piano
John – harmony and backing vocals
George – lead and rhythm guitar, possibly Hammond organ
George Martin – possibly Hammond organ
Mal Evans – possibly cowbell

Studio recording and mixing

29 March 1967 – Studio Two – Sgt Pepper session 51 out of 56
Takes 1–10
Tape reduction take 10 > take 11
Overdubs onto take 11 – vocals

30 March 1967 – Studio Two – Sgt Pepper session 52 out of 56
Overdubs onto take 11 – guitar, tambourine, bass, drums, timpani, organ, vocals

31 March 1967 – Studio Two control room
RM15 [1] – mono mix from take 11

7 April 1967 – Studio Two control room
RS3 [2] – stereo mix from take 11

1999 – EMI
[3] – stereo mix from take 11

2016/17 – EMI
[4] – stereo mix from edit of takes 1, 2
[5] – stereo mix from take 11

Releases   *UK/US peak*

Sgt Pepper's Lonely Hearts Club Band LP (1967) – Parlophone PMC 7027 [1], PCS 7027 [2]   1
Sgt Pepper's Lonely Hearts Club Band LP (US, 1967) – Capitol MAS 2653 [1], SMAS 2653 [2]   1

The Beatles 1967–1970 LP (1973) – Apple PCSP 718 [2]   2
The Beatles 1967–1970 LP (US, 1973) – Apple SKBO 3404 [2]   1
'Sgt Pepper's Lonely Hearts Club Band' / 'With A Little Help From My Friends' /
    'A Day In The Life' single (1978) – Parlophone R 6022 [2]   63
'Sgt Pepper's Lonely Hearts Club Band' / 'With A Little Help From My Friends' /
    'A Day In The Life' single (US, 1978) – Capitol 4612 [2]   71
Yellow Submarine Songtrack CD (1999) – Apple 5 21481 2 [3]   8/15
Sgt Pepper's Lonely Hearts Club Band Deluxe CD (2017) – Apple 0602557455328 [1] [4] [5]   1/3

NOTES

♪ The overdub session ended at
   7.30am, after shooting the LP
   cover.
♪ It is uncertain which George
   is playing organ – it is usually
   assumed that it is George Martin,
   but photos from the session show
   Beatle George at the keyboard.

Within You Without You

[Harrison]

George – lead vocals, tamboura, sitar, acoustic guitar
Neil Aspinall – tamboura
Session musicians – tabla, three dilrubas, tamboura, swarmandal, eight violins, three
   cellos

Studio recording and mixing

15 March 1967 – Studio Two – Sgt Pepper session 44 out of 56
Take 1

22 March 1967 – Studio Two – Sgt Pepper session 48 out of 56
Overdubs onto take 1 – dilrubas
Tape reduction of take 1 > take 2

3 April 1967 – Studio One – Sgt Pepper session 55 out of 56
Overdubs onto take 2 – strings, vocals, sitar, guitar

4 April 1967 – Studio Two control room
RM6–RM11 – mono mixes from part 1 of take 2
RM12 – mono mix from parts 2, 3 of take 2
[1] – edit of RM10, RM12, with overdub – laughter
RS1–RS3 – stereo mixes from part 1 of take 2
RS4, RS5 – stereo mixes from parts 2, 3 of take 2
[2] – edit of RS3, RS5, with overdub – laughter

1995 – EMI

[3] – stereo mix from instrumental from take 2

2004–06 – EMI

[4] – stereo mix from take 2, in medley with 'Tomorrow Never Knows' take 3: includes samples from 'Strawberry Fields Forever' (cymbal); 'Rain' (vocals); also possibly 'Sea Of Time' (tamboura) and 'Sea Of Monsters' (effects)

2016/17 – EMI

[5] – stereo mix from take 1
[6] – stereo mix from take 2

Releases _____ *UK/US peak*

Sgt Pepper's Lonely Hearts Club Band LP (1967) – Parlophone PMC 7027 [1], PCS 7027 [2]	1
Sgt Pepper's Lonely Hearts Club Band LP (US, 1967) – Capitol MAS 2653 [1], SMAS 2653 [2]	1
Anthology 2 CD (1996) – Apple 8 34448 2 [3]	1/1
Love CD (2006) – Apple 0946 3 80790 2 6 [4]	3/4
Sgt Pepper's Lonely Hearts Club Band Deluxe CD (2017) – Apple 0602557455328 [1] [5] [6]	1/3

=== NOTES ===

♪ George is the only Beatle on the recording, with Neil Aspinall on tamboura.
♪ The song was spilt into three parts for mixing.
♪ The laughter at the end, different in mono and stereo was added with the intention of providing a release after the seriousness of the track.

Wooden Heart

[Wise-Weisman-Twomey-Kaempfert]

Lead vocals, **Paul**. Played by the Beatles until 1962. From the Elvis Presley film *GI Blues*, it was a UK #1 in 1961 but not released in the US until 1964.

The Word

[Lennon-McCartney]

John – lead vocals, rhythm guitar
Paul – harmony vocals, bass, piano
George – harmony vocals, lead guitar
Ringo – drums, maracas
George Martin – harmonium

Studio recording and mixing

10 November 1965 – Studio Two – Rubber Soul session 14 out of 15
Takes 1–3
Overdubs onto take 3 – bass, maracas

11 November 1965 – Room 65
RM1 [1] – mono mix from take 3
RS1 [2] – stereo mix from take 3

15 November 1965 – Studio One control room
RS2 [3] – stereo mix from take 3

1987 – EMI
[4] – stereo mix from take 3

See 'Drive My Car' [5] for *Love* CD info.

Releases   *UK/US peak*

Rubber Soul LP (1965) – Parlophone PMC 1267 [1], PCS 3075 [3]	1
Rubber Soul LP (US, 1965) – Capitol T 2442 [1], ST 2442 [2]	1
Rubber Soul CD (1987) – EMI CDP 7 46440 2 [4]	60

NOTES

♪ The start of more lyrical bass playing by Paul.
♪ The US stereo version has the vocal-tracked throughout.

Words Of Love

[Holly]

John – vocals, rhythm guitar
Paul – vocals, bass
George – lead guitar
Ringo – drums, percussion

Studio recording and mixing

18 October 1964 – Studio Two – Beatles For Sale session 7 out of 8
Takes 1–3
Overdubs onto take 3 – guitar, handclaps, percussion

26 October 1964 – Studio Two control room
RM1 [1] – mono mix from take 3

4 November 1964 – Studio Two control room
RS1 [2] – stereo mix from take 3

BBC and other performances

16 July 1963 [3] – 20 August 1963 edition of *Pop Go The Beatles*

Releases	UK/US peak
Beatles For Sale LP (1964) – Parlophone PMC 1240 [1], PCS 3062 [2]	1
Beatles For Sale (No. 2) EP (1965) – Parlophone GEP 8938 [1]	5
Beatles VI LP (US, 1965) – Capitol T 2358 [1], ST 2358 [2]	1
Love Songs LP (1977) – Parlophone PCSP 721 / Capitol SKBL 11711 [2]	7/24
On Air – Live At The BBC Volume 2 CD (2013) – Apple 6025 37491698 [3]	12/7
1+ CD/DVD (2015) – Apple 6205 47567727 [3]	5/6

NOTES

♪ Released by Buddy Holly in June 1957, it didn't chart, although a cover by the Diamonds, released a month earlier, made the *Billboard* top 20.

♪ With Ringo on packing case.

♪ Played live by the Quarry Men/Beatles until 1962.

♪ The *1+* video is the promotional film for *On Air*, complete with sound effects.

The World Is Waiting For The Sunrise

[Seitz-Lockhart]

Recorded at Paul's house in June 1960 with **Paul** singing lead. John and Paul also performed the song at their only date as a duo – the Nerk Twins – in Caversham, Berkshire in April 1960. Les Paul and Mary Ford had a *Billboard* #3 hit with the song in 1951.

Ya Ya

[Dorsey-Lewis-Robinson]

Lead vocals, **John**. Played by the Beatles until 1962. Single by Lee Dorsey got to #7 in the US in 1961. Recorded by Tony Sheridan in 1962 and released on his *Ya Ya* EP, with backing by the Beat Brothers, and on the LP *Beatles First*. Also recorded for John's 1975 *Rock 'n' Roll* LP.

Yellow Submarine

[Lennon-McCartney]

Ringo – lead vocals, drums
John – backing vocals, acoustic guitar
Paul – backing vocals, bass

George – backing vocals, tambourine
George Martin, Mal Evans, Neil Aspinall, Brian Jones, Marianne Faithfull, Pattie Harrison and others – effects and backing vocals

Studio recording and mixing

26 May 1966 – Studio Three – Revolver session 23 out of 33
Takes 1–4
Overdubs onto take 4 – vocals
Tape reduction of take 4 > take 5

1 June 1966 – Studio Two – Revolver session 24 out of 33
Overdubs onto take 5 – vocals, effects, brass band, bass drum

3 June 1966 – Studio Two control room
RM5 [1] – mono mix from take 5

22 June 1966 – Studio Two control room
RS2 [2] – stereo mix from take 5

25 November 1968 – EMI
[3] – mono mix from [2]

1995 – EMI
[4] – stereo mix from take 5

1999 – EMI
[5] – stereo mix from takes 4, 5

2015 – EMI
[6] – stereo mix from takes 4, 5

Releases UK/US peak

	UK/US peak
Revolver LP (1966) – Parlophone PMC 7009 [1], PCS 7009 [2]	1
Revolver LP (US, 1966) – Capitol T 2576 [1], ST 2576 [2]	1
'Eleanor Rigby' / 'Yellow Submarine' single (1966) – Parlophone R 5493 [1]	1
'Eleanor Rigby' / 'Yellow Submarine' single (US, 1966) – Capitol 5715 [1]	2
A Collection Of Beatles Oldies LP (1966) – Parlophone PMC 7016 [1], PCS 7016 [2]	7
Yellow Submarine movie (1968) [1]	
Yellow Submarine LP (1969) – Apple PMC 7070 [3], PCS 7070 [2]	3
Yellow Submarine LP (US, 1969) – Apple SW 153 [2]	2
The Beatles 1962–1966 LP (1973) – Apple PCSP 717 [2]	3
The Beatles 1962–1966 LP (US, 1973)– Apple SKBO 3403 [2]	3
Reel Music LP (1982) – Parlophone PCS 7218 / Capitol SV-12199 [2]	–/19
20 Greatest Hits LP (1982) – Parlophone PCTC 260 [2]	10
'Real Love' single (1996) – Apple 8 82646 2 [4]	4/11
Yellow Submarine Songtrack CD (1999) – Apple 5 21481 2 [5]	8/15
1+ CD/DVD (2015) – Apple 6205 47567727 [6]	5/6

```
┌─────────────── NOTES ───────────────┐
│                                      │
```

♪ The 26 May session was the first recording session without George Martin.

♪ According to George Martin, the brass band was recorded in the studio; according to Geoff Emerick, an existing recording was cut up and used.

♪ [4] includes a spoken introduction by Ringo that was deleted from all other versions.

♪ Donovan claims credit for the line "sky of blue, sea of green".

Yer Blues

[Lennon-McCartney]

John – lead vocals, lead guitar
Paul – harmony vocals, bass
George – lead guitar
Ringo – drums

Studio recording and mixing

May 1968 – Kinfauns, Esher
Demo recording

13 August 1968 – Studio Two annexe – White Album session 42 out of 81
Takes 1–14
Tape reduction of take 6 > takes 15–17
Edit of takes 16, 17

14 August 1968 – Studio Two – White Album session 43 out of 81
Overdub onto edit of takes 16, 17 – vocals

14 August 1968 – Studio Two control room
RM1–RM4 – mono mixes from edit of takes 16, 17

20 August 1968 – Studio Three – White Album session 46 out of 81
Edit piece 1 – intro count-in
[1] – edit of RM3 and edit piece 1

14 October 1968 – Studio Two control room
RS5 [2] – stereo mix from edit of takes 16, 17 and edit piece 1

2018 – EMI
[3] – stereo mix from take 5
[4] – stereo mix from edit of takes 16, 17 and edit piece 1

Releases _____ *UK/US peak*

The Beatles LP (1968) – Apple PMC 7067–7068 **[1]**, PCS 7067–7068 **[2]** 1
The Beatles LP (US, 1968) – Apple SWBO-101 **[2]** 1
The Beatles Deluxe CD (2018) – Apple 0602567571957 **[3] [4]** 4/6

```
╔══════════ NOTES ══════════╗
║  ♪ The song was recorded in a   ║
║    small annex to Studio Two.   ║
║  ♪ The edit, at 3'17", was for  ║
║    the first time made on the   ║
║    original four-track tape     ║
║    rather than a mixed two-     ║
║    track tape.                  ║
╚═════════════════════════════╝
```

Yes It Is

[Lennon-McCartney]

John – lead vocals, acoustic rhythm guitar
Paul – harmony vocals, bass
George – harmony vocals, lead guitar
Ringo – drums, possibly tambourine

Studio recording and mixing

16 February 1965 – Studio Two – Help! session 2 out of 13
Takes 1–14
Overdubs onto take 14 – vocals, guitar

16 February 1965 – Studio Two control room
RM1 **[1]** – mono mix from take 14

23 February 1965 – Studio Two control room
RS1 **[2]** – stereo mix from take 14

14 May 1965 – Capitol
[3] – mastering of mock stereo from **[1]**

28 September 1977 – EMI
[4] – mock stereo from **[1]**

1995 – EMI
[5] – mono/stereo mix from takes 2, 14

Releases _____ *UK/US peak*

'Ticket To Ride' / 'Yes It Is' single (1965) – Parlophone R 5265 **[1]** 1
'Ticket To Ride' / 'Yes It Is' single (US, 1965) – Capitol 5407 **[1]** 46
Beatles VI LP (US, 1965) – Capitol T 2358 **[1]**, ST 2358 **[3]** 1

Love Songs LP (1977) – Parlophone PCSP 721 / Capitol SKBL 11711 **[4]**	7/24
Rarities LP (1978) – Parlophone PCM 1001, PSLP 261 **[1]**	71
Only The Beatles (Heineken promo cassette, 1986) – Stiletto/Parlophone SMMC 151 **[2]**	–
Past Masters 1 CD (1988) – EMI CDP 7 90043 2 **[2]**	49/–
Anthology 2 CD (1996) – Apple 8 34448 2 **[5]**	1/1

♪ NOTES

♪ The true stereo version was first released in 1986 on a cassette that was part of a promotion for Heineken – the release was not sanctioned by the Beatles, and so the promotional was short-lived.

♪ The Capitol single states "From the United Artists Release 'Eight Arms To Hold You'", although it didn't appear in the *Help!* film.

Yesterday

[Lennon-McCartney]

Paul – lead vocals, acoustic guitar
Session musicians – two violins, viola, cello

Studio recording and mixing

14 June 1965 – Studio Two – Help! session 11 out of 13
Takes 1–2
Overdubs onto take 2 – strings, vocals

17 June 1965 – Studio Two control room
RM1 **[1]** – mono mix from take 2

18 June 1965 – Studio Two control room
RS1 **[2]** – stereo mix from take 2

1987 – EMI
[3] – stereo mix from take 2

1995 – EMI
[4] – stereo mix from take 1

See 'Blackbird' **[4]** for *Love* CD info.

BBC and other performances

1 August 1965 **[5]** – *Blackpool Night Out* (Associated British Corp. TV, live)
14 August 1965 **[6]** – *The Ed Sullivan Show* broadcast on 12 September 1965 (CBS TV)
24 June 1966 – *Die Beatles* broadcast on 5 July 1966 (ZDF TV, Germany)

Releases   *UK/US peak*

Help! LP (1965) – Parlophone PMC 1255 **[1]**, PCS 3071 **[2]**	1

Yesterday EP (1966) – Parlophone GEP 8948 [1]	1
'Dizzy Miss Lizzy' / 'Yesterday' single (1965) – Parlophone DP 563 [1]	–
'Yesterday' / 'Act Naturally' single (US, 1965) – Capitol 5498 [1]	1
A Collection Of Beatles Oldies LP (1966) – Parlophone PMC 7016 [1], PCS 7016 [2]	7
"Yesterday" … And Today LP (US, 1966) – Capitol T 2553 [1], ST 2553 [2]	1
The Beatles 1962–1966 LP (1973) – Apple PCSP 717 [2]	3
The Beatles 1962–1966 LP (US, 1973) – Apple SKBO 3403 [2]	3
'Yesterday' / 'I Should Have Known Better' single (1976) – Parlophone R 6103 [1]	8
Love Songs LP (1977) – Parlophone PCSP 721 / Capitol SKBL 11711 [2]	7/24
The Beatles Ballads LP (1980) – Parlophone PCS 7214 [2]	17
20 Greatest Hits LP (US, 1982) – Capitol SV-12245 [2]	50
Help! CD (1987) – EMI CDP 7 46439 2 [3]	61
The Beatles 1962–1966 CD (1993) – EMI CDP 7 97036 2 [3]	3
Anthology 2 CD (1996) – Apple 8 34448 2 [4] [5]	1/1
The Four Historic Ed Sullivan Shows DVD (2003) – EREDV 372 [6]	
1+ CD/DVD (2015) – Apple 6205 47567727 [6]	5/6

NOTES

♪ The first use of strings on a Beatles recording.
♪ The first Beatles recording featuring just one Beatle.
♪ Like 'Eight Days A Week' earlier in the year, the US-only single reached #1 in the *Billboard* charts.
♪ The Parlophone DP single was released for export only.
♪ The song featured in the TV special *The Music Of Lennon & McCartney*, with Paul singing half of verse one, Marianne Faithfull singing the rest.

You Can't Do That

[Lennon-McCartney]

John – lead vocals, guitar
Paul – harmony and backing vocals, bass, cowbell
George – harmony and backing vocals, guitar
Ringo – drums, bongos
George Martin – piano (unused)

Studio recording and mixing

25 February 1964 – Studio Two – A Hard Day's Night session 2 out of 12
Takes 1–9
Overdubs onto take 9 – vocals, cowbell, bongos, guitar

26 February 1964 – Studio Two control room
RM2, RM4 [1] – mono mixes from take 9
RM3 [2] – mono mix from take 9

10 March 1964 – *Studio Two control room*
RS1 [3] – stereo mix from take 9

17 March 1964 – *Capitol*
[4] – mastering of mock stereo mix from [1]

22 May 1964 – *Studio Two* – *A Hard Day's Night session 8 out of 12*
Overdubs onto take 9 – piano > take 10

22 June 1964 – *Studio One control room*
RS1 [5] – stereo mix from take 9

1995 – *EMI*
[6] – mono mix from take 6

BBC and other performances

28 February 1964 – 30 March 1964 edition of *From Us To You*
31 March 1964 – 4 April 1964 edition of *Saturday Club*
26 April 1964 – *NME 1963–64 Annual Poll-Winners' Concert*
1 May 1964 – 18 May 1964 edition of *From Us To You*
17 June 1964 – *The Beatles Sing For Shell* broadcast on 1 July 1964 (Channel 9 TV, Australia)
14 July 1964 [7] – 16 July 1964 edition of *Top Gear*
23 August 1964 [8] – Hollywood Bowl (live)

Releases

	UK/US peak
A Hard Day's Night LP (1964) – Parlophone PMC 1230 [2], PCS 3058 [5]	1
'Can't Buy Me Love' / 'You Can't Do That' single (1964) – Parlophone R 5114 [2]	1
'Can't Buy Me Love' / 'You Can't Do That' single (US, 1964) – Capitol 5150 [1]	48
The Beatles' Second Album LP (US, 1964) – Capitol T 2080 [1], ST 2080 [4]	1
Long Tall Sally LP (Canada, 1964) – Capitol T 6063 [1], ST 6063 [3]	–
Rock 'n' Roll Music LP (1976) – Parlophone PCSP 719 / Capitol SKBO 11537 [5]	11/2
Anthology 1 CD (1995) – Apple 8 34445 2 [6]	2/1
On Air – Live At The BBC Volume 2 CD (2013) – Apple 6025 37491698 [7]	12/7
Live At The Hollywood Bowl CD (2016) – Apple 6025 57054972 [8]	3/7
Tomorrow Never Knows (2012) – iTunes [5]	44/24

═══ **NOTES** ═══

♪ The debut of George's 12-string Rickenbacker 360-12.
♪ A performance of the song was edited out of the movie.
♪ George Martin's piano overdub onto take 9 was not used.
♪ It's likely that [1] was not used, and that all mono releases are [2].
♪ Played in concert in 1964.

You Don't Understand Me

[Massey]

Lead vocals, **John**. Part of the Beatles' set until 1962. Released in 1960 by Bobby Freeman on the B-side of '(I Do The) Shimmy Shimmy'. The single was released on the Parlophone label in the UK, who credited him as 'Bobby Freem<u>e</u>n'.

You Know My Name (Look Up The Number)

[Lennon-McCartney]

John – lead and backing vocals, guitar, maracas
Paul – lead, harmony and backing vocals, piano, bass
George – guitar, vibraphone
Ringo – drums, bongos
Brian Jones – alto saxophone
Mal Evans – effects

Studio recording and mixing

17 May 1967 – Studio Two – Magical Mystery Tour session 6 out of 30
Part 1 takes 1–14

7 June 1967 – Studio Two – Magical Mystery Tour session 8 out of 30
Overdubs onto take 9 – flute, guitar, drums, organ, tambourine > takes 20–24

8 June 1967 – Studio Two – Magical Mystery Tour session 9 out of 30
Part 2 takes 1–12
Part 3 takes 1–4
Part 4 takes 1–6
Part 5 take 1

9 June 1967 – Studio Two control room
Edit of part 1 take 9, part 2 take 12, part 3 take 4, part 4 take 6 and part 5 take 1 > take 30
RM1 – mono mix from take 30

30 April 1969 – Studio Three – Let It Be session 12 out of 17
Overdubs onto take 30 – vocals, effects

30 April 1969 – Studio Three control room
RM1–RM3 – mono mixes from take 30

26 November 1969 – Studio Two control room
Tape copying of RM3 > RM4
[1] – edit of RM4

1995 – EMI
[2] – mono mix from take 30

Releases *UK/US peak*

'Let It Be' / 'You Know My Name (Look Up The Number)' single (1970) – Apple R 5833 [1]	2
'Let It Be' / 'You Know My Name (Look Up The Number)' single (1970) – Parlophone P-R 5833 [1]	–
'Let It Be' / 'You Know My Name (Look Up The Number)' single (US, 1970) – Apple 2764 [1]	–
Rarities LP (1978) – Parlophone PCM 1001, PSLP 261 [1]	71
Rarities LP (US, 1980) – Capitol SHAL 12060 [1]	21
Past Masters 2 CD (1988) – EMI CDP 7 90044 2 [1]	46/–
Anthology 2 CD (1996) – Apple 8 34448 2 [2]	1/1

=== NOTES ===

♪ Released nearly three years after the recording had started.
♪ Brian Jones of the Rolling Stones plays saxophone on the track.
♪ No stereo mix was made – the previous mono-only release was 'I'll Get You', from 1963.

You Know What To Do

[Harrison]

George – lead vocals, guitar
John – tambourine
Paul – bass

Studio recording and mixing

3 June 1964 – Studio Two – A Hard Day's Night session 11 out of 12
Take 1

3 June 1964 – Studio Two control room
RM1 [1] – mono mix from take 1

Releases *UK/US peak*

Anthology 1 CD (1995) – Apple 8 34445 2 [1]	2/1

=== NOTES ===

♪ Would likely have been on side 2 of *A Hard Day's Night* had Ringo not fallen ill meaning the song could not be completed.
♪ The tape of the session was re-discovered in 1993.
♪ Registered for copyright as 'You'll Know What To Do'.

You Like Me Too Much

[Harrison]

George – lead vocals, lead guitar
Paul – harmony vocals, bass, possibly piano

John – acoustic guitar, electric piano
Ringo – drums, tambourine
George Martin – piano

Studio recording and mixing

17 February 1965 – Studio Two – Help! session 3 out of 13
Takes 1–8
Overdubs onto take 8 – piano, electric piano, tambourine, vocals

18 February 1965 – Studio Two control room
RM1 [1] – mono mix from take 8

23 February 1965 – Studio Two control room
RS1 [2] – stereo mix from take 8

1987 – EMI
[3] – stereo mix from take 8

Releases   *UK/US peak*

Help! LP (1965) – Parlophone PMC 1255 [1], PCS 3071 [2]	1
Beatles VI LP (US, 1965) – Capitol T 2358 [1], ST 2358 [2]	1
Yesterday EP (1966) – Parlophone GEP 8948 [1]	1
Help! CD (1987) – EMI CDP 7 46439 2 [3]	61

> ═══ **NOTES** ═══
> ♪ 'You Like Me Too Much' and 'I Need You' were
>   the first time George had two songs on an LP,
>   although neither are mentioned in his 1980
>   memoir *I Me Mine*.
> ♪ The introduction has a Pianet played through a
>   Leslie speaker.

You Must Write Every Day

[Lennon-McCartney]

Lead vocals, **Paul**. Recorded at Paul's house in June 1960 and presumably part of the
Quarry Men/Beatles' set at the time.

You Never Give Me Your Money

[Lennon-McCartney]

Paul – lead and backing vocals, piano, bass, guitars, chimes
John – backing vocals, guitars
George – backing vocals, guitars, six-string bass
Ringo – drums, tambourine
George Martin – possibly piano

Studio recording and mixing

6 May 1969 – Olympic Sound – Abbey Road session 10 out of 42
Takes 1–36
Overdubs onto take 30 – guitar

1 July 1969 – Studio Two – Abbey Road session 11 out of 42
Overdubs onto take 30 – vocals

11 July 1969 – Studio Two – Abbey Road session 19 out of 42
Overdubs onto take 30 – bass

15 July 1969 – Studio Three – Abbey Road session 20 out of 42
Overdubs onto take 30 – vocals, chimes, tambourine

30 July 1969 – Studio Two control room
Tape reduction take 30 > takes 37–42

30 July 1969 – Studio Three – Abbey Road session 31 out of 42
Overdubs onto take 40 – organ

31 July 1969 – Studio Two – Abbey Road session 32 out of 42
Overdubs onto take 30 – bass, piano

5 August 1969 – Studio Two – Abbey Road session 35 out of 42
Sound effects takes 1–5

13 August 1969 – Studio Two control room
RS20–RS27 – stereo mixes from take 30 with sound effects take 5

14 August 1969 – Studio Two control room
[1] – stereo crossfade of RS23 with sound effects take 5

Releases   *UK/US peak*

Abbey Road LP (1969) – Apple PCS 7088 [1]	1
Abbey Road LP (US, 1969) – Apple SO 383 [1]	1

═══ **NOTES** ═══

♪ The start of the *Abbey Road* medley, this song itself consisting of four songs – 'You Never Give Me Your Money', 'That Magic Feeling', 'One Sweet Dream', and 'One, Two, Three, Four, Five, Six, Seven'.

You Really Got A Hold On Me

[Robinson]

John – lead vocals, rhythm guitar
George – harmony vocals, lead guitar
Paul – backing vocals, bass

Ringo – drums
George Martin – piano

Studio recording and mixing

18 July 1963 – Studio Two – With The Beatles session 2 out of 9
Takes 1–5
Overdubs onto take 5 – piano > takes 6–7
Edit piece overdubs takes 8–10 – vocals
Edit piece overdub take 11 "ending" (guitar riff)

21 August 1963 – Studio Three control room
RM7/10/11 [1] – mono mix from takes 7, 10 and 11

17 October 1963 – Studio Two – With The Beatles session 8 out of 9
Take 12

29 October 1963 – Studio Three control room
RS7/10/11 [2] – stereo mix from takes 7, 10 and 11

17 March 1964 – Capitol
[3] – mastering of stereo mix from [2]
[4] – mastering of mono mix from [2]

26 January 1969 – Apple Studio – Let It Be session 6 out of 17
Take 26.32 [5]

BBC and other performances

24 May 1963 [6]– 4 June 1963 edition of *Pop Go The Beatles*
16 July 1963 – 13 August 1963 edition of *Pop Go The Beatles*
30 July 1963 [7] – 24 August 1963 edition of *Saturday Club*
3 September 1963 [8] – 17 September 1963 edition of *Pop Go The Beatles*
24 October 1963 [9] – Karlaplansstudion, Stockholm (live)

Releases   UK/US peak

With The Beatles LP (1963) – Parlophone PMC 1206 [1], PCS 3045 [2]	1
The Beatles' Second Album LP (US, 1964) – Capitol T 2080 [4], ST 2080 [3]	1
Let It Be movie (1970) [5]	
Live At The BBC CD (1994) – Apple 8 31796 2 [7]	1/3
Anthology 1 CD (1995) – Apple 8 34445 2 [9]	2/1
The Beatles Bootleg Recordings 1963 (2013) – iTunes [6] [8]	–

═══════ **NOTES** ═══════

♪ Released by the Miracles in 1962, originally the B-side to 'Happy Landing'.
♪ The first recording made for *With The Beatles*.
♪ Part of the Beatles' live set 1962–63.

You Win Again

[Williams]

Lead vocals, **John**. Played by the Quarry Men/Beatles until the second Hamburg season. Released by Hank Williams on the B-side of 'Settin' The Woods On Fire' in 1952. Jerry Lee Lewis released his version on the B-side of 'Great Balls Of Fire' in 1957.

You Won't See Me

[Lennon-McCartney]

Paul – lead vocals, bass, piano
John – backing vocals, rhythm guitar
George – backing vocals, tambourine
Ringo – drums
Mal Evans – organ

Studio recording and mixing

11 November 1965 – Studio Two – Rubber Soul session 15 out of 15
Takes 1–2
Overdubs onto take 2 – piano, organ

15 November 1965 – Studio Two control room
RM1 [1] – mono mix from take 2
RS1 [2] – stereo mix from take 2

1987 – EMI
[3] – stereo mix from take 2

Releases   *UK/US peak*

Rubber Soul LP (1965) – Parlophone PMC 1267 [1], PCS 3075 [2]	1
Rubber Soul LP (US, 1965) – Capitol T 2442 [1], ST 2442 [2]	1
Nowhere Man EP (1966) – Parlophone GEP 8952 [1]	4
Rubber Soul CD (1987) – EMI CDP 7 46440 2 [3]	60

═══NOTES═══

♪ The recording debut of Mal Evans, on organ.
♪ The final recording session with Norman Smith, who had been the Beatles' recording engineer since their first Abbey Road session.

You'll Be Mine

[McCartney-Lennon]

Paul – lead vocals, acoustic guitar
John – vocals, acoustic guitar
Stuart Sutcliffe – bass

BBC and other performances

June 1960 – amateur recording made at the McCartney home, Liverpool

1995 – EMI

[1] – edited and reprocessed from source tape

Releases   *UK/US peak*

Anthology 1 CD (1995) – Apple 8 34445 2 [1]   2/1

```
╔══════════════ NOTES ══════════════╗
```
♪ Written by Paul, around 1959, in the style of
   an Ink Spots parody.
♪ The earliest John/Paul composition to be
   released commercially.
♪ With Stu Sutcliffe on bass.

You're Going To Lose That Girl

[Lennon-McCartney]

John – lead vocals, rhythm guitar
Paul – backing vocals, bass, piano
George – backing vocals, lead guitar
Ringo – drums, bongos

Studio recording and mixing

19 February 1965 – Studio Two – Help! session 5 out of 13
Takes 2–3
Overdubs onto take 3 – electric piano, guitar

30 March 1965 – Studio Two – Help! session 7 out of 13
Overdubs onto take 3 – piano, bongos, guitar

2 April 1965 – Studio Two control room
[1] – mono mix from take 3
RS3 [2] – stereo mix from take 3

1965 – Capitol
[3] – untrimmed stereo mix from [2]
[4] – mono mix from [3]

1987 – EMI
[5] – stereo mix from take 3

Releases   *UK/US peak*

Help! LP (1965) – Parlophone PMC 1255 [1], PCS 3071 [2]   1

Help! LP (US, 1965) – Capitol MAS 2386 [4], SMAS 2386 [3]   1
Love Songs LP (1977) – Parlophone PCSP 721 / Capitol SKBL 11711 [2]   7/24
Help! CD (1987) – EMI CDP 7 46439 2 [5]   61

=== **NOTES** ===

♪ The last song to be recorded before filming started.
♪ The song is performed in a studio in *Help!*, with Paul alternating between bass and piano, and Ringo between drums and bongos.
♪ [1] was given no RM number.
♪ Listed on the Capitol *Help!* LP (and on the 2006 reissue) as 'You're Gonna Lose That Girl'.

(You're So Square) Baby I Don't Care

[Leiber-Stoller]

Paul – lead vocals, guitar
John – bass
George – guitar
Ringo – drums

Studio recording and mixing

9 September 1968 – Studio Two – White Album session 56 out of 81
Studio jam

2018 – EMI
[1] – stereo mix from studio jam

Releases

UK/US peak

The Beatles Deluxe CD (2018) – Apple 0602567571957 [1]   4/6

=== **NOTES** ===

♪ Written in 1957 for the Elvis Presley film *Jailhouse Rock*.
♪ Buddy Holly's version got to #12 in the UK in 1961.

You've Got To Hide Your Love Away

[Lennon-McCartney]

John – lead vocals, acoustic guitar
Paul – bass, maracas
George – acoustic guitar
Ringo – brushes, tambourine
John Scott – flutes

Studio recording and mixing

18 February 1965 – Studio Two – Help! session 4 out of 13
Takes 1–9
Overdubs onto take 9 – tambourine, maracas, guitar, vocals

19 February 1965 – Studio Two – Help! session 5 out of 13
Overdubs onto take 9 – flute

20 February 1965 – Studio Two control room
RM1 [1] – mono mix from take 9

23 February 1965 – Studio Two control room
RS1 [2] – stereo mix from take 9

1965 – Capitol
[3] – mono mix from [2]

1987 – EMI
[4] – stereo mix from take 9

1995 – EMI
[5] – mono mix from edit of takes 1, 2, 5

Releases   UK/US peak

Help! LP (1965) – Parlophone PMC 1255 [1], PCS 3071 [2]	1
Help! LP (US, 1965) – Capitol MAS 2386 [3], SMAS 2386 [2]	1
The Beatles 1962–1966 LP (1973) – Apple PCSP 717 [2]	3
The Beatles 1962–1966 LP (US, 1973)– Apple SKBO 3403 [2]	3
Love Songs LP (1977) – Parlophone PCSP 721 / Capitol SKBL 11711 [2]	7/24
The Beatles Ballads LP (1980) – Parlophone PCS 7214 [2]	17
Reel Music LP (1982) – Parlophone PCS 7218 / Capitol SV-12199 [2]	–/19
Help! CD (1987) – EMI CDP 7 46439 2 [4]	61
The Beatles 1962–1966 CD (1993) – EMI CDP 7 97036 2 [4]	3
Anthology 2 CD (1996) – Apple 8 34448 2 [5]	1/1

=== NOTES ===
♪ The flautist was the first session musician on a
Beatles track since Andy White on 'Love Me Do'.

Young Blood

[Leiber-Stoller-Pomus]

George – lead vocals, lead guitar
John – backing vocals, rhythm guitar
Paul – backing vocals, bass
Ringo – drums

BBC and other performances

11 June 1963 [1] – 1 June 1963 edition of *Pop Go The Beatles*

Releases
UK/US peak

Live At The BBC CD (1994) – Apple 8 31796 2 [1]
1/3

═══ **NOTES** ═══

> ♪ B-side to 'Searchin'', the Coasters' single from March 1957.
> ♪ Sung by George from 1958 to 1962.
> ♪ Performed by Leon Russell at George's Concert for Bangladesh in 1971.

Your Feet's Too Big
[Benson-Fisher]

Paul – lead vocals, bass
John – rhythm guitar
George – lead guitar
Ringo – drums

BBC and other performances

December 1962 [1] – Star-Club, Hamburg (live)

Releases
UK/US peak

Live! At The Star-Club In Hamburg, Germany; 1962 LP (1977) – Lingasong LNL 1 /
Lingasong LS 2 7001 [1]
–

═══ **NOTES** ═══

> ♪ A hit for Fats Waller from 1939.
> ♪ A short film of Waller performing the song was made in 1941.

Your Mother Should Know
[Lennon-McCartney]

Paul – lead and backing vocals, bass, piano
John – backing vocals, organ
George – backing vocals, guitar
Ringo – drums, tambourine

Studio recording and mixing

22 August 1967 – Chappell Studios – Magical Mystery Tour session 10 out of 30
Takes 1–8
Overdubs onto take 8 – vocals

23 August 1967 · *Chappell Studios – Magical Mystery Tour session 11 out of 30*
Tape reduction of take 8 > take 9
Overdubs onto take 9 – vocals, guitar

16 September 1967 – *Studio Three – Magical Mystery Tour session 16 out of 30*
Remake takes 20–30

29 September 1967 – *Studio Two – Magical Mystery Tour session 21 out of 30*
Tape reduction of take 9 > takes 50–52
Overdubs onto take 52 – organ, bass, tambourine

2 October 1967 – *Studio Two control room*
RM25 [1] – mono mix from take 52

6 November 1967 – *Studio Three control room*
RS2 [2] – stereo mix from take 52

1995 – *EMI*
[3] – stereo mix from take 27

Releases

	UK/US peak
Magical Mystery Tour EP (1967) – Parlophone MMT-1 [1], SMMT-1 [2]	2
Magical Mystery Tour LP (US, 1967) – Capitol MAL 2835 [1], SMAL 2835 [2]	1
Anthology 2 CD (1996) – Apple 8 34448 2 [3]	1/1

═══ **NOTES** ═══

♪ The 23 August session was the last to be attended by Brian Epstein.
♪ The only Beatles recording made at Chappell Studios.

Your True Love

[Perkins]

Lead vocals, **George**. Part of the Quarry Men/Beatles' set until 1962. Sung by Paul and George on day 2 of the *Let It Be* sessions. Released by Carl Perkins on the B-side of 'Matchbox' in 1957.

Calendar of Recording Sessions 1963–1969

The dates of the recording sessions held by the Beatles are shown on the following pages, the dates shaded to indicate the relevant LP. Underlined dates signify that non-album material, principally singles, was also recorded, or exceptionally denote a recording session that did not involve the Beatles.

In addition, recording of the first two singles had taken place on 4 and 11 September and 26 November 1962.

1964

March
June
September
December

February
May
August
November

January
April
July
October

Beatles For Sale

A Hard Day's Night

1963

March
June
September
December

February
May
August
November

January
April
July
October

With The Beatles

Please Please Me

1966

January · February · March
April · May · June
July · August · September
October · November · December

Revolver · **Rubber Soul** · **Sgt. Pepper**

1965

January · February · March
April · May · June
July · August · September
October · November · December

Help! · **Rubber Soul**

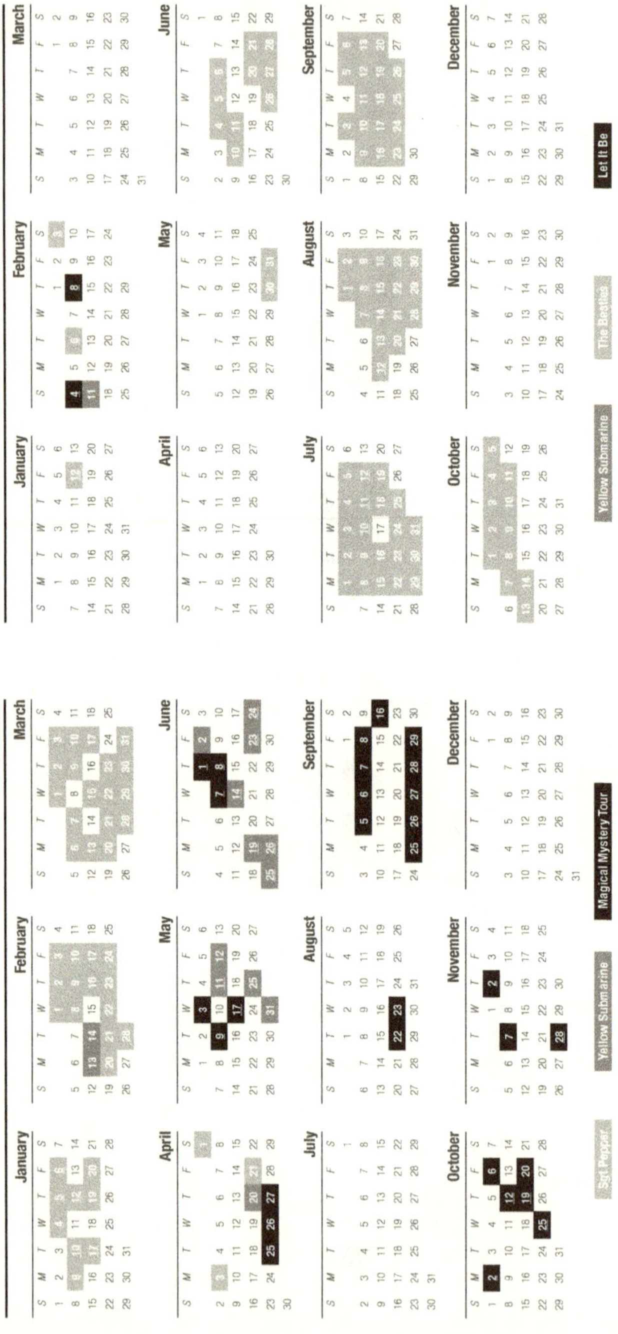
1967
1968
Sgt Pepper
Yellow Submarine
Magical Mystery Tour
Yellow Submarine
The Beatles
Let It Be

1969

	January	February	March

Abbey Road

Let It Be

Further recording for *Let It Be* also took place on 3, 4 and 8 January and 1 April 1970.

The Recording Sessions

The following tables show which songs were recorded in each in the series of LP sessions. The studio listed is Abbey Road Studio One, Two or Three, unless otherwise noted. As the bulk of *Let It Be* was recorded before *Abbey Road*, these two LPs are listed in that order.

Please Please Me

Session	Date	Studio	Tracks recorded
1	6 June 1962	Two	Besame Mucho; Love Me Do; P.S. I Love You; Ask Me Why
2	4 September 1962	Two	How Do You Do It; Love Me Do
3	11 September 1962	Two	P.S. I Love You; Love Me Do; Please Please Me
4	26 November 1962	Two	Please Please Me; Ask Me Why; Tip Of My Tongue
5	11 February 1963	Two	There's A Place; I Saw Her Standing There; A Taste Of Honey; Do You Want To Know A Secret; Misery; Hold Me Tight; Anna (Go To Him); Boys; Chains; Baby It's You; Twist And Shout
6	20 February 1963	One	Misery; Baby It's You
7	5 March 1963	Two	From Me To You; Thank You Girl; One After 909
8	13 March 1963	Two	Thank You Girl

With The Beatles

Session	Date	Studio	Tracks recorded
1	1 July 1963	Two	She Loves You; I'll Get You
2	18 July 1963	Two	You Really Got A Hold On Me; Money; Devil In Her Heart; Till There Was You

Session	Date	Studio	Tracks recorded
3	30 July 1963	Two	Please Mr Postman; It Won't Be Long; Money; Till There Was You; Roll Over Beethoven; All My Loving
4	11 September 1963	Two	I Wanna Be Your Man; Little Child; All I've Got To Do; Not A Second Time; Don't Bother Me
5	12 September 1963	Two	Hold Me Tight; Don't Bother Me; Little Child; I Wanna Be Your Man
6	30 September 1963	Two	Money; I Wanna Be Your Man
7	3 October 1963	Two	I Wanna Be Your Man; Little Child
8	17 October 1963	Two	The Beatles' Christmas Record; You Really Got A Hold On Me; I Want To Hold Your Hand; This Boy
9	23 October 1963	Two	I Wanna Be Your Man

A Hard Day's Night

Session	Date	Studio	Tracks recorded
1	29 January 1964	EMI Paris	Komm, Gib Mir Deine Hand; Sie Liebt Dich; Can't Buy Me Love
2	25 February 1964	Two	You Can't Do That; And I Love Her; I Should Have Known Better; Can't Buy Me Love
3	26 February 1964	Two	I Should Have Known Better; And I Love Her
4	27 February 1964	Two	And I Love Her; Tell Me Why; If I Fell
5	1 March 1964	Two	I'm Happy Just To Dance With You; Long Tall Sally; I Call Your Name
6	10 March 1964	Two	Can't Buy Me Love
7	16 April 1964	Two	A Hard Day's Night
8	22 May 1964	Two	You Can't Do That
9	1 June 1964	Two	Matchbox; I'll Cry Instead; Slow Down; I'll Be Back
10	2 June 1964	Two	Any Time At All; Things We Said Today; When I Get Home; Any Time At All
11	3 June 1964	Two	Any Time At All; Things We Said Today; You Know What To Do; No Reply
12	4 June 1964	Two	Slow Down

Beatles For Sale

Session	Date	Studio	Tracks recorded
1	11 August 1964	Two	Baby's In Black
2	14 August 1964	Two	I'm A Loser; Mr Moonlight; Leave My Kitten Alone
3	29 September 1964	Two	Every Little Thing; I Don't Want To Spoil The Party; What You're Doing
4	30 September 1964	Two	Every Little Thing; What You're Doing; No Reply
5	6 October 1964	Two	Eight Days A Week
6	8 October 1964	Two	She's A Woman
7	18 October 1964	Two	Eight Days A Week; Kansas City/Hey, Hey, Hey, Hey; Mr Moonlight; I Feel Fine; I'll Follow The Sun; Everybody's Trying To Be My Baby; Rock And Roll Music; Words Of Love
8	26 October 1964	Two	Honey Don't; What You're Doing; Another Beatles Christmas Record

Help!

Session	Date	Studio	Tracks recorded
1	15 February 1965	Two	Ticket To Ride; Another Girl; I Need You
2	16 February 1965	Two	I Need You; Another Girl; Yes It Is
3	17 February 1965	Two	The Night Before; You Like Me Too Much
4	18 February 1965	Two	You've Got To Hide Your Love Away; If You've Got Trouble; Tell Me What You See
5	19 February 1965	Two	You're Going To Lose That Girl; You've Got To Hide Your Love Away
6	20 February 1965	Two	That Means A Lot
7	30 March 1965	Two	That Means A Lot; You're Going To Lose That Girl
8	13 April 1965	Two	Help!
9	10 May 1965	Two	Dizzy Miss Lizzy; Bad Boy
10	24 May 1965	CTS	Help!
11	14 June 1965	Two	I've Just Seen A Face; I'm Down; Yesterday

Session	Date	Studio	Tracks recorded
12	15 June 1965	Two	It's Only Love
13	17 June 1965	Two	Act Naturally; Wait

Rubber Soul

Session	Date	Studio	Tracks recorded
1	12 October 1965	Two	Run For Your Life; Norwegian Wood (This Bird Has Flown)
2	13 October 1965	Two	Drive My Car
3	16 October 1965	Two	Day Tripper; If I Needed Someone
4	18 October 1965	Two	If I Needed Someone; In My Life
5	20 October 1965	Two	We Can Work It Out
6	21 October 1965	Two	Norwegian Wood (This Bird Has Flown); Nowhere Man
7	22 October 1965	Two	In My Life; Nowhere Man
8	24 October 1965	Two	I'm Looking Through You
9	29 October 1965	Two	We Can Work It Out
10	3 November 1965	Two	Michelle
11	4 November 1965	Two	What Goes On; 12-Bar Original
12	6 November 1965	Two	I'm Looking Through You
13	8 November 1965	Two	Think For Yourself; The Beatles Third Christmas Record
14	10 November 1965	Two	The Word; I'm Looking Through You
15	11 November 1965	Two	You Won't See Me; Girl; Wait; I'm Looking Through You

Revolver

Session	Date	Studio	Tracks recorded
1	6 April 1966	Three	Tomorrow Never Knows
2	7 April 1966	Three	Tomorrow Never Knows; Got To Get You Into My Life
3	8 April 1966	Two	Got To Get You Into My Life
4	11 April 1966	Two	Got To Get You Into My Life; Love You To

Session	Date	Studio	Tracks recorded
5	13 April 1966	Three	Love You To; Paperback Writer
6	14 April 1966	Three	Paperback Writer; Rain
7	16 April 1966	Two	Rain
8	17 April 1966	Two	Doctor Robert
9	19 April 1966	Two	Doctor Robert
10	20 April 1966	Two	And Your Bird Can Sing; Taxman
11	21 April 1966	Two	Taxman
12	22 April 1966	Two	Taxman; Tomorrow Never Knows
13	26 April 1966	Two	And Your Bird Can Sing
14	27 April 1966	Three	I'm Only Sleeping
15	28 April 1966	Two	Eleanor Rigby
16	29 April 1966	Three	Eleanor Rigby; I'm Only Sleeping
17	5 May 1966	Three	I'm Only Sleeping
18	6 May 1966	Two	I'm Only Sleeping
19	9 May 1966	Two	For No One
20	16 May 1966	Two	Taxman; For No One
21	18 May 1966	Two	Got To Get You Into My Life
22	19 May 1966	Three	For No One
23	26 May 1966	Three	Yellow Submarine
24	1 June 1966	Two	Yellow Submarine
25	2 June 1966	Two	I Want To Tell You
26	3 June 1966	Two	I Want To Tell You
27	6 June 1966	Three	Eleanor Rigby
28	8 June 1966	Two	Good Day Sunshine
29	9 June 1966	Two	Good Day Sunshine
30	14 June 1966	Two	Here, There And Everywhere
31	16 June 1966	Two	Here, There And Everywhere
32	17 June 1966	Two	Here, There And Everywhere; Got To Get You Into My Life
33	21 June 1966	Two	She Said She Said

Sgt Pepper's Lonely Hearts Club Band

Session	Date	Studio	Tracks recorded
1	24 November 1966	Two	Strawberry Fields Forever
2	25 November 1966	Dick James	Pantomime: Everywhere It's Christmas
3	28 November 1966	Two	Strawberry Fields Forever
4	29 November 1966	Two	Strawberry Fields Forever
5	6 December 1966	Two	Christmas Messages; When I'm Sixty-Four
6	8 December 1966	One; Two	When I'm Sixty-Four; Strawberry Fields Forever
7	9 December 1966	Two	Strawberry Fields Forever
8	15 December 1966	Two	Strawberry Fields Forever
9	20 December 1966	Two	When I'm Sixty-Four
10	21 December 1966	Two	When I'm Sixty-Four; Strawberry Fields Forever
11	29 December 1966	Two	Penny Lane
12	30 December 1966	Two	Penny Lane
13	4 January 1967	Two	Penny Lane
14	5 January 1967	Two	Penny Lane; Carnival Of Light
15	6 January 1967	Two	Penny Lane
16	9 January 1967	Two	Penny Lane
17	10 January 1967	Three	Penny Lane
18	12 January 1967	Three	Penny Lane
19	17 January 1967	Two	Penny Lane
20	19 January 1967	Two	A Day In The Life
21	20 January 1967	Two	A Day In The Life
22	1 February 1967	Two	Sgt Pepper's Lonely Hearts Club Band
23	2 February 1967	Two	Sgt Pepper's Lonely Hearts Club Band
24	3 February 1967	Two	A Day In The Life
25	8 February 1967	Two	Good Morning Good Morning
26	9 February 1967	Regent	Fixing A Hole
27	10 February 1967	One	A Day In The Life
28	16 February 1967	Three	Good Morning Good Morning
29	17 February 1967	Two	Being For The Benefit Of Mr Kite!

Session	Date	Studio	Tracks recorded
30	20 February 1967	Three	Being For The Benefit Of Mr Kite!
31	21 February 1967	Two	Fixing A Hole
32	22 February 1967	Two	A Day In The Life; Drum Track
33	23 February 1967	Two	Lovely Rita
34	24 February 1967	Two	Lovely Rita
35	28 February 1967	Two	Lucy In The Sky With Diamonds
36	1 March 1967	Two	A Day In The Life; Lucy In The Sky With Diamonds
37	2 March 1967	Two	Lucy In The Sky With Diamonds
38	3 March 1967	Two	Sgt Pepper's Lonely Hearts Club Band
39	6 March 1967	Two	Sgt Pepper's Lonely Hearts Club Band
40	7 March 1967	Two	Lovely Rita
41	9 March 1967	Two	Getting Better
42	10 March 1967	Two	Getting Better
43	13 March 1967	Two	Good Morning Good Morning
44	15 March 1967	Two	Within You Without You
45	17 March 1967	Two	She's Leaving Home
46	20 March 1967	Two	She's Leaving Home
47	21 March 1967	Two	Getting Better; Lovely Rita
48	22 March 1967	Two	Within You Without You
49	23 March 1967	Two	Getting Better
50	28 March 1967	Two	Good Morning Good Morning; Being For The Benefit Of Mr Kite!
51	29 March 1967	Two	Good Morning Good Morning; Being For The Benefit Of Mr Kite!; With A Little Help From My Friends
52	30 March 1967	Two	With A Little Help From My Friends
53	31 March 1967	Two	Being For The Benefit Of Mr Kite!
54	1 April 1967	One	Sgt Pepper's Lonely Hearts Club Band (Reprise)
55	3 April 1967	One	Within You Without You
56	21 April 1967	Two	Run-out Groove

Magical Mystery Tour

Session	Date	Studio	Tracks recorded
1	25 April 1967	Three	Magical Mystery Tour
2	26 April 1967	Three	Magical Mystery Tour
3	27 April 1967	Three	Magical Mystery Tour
4	3 May 1967	Three	Magical Mystery Tour
5	9 May 1967	Two	Untitled
6	17 May 1967	Two	You Know My Name (Look Up The Number)
7	1 June 1967	De Lane Lea	Untitled
8	7 June 1967	Two	You Know My Name (Look Up The Number)
9	8 June 1967	Two	You Know My Name (Look Up The Number)
10	22 August 1967	Chappell	Your Mother Should Know
11	23 August 1967	Chappell	Your Mother Should Know
12	5 September 1967	One	I Am The Walrus
13	6 September 1967	Two	I Am The Walrus; The Fool On The Hill; Blue Jay Way
14	7 September 1967	Two	Blue Jay Way
15	8 September 1967	Three	Flying
16	16 September 1967	Three	Your Mother Should Know
17	25 September 1967	Two	The Fool On The Hill
18	26 September 1967	Two	The Fool On The Hill
19	27 September 1967	One; Two	I Am The Walrus; The Fool On The Hill
20	28 September 1967	Two	Flying
21	29 September 1967	Two	Your Mother Should Know
22	2 October 1967	Two	Hello Goodbye
23	6 October 1967	Two	Blue Jay Way
24	12 October 1967	Three	Shirley's Wild Accordion
25	19 October 1967	One	Hello Goodbye
26	20 October 1967	Three	The Fool On The Hill; Hello Goodbye
27	25 October 1967	Two	Hello Goodbye
28	2 November 1967	Three	Hello Goodbye
29	7 November 1967	One	Magical Mystery Tour
30	28 November 1967	Three	Christmas Time (Is Here Again)

Yellow Submarine

Session	Date	Studio	Tracks recorded
1	13 February 1967	Two	Only A Northern Song
2	14 February 1967	Two	Only A Northern Song
3	20 April 1967	Two	Only A Northern Song
4	11 May 1967	Olympic	Baby You're A Rich Man
5	12 May 1967	Two	All Together Now
6	25 May 1967	De Lane Lea	It's All Too Much
7	31 May 1967	De Lane Lea	It's All Too Much
8	2 June 1967	De Lane Lea	It's All Too Much
9	14 June 1967	Olympic	All You Need Is Love
10	19 June 1967	Three	All You Need Is Love
11	23 June 1967	One	All You Need Is Love
12	24 June 1967	One	All You Need Is Love
13	25 June 1967	One	All You Need Is Love
14	26 June 1967	Two	All You Need Is Love
15	11 February 1968	Three	Hey Bulldog

The Beatles

Session	Date	Studio	Tracks recorded
1	12 January 1968	EMI Bombay	The Inner Light
2	3 February 1968	Three	Lady Madonna
3	6 February 1968	One	The Inner Light; Lady Madonna
4	30 May 1968	Two	Revolution 1/Revolution 9
5	31 May 1968	Three	Revolution 1
6	4 June 1968	Three	Revolution 1
7	5 June 1968	Three	Don't Pass Me By
8	6 June 1968	Two	Don't Pass Me By; Revolution 9
9	10 June 1968	Three	Revolution 9
10	11 June 1968	Two; Three	Blackbird; Revolution 9
11	20 June 1968	One; Two; Three	Revolution 9
12	21 June 1968	Two	Revolution 1; Revolution 9

Session	Date	Studio	Tracks recorded
13	26 June 1968	Two	Everybody's Got Something To Hide Except Me And My Monkey
14	27 June 1968	Two	Everybody's Got Something To Hide Except Me And My Monkey
15	28 June 1968	Two	Good Night
16	1 July 1968	Two	Everybody's Got Something To Hide Except Me And My Monkey
17	2 July 1968	Two	Good Night
18	3 July 1968	Two	Ob-La-Di, Ob-La-Da
19	4 July 1968	Two	Ob-La-Di, Ob-La-Da
20	5 July 1968	Two	Ob-La-Di, Ob-La-Da
21	8 July 1968	Two	Ob-La-Di, Ob-La-Da
22	9 July 1968	Three	Ob-La-Di, Ob-La-Da
23	10 July 1968	Three	Revolution
24	11 July 1968	Three	Revolution; Ob-La-Di, Ob-La-Da
25	12 July 1968	Two	Don't Pass Me By; Revolution
26	15 July 1968	Two	Ob-La-Di, Ob-La-Da; Cry Baby Cry
27	16 July 1968	Two	Cry Baby Cry
28	18 July 1968	Two	Cry Baby Cry; Helter Skelter
29	19 July 1968	Two	Sexy Sadie
30	22 July 1968	One	Don't Pass Me By; Good Night
31	23 July 1968	Two	Everybody's Got Something To Hide Except Me And My Monkey
32	24 July 1968	Two	Sexy Sadie
33	25 July 1968	Two	While My Guitar Gently Weeps
34	29 July 1968	Two	Hey Jude
35	30 July 1968	Two	Hey Jude
36	31 July 1968	Trident	Hey Jude
37	1 August 1968	Trident	Hey Jude
38	7 August 1968	Two	Not Guilty
39	8 August 1968	Two	Not Guilty
40	9 August 1968	Two	Not Guilty; Mother Nature's Son
41	12 August 1968	Two	Not Guilty

Session	Date	Studio	Tracks recorded
42	13 August 1968	Two; Annexe	Sexy Sadie; Yer Blues
43	14 August 1968	Two	Yer Blues; What's The New Mary Jane
44	15 August 1968	Two	Rocky Raccoon
45	16 August 1968	Two	While My Guitar Gently Weeps
46	20 August 1968	Three; Two	Yer Blues; Mother Nature's Son; Wild Honey Pie
47	21 August 1968	Two	Sexy Sadie
48	22 August 1968	Two	Back In The U.S.S.R.
49	23 August 1968	Two	Back In The U.S.S.R.
50	28 August 1968	Trident	Dear Prudence
51	29 August 1968	Trident	Dear Prudence
52	30 August 1968	Trident	Dear Prudence
53	3 September 1968	Two	While My Guitar Gently Weeps
54	5 September 1968	Two	While My Guitar Gently Weeps
55	6 September 1968	Two	While My Guitar Gently Weeps
56	9 September 1968	Two	Helter Skelter
57	10 September 1968	Two	Helter Skelter
58	11 September 1968	Two	Glass Onion
59	12 September 1968	Two	Glass Onion
60	13 September 1968	Two	Glass Onion
61	16 September 1968	Two	I Will; Can You Take Me Back; Los Paranoias; Step Inside Love; Glass Onion
62	17 September 1968	Two	I Will
63	18 September 1968	Two	Birthday
64	19 September 1968	One; Two	Piggies
65	20 September 1968	Two	Piggies
66	23 September 1968	Two	Happiness Is A Warm Gun
67	24 September 1968	Two	Happiness Is A Warm Gun
68	25 September 1968	Two	Happiness Is A Warm Gun
69	26 September 1968	Two	Glass Onion
70	1 October 1968	Trident	Honey Pie
71	2 October 1968	Trident	Honey Pie
72	3 October 1968	Trident	Savoy Truffle

Session	Date	Studio	Tracks recorded
73	4 October 1968	Trident	Martha My Dear; Honey Pie
74	5 October 1968	Trident	Savoy Truffle; Martha My Dear
75	7 October 1968	Two	Long Long Long
76	8 October 1968	Two	Long Long Long; I'm So Tired; The Continuing Story Of Bungalow Bill
77	9 October 1968	Two; One	Long Long Long; Why Don't We Do It In The Road
78	10 October 1968	Two; Three	Piggies; Glass Onion; Why Don't We Do It In The Road
79	11 October 1968	Two	Savoy Truffle
80	13 October 1968	Two	Julia
81	14 October 1968	Two	Savoy Truffle

Let It Be

Session	Date	Studio	Tracks recorded
1	3 February 1968	Three	Across The Universe
2	4 February 1968	Three	Across The Universe
3	8 February 1968	Two	Across The Universe; The Inner Light
4	24 January 1969	Apple*	Maggie Mae; Dig It
5	25 January 1969	Apple*	For You Blue
6	26 January 1969	Apple*	Dig It; The Long And Winding Road
7	27 January 1969	Apple*	Get Back
8	28 January 1969	Apple*	Get Back; Don't Let Me Down
9	30 January 1969	Apple roof*	I've Got A Feeling; Dig A Pony; One After 909; Get Back
10	31 January 1969	Apple*	Two Of Us; Let It Be
11	7 April 1969	Olympic	Don't Let Me Down
12	30 April 1969	Three	Let It Be; You Know My Name (Look Up The Number)
13	26 November 1969	Two	What's The New Mary Jane
14	3 January 1970	Two	I Me Mine
15	4 January 1970	Two	Let It Be
16	8 January 1970	Olympic	For You Blue

Session	Date	Studio	Tracks recorded
17	1 April 1970	One	Across The Universe; The Long And Winding Road; I Me Mine

Abbey Road

Session	Date	Studio	Tracks recorded
1	22 February 1969	Trident	I Want You (She's So Heavy)
2	14 April 1969	Three	The Ballad Of John And Yoko
3	16 April 1969	Three	Old Brown Shoe; Something
4	18 April 1969	Three; Two	Old Brown Shoe; I Want You (She's So Heavy)
5	20 April 1969	Three	I Want You (She's So Heavy); Oh! Darling
6	26 April 1969	Two	Oh! Darling; Octopus's Garden
7	29 April 1969	Three	Octopus's Garden
8	2 May 1969	Three	Something
9	5 May 1969	Olympic	Something
10	6 May 1969	Olympic	You Never Give Me Your Money
11	1 July 1969	Two	You Never Give Me Your Money
12	2 July 1969	Two	Her Majesty; Golden Slumbers/Carry That Weight
13	3 July 1969	Two	Golden Slumbers/Carry That Weight
14	4 July 1969	Two	Golden Slumbers/Carry That Weight
15	7 July 1969	Two	Here Comes The Sun
16	8 July 1969	Two	Here Comes The Sun
17	9 July 1969	Two	Maxwell's Silver Hammer
18	10 July 1969	Two	Maxwell's Silver Hammer
19	11 July 1969	Two	Maxwell's Silver Hammer; Something; You Never Give Me Your Money
20	15 July 1969	Three	You Never Give Me Your Money
21	16 July 1969	Three; Two	Here Comes The Sun; Something
22	17 July 1969	Three; Two	Oh! Darling; Octopus's Garden
23	18 July 1969	Three	Oh! Darling; Octopus's Garden
24	21 July 1969	Three	Come Together
25	22 July 1969	Three	Oh! Darling; Come Together
26	23 July 1969	Three	Oh! Darling; Come Together; The End

Session	Date	Studio	Tracks recorded
27	24 July 1969	Two	Come And Get It; Sun King/Mean Mr Mustard; Ain't She Sweet
28	25 July 1969	Two	Sun King/Mean Mr Mustard; Come Together; Polythene Pam/She Came In Through The Bathroom Window
29	28 July 1969	Three	Polythene Pam/She Came In Through The Bathroom Window
30	29 July 1969	Three	Come Together; Sun King/Mean Mr Mustard
31	30 July 1969	Three	Come Together; Polythene Pam/She Came In Through The Bathroom Window; You Never Give Me Your Money; Golden Slumbers/Carry That Weight
32	31 July 1969	Two	You Never Give Me Your Money; Golden Slumbers/Carry That Weight
33	1 August 1969	Two	Because
34	4 August 1969	Two	Because
35	5 August 1969	Three; Room 43; Two	You Never Give Me Your Money; Because; The End
36	6 August 1969	Three; Room 43; Two	Here Comes The Sun; Maxwell's Silver Hammer
37	7 August 1969	Three	The End
38	8 August 1969	Two; Three	The End; I Want You (She's So Heavy); Oh! Darling
39	11 August 1969	Two	I Want You (She's So Heavy); Oh! Darling; Here Comes The Sun
40	15 August 1969	One	Golden Slumbers/Carry That Weight; The End; Something; Here Comes The Sun
41	18 August 1969	Two	The End
42	19 August 1969	Two	Here Comes The Sun

(* tracks released on the *Let It Be* LP and as singles only)

Catalogue of Releases

The following is a catalogue of the principal official Parlophone/Capitol/Apple releases, along with various notable releases, all of which are included in this book. The releases are UK, unless otherwise noted. For convenience, multi-format album releases after 1982 are given in the CD format only.

Singles

'Ain't She Sweet' / 'If You Love Me Baby' – Polydor NH 52317
Released: 29 May 1964; UK chart peak: 29

'Ain't She Sweet' / 'Nobody's Child' (US) – Atco 45-6308
Released: 6 July 1964; US chart peak: 19, –

'All My Loving' / 'This Boy' (Canada) – Capitol 72144
Released: 9 March 1964; US chart peak: 45, –

'All You Need Is Love' / 'Baby You're A Rich Man' – Parlophone R 5620
Released: 7 July 1967; UK chart peak: 1

'All You Need Is Love' / 'Baby You're A Rich Man' (US) – Capitol 5964
Released: 17 July 1967; US chart peak: 1, 34

'And I Love Her' / 'If I Fell' (US) – Capitol 5235
Released: 20 July 1964; US chart peak: 12, 53

'Baby It's You' – Apple 8 82073 2
Released: 20 March 1995; UK chart peak: 7, US chart peak: 67

'Back In The U.S.S.R.' / 'Twist And Shout' – Parlophone R 6016
Released: 25 June 1976; UK chart peak: 19

'The Ballad Of John And Yoko' / 'Old Brown Shoe' – Apple R 5786
Released: 30 May 1969; UK chart peak: 1

'The Ballad Of John And Yoko' / 'Old Brown Shoe' (US) – Apple 2531
Released: 4 June 1969; US chart peak: 8, –

'The Beatles' Movie Medley' / 'I'm Happy Just To Dance With You' – Parlophone R 6055
Released: 24 May 1982; UK chart peak: 10

'The Beatles' Movie Medley' / 'I'm Happy Just To Dance With You' (US) – Capitol B 5107
Released: 22 March 1982; US chart peak: 12

'Can't Buy Me Love' / 'You Can't Do That' – Parlophone R 5114
Released: 20 March 1964; UK chart peak: 1

'Can't Buy Me Love' / 'You Can't Do That' (US) – Capitol 5150
Released: 16 March 1964; US chart peak: 1, 48

'Cry For A Shadow' / 'Why (Can't You Love Me Again)' – Polydor NH 52275
Released: 28 February 1964; did not chart

'Dizzy Miss Lizzy' / 'Yesterday' – Parlophone DP 563
Released: October 1965; for export – did not chart

'Do You Want To Know A Secret' / 'Thank You Girl' (US) – Vee Jay VJ 587
Released: 23 March 1964; US chart peak: 2, 35

'Do You Want To Know A Secret' / 'Thank You Girl' (US) – Capitol Starline 6064
Released: 11 October 1965; did not chart

'Eight Days A Week' / 'I Don't Want To Spoil The Party' (US) – Capitol 5371
Released: 15 February 1965; US chart peak: 1, 39

'Eleanor Rigby' / 'Yellow Submarine' – Parlophone R 5493
Released: 5 August 1966; UK chart peak: 1

'Eleanor Rigby' / 'Yellow Submarine' (US) – Capitol 5715
Released: 8 August 1966; US chart peak: 11, 2

'Free As A Bird' – Apple 8 82587 2
Released: 4 December 1995 (UK), 12 December 1995 (US); UK chart peak: 2, US chart peak: 6

'From Me To You' / 'Thank You Girl' – Parlophone R 5015
Released: 11 April 1963; UK chart peak: 1

'From Me To You' / 'Thank You Girl' (US) – Vee Jay VJ 522
Released: 27 May 1963; US chart peak: 116, –

'Get Back' / 'Don't Let Me Down' – Apple R 5777
Released: 11 April 1969; UK chart peak: 1

'Get Back' / 'Don't Let Me Down' (US) – Apple 2490
Released: 5 May 1969; US chart peak: 1, 35

'Got To Get You Into My Life' / 'Helter Skelter' (US) – Capitol 4274
Released: 31 May 1976; US chart peak: 7

'A Hard Day's Night' / 'I Should Have Known Better' (US) – Capitol 5222
Released: 13 July 1964; US chart peak: 1, 53

'A Hard Day's Night' / 'Things We Said Today' – Parlophone R 5160
Released: 10 July 1964; UK chart peak: 1

'Hello, Goodbye' / 'I Am The Walrus' – Parlophone R 5655
Released: 24 November 1967; UK chart peak: 1

'Hello, Goodbye' / 'I Am The Walrus' (US) – Capitol 2056
Released: 27 November 1967; US chart peak: 1, 56

'Help!' / 'I'm Down' – Parlophone R 5305
Released: 23 July 1965; UK chart peak: 1

'Help!' / 'I'm Down' (US) – Capitol 5476
Released: 19 July 1965; US chart peak: 1, 101

'Hey Jude' / 'Revolution' – Apple R 5722
Released: 30 August 1968; UK chart peak: 1

'Hey Jude' / 'Revolution' – Parlophone DP 570
Released: 31 August 1968; for export – did not chart

'Hey Jude' / 'Revolution' (US) – Apple 2276
Released: 26 August 1968; US chart peak: 1, 12

'I Feel Fine' / 'She's A Woman' – Parlophone R 5200
Released: 27 November 1964; UK chart peak: 1

'I Feel Fine' / 'She's A Woman' (US) – Capitol 5327
Released: 23 November 1964; US chart peak: 1, 4

'I Want To Hold Your Hand' / 'I Saw Her Standing There' (US) – Capitol 5112
Released: 26 December 1963; US chart peak: 1, 14

'I Want To Hold Your Hand' / 'This Boy' – Parlophone R 5084
Released: 29 November 1963; UK chart peak: 1

'I Want To Hold Your Hand' / 'This Boy' (Australia) – Parlophone A 8103
Released: 12 December 1963; did not chart in the UK or US, Australia chark peak: 1

'I'll Cry Instead' / 'I'm Happy Just To Dance With You' (US) – Capitol 5234
Released: 20 July 1964; US chart peak: 25, 95

'If I Fell' / 'Tell Me Why' – Parlophone DP 562
Released: 16 October 1964; for export – did not chart

'Kansas City/Hey, Hey, Hey, Hey' / 'Boys' (US) – Capitol Starline 6066
Released: 11 October 1965; US chart peak: –, 102

'Komm, Gib Mir Deine Hand' / 'Sie Liebt Dich' (Germany) – Odeon O 22671
Released: 5 March 1964; did not chart in UK or US, Germany chart peak: 1, 7

'Lady Madonna' / 'The Inner Light' – Parlophone R 5675
Released: 15 March 1968; UK chart peak: 1

'Lady Madonna' / 'The Inner Light' (US) – Capitol 2138
Released: 18 March 1968; US chart peak: 4, 96

'Let It Be' / 'You Know My Name (Look Up The Number)' – Apple R 5833
Released: 6 March 1970; UK chart peak: 2

'Let It Be' / 'You Know My Name (Look Up The Number)' – Parlophone P-R 5833
Released: April 1970; for export – did not chart

'Let It Be' / 'You Know My Name (Look Up The Number)' (US) – Apple 2764
Released: 11 March 1970; US chart peak: 1

'The Long And Winding Road' / 'For You Blue' (US) – Apple 2832
Released: 11 May 1970; US chart peak: 1

'Love Me Do' / 'P.S. I Love You' – Parlophone 45-R 4949
Released: 5 October 1962; UK chart peak: 17 (1982 peak: 4)

'Love Me Do' / 'P.S. I Love You' (US) – Tollie 9008
Released: 27 April 1964; US chart peak: 1, 10

'Love Me Do' / 'P.S. I Love You' (US) – Capitol Starline 6062
Released: 11 October 1965; did not chart

'Matchbox' / 'Slow Down' (US) – Capitol 5255
Released: 24 August 1964; US chart peak: 17, 25

'Michelle' / 'Drive My Car' – Parlophone DP 564
Released: 8 July 1966; for export – did not chart

'My Bonnie' / 'The Saints (When The Saints Go Marching In)' (Germany) – Polydor NH 24673
Released: 23 October 1961; did not chart in UK or US, Germany chart peak: 32 in 1964

'My Bonnie' / 'The Saints (When The Saints Go Marching In)' – Polydor NH 66833
Released: 5 January 1962; ; UK chart peak: 48 (January 1963)

'My Bonnie' / 'The Saints (When The Saints Go Marching In)' (US) – Decca 31382
Released: 11 April 1962; did not chart

'My Bonnie (My Bonnie Lies Over The Ocean)' / 'The Saints (When The Saints Go Marching In)' (US)
    – MGM K13213
Released: 27 January 1964; US chart peak: 26, –

'Nowhere Man' / 'What Goes On' (US) – Capitol 5587
Released: 21 February 1966; US chart peak: 3, 81

'Ob-La-Di, Ob-La-Da' / 'Julia' (US) – Capitol 4347
Released: 8 November 1976; US chart peak: 49

'Paperback Writer' / 'Rain' – Parlophone R 5452
Released: 10 June 1966; UK chart peak: 1

'Paperback Writer' / 'Rain' (US) – Capitol 5651
Released: 30 May 1966; US chart peak: 1, 23

'Please Please Me' / 'Ask Me Why' – Parlophone 45-R 4983
Released: 11 January 1963; UK chart peak: 2

'Please Please Me' / 'Ask Me Why' (US) – Vee Jay VJ 498
Released: 25 February 1963; did not chart

'Please Please Me' / 'From Me To You' (US) – Vee Jay VJ 581
Released: 30 January 1964; US chart peak: 3, 41

'Please Please Me' / 'From Me To You' (US) – Capitol Starline 6063
Released: 11 October 1965; did not chart

'Real Love' – Apple 8 82646 2
Released: 4 March 1996 (UK), 5 March 1996 (US); UK chart peak: 4, US chart peak: 11

'Roll Over Beethoven' / 'Misery' (US) – Capitol Starline 6065
Released: 11 October 1965; did not chart

'Roll Over Beethoven' / 'Please Mister Postman' (Canada) Capitol 72133
Released: 9 December 1963; US chart peak: 68, –

'Sgt Pepper's Lonely Hearts Club Band' – 'With A Little Help From My Friends' / 'A Day In The Life' –
   Parlophone R 6022
Released: 30 September 1978; UK chart peak: 63

'Sgt Pepper's Lonely Hearts Club Band' – 'With A Little Help From My Friends' / 'A Day In The Life' (US)
   – Capitol 4612
Released: 14 August 1978; US chart peak: 71

'She Loves You' / 'I'll Get You' – Parlophone R 5055
Released: 23 August 1963; UK chart peak: 1

'She Loves You' / 'I'll Get You' (US) – Swan 4152
Released: 16 September 1963; did not chart

'Sie Liebt Dich' / 'I'll Get You' (US) – Swan 4182
Released: 21 May 1964; US chart peak: 97, –

'Something' / 'Come Together' – Apple R 5814
Released: 31 October 1969; UK chart peak: 4

'Something' / 'Come Together' (US) – Apple 2654
Released: 6 October 1969; US chart peak: 1

'Strawberry Fields Forever' / 'Penny Lane' – Parlophone R 5570
Released: 17 February 1967; UK chart peak: 2

'Strawberry Fields Forever' / 'Penny Lane' (US) – Capitol 5810
Released: 13 February 1967; US chart peak: 8, 1

'Sweet Georgia Brown' / 'Nobody's Child' (Germany) – Polydor 52906
Released: 31 January 1964; did not chart

'Sweet Georgia Brown' / 'Take Out Some Insurance On Me Baby' (US) – Atco 45-6302
Released: 1 June 1964; did not chart

'Ticket To Ride' / 'Yes It Is' – Parlophone R 5265
Released: 9 April 1965; UK chart peak: 1

'Ticket To Ride' / 'Yes It Is' (US) – Capitol 5407
Released: 19 April 1965; US chart peak: 1, 46

'Twist And Shout' / 'There's A Place' (US) – Tollie 9001
Released: 2 March 1964; US chart peak: 2, 74

'Twist And Shout' / 'There's A Place' (US) – Capitol Starline 6061
Released: 11 October 1965; did not chart

'We Can Work It Out' / 'Day Tripper' – Parlophone R 5389
Released: 3 December 1965; UK chart peak: 1

'We Can Work It Out' / 'Day Tripper' (US) – Capitol 5555
Released: 6 December 1965; US chart peak: 1, 5

'Why' / 'Cry For A Shadow' (US) – MGM K13227
Released: 27 March 1964; did not chart

'Yesterday' / 'Act Naturally' (US) – Capitol 5498
Released: 13 September 1965; US chart peak: 1, 47

'Yesterday' / 'I Should Have Known Better' – Parlophone R 6103
Released: 6 March 1976; UK chart peak: 8

EPs

All My Loving – Parlophone GEP 8891
Released: 7 February 1964; UK chart peak: 1

The Beatles – Parlophone SGE 1
Released: 7 December 1981; did not chart

The Beatles – Parlophone SGE 1 (CD issue)
Released: 15 June 1992; did not chart

Beatles For Sale – Parlophone GEP 8931
Released: 6 April 1965; UK chart peak: 1

Beatles For Sale (No. 2) – Parlophone GEP 8938
Released: 4 June 1965; UK chart peak: 5

The Beatles' Hits – Parlophone GEP 8880
Released: 6 September 1963; UK chart peak: 1

The Beatles' Million Sellers – Parlophone GEP 8946
Released: 6 December 1965; UK chart peak: 1

The Beatles (No. 1) – Parlophone GEP 8883
Released: 1 November 1963; UK chart peak: 2

The Beatles' Second Album (US) – Capitol SXA 2080
Released: April 1964; did not chart

Extracts From The Album 'A Hard Day's Night' – Parlophone GEP 8924
Officially released: 6 November 1964; UK chart peak: 7

Extracts From The Film 'A Hard Day's Night' – Parlophone GEP 8920
Released: 4 November 1964; UK chart peak: 1

Four By The Beatles (US)– Capitol EAP 1-2121
Released: 11 May 1964; US chart peak: 92

4 – By The Beatles (US) – Capitol R 5365
Released: 1 February 1965; US chart peak: 68

Long Tall Sally – Parlophone GEP 8913
Released: 19 June 1964; UK chart peak: 1

Magical Mystery Tour – Parlophone MMT-1, SMMT-1
Released: 8 December 1967; UK chart peak: 2

Meet The Beatles! (US) – Capitol SXA 2047
Released: February 1964; did not chart

Nowhere Man – Parlophone GEP 8952
Released: 8 July 1966; UK chart peak: 4

Something New (US) – Capitol SXA 2108
Released: July 1964; did not chart

Souvenir Of Their Visit To America (US) – Vee Jay VJEP 1903
Released: 23 March 1964; did not chart

Twist And Shout – Parlophone GEP 8882
Released: 12 July 1963; UK chart peak: 1

Ya Ya (Germany) – Polydor 21485
Only one track, 'Sweet Georgia Brown,' features the Beatles
Released: October 1962; did not chart

Yesterday – Parlophone GEP 8948
Released: 4 March 1966; UK chart peak: 1

LPs

Certain compilation LPs are included because they were first to include the specific mix of a track, such as the Australian *Greatest Hits Volume 2*, which marked the first appearance of the stereo version of 'She's A Woman'. The reason for the inclusion of these LPs is noted, where applicable.

Abbey Road – Apple PCS 7088
Released: 26 September 1969; UK chart peak: 1

Abbey Road (US) – Apple SO 383
Released: 1 October 1969; US chart peak: 1

The Beatles – Apple PMC 7067–7068, PCS 7067–7068
Released: 22 November 1968; UK chart peak: 1

The Beatles (US) – Apple SWBO-101
Released: 25 November 1968; US chart peak: 1

The Beatles 1962–1966 – Apple PCSP 717
Released: 19 April 1973; UK chart peak: 3

The Beatles 1962–1966 (US)– Apple SKBO 3403
Released: 2 April 1973; US chart peak: 3

The Beatles 1967–1970 – Apple PCSP 718
Released: 19 April 1973; UK chart peak: 2

The Beatles 1967–1970 (US) – Apple SKBO 3404
Released: 2 April 1973; US chart peak: 1

Beatles '65 (US) – Capitol T 2228, ST 2228
Released: 15 December 1964; US chart peak: 1

The Beatles At The Hollywood Bowl – Parlophone EMTV 4
Released: 6 May 1977; UK chart peak: 1

The Beatles At The Hollywood Bowl (US) – Capitol SMAS 11638
Released: 4 May 1977; US chart peak: 2

The Beatles Ballads – Parlophone PCS 7214
Includes alternative mix of 'Norwegian Wood'
Released: 13 October 1980; UK chart peak: 17

Beatles First – Polydor 236 201
UK release of 1964 German LP. Contains tracks by Tony Sheridan, and some not featuring the Beatles
Released: 4 August 1967; did not chart

Beatles For Sale – Parlophone PMC 1240, PCS 3062
Released: 4 December 1964; UK chart peak: 1

The Beatles' Greatest (Germany) – Odeon SMO 83 991
Includes first stereo mix of 'I Want To Hold Your Hand'
Released: 8 June 1965; did not chart in UK or US, Germany chart peak: 38

The Beatles' Second Album (US) – Capitol T 2080, ST 2080
Released: 10 April 1964; US chart peak: 1

Beatles VI (US) – Capitol T 2358, ST 2358
Released: 14 June 1965; US chart peak: 1

A Collection Of Beatles Oldies – Parlophone PMC 7016, PCS 7016
Released: 9 December 1966; UK chart peak: 7

The Early Beatles (US) – Capitol T 2309, ST 2309
Released: 22 March 1965; US chart peak: 43

From Then To You – Apple LYN 2153/2154
Released: 18 December 1970; did not chart

Greatest Hits Volume 2 (Australia) – Parlophone PCSO 7534
Includes first release of stereo mix of 'She's A Woman'
Released: 16 February 1967; did not chart in UK or US, Australia chart peak: 9

A Hard Day's Night – Parlophone PMC 1230, PCS 3058
Released: 10 July 1964; UK chart peak: 1

A Hard Day's Night (US) – United Artists UAL 3366, UAS 6366
Released: 26 June 1964; US chart peak: 1

Help! – Parlophone PMC 1255, PCS 3071
Released: 6 August 1965; UK chart peak: 1

Help! (US) – Capitol MAS 2386, SMAS 2386
Released: 13 August 1965; US chart peak: 1

Hey Jude (US) – Apple SW 385
Released: 26 February 1970; US chart peak: 2

Introducing... The Beatles (US) – Vee Jay VJLP 1062, VJSR 1062
Released: January 1964; US chart peak: 2

Let It Be – Apple PXS1, PCS 7096
Released: 8 May 1970; UK chart peak: 1

Let It Be (US) – Apple AR 34001
Released: 18 May 1970; US chart peak: 1

Live! At The Star-Club In Hamburg, Germany; 1962 – Lingasong LNL 1
Released: 8 April 1977; did not chart

Live! At The Star-Club In Hamburg, Germany; 1962 (US) – Lingasong LS 2 7001
Released: April 1977; US chart peak: 111

Long Tall Sally (Canada) – Capitol T 6063, ST 6063
Released: 27 April or 11 May 1964; did not chart

Love Songs – Parlophone PCSP 721
'This Boy' and 'Yes It Is' have mock stereo mixes, 'Norwegian Wood' and 'Girl' have alternative stereo mixes
Released: 19 November 1977; UK chart peak: 7

Love Songs (US) – Capitol SKBL 11711
See UK version
Released: 21 October 1977; US chart peak: 24

Magical Mystery Tour (US) – Capitol MAL 2835, SMAL 2835
Released: 27 November 1967; US chart peak: 1, UK chart peak: 31

Magical Mystery Tour (Germany) – Hör Zu SHZE 327 / Apple 1C 072-04449
Released: 16 September 1971; did not chart

Meet The Beatles! (US) – Capitol T 2047, ST 2047
Released: 20 January 1964; US chart peak: 1

No One's Gonna Change Our World – Regal Starline SRS 5013
Released: 12 December 1969; did not chart

Please Please Me – Parlophone PMC 1202, PCS 3042
Released: 22 March 1963 (mono), 26 April 1963 (stereo); UK chart peak: 1

Rarities – Parlophone PCM 1001, PSLP 261
Released: 2 December 1978; UK chart peak: 71

Rarities (US) – Capitol SHAL 12060
Released: 24 March 1980; US chart peak: 21

Reel Music – Parlophone PCS 7218
Released: 29 March 1982; did not chart

Reel Music (US) – Capitol SV-12199
Includes edited version of 'I Should Have Known Better'
Released: 22 March 1982; US chart peak: 19

Revolver – Parlophone PMC 7009, PCS 7009
Released: 5 August 1966; UK chart peak: 1

Revolver (US) – Capitol T 2576, ST 2576
Released: 8 August 1966; US chart peak: 1

Rock 'n' Roll Music – Parlophone PCSP 719
Includes alternative mixes of 'I Call Your Name' and 'Long Tall Sally'
Released: 11 June 1976; UK chart peak: 11

Rock 'n' Roll Music (US) – Capitol SKBO 11537
Also includes alternative mixes of 'Twist And Shout', 'I Saw Her Standing There', 'I Wanna Be Your Man', 'Boys', 'Money', 'Bad Boy' and 'Roll Over Beethoven'
Released: 7 June 1976; US chart peak: 2

Rubber Soul – Parlophone PMC 1267, PCS 3075
Released: 3 December 1965; UK chart peak: 1

Rubber Soul (US) – Capitol T 2442, ST 2442
Released: 6 December 1965; US chart peak: 1

Sgt Pepper's Lonely Hearts Club Band – Parlophone PMC 7027, PCS 7027
Released: 1 June 1967; UK chart peak: 1

Sgt Pepper's Lonely Hearts Club Band (US) – Capitol MAS 2653, SMAS 2653
Released: 2 June 1967; US chart peak: 1

Something New (US) – Capitol T 2108, ST 2108
Released: 20 July 1964; US chart peak: 2

Something New (Germany) – Odeon STO 83 756
Includes version of 'And I Love Her' with extended intro
Released: 10 September 1964; did not chart in UK or US, Germany chart peak: 8

With The Beatles – Parlophone PMC 1206, PCS 3045
Released: 22 November 1963; UK chart peak: 1

With The Beatles (Germany) – Odeon O 83 991, Odeon STO 83 568
Released: November 1963; did not chart in UK or US, Germany chart peak: 1

Yellow Submarine – Apple PMC 7070, PCS 7070
Released: 17 January 1969; UK chart peak: 3

Yellow Submarine (US) – Apple SW 153
Released: 13 January 1969; US chart peak: 2

"Yesterday" … And Today (US) – Capitol T 2553, ST 2553
Released: 20 June 1966; US chart peak: 1

20 Greatest Hits – Parlophone PCTC 260
Released: 18 October 1982; UK chart peak: 10

20 Greatest Hits (US) – Capitol SV-12245
'Hey Jude' is edited to 5:05 for timing reasons
Released: 11 October 1982; US chart peak: 50

CDs and other audio

Some CD equivalents of LPs are included because they include different mixes of one or more tracks. The reason for inclusion is noted, where applicable.

1+ CD/DVD – Apple 6205 47567727
Released: 6 November 2015; UK chart peak: 5, US chart peak: 6

Anthology 1 CD – Apple 8 34445 2
Released: 21 November 1995; UK chart peak: 2, US chart peak: 1

Anthology 2 CD – Apple 8 34448 2
Released: 18 March 1996; UK chart peak: 1, US chart peak: 1

Anthology 3 CD – Apple 8 34451 2
Released: 28 October 1996; UK chart peak: 4, US chart peak: 1

The Beatles Deluxe CD – Apple 0602567571957
Released: 9 November 2018; UK chart peak: 4, US chart peak: 6

The Beatles 1962–1966 CD – EMI CDP 7 97036 2
All tracks have different mixes to those on the LP for various reasons, apart from 'Eleanor Rigby' and 'Yellow Submarine'
Released: 20 September 1993; UK chart peak: 3

The Beatles 1967–1970 CD – EMI CDP 7 97039 2
Mixes of 'Strawberry Fields Forever' and 'A Day In The Life' are different to those on the LP; 'Penny Lane', 'I Am The Walrus' and 'Hello, Goodbye' have different mixes on the UK and US LPs – the UK mixes are used for the CD
Released: 20 September 1993; UK chart peak: 4

The Beatles Bootleg Recordings 1963 – iTunes
Released: 17 December 2013; did not chart

The Early Tapes Of The Beatles CD – Polydor 823701-2
Released: 10 December 1984; did not chart

Help! CD – EMI CDP 7 46439 2
Released: 30 April 1987; UK chart peak: 61

Let It Be... Naked CD – Apple 24359 57142
Released: 17 November 2003; UK chart peak: 7, US chart peak: 5

Live At The BBC CD – Apple 8 31796 2
Released: 30 November 1994; UK chart peak: 1, US chart peak: 3

Live At The Hollywood Bowl CD – Apple 6025 57054972
Released: 9 September 2016; UK chart peak: 3, US chart peak: 7

Love CD – Apple 0946 3 80790 2 6
Released: 20 November 2006; UK chart peak: 3, US chart peak: 4

Magical Mystery Tour cassette – Parlophone TC-PCS 3077
Released: 19 November 1976 (UK); did not chart

Magical Mystery Tour CD – EMI CDP 7 48062 2
Released: 21 September 1987; UK chart peak: 52

Mono Masters CD – Apple 6 849582 4
Released: 9 September 2009; did not chart

On Air – Live At The BBC Volume 2 CD – Apple 6025 37491698
Released: 11 November 2013; UK chart peak: 12, US chart peak: 7

Only The Beatles (Heineken promo cassette) – Stiletto/Parlophone SMMC 151
Released: June 1986; did not chart

Past Masters 1 CD – EMI CDP 7 90043 2
Released: 7 March 1988; UK chart peak: 49

Past Masters 2 CD – EMI CDP 7 90044 2
Released: 7 March 1988; UK chart peak: 46

Past Masters CD – EMI CDP 2 43807 2
Released: 9 September 2009; UK chart peak: 31

Rubber Soul CD – EMI CDP 7 46440 2
Released: 30 April 1987; UK chart peak: 60

Sgt Pepper's Lonely Hearts Club Band Deluxe CD – Apple 0602557455328
Released: 26 May 2017; UK chart peak: 1, US chart peak: 3

Tomorrow Never Knows – iTunes
Released: 24 July 2012; UK chart peak: 44, US chart peak: 24

Yellow Submarine Songtrack CD – Apple 5 21481 2
Released: 13 September 1999; UK chart peak: 8, US chart peak: 15

Films and DVDs

Anthology DVD – Apple 4 92969 9
Released: 1 April 2003

The Four Historic Ed Sullivan Shows DVD – EREDV 372
Released: 28 October 2003

A Hard Day's Night movie
Released: 6 July 1964 (UK), 11 August 1964 (US)

Help! movie
Released: 28 July 1965 (UK), 9 August 1965 (US)

Let It Be movie
Released: 20 May 1970 (UK), 13 May 1970 (US)

Magical Mystery Tour movie
First broadcast: 26 December 1967

Yellow Submarine movie
Released: 17 July 1968 (UK), 13 November 1968 (US)